Ace the
Technical
Interview

Ace the Technical Interview

Michael Rothstein

McGraw-Hill, Inc.
New York   San Francisco   Washington, D.C.   Auckland   Bogotá
Caracas   Lisbon   London   Madrid   Mexico City   Milan
Montreal   New Delhi   San Juan   Singapore
Sydney   Tokyo   Toronto

Library of Congress Cataloging-in-Publication Data

Rothstein, Michael F.
    Ace the technical interview / Michael Rothstein.
        p.   cm.
    Includes bibliographical references and index.
    ISBN 0-07-054030-6 (pc) :
    1. Computer science—Vocational guidance. 2. Employment
interviewing. I. Title.
QA76 .25.R68 1994
004'.023'73—dc20   93-20953
                                      CIP

   3 4 5 6 7 8 9 0 DOH/DOH 9 9 8 7 6 5 4

ISBN 0-07-054030-6

The sponsoring editor for this book was Jerry Papke, the editing supervisor was Christine H. Furry, and the production supervisor was Pamela Pelton. It was set in Palatino by North Market Street Graphics.

Printed and bound by R. R. Donnelley & Sons Company.

This book is respectfully dedicated to:
Marion Rothstein, my mother
David Rothstein, my brother
and to
Dan Rones, a friend . . . a special person
who is remembered. May he rest in peace.

Contents

Contributors

Paul H. Baneky (CHAPTER 5) specializes in assisting clients to manage technology transition. He is well versed in both mainframe and the newer Client/Server technologies. He has been a senior operations and systems engineering officer at White Weld, First Boston, Lehman Brothers, and group manager at Merrill Lynch Capital Markets. His most recent assignments have ranged from Huron environment porting to design and setup of the OS/2 technical support function for IBM. He is well known for his innovative strategies in managing information systems business operations.

Scott Boyajian (CHAPTER 11) works for the IBM Corporation, where he is responsible for RS/6000 and AIX client support.

Daniel Robert Cohen (CHAPTER 7) is a senior programming analyst with Orix Credit Alliance, Inc., Secaucus, New Jersey, a company that specializes in financing companies that lease and buy construction equipment. He is responsible for designing, coding, testing, debugging, and maintaining software on Orix's invoicing and accounting systems, as well as implementing these changes into production. He is an RPG/400 and AS/400 command language specialist with extensive IBM midrange experience on the AS/400, System/38, and IBM PC platforms.

John Cornetto, Jr. (CHAPTER 14) is an officer with J.P. Morgan. He has over 13 years' experience in the data processing field, with an emphasis in the analysis, design, and development of CICS, DB2, and COBOL systems. For CAP GEMINI AMERICA, his clients included Drexel, Merrill Lynch, Brown Brothers, and MONY, where as senior programmer/analyst he implemented a variety of CICS systems.

David Dodge (CHAPTER 19) is the U.S. practice leader for IBM's End-User Systems (Client/Server) Consulting Group. He is responsible for IBM consulting in the areas of Client/Server application design and development, data warehouse design and implementation, decision support systems, office systems integration, and end-user resource management. He led the development of IBM's Client/Server Consulting Methodology and is spearheading the establishment of this facet of

IBM's consulting nationwide. He is currently managing a Client/Server transition project for an international nonprofit agency. Mr. Dodge is a graduate of the U.S. Naval Academy, with advanced degrees from George Washington University, including an M.S.A. degree in Personnel Administration and a law degree.

Walter N. Eachus (CHAPTER 28) has over 20 years' experience in data processing with skills in project management, problem analysis, system integration, and logical and physical database design across various technologies and platforms. He has extensive experience with the Bachman CASE toolset over a wide range of applications. His B.S. and M.S. degrees in Theology are from Bob Jones University.

Arnie G. Fonseca (CHAPTER 13) is a programmer analyst with S.A.F. and Associates, Inc., New Jersey. He has had over 10 years' experience in CICS application programming and has provided consulting services to a number of financial corporations, including U.S. Trust Bank, Metropolitan Life Insurance Co., and Chemical Banking Corporation, where he enhanced existing VS/COBOL and COBOL II applications using CICS VSAM and DB2. His B.S. degree is from the University of Puerto Rico.

Barry Glasgow, Ph.D. (CHAPTER 3) is vice president and manager of an advanced technology group at a major retail brokerage firm. Since 1987 he has been principally concerned with aligning business needs and technology. His main areas of concentration have been on AI, CASE, and EDI. For the past 15 years he has developed brokerage systems and applied emerging technologies for Wall Street firms. He is a founding member and vice president for meetings of the Metropolitan New York CASE Users Group, a member of AAAI, IEEE, ACM, and Smart F$.

Julian T. Glyck (CHAPTER 18) has over 14 years' experience in business and system analysis, specializing in payroll/human resource applications. He developed and marketed ADLI, a utility to access and update segments in any IMS database on an ad hoc basis via CICS and IMS Supertest, a software package designed to speed testing and maintenance of IMS-based applications. Major clients include Wal-Mart, Tenneco Gas, Mercedes-Benz, and BASF. Other clients include Merrill Lynch, Exxon Office Systems, and Bankers Trust. His B.S. degree in Industrial Engineering and Operations Research is from Columbia University; his M.B.A. degree in Computer Systems and Information Science is from Pace University in New York.

Sheryl Hert Harawitz (CHAPTER 24) is a computer software specialist with the New York City Housing Authority, responsible for data analysis and accuracy of data and programs. She has developed and taught computer courses in both SAS and dBASE. She is the author of *Psych Lab* (1987), an introductory text in designing and conducting psychological experiments with computers. Her M.A. degree in Psychology is from Hunter College.

George W. Harrison (CHAPTER 17), since 1979, has been with the New York City Housing Authority. Currently, he is manager of the Technical Assistance Group for Computer Operations, responsible for conversion of applications from DOS/VSE to MVS/XA, and DASD management advice and support functions. He has worked in a number of capacities, including systems programmer and assistant chief, Computer Operations.

Jeff Kaplan (CHAPTERS 9 & 10) is a senior technical consultant with extensive experience in all phases of systems engineering. He has experience in the installation, maintenance, modification, and tuning of VM/XA/SP, SQL/DS, CICS/VS, VTAM, NCP/EP, and numerous other program products. He has evaluated operating environments, made hardware and software recommendations, and trained staff. He has served as a technical adviser in the application of new technologies. He is an expert on all IBM mainframe and midrange platforms, as well as IBM system and applications software for these systems. His B.S. degree in Computer Science is from Brooklyn College.

Paul King (CHAPTER 16) is a senior database consultant with over 18 years' experience as a programmer/analyst and over 14 years' experience in IDMS database logical design, physical design, implementation, programming, and tuning from release 4.5–10.2. He was chairman of the IDMS User Association Technical Advisory Committee from 1979 to 1987 and on the association's board of directors from 1984 to 1987. He has served as an expert witness on computer databases in Federal Court.

James Fee Langendoen (CHAPTER 12) has over 21 years of successful business experience, including over 12 years of computer experience, the last 6 years as an independent computer consultant. He has been an instructor at Columbia University's Computer Technology and Applications Program, specializing in relational database and structured design (including CASE), using ORACLE as the relational database management system for his coursework. He is a member of the New York ORACLE User Group, the Metropolitan New York CASE User Group, IEEE Computer Society, and serves on the IEEE Technical Committee on Software Engineering.

John H. Lister (CHAPTER 20) is vice president of communications software at Shearson Lehman Brothers, New York. He is responsible for the development and maintenance of a large SNA network consisting of seven mainframe hosts and approximately 20,000 devices. The Shearson SNA network has connections to approximately 20 other SNA networks. He coordinated the planning for the introduction of token-ring technology within Shearson Lehman Brothers, which now supports approximately 7000 users in the downtown Manhattan locations. He also coordinated the introduction of TCP/IP protocols to mainframes within Shearson and supports a substantial amount of communications with UNIX workstations and servers. He was previously with Manufacturers Hanover Trust, New York, and National Westminster Bank, London. His B.A. degree in Mathematics is from King's College, London.

Maria I. Martins (CHAPTER 4) is presently a technical analyst, DB/Technical Services, CIS at Brown University. She is responsible for implementing new large systems which run under MVS. She works with MVS/JCL, streamlines procedures for production support, performs analysis and recovery on complex abends, trains others on new procedures, and writes documentation. Since 1979 she has held a number of responsible positions dealing with applications development, production services, and technical services. She has extensive programming skills applicable to MVS and VM environments.

Richard Miller (CHAPTER 23) is a consultant with the New York City Housing Authority presently involved as a consultant project analyst for the Human Resources Information System (HRIS) system study. He was responsible, among other things, for the analysis of existing computing capabilities and the IDMS/R database and for analyzing DB2 and related productivity tools. He also installed and implemented DB2, CSP, COBOL II, and the Human Resources Application Software. He previously consulted with Metro North Commuter Railroad, the New

York City Transit Authority, and the New York City Police Department. His B.S. degree in Business Administration is from Northeastern University, Boston.

Jeffrey O. Milman (CHAPTER 27) is cofounder of Applied Intelligence Systems, New York, which was created to succeed Expert Systems, Inc. as a supplier of expert system software for the life insurance industry. Applied Intelligence Systems created a successful life underwriting expert system, called ELUS, for a major mutual life insurance company. He is presently director of licensing with AMSCAN, Inc., Harrison, New York. Previously, he was Ideal Toy Corporation's Controller and also had major accounting positions with Kane-Miller Corp., Tarrytown, New York and Price Waterhouse & Co., New York. He has an M.B.A. degree in Finance and Accounting from Stanford University. His B.A. degree in Economics is from Cornell University. He's a Certified Public Accountant in New York State.

Robert Pesner (CHAPTER 8) is president of PC Dialogs, Inc., New York City, a firm that develops and conducts classes on various computer-related topics including OS/2, LANs, distributed processing, APPC, VM, REXX, and ISPF, in addition to custom designing applications that focus on distributed processing. He was previously manager, OS/2 curriculum with Software Education Corporation in Marlboro, New Jersey and manager of VM systems programming with Shearson Lehman Hutton, New York City. His M.A. degree is from the University of California, Irvine.

Arthur D. Rosenberg (CHAPTER 1) specializes in analyzing and translating business requirements into software applications; producing accurate and readable documentation; designing and conducting training programs; developing RFPs and proposals. He is the editor of *Interface*, a monthly newsletter from Independent Computer Consultants Association, New York/New Jersey chapter. He has authored several books, including a bestseller—*The Résumé Handbook*—now in a successful second edition.

Burt Rosner (CHAPTER 26) is divisional vice president, Paine Webber, New Jersey, responsible for introducing MIS wide methodology and standards, CASE tools and concepts, and project management tools in a strategic systems planning environment. He previously served as a vice president project manager for Paine Webber. Prior to joining Paine Webber he was a data systems manager and project manager for AT&T. He is the coauthor of *The Professional's Guide to Database Systems Project Management* (Wiley, 1990) and coauthor of *Structured Analysis and Design for the CASE User* (McGraw-Hill, 1993). He lectures widely on CASE-related topics. His B.S. degree in Accounting is from Pace University, New York.

Joseph S. Rubenfeld (CHAPTER 27) is senior knowledge engineer with Inference Corporation, Stamford, Connecticut. He has over 20 years' experience in the design and development of applications software and systems ranging from programming to systems analysis and knowledge engineering to project and corporate management. Prior to joining Inference Corporation, he was with Applied Intelligence Systems, New York; Paine Webber, New York; NBC in New York as senior systems analyst; Decision Systems, Inc., Mahwah, New Jersey; and Loeb, Rhoades & Co., New York. Among his many accomplishments, he wrote a chess-playing program which became one of the top-ranked programs in the world. His B.S. degree in Electrical Engineering is from Carnegie-Mellon University, Pittsburgh. His M.S. degree in Computer Science is from the University of Pittsburgh.

Marvin Rubenstein (CHAPTER 25) is a hands-on information engineering management consultant specializing in modern system development quality and productivity methods, techniques, and tools. He is a certified Fast/JAD facilitator experienced in over 20 JAD facilitations. He is a data modeler/system architect, a methodologist who developed two in-house methodologies for Fortune 100 companies, an information engineering/CASE hands-on project development expert, and a project management expert. In March, 1990, *Software Magazine* called him ". . . one of the 5 most outstanding software innovators in the United States." Earlier, *IEEE Software* said that "Rubenstein runs what may be the most successful Application Development Center in the country." His B.B.A. degree is from City College of New York. He is a member of ACM and IEEE.

Michael A. Senatore (CHAPTER 15) is a database administrator with over 12 years of experience in data processing. His current skills include DB2 design and maintenance, DB2 COBOL and CSP project management, and the use of CASE tools. He is the coauthor of *Structured Analysis and Design for the CASE User,* recently published by McGraw-Hill. He has also been involved in Yourdon/Constantine methodologies, data and process modeling, and relational database design. His clients have included Metropolitan Life Insurance Company, Manufacturers Hanover Trust, New York City Housing Authority, and others. His B.A. degree is from Brooklyn College, with advanced training at NYU and Columbia University.

Michael Sichel (CHAPTER 2), since 1978, has directed a successful technical and executive staffing and outplacement facility—RMS Computer Corporation, located in mid-Manhattan. He has over 20 years of diversified management experience. His consulting activities in both North America and Western Europe include corporate experience with major industries such as aerospace, communications, and diversified conglomerates. His B.S. degree is from Cornell University and he has completed additional graduate work at Columbia University's Graduate School of Business.

Michael J. Talbot (CHAPTER 22) is vice president, Database Systems, for Bankers Trust Company, New York, where he directed the implementation, customization, and deployment of the latest relational database software from major vendors, including IBM, Candle, Platinum, IBI, Bachman, DBT, and Legent. Prior to joining Bankers Trust in 1986, he spent 15 years with NYNEX Service Company in a variety of capacities. His B.S.E.E. degree is from Manhattan College, Bronx, New York. He also has an M.S. degree in Engineering from RPI, Troy, New York, and an M.S. degree in Computer Science from New York Institute of Technology, Old Westbury, New York.

Chayim Leib Weiss (CHAPTER 6) has had 11 years' experience in the management, design, administration, and maintenance of UNIX workstations and servers. He is responsible for hardware and software installations, network configuration, system tuning, backups, and troubleshooting. He is a specialist in Wide Area Communications and routing. He spent 10 years with the New York City Housing Authority in a variety of positions, including UNIX section manager and computer services manager.

Candice Zarr (CHAPTER 21) is assistant vice president, Technical Planning, with Shearson Lehman Brothers, New York, responsible for assessing and identifying opportunities in software technology and methodology to improve/support the creation and maintenance of business applications. Her specialties include CASE, reengineering, object-oriented technology, project management, metrics, and methodologies. She was previously director, Systems Integration, with the New York City Transit Authority as a CASE specialist, as well as having responsibilities for introducing PC technology to the organization.

Preface

Looking for a job is hard work. Being out of work is worse. At least when you have a job, money is still coming in . . . bills can be paid. Whatever the circumstances, when one is looking for a new position one is in *constant competition* . . . in competition with all those out there who are trying to get the same job that you are trying for. To succeed, to be the one that gets the job, you are going to have to be better than anyone else, at least in the eyes of those offering the position. You are going to have to be the *best*.

When applying for a technical position there are at least two things you have to be able to do (or appear to do) better than all the others applying for the same position:

1. You are going to have to answer the general types of questions, like *Why do you want to work here? Why do you want to leave your current position? What do you know about the company (offering the job)?* In addition, you have to know how to appear prosperous, confident, and not be a potential threat to those offering the job.

2. You are going to have to be *technically current*. You are going to have to be able to show that you know as much as, if not more than, someone who has been working continuously in that technical area.

Providing information on a variety of subjects that you can use to help you do well during an interview, as well as answering all types of technical questions, is what this book is all about.

Each chapter has been written by a professional who has specialized in the material covered in his or her chapter. The book brings together the know-how of 28 professionals, each with years of experience—each with an understanding as to what one needs to know to pass a technical interview. In addition to being technically proficient, they have given interviews and have been responsible for hiring people.

About This Book

The book covers two broad areas. The first part discusses the interview process—
knowing what is involved in successful interviews, as well as how to control an
interview. The second part contains 25 chapters, each providing in terms of scope
and depth the technical information that you will need to *show an interviewer that
you are current, up-to-date, and that you know what you are talking about . . . you know
the subject . . . you know your stuff.*

During my professional career as a candidate for permanent, as well as for consulting, positions I have been through the interview process more times than I like
to think about. This material has been brought together because it can be of tremendous help to a job applicant. It would have helped me if I had had access to such a
book. Especially in today's job market, we can use all the support we can get. Read,
review, and even memorize the material covered. You will be better equipped to
get a good job. *This book gives you the competitive edge in getting your next job.*

If you have any comments, recommendations, or contributions as to what
should be included in future editions, please do not hesitate to write to me in care
of the publisher. I hope you will enjoy this book.

Good luck, and enjoy your new job.

Michael Rothstein

Acknowledgments

This book was a team effort from the very start. As it is a book that took a lot of work on the part of many people, I would like to take this opportunity to thank the following:

- The contributors/writers of each chapter. While their names and biographies are included elsewhere, I still would like to acknowledge their efforts . . . without them there would not have been a book.

- I would like to thank Jerry Papke and Rachel Hirschfield of McGraw-Hill and Sheryl Harawitz for their support, their ideas, and their recommendations.

- For those who took the time to read and review various chapters, I would like to thank:

  Valentin Carciu for his review of "Unix"
  Patricia Fitzpatrick for reviewing "COBOL/COBOL II"
  Tom Hutcherson and Patti Curran for their review of "The AS/400"
  Alexander Katz for reviewing "MVS for the System Programmer"
  Arthur Rosenberg for his review of "You and the Employment Agency"
  Mike Senatore for reviewing "IBM's DB2"
  Stephen Spiro for reviewing "CICS"

- And last . . . but definitely not least . . . to my friends who understood (I surely hope) my many absences while burning the proverbial midnight oil:

  Carmela and Joseph Bernstein
  Miryam and Harry Frei
  Lea and David Melamed
  Lya and Eugene Quitt
  Miriam and Carl Stern
  Mireille and Jerry Zarin
  Thanks for being understanding.

Michael Rothstein

Ace the Technical Interview

1

The Interview: Preparation and Interaction

Arthur D. Rosenberg

Defining Terms

An interview for a full-time position or a consulting assignment is, for our purposes, a *job interview*. Job interviews include interviews with potential employers and with agencies and other screening go-betweens.

Job interviews occur between one or more interviewers and an interviewee. Occasionally, two or more individuals may be interviewed together. Sometimes an interviewee may be accompanied by an agent, but most often the interviewee is on his or her own.

This chapter has been designed to assist the recent graduate seeking an entry-level position, the career-oriented professional moving up the corporate ladder, the executive who is reaching toward the top, and the consultant looking for another contract. The major difference between full-timer and consultant interviews is the amount of interest focused by the interviewer on the interviewee's character and personality. These distinctions are pointed out, where appropriate, throughout this chapter.

Another important difference to be aware of is between the screening interview and the decision interview, discussed later in the chapter under "Different Types of Interviewers."

Finally, we remind the reader that this chapter, like the entire book, is oriented toward the data processing industry. Although the basic principles of interviewing are common to most professions, we believe that the computer environment is unique in its demands and standards. Data processing is a profession in which skill cannot be forged, where experience is truly valued.

Getting the Interview

Prior to preparing for an interview, you must first *get* the interview. This obvious and necessary step is generally accomplished through personal contacts, agencies, postings, and advertisements.

Agencies

Placement and consulting agencies often have valuable contacts with clients who are seeking employees and/or consultants. Most are experienced at evaluating and matching skills such as yours with client needs. Bear in mind, though, that the agency traditionally receives their fees from the employer, and so their loyalties are naturally inclined in that direction.

When you negotiate a salary or rate with an agency, you have to balance two opposing facts of life: the less you agree to, the less you will have to live with; and the more you demand, the more attractive the competition may appear.

The Résumé

Whether you go through an agency or contact the client directly, you need a current résumé to help you stand out among the hundreds, perhaps thousands, of others who may be competing with you for the job. According to the *Résumé Handbook* (Arthur D. Rosenberg and David V. Hizer, Bob Adams, Inc., 2d edition, 1990), only one interview is granted for every 245 résumés received.

If you're looking for a full-time job, your résumé should be chronologically organized (unless there are significant gaps of time between jobs) to show growth, responsibility, and consistency. A consultant's résumé can be functionally organized to display technical and related skills, experience, and clients. A résumé should be limited to two or three pages (one for recent graduates and people with limited work experience); lists of publications, patents, and other relevant credits should be attached. It doesn't hurt to maintain your résumé on a word-processor to keep it up-to-date, and to quickly produce variations that emphasize any specific skills and applications that may be of interest to a potential client.

Your résumé must be clearly organized and detailed without being cumbersome. Particularly for consultants, it also helps to have professional business cards, an answering machine, and a fax.

Preinterview Preparations

If you are seeking a full-time position, you must be prepared for questions not only about the job for which you are applying, but also more personal inquiries, such as why you left your last (or are considering leaving your current) employer, why you'd like to join company X, and more subtle queries intended to reveal your character. As a consultant, potential clients are more concerned with your job-related track record—specifically, the hardware, software, and applications you have mastered. Regarding the latter, it is important to be candid and objective, for it is difficult to fool people for long in a data processing environment.

Doing Your Homework

The first step in getting ready for an interview is preparing for the kinds of questions you are likely to be asked. Ask your contact or intermediary about the specific job requirements and related issues. Job requirements may include hardware, software, applications, and responsibilities such as design, installation, supervision, and management. Related issues cover location, hours, and potential future to career-minded applicants. If a technical skill is required, update your memory and knowledge by referring to the appropriate chapter of this book. Ask yourself what you would ask a potential candidate if you were conducting the interview, and be prepared to answer no less than that.

Try also to find out who your interviewer is likely to be—the president of the company, the MIS director, a project leader or manager, or someone from the personnel department (see "Different Types of Interviewers" in this chapter). Is the interviewer a decision maker, or merely screening for someone else?

Objectives

Just as the objective of a résumé is to get the interview, the objective of an interview is to convince the screener to pass you on to the decision maker, or to convince the decision maker to offer you the job. When you go on an interview, always give it your best shot, with confidence and enthusiasm. Don't waste the interviewer's time—or your own—with an *I don't really want this job* type attitude. And don't shoot yourself in the foot with a *you probably won't offer me the job* type air because, in that case, they probably won't. Whether you are seeking a career position or a consulting assignment, the bottom line is winning the offer. You may later decide not to accept the job if you feel it isn't right for you, or if something better is available, but that decision lies in the future. At worst—if they do not offer you the job—you will have gained the experience of the interview for the investment of your time.

Psyching Up

Everyone, from the beginner to the seasoned pro, needs to be mentally ready for an interview in order to be at their impressive best. When all other things are more or less equal (i.e., when two or more candidates are of comparable competence and experience), then confidence and enthusiasm for the job may serve as the tiebreaker.

Let's face it, if you're an unusually heavyweight tech, a guru among experts, clients are very likely lined up for your services despite any apparent negatives (e.g., coffee-stains on your apparel, creased clothes, or a passive attitude). They put up with you because they have to. But if you haven't yet outdistanced the competition, your appearance and attitude can work for or against you. Nobody wants to work with a negative individual, a complainer, or a sourpuss if there are more agreeable alternatives available.

Personal Appearance

While we are not supposed to judge others by *their* personal appearance, we should nevertheless make sure that *ours* is "correct." Reality, of course, is that personal appearance strongly influences the expectations of those who meet us for the first time.

With regard to grooming and dress, common sense dictates that the closer you conform to the norm (what you see around you), the more you look the part. Since data processing is a relatively conservative environment, men with long hair, women with flashy makeup, and anyone unusually dressed are apt to divert attention from their skills and may be taken less than seriously.

If you have reason to anticipate an extended interviewing process that may last for several hours, wear clothing that will maintain its neatness throughout the day.

References

Give references that will enhance your credibility as an employee/consultant in the job for which you are interviewing. Former employers, supervisors, and colleagues count for more than friends and casual acquaintances. By all means, use academic references if you are a recent graduate, but try to avoid using any references with whom you have had no contact for a number of years. It is customary to ask permission of the person involved to use his or her name. Besides being the polite thing to do, it alerts the person giving the reference to expect calls. If you are uncertain about what someone may say about you, check them out by having a friend call them as a potential employer, or just don't use them. A poor reference is worse than no reference at all.

Disabilities

If you have any handicaps that might interfere with your ability to perform activities normally associated with the job for which you wish to interview, reveal them up front. In this manner, you are more likely to overcome any doubts the interviewer may have (but may be hesitant to ask) about your ability to perform.

Different Types
of Interviewers

Before getting into the potential idiosyncrasies of individual interviewers, let's take a moment to identify the two major camps by objectives: those who screen, and those who decide.

Screeners

The screening interview is usually a formal, impersonal meeting conducted by a professional interviewer in the personnel department. It is most often required for a career position, to a lesser degree for a consulting assignment. The purpose of this process is to weed out the more obviously inappropriate candidates by verifying their background, credentials, appearance, and any overt character-istics.

The screening interviewer is likely to be skilled at the kinds of techniques that encourage you to put your foot in your mouth by revealing facts you'd rather not discuss (e.g., discrepancies between what you say and what is written on your résumé, or perhaps the real reason why you left a certain company). The screener probably doesn't know a whole lot about the job for which you are interviewing, so they are unlikely to ask any technical questions. Their purpose is to gather enough relevant information about you to enable them to make a safe decision as to whether to pass you on to the decision maker or show you the door.

Since this is likely to be the only time you ever meet the screeners (even if you get the job), they are less interested in you personally than would be a potential supervisor or colleague. In a very real sense, screeners are more focused in uncov-ering reasons to stop you from getting any further than in your finer attributes. So it is more important that they do not find anything wrong with you than that they like you.

Your objective in a screening interview is to pass. This means providing the screener with solid facts that fit into a wholesome picture. You need only to satisfy screeners, not impress them. Avoid any hint of suspicion or controversy. Respond clearly and fully to all questions while volunteering absolutely nothing. If the screeners are not impressed with you, you won't be able to charm or fast-talk your way past them; and if they are satisfied with your credentials, the more you talk, the wider and deeper the potential pitfall.

Deciders

The decision (hiring) interview is commonly conducted by a department head, project leader, supervisor, or any combination of these. Unlike the screener, deci-sion makers most likely know a lot more about the job and related technical details than about interviewing techniques. They are concerned with your ability to do the work, and how you will fit into the environment. They may have to deal with you on a daily basis, and so it matters, to some extent, whether or not they like you.

Since the decision-making interviewer isn't usually a professional interviewer, the decision interview tends to be a less structured affair. This is where you must be prepared for technical questions and informal conversations on a more personal level. This is where you may have to convince potential supervisors and colleagues that you are—in addition to being competent—a reasonably agreeable person. This is where you may use your interpersonal skills to direct the interview in a positive (for you) direction. And this is where you get the information and the *vibes* that help you to make up your own mind about the job.

Personalities

Whenever people with different objectives get together, potential hazards come into play. Despite the best of intentions, objectivity can give way to personal inclination when certain types of individuals confront each other. A few of the more obvious examples include status and authority, male-female, short-tall, and older-younger. Differences of national origin, accent, and style (e.g., flamboyance versus restraint) may also influence an interaction. This is especially true of job interviews.

While confidence and attention are assets in most interview situations, the following conditions call for heightened sensitivity. Since we cannot cover all of the possible personality combinations in a single chapter, we offer these examples as representative of the kinds of efforts that may be needed on both sides of the interview.

Upper management.   The president, the chairperson, and certain department heads may have large egos. When you interview with a bigwig, treat that person with the respect to which he or she is accustomed. Manifest your confidence within the confines of your arena, and tread lightly on their comfort zones.

Consultant-employee.   Interviewing with a manager or project leader who knows, and perhaps resents, the fact that you are making more money (and having a lot more fun) than they is a common situation. The best way to deal with this is to focus on the job to be done and your ability to do the job, and downplay any reference to your lifestyle. Your tack is to convince the interviewer that you are a reliable team player who will make the interviewer look good.

Male-female.   Both should be careful to avoid any innuendo that might be interpreted in a sexual manner. Both male and female candidates should keep their eyes up to face level and feel free to manifest their natural self-confidence by sitting in a conservative manner and refraining from remarks that could possibly be "sexually" misconstrued.

Short-tall.   People whose physical dimensions are considered to be within the norm are often unaware of the sensitivities of exceptionally tall, short, overweight, and otherwise visually unusual individuals. Avoid making any references to these characteristics—your remarks may be misinterpreted.

Older-younger.   When there is a significant difference in age, the elder interviewee should strive to be energetic and careful not to condescend. The younger interviewee should be calm, respectfully confident, and an especially good listener.

One-on-One

As mentioned earlier, personal predispositions can be difficult to avoid, even during a professional interview. Focus your attention on the interviewer rather than on the impression you are trying to make. Listen carefully to what interviewers say, and try to read their reactions to you. If they appear to lose interest in what you're saying, change course by asking them a question; for example,

"Have I answered the question to your satisfaction?"

"Was there something else you wanted me to address?"

"Do you want me to go into (technical) detail?"

"How many people are there in your department?"

"When do you plan to make a decision on this position?"

Outnumbered

When you are being interviewed by two or more potential employer/clients, it may be useful to have some samples of your work, or extra copies of your résumé, to divert their attention. Try to learn, if you don't already know, who has the most authority, and be sure to address that individual at least as often as the others. Pay attention to them all by looking at them, one by one, as you talk. Get them to do most of the talking, if you can, by asking questions based on what they tell you. Answer every question as accurately and completely as you can.

If someone asks a stupid question, focus on any aspect of it that may be sensible; or divert it toward relevancy, if possible, without embarrassing the one who asked it. Example: You are interviewing for a three-to-six-month assignment, and someone asks, "Why are you interested in working for our company?" Instead of shrugging it off, gaping in disbelief, or resorting to sarcasm, try to come up with a face-saver, like, "I've been hearing about your company's accomplishments/innovations in recent months, and this is a chance to learn more about it/them," or "I've been learning a good deal about CASE (DB, etc.), and this looks like an excellent opportunity to apply that knowledge." The point is that even if the individual who asked the silly question does not recognize or appreciate your tact, the others will.

The Interview

When you succeed in getting the interview, be punctual. Plan to arrive early enough that unforeseen delays will not make you late. Excuses for arriving late are just that—*excuses*—even if they are true. Being late is failing to arrive on time, and you don't want a potential employer's initial experience with you to be tainted with any kind of failure.

If you are going to be unavoidably delayed, call the interviewer before the time of the scheduled interview to apologize for inconveniencing him or her, and ask if it would be more convenient to delay the interview or reschedule it.

Credibility is the most important impression to create during an interview. This is accomplished by appearing honest, confident, enthusiastic, courteous, and inoffensive. Speak in a manner that is natural for you; if you have memorized a bunch of technical details, deliver them in a conversational manner, not as if reading from a list. Avoid slang ("like, real cool," "right on," etc.); bad English ("so he goes, 'well, yeah,' and I go, . . ."); profanity of any kind; and criticism (especially of a past employer or someone known to the interviewer). Avoid frequent use of "well," "umm," "y' know," and such.

Try to enjoy the interview itself; this can help you to relax and make a positive impression on the interviewer. Memorize the interviewer's name, and be sure to pronounce it correctly when addressing him or her. And—forgive us for adding the obvious—do not smoke, chew gum, or eat food or candy during an interview. It's OK to accept coffee, tea, or water if offered, although it may be safer to decline. Remember that the interviewer—especially the professional interviewer—is watching you and evaluating your behavior.

Body Language

Eye contact is the dominant feature in nonverbal communications. The way you meet or avoid someone's gaze can reveal volumes about your character and your feelings. Consciously and unconsciously, our eyes contribute to the messages we give out. For example, looking away from the listener while speaking means *don't interrupt me even if I pause for a moment;* looking at the listener when you stop speaking is a signal that you're finished; and looking away from the person who is speaking suggests impatience or dissatisfaction with whatever that person is saying.

It has been estimated that as much as 70 percent of all face-to-face communication is nonverbal. While volumes have been written on this subject, we have summarized the function into a few action verbs:

- *Reach out* to potential employers and clients with a firm handshake on arriving and departing.
- *Smile* as pleasantly as your personality allows.
- *Look* at people when they speak, and make eye contact with each of them in turn when you are talking.

- *Relax* your body, especially your head and hands; avoid abrupt or jerky motions, fidgeting, crossing your arms, or covering your mouth with your hands.

- *Lean* slightly forward, without slouching.

- *Nod* affirmatively to show attention and agreement, and to encourage the interviewer to continue talking, but avoid nodding when they say something with which you disagree.

Evaluating

Winning teams are those that make quick adjustments to what their opponents are doing. A successful interviewee pays attention to what the interviewer says and does, and reacts accordingly. For example, if you are describing your last job or assignment, and the interviewer's eyes begin to wander around the room, it's time to change the topic or to ask a question. If the interviewer glances frequently at the clock on the wall or his or her watch, it may be wise to keep your answers brief. When you do manage to catch the interviewer's interest, hold to that subject, and to similar topics, as long as may be reasonable.

Always listen carefully to what the interviewer says, whether it is what you want to hear or not. Skilled interviewers tell you precisely what they want you to know; unskilled interviewers may reveal more than they realize. In either case, the information an interviewer provides can help you to evaluate the interviewer, the company, and the job, and to respond in an appropriate and relevant manner.

If the interviewer is terse, tense, or unpleasant, don't take it personally. He or she may be having a bad day, or perhaps that's just the personality of the interviewer. Continue to conduct yourself with professional courtesy and enthusiasm, and hope for the best. Unless you experience this sort of unpleasantness often, chances are it isn't worth a second thought.

Responding

Try to answer every question clearly, accurately, and thoroughly without overexplaining or repeating yourself. Maintain consistency between different questions. This is most easily achieved by telling the truth. Be ready for the open-ended type of question, such as, "Tell me about yourself," or "What do you consider to be your major strengths and weaknesses?" In such cases, represent yourself in a believable and work-related manner; discuss your assets in a matter-of-fact manner without overselling them. And try to portray the weakness you choose to reveal as a borderline asset (e.g., "Sometimes I'm a bit of a perfectionist, but I like to get things right," or, "I may get a little impatient when people hold me back, but I've learned to be a team player").

And, above all, assume that if you are telling the truth, you are being believed. With a skilled interviewer, the way you respond to questions can be even more important than the answers; clear, decisive answers contribute to the image of intelligence and credibility.

- *Qualify.*   Ask questions that help to define or clarify what is being asked of you. Example: "Are you more interested in how I designed the system, or in how I applied the methodology?" This keeps you from taking a false path, and gives you a few extra moments to prepare your answer.

- *Clarify.*   After answering a question, check the interviewers' demeanor. If they seem to be satisfied (e.g., they smile or nod), then pause to let them comment or ask another question. If they do not appear comfortable, ask if you have answered the question to their satisfaction and if there are any additional points they would like you to address.

- *Specify.*   Tell what *you* did in your last job, or in your last job related to the position/assignment for which you are applying, aside from the team on which you worked.

- *Quantify.*   Try to put your accomplishments in a meaningful context. Examples: "I wrote a hundred programs averaging half a million lines of code in two years," "We were the only group to complete our project on schedule," or "When my assignment was completed, I was assigned another task by the project leader."

- *Do not lie.*   Plausible exaggeration is the outer limit of creative expression when describing your experience and accomplishments. Employers tend to check up on their prospective employees thoroughly, and a consultant's reputation is his or her lifeline to success. Never tell a verifiable lie to a potential employer/client—even the possibility of its discovery will haunt you.

Controlling the Interview

Projecting an Image

There are three separate aspects of your behavior of which you need to be aware: how you really feel, the image you would like to project, and the interviewer's perception of your behavior.

Your personal feelings are private. You may wish to allow some of them into your projected image, but most of us prefer to filter out at least some of our innermost views and characteristics.

Projecting an image requires an awareness of how others perceive us. Alas, many otherwise clever individuals harbor self-images which are not uniformly shared by those who meet them.

To compensate for potential discrepancies, we suggest the following kind of reality check: ask three or four trusted friends and colleagues of both genders what they consider to be your two or three strongest personality characteristics, both positive and negative. Examples: nice smile, good speaking voice, nervous hand gestures, avoiding eye contact. Use these lists to make up your own list, emphasizing traits which were mentioned more than once, plus any negative traits of which you are already aware. Do not delete any negatives, no matter how strongly you may disagree, or this exercise will be worthless. Remember, you are focusing on how others perceive you, aside from what you may see in yourself. Next, ask three or four of your closest friends and family members to rearrange the list, beginning with your strongest tendencies. The combination of the rearranged lists will likely give you some idea of your public image, pro and con. Then it's up to you to work on what you want to do about it. Note that even positive qualities, when carried to excess, can be negative.

Influencing the interviewer's perception of you, as discussed earlier under "Evaluating," depends on paying careful attention to what the interviewer says and does, perceiving what he or she wants and does not want, and adjusting your approach accordingly. Always bear in mind that what the interviewer wants to hear is more important than what the interviewee wants to say. The closer you come to emphasizing those of your qualities which relate specifically to what the interviewer is looking for, the more successful you will be. Just as it may be counterproductive to ramble on about your IDMS background in a DB2 environment, don't push any skills in which the interviewer appears uninterested.

Turning the Interview Around: Interviewing the Interviewer

Note: this tactic is intended primarily for the decision interview; it is rarely successful with the professional screening interviewer.

One of the most successful interviewee tactics is getting the interviewer to do most of the talking. It is a given that people who talk a lot enjoy talking. So even if you do not get to make all the points you'd like to make, avoid the temptation of interrupting a chatty interviewer. An interview dominated by the interviewer is likely to leave that interviewer with a comfortable feeling about the interviewee.

When interviewers show a tendency to talk about themselves, their company, the surf at Malibu, Bogart movies, or any other subject, let them do so with a minimum of interruption. One way to discover what makes them tick is to politely ask semipersonal questions, such as: "How long have you been working here, if you don't mind my asking?" or "Do you have a long commute?" or (in response to their question) "We have three children; how about you?" You never know what might get them going.

On the other hand, don't get too personal, avoid politics, and stay clear of references to any unusual physical characteristics. Remember, small talk can be a double-edged sword.

Fielding Hard-to-Handle Questions

Before responding to a difficult question, pause just long enough to check your body language and to compose your thoughts.

If you get a technical question for which you are unprepared, tell what (if anything) you know, and admit your ignorance in a straightforward manner (e.g., "I have relatively little background in IDMS—is it essential to this position?" or "I would welcome the opportunity to sharpen my skills on the AS/400" or "I was not informed that C was a prerequisite for this assignment"). Then try to draw attention to an area in which you are more knowledgeable.

Managing Uncomfortable Situations

The *pressure interview* is more frequently encountered by potential employees than consultants, but every interviewee should be prepared for it. Most often, pressure interviews are devised to find out how the candidate will respond to unexpected circumstances; occasionally, they may be inadvertent, the result of internal pressure, an incompetent interviewer, etc. But generally they are intentional, premeditated ploys to see how you react to stress.

The rule of thumb when under pressure is courtesy, tact, and confidence. Don't blow your cool; never let yourself be baited into rudeness, anger, impatience, or agreeing with a point of view with which you really disagree. You can acknowledge the interviewer's point without agreeing ("I understand your point"), and you can politely disagree ("Your point is well taken, although I find that . . .").

If the interviewer stares at you strangely (e.g., in apparent disbelief), don't feel that you must justify whatever you just said. If your statement is challenged, don't back down; show confidence in your position without arguing or becoming flustered. If the interviewer lapses into a prolonged silence after you have finished talking, just sit there calmly, meeting his or her stare as pleasantly as possible, until the interviewer resumes. Don't let interviewers lure you into qualifying, overexplaining, taking back what you have told them, or fidgeting. If they haven't asked a question, you don't have to answer one. If you have been honest with interviewers, you have nothing to feel guilty about. When experienced interviewers behave strangely, their purpose is to see how you respond. Tell yourself that they are testing you, and you will very likely pass the test.

In the following scenarios, you are presented with stressful situations and a number of sample options. The choices are yours. There are no right or wrong answers, only a range of options. It is important to be aware of these potential courses of action, and to be ready to exercise them in time of need. The likely consequences of these options are fairly obvious; your choice is a reflection of your personality and values.

Scenario 1.   You arrive for an interview and are seated by a secretary/receptionist in a typical meeting room containing a table and chairs. This person tells you that Mr./Mrs. Something-or-Other will be there shortly, and leaves. The minutes pass, and no one shows up. You recognize that you are being tested, or that the interviewer has other priorities. How long do you wait (15 minutes? 30? an hour or two or three?) before:

1. Asking the secretary to contact the interviewer
2. Telling the secretary that you have to leave at a certain time
3. Jotting a note on the back of your card and leaving
4. Just leaving

Or do you just sit back and wait, no matter how long it takes? To what extent are you influenced by how badly you want the job? How much are you willing to put up with in order to get the job? One answer is that you should wait until you begin to feel annoyed or that you are being put upon. Why? Because it is better to reschedule the interview than to have your annoyance interfere with the interview—and interfere it will, because it is difficult to hide annoyance.

Scenario 2. After keeping you waiting for an hour or more, the interviewer arrives without apologizing, complaining that there isn't enough time to do all the things he or she needs to do (as if you are responsible for the inconvenience). Throughout the interview the interviewer takes obvious and frequent time checks and repeatedly interrupts you before you can finish what you're saying. What do you do?

1. You ignore the interruptions and continue as if everything were perfectly normal. *If interruptions really do not bother you, no problem!*
2. You ask the interviewer if it might not be preferable to reschedule the interview for a more convenient time. *This is a polite way of letting the interviewer know that you are not prepared to continue.*
3. You tell the interviewer that you do not believe you are receiving a proper opportunity to present your credentials for the job. *There are times when a degree of aggressiveness may be appropriate, as long as it suits your personality.*
4. You suggest (preferably without sarcasm) that both of you might be more comfortable if someone else continued the interview with you. *This is likely to impress the interviewer, although the impression may be negative. On the other hand, there's an outside chance that this was just what the interviewer was looking for.*
5. You refuse to put up with it and leave. *Of course, this will probably end any chance of your getting the job.*

Scenario 3. You arrive for an interview in a conference-room-sized office. The interviewer, who is seated to one side of the room behind a desk, tells you that he or she will be with you in a minute. The only chairs in the room, aside from the interviewer's, are around the table at the opposite end of the room. What do you do?

As in the preceding scenarios, your choice should be the one with which you are most comfortable and for which you are prepared to accept the consequences.

1. You quietly wait for the interviewer to tell you what to do. *After all, the interviewer is running the show.*

2. You ask the interviewer where to sit. *This is the polite thing to do.*

3. You wander around the office, waiting for the interviewer to act. *The interviewer will get around to you when he or she is ready; meanwhile, you'll do your thing.*

4. You invite the interviewer to join you at the table. *This is a polite way of asserting yourself.*

5. You bring a chair from the table to the desk and sit down. *This is an aggressive way to assert yourself.*

6. You sit in a chair at the table, and wait. *Patience is a virtue.*

7. You sit in a chair at the table and read a newspaper (pretend to make notes in a notebook, etc.). *Two can play that game.*

8. You sit on a corner of the table and glance at your watch from time to time. *You are not intimidated, and you haven't got all day.*

9. You turn around and leave. *You don't need this.*

10. You tell the interviewer off, and then leave. *Who do they think they are, anyway?*

Postinterview Follow-Up

Communicating

If your interview was arranged by an agency, call your contact no later than the afternoon following a morning interview, or the very next morning after an afternoon interview (unless the interviewer calls you first). Avoid the temptation to call or write directly to the interviewer, unless he or she is expecting you to follow up with information.

Negotiating for a Salaried Position

Do your best to find out the company's salary range for the job you want, and how much you can reasonably expect them to pay you. Then consider the least you are willing to accept. Now you're ready to negotiate.

Never bring up the question of salary yourself; try to avoid revealing what you are currently earning, unless they insist, with a comment like, "I would rather not discuss that." If they say they need to know what you are earning in order to make you an offer, you can suggest a figure that you know to be within their range. Once you ask for a certain amount, unless you are willing to negotiate, be prepared to stick to it. If their offer is final but a little on the low side, you could ask that, if they are satisfied with your performance after six months (for example), they then give you a salary review (i.e., more money). It never hurts to try.

Negotiating for a
Consulting Contract

Once your qualifications for the job have been established, try to find out what the client/agency is willing to pay. Of course, agencies are skilled negotiators, and they may have alternative resources from which to choose. Typically, they will ask you your rate. If you give them a precise number, there is little chance of their offering you more; if you give them a range, there may be room for discussion without scaring them away. If you are adamant, obviously there is no room for negotiation.

To negotiate your rate successfully, you must be aware of what the market will bear in your specialty. Your willingness to accept a lower rate than you would like, for a period of time, depends upon your need.

Managing Your Expectations

Just as you convinced the interviewer—and yourself—that you wanted the job during the interview, consider afterward the possibility that you may not get it. Try not to let any one position or contract become so important that you will be severely disappointed if it doesn't work out. Conversely, don't talk yourself into believing that you did a bad job at the interview.

Remember that—whether you get it or not—it's only a job.

Summary

The job interview is a necessary part of earning a living. Interviewing is hard work and, fortunately, a skill at which one can improve. It is definitely worth the effort. Consider it an investment not only in obtaining a job but also in keeping a job and moving on to better jobs. Keep in mind that the fundamental principles of successful interviewing (preparation and presentation) are the building blocks of nearly every aspect of your professional career.

2
You and the Employment Agency

Michael Sichel

Looking for a new job is serious work. The job seeker may suddenly find him or herself in the position of asking some difficult questions, such as, "What kind of work do I really want to do?" and "How much can I expect to earn?"

These questions call for realistic self-examination and appraisal, and perhaps some conversations with a few close friends and associates. Only after they have been resolved is the job seeker ready to initiate consultations with qualified employment agents.

Types of Employment Agencies

Private employment agents or agencies are grouped by the method in which they receive compensation. The major categories are *fee-paid, retained-search,* and *fee paid by applicant.*

Fee-paid agencies receive their compensation from the employer only after successfully placing the applicant within that company. The determination of fee is made between the company and the agent; the applicant is in no way responsible for any payment to the agent.

Fee-paid agents provide professional guidance because they are paid by hiring companies to do so. These counselors are paid for successful performance, which is measured by getting the job seeker an appropriate job (i.e., one which correctly matches the needs of the candidate and the employer). Only a fee-paid agency will provide a combination of professional evaluation, tailored job search, and interview preparation at no cost to the job seeker.

Retained-search agencies receive their compensation from the employer at the inception of the search procedure. These firms also differ from fee-paid agencies in that they rigidly search out those who possess a preestablished set of experience and credentials. A retained-search firm is not likely to be interested in a candidate who does not meet their client's criteria; they will neither counsel nor assist those job seekers whose experience deviates from predetermined requirements.

Fee paid by applicant agencies receive their compensation from the job seeker. Payment may be made in full at the beginning of the search (on the guarantee of presenting the candidate's résumé to a given number of companies), or on the installment plan after the candidate has begun work for an employer to whom they were presented by the agency. In either event, the job seeker signs a binding agreement to pay them a fee out of his or her own pocket.

Selecting Employment Agencies

Assuming you opt for a fee-paid agency, your next step is to select at least three such agents or agencies in the data processing industry for optimum coverage. The best selection method is word of mouth. If, for instance, your specialty is in the mainframe area, you might do well to ask other large-systems people about the agencies that placed them in their current job. If you do not know anyone who has the kind of job you're seeking, contact local user groups to ask for referrals to quality agents. Be sure to identify your level of experience to your contact—a recent graduate with a B.S. degree in Computer Science should seek an agency that specializes in placing beginners rather than one that focuses on placing MIS directors.

When you are given the name of an agency, try to have your source also provide you with the name of a specific counselor who specializes in placing individuals at your career level. This distinction is very important, because counselors tend to specialize in specific industry niches. You will profit most from dealing with a counselor whose interest lies in your unique market.

After collecting a list of three such specialists, take the time to update your résumé; be sure to list your education, job experience, and references. If you have never written a résumé, check with your local bookstore for a copy of a leading résumé book. Use a common word processing software package, if available, to create a draft of your résumé, or pay someone to input it for you. You can always make adjustments, such as those suggested by your employment counselors, later on.

With your résumé and your list of agents and agencies before you, you're now ready to phone the counselors to arrange initial evaluation meetings. Bear in mind that although a counselor may appear less formal than a prospective employer, the counselor will nevertheless evaluate your professionalism, poise, and communication skills against those of other candidates. While you should try to relax and behave in an open and friendly manner, remember that you are initiating a business relationship.

Explain briefly to the agent the reason for your call, and be prepared to give a synopsis of your experience and goals. It's best to leave the subject of salary open, but don't be too evasive about past or current compensation. Close the conversation by asking for an appointment at the agent's earliest convenience. Remember, too, that the phrase, "thank you for your time" is still one of the most underused and overappreciated phrases in business. In the event that the counselor asks you to send a fax of your résumé prior to the interview, don't forget to include a brief cover letter—a paragraph is sufficient. It is important to realize that the agent's only estimate of how you will handle yourself with their treasured clients will be based on how you interact with them.

Employment Agency Interview

Your personal interview with the employment agent will define the way your personal traits, professional history, educational background, and goals conform to job opportunities in your selected area. Prepare by bringing with you your résumé, a pad for notes, a proper (preferably dark) interview suit, and an open mind. The agent's initial impression of you is likely to set the tone for the entire business relationship, and whether you get presented to their "A" or "B" list companies. Remember to smile, offer a firm handshake, and speak up in a confident tone.

As a general rule, you and the agent will begin with a review of your history as documented in the résumé. This is where you may begin to note changes in form or emphasis. A general discussion to fill in any blanks may follow. Normally, such talks will be led with open questions which invite a free discussion (e.g., "What is your current job like?" or "What do you see yourself doing in five years?"). By contrast, a closed question is designed to produce a much shorter response by narrowing your answer to a specific area. Examples include: "How much was your gross pay in 1992?" or "What is your address?"

After determining your experience and career goals, the agent may ask you to take a standard industry test in your skill set. You are advised to take this opportunity to show the agent what you know and how you handle yourself, even if the test is presented informally. Don't be defensive or consider a test as a personal attack, and avoid behaving defensively, or you may dampen the agent's interest in promoting you to their clients.

Following this evaluation, the agent will typically begin to explore specific job opportunities. With the full range of your qualifications in mind, the agent is ready to assess your interest in current positions which meet your unique experience and skills. This process also serves to help the agent fine-tune his or her understanding of what you're looking for. Once a group of job opportunities has been uncovered, the agent may advise you how best to present your credentials on paper.

After revising the outline, content, and emphasis of your résumé, the agent may ask about your availability for interviews. Of course, agents understand that if you are currently employed, your time is not entirely your own. In fact, most counselors respect your loyalty to your current job, even though you plan to leave it for a better job. This demonstrates your conscientiousness and professionalism.

Communications procedures (when and where to call each other) are the final part of this initial meeting. Be sure to let the agent know how much notice you require for an interview, and when your revisions to the résumé will be complete.

Preparation for the Job Interview

During the week following submission of the complete résumé, you may expect a call from the agent with a time and date for your first client interview. Typically, the agent will ask you to drop by the office an hour or two before the interview for a discussion of any issues peculiar to the client and department. After a brief discussion, which may cover appropriate dress for the interview and what to bring, don't forget the little courtesies that translate into polished interpersonal skills and are likely to keep your résumé on the top of the agent's list.

At the interview strategy meeting, the agent may provide you with a complete review of the client company, position at hand, interviewer, hiring cycle, and other related information. These details may include the size of the firm, gross sales, number of employees, product line, and so on. This overview will be geared toward your job's place in the scheme of things. You should also receive information related to tangible realities, such as upward mobility within your potential department, the general culture of the company, its history, and perhaps some details about one or two of your potential colleagues.

Most importantly, the agent will review with you the complete job description, including duties and responsibilities, a history of the last person to have held this post, technical data on the department mechanisms which may affect you, an explanation of why the job is open, the person to whom you will report, salary range, and so forth. Of course, some of these details, especially those concerning personalities, are off the record.

The interview strategy meeting continues with a review of the process through which candidates proceed at this particular company. This process is referred to as the *hiring cycle*. You will be apprised of any tests you may be expected to take, the need for any peer interviews, personnel evaluations, department-head interviews, bonding exams, etc. Thus you will know what to expect throughout the hiring procedure.

Every interview is an opportunity to learn. The best way to approach an interview is with confidence in the fact that you will learn from the experience. Adjust your expectations accordingly. Don't go to the interview with a desire to prove or disprove, or to earn points or pass out judgments. Instead, be ready to give and receive information. There is no need to be nervous when you are well prepared. Always ask the client interviewer for company literature at the close of the interview.

The rule of thumb in any client follow-up situation is to contact the agent immediately following the interview; do not send any letters or information which has not been personally reviewed by the agent to the client company. On occasion, the client interviewer will request that certain additional documentation be brought with you to subsequent interviews. This request might be for anything from a college diploma to a writing sample.

With three professional agents dialing the phones on your behalf, discretion is your part of the bargain. If asked, let each agent know that you are working with other counselors, but keep their names to yourself. In particular, hold the names of the companies with which you are currently interviewing in the strictest of confidence. Since agents are in constant competition with each other, such information is their stock-in-trade; sharing it with another agent would constitute a serious breach of trust which may also hurt you in the long run.

The initial client interview will also help you to narrow or, in some cases, expand the focus of the job search. During your follow-up conversation with the agent, share your thoughts and feelings about the job and department; describe the place within the department which is of most interest to you. It is not uncommon to hear an applicant make a comment like, "The posting department is the front end of the business; although I am still interested in similar jobs, I couldn't help becoming curious about the research group."

As mentioned earlier, the interviewing process can be a learning experience; it may be to your advantage to keep an open mind to various job opportunities presented by the agent. The interaction between agent and job seeker is flexible by nature—there should be room for change within the parameters of career goals and compensation set up at the evaluation stage. It is the agent's duty to provide the job seeker with a variety of options, and it is the job seeker's prerogative to either accept or decline pursuit of those options.

The second meeting with the client company is usually with the hiring manager (who may be your immediate boss) and one or two peers. This is followed by a collective assessment of how well you meet both the required professional skills necessary to successfully perform the job function and also the intangible qualities required to fit in with the department. To properly prepare for this step, you need a strategy meeting with the agent.

The agent will counsel you on the setup of the department. You will be clued in on the variety of power structures, skills, personalities, and peculiarities of the department's inhabitants. For example, an individual manager might look for a person who can take the ball and run with it—failure to respond to his or her questions or comments with an extemporaneous solution might damage your hopes of landing the job. An experienced and qualified counselor should prepare you to safely avoid many hidden pitfalls, and you must use this information to your advantage.

The manner in which a job is initially presented by the personnel department and the reality of the day-to-day duties performed at the functional level may differ substantially. In this area of disparity, the agent may prove to be an invaluable guide in determining more accurately what is expected of the new employee. The agent may be able to provide you with a report of the current projects in the hiring manager's department, preparing you to make some positive analogies between your past experience and some current problems with which the department is dealing.

In some cases, a third party may be perceived as less threatening and therefore more effective in a fact-finding role. The agent may be viewed by the hiring company as an extension of the human resource department, a benign helper who is part of the team. In the purest sense, the agent is all of these and, as your counselor, he or she is also your advocate. The agent will not, of course, misrepresent the skills or abilities of the candidate to the hiring company. They will, however, provide the job seeker with the necessary information required to allow his or her full abilities to be fairly evaluated. In this sense, the interests of both parties are effectively served.

After your meetings with the hiring department, a follow-up call or (preferably) a meeting is scheduled to assess the potential fit of opportunity and job candidate. Here again, you should openly express both your doubts and your interest in the job opportunity.

Negotiating
the Employment Offer

There is always a thrill, and a sense of pride and achievement, when the agent informs you of a positive client response. All of the work and effort have proved fruitful, and an exhilarating sense of accomplishment is well deserved. At this point, the employment agency must address the issues of compensation, benefits, and advancement. The agent has to conceive an accurate picture of the essential needs and limits of both parties in order to accurately present to each the desires of the other. The deliberateness of the coordinated effort and the appearance of natural progression are the skills of a qualified agent.

To provide you with full and accurate details of the offer, the agent provides the client with a review of the duties, compensation, and benefits acceptable to you and requests that the client draft an offer letter. It is rare to see a placement which does not require a negotiation of the offer. To this end, it is the agent's job to use his or her negotiating skills to produce a successful conclusion.

The review of the offer letter is always done in person. A career move is an important turning point in your life. Be aware of the fact that you will spend the major portion of your waking hours with the people in their department, and that your success or failure may hinge on your ability to effectively interact with them. You may want to have the reporting structures spelled out. Perhaps you would feel more comfortable with a written determination of your duties.

Once an accurate adjustment of the offer has been made, the agent will inform the client company of the amendments to the offer which meet the candidate's needs. Most often, the parties are closer to agreement than may have been initially believed. Here also, the agent is an invaluable resource; having the unique view of an objective party enables the agent to suggest solutions based on the interests of both client company and job seeker.

In summary, the employment agent and the job seeker are most evenly complemented on the fee-paid level. Your value to the agent is as a respected professional, with a salable set of assets and abilities. The agent's value to you is as a qualified professional with the ability to immeasurably simplify the job-getting process and to increase the probability of successful conclusion through professional know-how.

As you use the tried and proven concepts detailed in this chapter, it is my hope that you may find them to be as beneficial to your job search as they have been to the literally hundreds of candidates who have been assisted over the years. Good hunting.

3

Interviewing Frameworks

Barry Glasgow, Ph.D.

Introduction

The purpose of this chapter is to give the reader an insight into what MIS managers are looking for when interviewing a job candidate. MIS managers want to:

1. Find out if the job applicant is suitable for the position.
2. Provide sufficient information for the applicant to realistically evaluate the position and the company.

The ultimate goal of the employment process is to hire a competent employee who can perform the current job, has potential for future growth, and is reasonably happy with the position.

It would be nice if the manager could describe the position, its responsibilities and technical requirements, and then ask the applicant to rate his or her qualifications and abilities to handle the position. Unfortunately, this naive approach does not work. The interview process should be structured to essentially achieve this result.

To facilitate hiring, the MIS manager should concurrently use several frameworks or views to organize, analyze, and collect the data.

This chapter discusses:

- Three frameworks for achieving this goal
- Knowledge to be collected from each phase
- Purpose and analysis of this data
- Interviewing techniques

This chapter is concerned with general issues, and does not concentrate on a particular job description (e.g., programmer analyst, communication engineer, C/UNIX programmer) or technology (e.g., information engineering, COBOL, DB2). Subsequent chapters will present detailed domain questions from these areas.

Does every interviewer use these frameworks? No. Some interviewers will have alternative sets of frameworks but, although the organization may be different, there will be a large overlap of questions. Other interviewers will not have taken the time or expended the effort to organize their goals for this meeting.

Three frameworks I use during the job interview and applicant evaluation are:

- The Input-Analysis-Output (IAO) model
- Evidence-Analysis (EA) procedure
- The Job-Employee-Employer (JEE) model

The Input-Analysis-Output (IAO) Model

The IAO model addresses two concerns: the employer's and the applicant's.

The employer analyzes the information presented by the employee to produce the required outputs for judging the individual suitability for the position requirements as documented in the JEE model.

The Inputs to This Model Include the Applicant's
- Résumé
- Physical appearance
- Answers during the interview
- Written work, including tests and previous work
- Questions asked by the applicant
- Education, transcripts
- References

The Outputs of This Model Include
- Appraisal of job skills, including:
  Technical competency
  Business knowledge
  Communication skills, both verbal and written
- Work ethics evaluation, including:
  Ability to work with others
  Handling long hours, emergencies, pressure
  Honesty/integrity

- Job satisfaction forecast, including:

   Probability that applicant will stay at least two years

   Salary and benefit expectations

   Growth potential

The applicant has less physical evidence to go on:

- Annual reports, recent news articles
- Information from company's human resource department
- Answers and questions during the interview

The Applicant Goal Is to Assess

- What the position entails:

   Job description

   Technical skills required

   Hardware platform

   Software

   Maintenance versus development

   Chance to learn new technical skills

- Working environment, including:

   Project team or independent work

   Amount of client contact

   Overtime responsibility

   Work at home, emergencies, time and financial compensations

- Career path opportunity:

   Chances of advancement

   Current salary, potential for increases, bonus

   Benefits, education, training

   Stability of position, chances of a layoff

Evidence-Analysis (EA) Procedure

A special type of analysis beyond the IAO must be done to verify and validate the information presented. Verification is the process of checking individual facts about the employee (e.g., if the applicant actually worked at a particular company for the time period specified on the résumé). Validation looks at the applicant's total image for consistency (e.g., the applicant claims to have a master's degree in engineering from a foreign university; no transcript is available, but the applicant cannot answer questions about calculus).

The applicant wants to convey his or her competence and ability to do the job. Unless there is a total mismatch, the applicant never wants to reject the position during an interview. The employer wants to convey that this is a good opportunity, one that will advance the applicant's career. The manager, assuming it is not a complete mismatch, wants to hold out the promise that a reasonable applicant may be hired. The manager does not know if future applicants will be as good or whether a previous better applicant will accept the position.

Given the deviousness and cross-purposes of each party, it is the responsibility of each party to verify and validate what has been said and what conclusions have been reached.

It behooves each party to:

- Test the information for consistency and completeness
- When required, expand and ask for additional explanations
- Interpret

The applicant has less physical evidence to validate than the employer. His or her sources of information include the company's annual reports (if a publicly held company), individuals the applicant knows who have worked for the company or manager, and company policy as written in employee handbooks and literature.

The employer has references, previous work history, and educational records that can be verified. Data relating to work done, people supervised, courses taken, and salary history have to be checked.

The Job-Employee-Employer (JEE) Model

In the JEE framework the particular requirements of the position are assessed. The employer, through an accurate job description and understanding of the position responsibilities, attaches weights to these requirements and emphasizes them during the employment process. Similarly, it helps the employee to understand how his or her strengths relate to the particular position. JEE provides a weighting factor (on a scale from 1 to 10) to evaluate the importance of each requirement.

A programmer working on a particular algorithm may require technical competence above all else, whereas a business analyst will need balance between business knowledge, communication skills, and technical competence.

Interplay between IAO and JEE Frameworks

IAO determines how well (on a scale from 1 to 10) the applicant scored on each requirement. JEE attaches the weights to these requirements based on the particulars of the job description and the employer's needs. The applicant's score can be found by multiplying his or her grade on each requirement (from IAO) by the importance placed on that requirement (from JEE) and summing across all requirements.

Questions and Answers

Remember, the answer to a question is assembled from all the inputs described in the IAO model. The résumé will provide initial chronological ordering of your work history and highlight relevant skills for the job. The interviewer will want you to elaborate and expand on areas relevant to the position.

Question-asking is an iterative nonlinear process. The initial data supplied by your inputs, driven by the goals from JEE, suggest successive series of questions. The interviewer will sometimes focus a series of questions to clarify a detail, or ask open questions to get new material not previously covered or suspected.

A good question gets new information from you, something the interviewer did not already know, whether favorable or unfavorable. The best answer you can give is an honest answer that gives the interviewer the required information and also suggests other questions that will accentuate your positives and allow you to talk about your strengths.

Sample Questions and Analysis

Why an interviewer asks a question and what his or her goals are is germane to how you answer. I have indicated the framework or, in some cases, the multiple frameworks in which the information from a question will be used.

Technical questions will be found in the appropriate chapters. We will concentrate on questions that establish the applicant's work ethic, preferred style of work, and desired career path.

Q: *Why are you leaving your current position?*
A: (IAO, EA.) Interviewer is trying to find out if (1) you are leaving voluntarily or (2) you were let go. If (1), what are your motives (i.e., primarily financial, career enhancement, dissatisfaction with your current position)? If (2), what was the reason (i.e., being a casualty of an overall downsizing, lack of technical skills, work ethics, working relations with fellow workers)?

References and your total work history will be used to collaborate and verify your answer.

Q: *Why have you left your last several positions after a short period (less than two years)?*
A: (EA, IAO.) A pattern of frequent job changes has to be explained.

Q: *How did you get along with your coworkers, superiors, clients?*

A: (IAO, JEE.) "I got along fine with everyone." Analysis: too general, a platitude. If you had a problem, it may be helpful and informative to describe how you solved it. Reality is that you can't have a perfect relationship with everyone, so explain how you handled a problem.

Q: *How did you communicate with your coworkers, superiors, clients?*

A: (IAO, JEE.) This is an alternate form of the previous question which can be used to probe for writing skills, familiarity with E-mail, and whether or not you use PCs.

Q: *Did you work as a team member (how many people on the team) or individually?*

A: (IAO, JEE.) How did the employee relate to a team? What role was assumed? Was the applicant a leader or a follower? (Both can be valuable depending upon the particular position.)

Q: *Do you want management responsibilities?*

A: (JEE, IAO.) Employee has shown technical ability in previous job, but this is the first position where applicant will be a project leader and assume supervisory responsibility.

Q: *Did you have management responsibilities?*

A: 1. *Project management.* (JEE.) Managing a multiperson, multiphase software project is a distinct skill. The interviewer is looking for familiarity with different project and task representations, such as PERT or Gantt charts, and with concepts such as critical path, resource loading, slack and lead time.

   2. *Budgeting.* (IAO, JEE.) You may have experience being a project leader, but not the responsibilities for budgeting the project.

   3. *Supervisory experience.* How did you deal with a difficult employee (incompetent, poor work habits)? (IAO, EA.) Dealing with a problem employee is a critical success factor in management. Poorly handled, it can result in an employee being fired or a project team being demoralized. The interviewer is trying to learn something about your style, how you approach interpersonal work relations. Also, if you have inflated your previous management experience, it may be hard for you to describe how you have dealt with a difficult employee.

Q: *Did you have to write? What type of documents? (JEE, IAO.) If the position involves heavy analysis, contact with operations (either computer and/or back office), or client contact, then the ability to communicate in written and verbal form is very important.*

A: Contrast these two answers:

   1. Answer A: "I write memos when I have to."

   2. Answer B: "I have prepared formal documents including graphical elements using a word processor and incorporating outputs from a spread sheet."

Q: *Have you made presentations to management and/or clients?*
A: (JEE, IAO.) An important skill for an analyst or project manager is the ability to present information.

Q: *Can you use a PC for presentations, word processing?*
A: (IAO.) You have begun to pursue new technology.

Q: *What is your salary history?*
A: (JEE, EA.) This information should already be known to the interviewer. Your answers to this question and the next allow a manager to judge how important financial considerations are in order for you to accept the job. Your answer should be factual and correct.

Q: *What are your expectations for future raises and a bonus?*
A: (IAO, EA.) The interviewer is trying to ascertain whether you will be happy, from a financial perspective, at this job. Also, if you are aggressive in your financial requirements, there is an inference that this may relate to why you are leaving your current position.

Q: *Will you be going to school, college, graduate school?*
A: (IAO, JEE.) On the positive side, going to school indicates the desire to improve your skills and motivation to stay current (assuming that your classwork relates to the required skills of the position). On the negative side, it represents time you cannot spend on the job. If the new position requires tight deadlines, overtime, and resolution of frequent production problems, then you must explain how schooling can be handled in this context. It is important to indicate whether your schooling is degree-related and to determine what the tuition reimbursement policy is.

Q: *Do you like to work independently or on teams?*
A: (JEE.) There is no right answer to this question. It gets down to your personality. Some MIS jobs are extremely technical and relatively isolated, where an asocial hacker might be acceptable. On the other hand, many MIS projects are large and require a team effort where cooperation, negotiation, and people skills are important.

Q: *Do you want to work directly with clients or from specifications?*
A: (JEE, IAO.) This is similar to the previous question. The nature of the position will dictate the amount of contact. An analyst's job will require heavy user interface. Hopefully, unless you are desperate, you are applying for jobs that emphasize your abilities and your likes.

Q: *Have you worked with clients?*
A: (JEE, IAO.) Again, similar to the previous question.

Q: *What is your ideal position?*
A: (IAO.) What you say, what you don't say, and how you say it are all important. Do you emphasize personal growth, the ability to be visible, the chance to help your colleagues, financial reward?

Q: *Rate your skill level.*

A: (IAO, JEE, EA.) You know your own ability better than anyone else. The interviewer is trying to get your own evaluation. However, the interviewer has probably formed an opinion of your strengths and weaknesses already. If your evaluation basically validates the interviewer, fine; if there is a large variance, then be prepared for detailed questions to clarify the difference in opinions.

Q: *How confident are you that you can perform this job?*

A: (EA, IAO, JEE.) Employers want confident employees, especially if they believe you are being honest. If the job is a real leap for you, it may be realistic to express some of the fears you have about the position, but the employer still expects you to feel comfortable that you can handle the new position.

Q: *What do you think is the hardest part of this job? Your past jobs?*

A: (EA, JEE.) A really bad answer is, "This is an easy job. There are no problems." Whereas the employer wants you to be confident, he or she does not expect you to think of this new position as trivial.

   If you have been listening, and if the interviewer has been discussing the position, you should have formed some opinion of what will be difficult for you to do in this new position. By highlighting these areas, you show that you have a good understanding of the job.

Q: *What is the easiest part of this job? Your past jobs?*

A: (EA, JEE.) This is a complementary form of the previous question.

Q: *What do you know about the business domain?*

A: (JEE, IAO.) The quality of software built improves if the programmer understands the business context of the system. If you do not currently understand the business domain, are you interested in learning it?

Q: *Can you handle the pressure, deadlines, and production problems?*

A: (JEE.) If you have personal or other commitments such that you cannot handle deadlines or production problems, it is important to discuss the implications of these constraints. It may cost you a position, but getting a pressure position that you cannot manage is worse.

Q: *Can you work at home or come into the office if a problem occurs outside of your normal work hours?*

A: (JEE, IAO.) If the position involves a critical application, you will be responsible for resolving production problems.

Q: *What skills do you want to learn or improve?*

A: (IAO.) The interviewer wants to know if you have a realistic understanding of your good and bad points and a plan for improving your weak areas and capitalizing on your strengths.

Q: *Where do you want to be in two, five years?*
A: (IAO.) If your goals are too aggressive, you may not be happy with the position. If you have no aspirations for advancement, you may not be alert to the challenge of the position.

Q: *Why do you want this job?*
A: (IAO, JEE, EA.) This is an open-ended question which gives you a chance to:
   Show that you understand the position
   Summarize your strengths and how they dovetail with the requirements for the position
   Identify any issues that have to be resolved

In summary, we have presented a model of the interaction between the interviewee and interviewer. For the employer this framework provides guidelines as to how information can be extracted from the interview process.

4
MVS for the Application Programmer

Maria I. Martins

Introduction

Multiple Virtual Storage (MVS) is currently available in three versions: MVS/SP, MVS/XA, and MVS/ESA. MVS dates back to the 1970s with the introduction of OS that ran on the System/370. As time passed, the MVS system expanded to address needs which have arisen. Some other models of computers which utilize MVS are: the IBM 43xx, 30xx, and 9370. In 1990, IBM introduced the System/390. MVS/SP and MVS/XA run on the System/370. System/390 also utilizes MVS/ESA.

The main/major components of MVS are Job Management, Task Management, Data Management, Storage Management, Resource Management, Recovery Termination Management, and Systems Application Architecture. The following is a brief description of the major functions performed by these features:

1. Job Management (job entry subsystem)
   - Controls reading and scheduling of jobs
   - Controls initiation and allocation tasks for jobs
   - Controls execution and termination of jobs
   - Sends output to proper devices
   - Allows remote users to submit jobs as easily as those located near the computer
2. Task Management
   - Supervises the dispatching and service requests of work in the system

3. Data Management
   - Stores and retrieves data
   - Provides sequential, partitioned, and Virtual Storage Access Method (VSAM) dataset support

4. Storage Management (storage management subsystem)
   - Is used to manage user (disk) datasets
   - Allows datasets to be migrated to tape for long-term storage based on usage and importance
   - Consolidates fragmented disk space and moves datasets around on the disk packs to balance usage
   - Makes JCL easier for programmers because the operating system calculates an optimum block size for all datasets if the user does not supply one
   - Is available only with MVS/ESA

5. Resource Management
   - Allocates computer resources
   - Utilizes time-sharing options (such as TSO, CICS, and VTAM, which allow simultaneous use by a large number of users)
   - Supports multiprogramming, which is used to maximize the efficiency of the system

6. Recovery Termination Management
   - Ensures proper recovery from system and hardware failures

7. Systems Application Architecture (SAA)
   - Common User Access, which makes applications look alike to the user
   - Common Programming Interface, which provides the same computer languages and program services across IBM platforms
   - Common Communications Support, which allows IBM computers to talk to each other
   - Common Applications, which allows application programs to run on various IBM platforms

Virtual Storage. Virtual storage is the component of the MVS system that allows application programs to have storage addresses independent of the addresses of the computer's central storage. When a program begins execution, the system loads it onto virtual storage and, as resources become available, it loads pages of the program into real storage to be executed. With virtual storage, a program occupies only a small amount of real storage. This gives the ability to run a program whose size exceeds the central storage available. Virtual storage also allows many programs to run on the computer simultaneously through the use of multiprogramming.

Multiprogramming. Multiprogramming attempts to maximize the efficiency of the computer by keeping the major components (such as the CPU, I/O devices, and central storage) busy. A multiprogramming system can keep several jobs inside the computer and switch back and forth between them. It is able to do this because most jobs do not use all the storage, all the I/O devices, and the CPU at the same time.

Job Entry Subsystem (JES). Job Entry Subsystem (JES2 or JES3) interfaces with JCL. JES2 and JES3 are subsystems which provide similar functions, as if one had several computers linked together. They keep track of jobs that enter the system, determine when jobs are executed, and send output to the appropriate device—normally, a printer.

Terminology

MVS/SP: Multiple Virtual System/Systems Program.

MVS/XA: Multiple Virtual System/Extended Architecture.

MVS/ESA: Multiple Virtual System/Enterprise Systems Architecture.

Address space: A "complete" range of addresses. The maximum size of an address space is limited by the number of digits used to represent addresses.

JES: Job Entry Subsystem. Keeps track of jobs that enter the system, determines when they are executed, and sends each job's printed output to the correct printer.

SMS: Storage Management Subsystem. Manages user disk datasets.

SAA: Systems Application Architecture. A concept used to make IBM's major product lines (such as MVS and VM, AS/400, and PS/2) compatible.

Partitioned dataset: Often called PDS or library. It consists of a directory and one or more members. A PDS directory is a list of the members in a library. A member has a one-to-eight-character member name.

Master catalog: Contains catalog entries for system files and files that begin with SYS1, and user catalogs.

User catalog: Contains catalog entries for user's datasets.

Questions and Answers

Abends

Q: *What is a system completion code?*

A: A system completion code is a three-position identifier controlled by MVS. Programs have no access to it. It is prefaced under MVS with literal 'S' in the form of 'Snnn'. NNN stands for a three-position hexadecimal number. The error message will print on the JCL in the format of 'Snnn-rc'. RC stands for the return code associated with the system message which further describes the error.

Q: *What is an operation exception error?*

A: An operation exception error indicates that an operation code is not assigned or the assigned operation is not available on a particular computer model. The machine did not recognize the instruction or operation used. A possible reason is a subscript error. This error could also be caused by an attempt to read a file that was not opened, a misspelled ddname, or a missing DD statement. The system completion code is 0C1.

Q: *What is a protection exception error?*

A: A protection exception error occurs when the program is attempting to access a memory address that is not within the memory area that the program is authorized to use. Some of the causes may be a subscript or index that is not initialized or has taken on a value outside the bounds of the table with which it is associated, an attempt to read an opened file, or an incorrect or missing DD statement. The system completion code is 0C4.

Q: *What is an addressing exception error?*

A: An addressing exception error occurs when a program is attempting to access a memory location which is outside the bounds of available real storage on the machine. This can be caused by a dataset not being opened at the time an I/O was directed to it, an attempt to close a dataset a second time, incorrectly called module parameters or coding, improper exit from a performed paragraph, or uninitialized subscript or index. The system completion code is 0C5.

Q: *What is a data exception error?*

A: A data exception error indicates an attempt to perform an arithmetic operation on nonnumeric data. It can also occur from incorrect input data to a program that is not performing sufficient numeric testing on it before attempting arithmetic. The system completion code is 0C7.

Q: *What return code can be issued when the operator cancels a job?*

A: There are two return codes which can be produced when the operator cancels a job. They are 122 and 222. A 122 indicates the operator canceled the job and requested a dump. A 222 indicates the operator canceled the job without a dump. It is important to ask the operator why the job was canceled. Some of the reasons this may occur are: the program needed a resource that was not available; the program appeared to be stalled in a wait state; or the program was in an apparent loop.

Q: *What return code is issued if a job or job step exceeded the time limit?*

A: The system will issue a system code of 322 when a job or job step has exceeded the time limit. If the time parameter was used on the JOB or EXEC statement, it may not have allowed enough time for the job or job step to complete. If the time parameter was not used, then it is important to check the program for possible logic loops.

Q: *When the system cannot find enough virtual storage, which system abend is issued?*

A: When the system cannot find enough virtual storage during a GETMAIN macro instruction, it generates a system abend of 804 or 80A. Check for program errors that incorrectly modify the storage request. If the REGION parameter has been used, either on the JOB or EXEC statement, it may need to be increased to satisfy the request.

Q: *Which system completion code is issued when a program module cannot be found?*

A: A system completion code of 806 will be issued when a program module cannot be found. Some of the causes may be missing the STEPLIB statement from the step or missing the JOBLIB statement from the job stream. Most likely the program name was misspelled on the EXEC statement or in a source code CALL.

Q: *What are some of the abends generated when not enough disk space is available and what do they mean?*

A: Some of the abends generated due to a lack of available disk space are:

1. B37—Disk volume out of space, cannot write output. The system gave all the primary space and as much secondary space as it could.

2. D37—Primary disk space was exceeded and either no secondary space allocation was specified or it was insufficient. One should increase the primary space as well as provide adequate secondary space allocation to eliminate this error.

3. E37—There was insufficient space on the volume. One way to solve this problem is to specify more volumes on the JCL.

Q: *Which abend is issued when the system cannot find a member on a partitioned dataset?*

A: An S013-18 abend occurs when the specified member on the JCL is not found on the indicated PDS (Partitioned Dataset). Determine if the member is spelled correctly on your JCL. If it is not, then fix member name and resubmit job. If it is correct, then determine why it is not on the PDS, take the necessary steps to place it on the PDS, and resubmit the job.

Q: *What normally causes an S013-20 abend?*

A: An S013-20 is normally caused by the block size not being a multiple of the record length or being incorrect for variable-length records. Divide your BLKSIZE by the record length to make sure it is a multiple of the BLKSIZE. If not, correct it and resubmit job. For variable-length records, it is necessary to have your BLKSIZE be at least 4 bytes greater than your record length.

Q: *What can be done to eliminate a 'NOT CATLG 2' for a particular dataset?*

A: To eliminate a 'NOT CATLG 2' message, one may take one of the following options:

1. Add a step to the beginning of the JOB which creates the dataset to first purge the dataset. One may wish to use utility IEFBR14 to perform this task.
2. Set up a job to purge the dataset and run it before the job which creates it.
3. Purge the dataset before running the job which creates it.

Q: *If a job step is in a wait state for 30 minutes or more with no activity, which abend does one receive?*

A: If a job step is in a wait state for 30 minutes or more with no activity, the job abends with an S522 indicating the time was exceeded for the wait state. This type of cancellation is unusual and is often caused by a program error or unavailable datasets/resources.

Q: *A system completion code of 813-04 is generated when a dataset name and volume serial number for a tape are not consistent with the information contained in the tape dataset label. What can be done to fix this problem?*

A: When a system completion code of 813-04 is received, one must check the spelling of the dataset name in the JCL and the volume serial number specified. If possible, dump the dataset label to see the actual dataset name on the tape. Once the problem has been identified, correct it and resubmit the job.

Q: *How does one fix a 'PROCEDURE NOT FOUND' ERROR?*

A: If one receives a 'PROCEDURE NOT FOUND' message, it indicates that it could not find the procedure on the procedure library specified on the JCL. Check the spelling of the procedure name on the EXEC statement to make sure it is correct. If it is not, fix it and resubmit the job.

If the JCL is correct, then check to make sure the procedure has been cataloged into the procedure library. If not, have it cataloged and resubmit the job.

Generation Data Groups

Q: *What is a Generation Data Group (GDG)?*

A: A Generation Data Group is a group of chronologically or functionally related datasets. GDGs are processed periodically, often by adding a new generation, retaining previous generations, and sometimes discarding the oldest generation.

Q: *How is a GDG base created?*

A: A GDG base is created in the system catalog and keeps track of the generation numbers used for datasets in the group. IDCAMS utility is used to define the GDG base for MVS/SP, MVS/XA, and MVS/ESA. Older systems required that the IEHPROGM utility be used.

Q: *What is model dataset label (Model DSCB)?*

A: A model dataset label is a pattern for the dataset label created for any dataset named as part of the GDG group. The system needs an existing dataset to serve as a model to supply the DCB parameters for the generation data group one wishes to create. The model dataset label must be cataloged. The model DSCB name is placed on the DCB parameter on the DD statement that creates the generation data group.

Q: *What is the advantage of using generation data groups?*
A: The advantage of using generation data groups is that all datasets have the same name, and the system keeps track of adding and deleting successive generations. The JCL does not need to be changed between runs.

Q: *How are GDGs concatenated?*
A: Generation data groups are concatenated by specifying each dataset name and the generation number for all generations of the generation data group. To retrieve all generations of a generation data group, omit the generation number. The DD statement will refer to all generations. The result is the same as if all individual datasets were concatenated. If generations are not on the same volume, this will not work.

Q: *How are different generations specified?*
A: Different generations are specified by providing the dataset name and generation number for each GDG desired.

Q: *What is the status of a GDG when an abend occurs?*
A: The GDG is in a bad state because it may consist of partial information. If used in this state, it is possible to get incorrect or improper results. It is recommended to reset the current generation by deleting the bad generation before executing the job which will re-create a new generation.

Q: *How is a previous GDG coded?*
A: Previous GDGs are coded as (−1) after the dataset name. An example would be DSN=JAN.DATA(−1).

Q: *How is the current GDG coded?*
A: Current GDGs are coded as (0), (+0), or (−0) after the dataset name as follows: DSN=JAN.DATA(0). The (+0) and (−0) have the same effect as (0). Normally, it is coded as (0).

Q: *How is a new GDG coded?*
A: A new GDG is coded as (+1) after the dataset name as follows: DSN=JAN.DATA(+1). This will cause all generations to be pushed down one level at the end of the job.

DD Statements

Q: *What is the purpose of the Data Definition (DD) Statement?*
A: Data Definition statements describe each dataset (a file on a direct-access storage device, tape, or printed output) and request the allocation of I/O devices.

Q: *Describe what the DISP parameter does.*

A: The DISP parameter describes the current status of the dataset and directs the system on the disposition of the dataset either at the end of the job or when the step abnormally terminates. DISP is always required unless the dataset is created and deleted in the same step.

Q: *How many subparameters does the DISP parameter consist of and what is the meaning of each?*

A: The DISP parameter consists of three subparameters: start-status, end-status-normal and end-status-abend. Start-status indicates the status of a dataset at the beginning of the job step. End-status-normal tells MVS what needs to be done with the dataset when the job step ends. End-status-abend indicates the desired disposition of the dataset if the job step abends. It is also known as the *conditional disposition.*

Q: *What are the meanings of the parameters used (within) the DISP parameter at the beginning of the job step?*

A: The status NEW, MOD, OLD, or SHR is the status of the dataset at the beginning of the step. If the dataset is NEW, the system creates a dataset label; if it is OLD, the system locates the dataset and reads its label. MOD allows records to be added to an existing dataset. The system gives a program exclusive control of a dataset except when SHR is used.

Q: *What are the "normal" dispositions of the DISP parameter?*

A: The normal disposition indicates the disposition of the dataset when the dataset is closed or when the job terminates normally. Normal dispositions are: KEEP, DELETE, PASS, CATLG, UNCATLG.

Q: *What are the "abnormal" dispositions of the DISP parameter?*

A: The abnormal dispositions will be in effect only if the step abnormally terminates. They are the same as normal dispositions, except that PASS is not allowed. KEEP, CATLG, UNCATLG, and DELETE are all permitted.

Q: *When should DISP=SHR be used?*

A: DISP=SHR must be used when it is necessary to share the datasets. SHR should be used only for input datasets.

Q: *When should DISP=MOD be used?*

A: DISP=MOD is used to either extend an existing sequential dataset or to create a dataset if it does not exist. If the dataset exists, then records are appended to the dataset at the end of the existing dataset. If the dataset does not exist, the system treats MOD as if it were NEW, provided that the volume parameter has not been used. If the volume parameter is used, the system terminates the job and does not create the new dataset. MOD can be used to add to a dataset that extends onto several volumes. Always specify a disposition of CATLG with MOD for cataloged datasets, even if they are already cataloged, so that any additional volume serial numbers will be recorded in the catalog.

Q: *When should DISP=OLD be used?*
A: DISP=OLD should be used for an existing dataset. It can be used with an input dataset to read, or an output dataset to rewrite. The step which uses DISP=OLD will have exclusive control of the dataset. If an OLD dataset is cataloged, the DSN parameter is usually the only other parameter needed. If an OLD dataset is not cataloged, UNIT and VOL parameters are required.

Q: *When should DISP=NEW be used?*
A: DISP=NEW should be used when it is desired to create a new dataset. The UNIT parameter is usually required for datasets on direct access volumes.

Q: *How is a dataset passed from one step to another?*
A: A dataset is passed from one step to another based on what is coded on the DISP parameter. The dataset can only be passed to subsequent steps if PASS was used on the disposition parameter.

Q: *If a dataset is passed and the subsequent steps do not use it, what happens to the dataset at the end of the job?*
A: If a dataset is passed to subsequent steps and it is not used, at the end of the job the dataset is deleted, since DELETE is assumed for all NEW datasets, temporary or nontemporary.

Q: *What is the default for the disposition parameter if it's not coded on the DD statement for a dataset?*
A: The default disposition used on a dataset which was coded without a disposition parameter is NEW. The disposition of NEW implies exclusive control of the dataset.

Q: *How are datasets concatenated?*
A: Datasets are concatenated by writing a normal DD statement for the first dataset and then adding a DD statement without a DDNAME for each dataset to be concatenated in the order they are to be read. The following is an example of three datasets concatenated:

```
//INSMP   DD DSN=JAN.DATA,DISP=SHR
//        DD DSN=FEB.DATA,DISP=SHR
//        DD DSN=MAR.DATA,DISP=SHR
```

Q: *Can datasets of a different record length (LRECL) be concatenated?*
A: Datasets with different LRECLs can be concatenated as long as the dataset with the largest block size appears first.

Q: *Can Partitioned Datasets (PDSs) be concatenated?*
A: Partitioned Datasets can be concatenated. This is often done for program libraries so that the system can search several libraries for a member.

Q: *What is a Data Control Block (DCB)?*
A: The Data Control Block is a table of data, in storage, that describes each dataset used by the program.

Q: *What are three different places from which DCB information can be obtained and in what order?*

A: Data information can be obtained from three places in the following order:

1. The data control block, from application program, is used first.
2. Information supplied on the DD statement is used second.
3. Dataset label information for the DCB is used third.

Q: *What is the purpose of using a dataset referback?*

A: A dataset referback is used to copy a dataset name from a prior job step.

Q: *What are the disadvantages of using a dataset referback?*

A: The disadvantages of using dataset referbacks is that they tend to make JCL more difficult to maintain because close attention, scrutiny, and manual examination of preceding steps is needed to understand what a given job-stream is doing. They also complicate the restart of a job if a failure or interruption occurs.

Q: *Under which circumstances is the disposition parameter not performed?*

A: Disposition is not performed under the following circumstances:

1. The step does not start because of JCL errors.
2. The step is bypassed because of the COND parameter in the JOB or EXEC statement.
3. The step abnormally terminates because it could not find enough space to satisfy the request.
4. DUMMY or DSN=NULLFILE is coded on the DD statement.

JOB Card, EXEC Statements, and PARM Parameters

Q: *What is the purpose of the JOB statement?*

A: The purpose of the JOB statement is to inform the operating system of the start of a job, give necessary accounting information, and supply run parameters. Each job must begin with a single JOB statement.

Q: *How does one identify a job to the operating system?*

A: A job is identified to the system by the use of Jobname. Jobnames can range from one to eight alphanumeric characters. The first character must begin in column 3 and be alphabetic (A–Z). Jobs should be given unique names since duplicate jobnames will not execute until any job having the same jobname completes execution.

Q: *What does the Accounting Information consist of?*

A: Accounting Information consists of the account number to which the job is charged and any additional information established by the installation.

Q: *What does the parameter CLASS in the JOB statement mean?*
A: Parameter CLASS specifies the job class. There are 36 possible job classes (A–Z, 0–9). Installations usually attempt to establish job classes that achieve a balance between I/O-bound and CPU-bound jobs. Job classes also determine the overall priority of a job, along with the PRTY parameter. PRTY may be coded to give special priority to a job. It may also be set by the operator.

Q: *What is parameter MSGCLASS in the JOB statement used for?*
A: The MSGCLASS parameter is used to specify the job scheduler message output class. The output class is (A–Z, 0–9). Job scheduler messages include all messages not printed by the actual job steps being executed. Some of these are: JCL statements and error messages, device allocations, dataset disposition, and accounting information.

Q: *What does parameter MSGLEVEL on the JOB statement mean and what is the advantage of using it?*
A: MSGLEVEL indicates whether or not one wishes to print the JCL statements and allocation messages. The MSGLEVEL parameter can save paper. After a job is debugged, there may be no need to print all the JCL and allocation messages each time it runs. To reduce printing to a minimum, one may wish to code MSGLEVEL=(0,0).

Q: *Which parameter allows one to run a syntax check on the JCL without executing it?*
A: TYPRUN=SCAN parameter is used to check the JCL for syntax errors and suppress the execution of the job. This checking does *not* include checking for duplicate datasets on volumes, insufficient space, or region size for job steps.

Q: *What does parameter TYPRUN=HOLD mean?*
A: The parameter TYPRUN=HOLD holds a job in the input queue for later execution. The job is held until the operator releases it. TYPRUN=HOLD is useful for when one job must not run until another job completes. Operator intervention is required to release the job.

Q: *What is the purpose of the EXEC statement?*
A: The purpose of the EXEC statement is to name a program or procedure to be executed. It follows the JOB statement. A job or cataloged procedure can contain several EXEC statements. A job may have up to 255 EXEC statements.

Q: *What is the stepname on the EXEC statement used for, and is it a required parameter?*
A: Stepname on the EXEC statement is used to name the job step. It is required if subsequent JCL statements refer to it or if one wishes to restart the job from the step; otherwise, it is optional. Stepnames are recommended and should have unique names. The names must begin in column 3 with an alphabetic or national character (A–Z, @ $ #).

Q: *Which parameter is used to name a program in the EXEC statement?*

A: The parameter 'PGM=' is used to name a program or utility to be executed. For example, to code a program named 'FIRST', one would code 'PGM=FIRST'. For a utility named 'IEBGENER', it would be coded as 'PGM=IEBGENER'.

Q: *What are the most commonly used parameters on the EXEC statement and what do they mean?*

A: The most commonly used parameters on the EXEC statement are: COND, PARM, REGION, and TIME. They stand for:

1. COND—Specifies conditions to execute subsequent job steps if the previous step(s) fail.
2. PARM—Passes parameters to the job step.
3. REGION—Specifies the REGION size to allocate for the job/job step.
4. TIME—Imposes a time limit on the job or job step.

Q: *What is the default for the TIME parameter if it is not coded on the EXEC statement?*

A: If the TIME parameter is omitted from the EXEC statement, the default is 30 minutes of CPU time.

Q: *What is the difference between the JOBLIB and STEPLIB statements?*

A: The JOBLIB statement is placed after the JOB statement and is effective for all job steps. It cannot be placed in a cataloged procedure. The STEPLIB statement is placed after the EXEC statement and is effective for that job step only. Unlike the JOBLIB statement, the STEPLIB can be placed in a cataloged procedure.

Q: *What can be done to resolve a JCL error that reads 'DATASET NOT FOUND'?*

A: Some of the actions one can take to resolve a JCL error of 'DATASET NOT FOUND' are:

1. One must examine the job log and the allocation/deallocation report and identify the step and DDname involved.
2. Determine whether or not the dataset name does indeed exist on the system.
3. Check the JCL to make sure the dataset name is spelled correctly.
4. If the job has more than one step and the abend is not on the first step, check to see if the dataset on the previous step was deleted.
5. Fix the problem and resubmit the job.

Q: *Does a 'DD STATEMENT MISSING' message normally abend the job?*

A: A DD statement missing message normally does not abend the job, but if not fixed it could later cause problems when least expected. It is advisable to determine why this message was generated and take action to rectify the problem.

Q: *Parameters COND, REGION, and TIME can be coded on both the JOB and the EXEC statements. What are the differences between using them on the JOB versus the EXEC statement, and in which statement are they most commonly used?*

A: Parameters COND, REGION, and TIME, when used on the JOB statement, will be in effect for the entire job. When used on the EXEC statement, they will be in effect for the job step only. The COND parameter is normally used on the EXEC statement. The REGION parameter is normally not used unless a particular program requires a lot of storage and it is necessary to override the installation's REGION default. If the REGION parameter is used on both the JOB and EXEC statements, then the parameter from the JOB statement will be in effect. The TIME parameter is most often used on the JOB statement.

Q: *Explain how virtual storage works in MVS/SP.*

A: MVS/SP stands for Multiple Virtual System/System Program. A major architectural component of MVS is virtual storage. With virtual storage, storage addresses of an application program are independent of the addresses of the computer's central storage. A hardware feature, paging supervisor, translates the user's virtual storage addresses to the computer's central addresses during execution. With virtual storage, a program needs to occupy only a relatively small amount of central storage. This allows programs to be run whose size exceeds the central storage available on the computer.

Q: *What are some of the main features of MVS/XA?*

A: MVS/XA stands for Multiple Virtual System/Extended Architecture. MVS/XA uses 32 bits for addressing. This gives an address space of approximately 2 billion bytes. The extended architecture also consists of more sophisticated input/output channels for faster I/O. Also, a separate version of the operating system is required. One of the differences is that a program for MVS/XA can go up to 2 billion bytes. Programs running under MVS/SP can go up to only 16 million bytes.

Q: *What are the "basic architecture" features of MVS/ESA?*

A: MVS/ESA stands for Multiple Virtual System/Enterprise Systems Architecture. MVS/ESA permits an application to have multiple 2-gigabyte address spaces. This allows huge applications to be segregated into functional parts. For ESA, the first address space is called *application space,* and programs can only execute in it. The other address spaces are called *dataspaces* and they contain only data. MVS/ESA also has the facility for hyperspaces, which allows temporary data to be stored or retrieved in 4-kbyte blocks under program control. Maximum address space is up to 2 trillion bytes in multiple 2-billion-byte address spaces.

Q: *What is the meaning of the "line"?*

A: The "line" indicates the maximum address space that is available for the MVS system. For MVS/SP it is 16 million bytes, for MVS/XA it is up to 2 billion bytes, and for MVS/ESA it is up to 2 trillion bytes in multiple 2-billion-byte address spaces.

Q: *When would a program run "below the line"?*
A: A program would run "below the line" if it did not exceed the maximum address space available.

Q: *When would a program run "above the line"?*
A: A program would run "above the line" if it required more than 16 megs or if it is competing with other programs which are using the same address space. Special parameters must be set for compilation and linkage editing in order for a program to run above the 16-meg line.

Procs

Q: *How are in-stream procedures (procs) built?*
A: In-stream procedures are built by coding a set of statements and placing them after the JOB statement and before the EXEC statement. In-stream procedures begin with a PROC statement and end with a PEND statement. Up to 15 in-stream procedures can be included in a single job. Each in-stream procedure may be invoked several times within the job. In-stream procedures can use symbolic parameters in the same way as cataloged procedures.

Q: *What is the difference between an in-stream procedure and a cataloged procedure?*
A: An in-stream procedure is basically the same as a cataloged procedure. The difference is that to execute an in-stream procedure one places it after the JOB statement and before the EXEC statement and must end it with the PEND statement. A cataloged procedure is cataloged on a procedure library and is called by specifying the procedure name on the EXEC statement. An in-stream procedure is useful to test the procedure before making it a cataloged procedure.

Q: *Name some of the JCL statements that are not allowed in procs.*
A: Some of the JCL statements which are not allowed in procedures are:
1. JOB, Delimiter (/*), or Null (//) statements
2. JOBLIB or JOBCAT DD statements
3. DD * or DATA statements
4. Any JES2 or JES3 control statements

Q: *What parameters are good candidates to make symbolic parameters?*
A: Any parameter, subparameter, or value in a procedure which may vary each time the procedure is called is a good candidate to be coded as a symbolic parameter.

Q: *Which type of override parameter requires that one know the parameters that can be overridden?*
A: Regular parameters require that one know the parameters that can be overridden, such as the stepnames within the procedure, the DDnames of the statements overridden, and the order of the DD statements.

Q: *How is a symbolic parameter coded?*
A: A symbolic parameter is preceded by an ampersand (&) and followed by a name (&FIRST). The first character must be alphabetic. Symbolic parameters can be coded only in the operand field of JCL statements; they cannot appear in the name or operation field. If more than one value is assigned to a symbolic parameter on a PROC or EXEC statement, only the first one is used. Symbolic parameters may be coded in any order on the PROC or EXEC statement.

Q: *How are values assigned to symbolic parameters?*
A: Values can be assigned to symbolic parameters on the PROC statement, on the EXEC statement, or on a SET command. Values containing special characters other than blank must be enclosed in apostrophes. The value assigned to a symbolic parameter can be of any length, but it cannot be continued onto another line.

Q: *Can symbolic parameters be concatenated?*
A: Symbolic parameters can be concatenated with other symbolic parameters, regular parameters, or with portions of regular parameters as follows:

Symbolic/symbolic	PARM=&FIRST&LAST
Symbolic/regular	SPACE=&SPACES
Symbolic/portion	SPACE=(TRK,&PRIMARY)

Q: *What are some of the rules involved in overriding parameters on the EXEC statements in a procedure?*
A: To override EXEC parameters one should follow these rules:
1. A PGM parameter cannot be overriden.
2. The parameters for each step do not need to be coded in the same order as they appear on the procedure EXEC statement.
3. To add or override a parameter on an EXEC statement, code it as follows: parameter.procstepname=value.
4. If a parameter which does not exist is coded on the EXEC statement, the parameter will be added.
5. All parameters for each step must be coded in order: the first step must be coded first, second step second, third step third, etc.

Q: *What are some of the rules involved in overriding DD statements in procs?*
A: The following rules apply when overriding a DD statement:
1. DD statement overrides precede the DDname with the procstepname.
2. The JCL parameter is replaced, unless it does not exist on the original statement, in which case it is added. For the DCB parameter, each subparameter can be overridden.
3. DD statement overrides should carry DDnames that already exist in the step they are to effect.
4. DD statement overrides must be coded preceding any added DD statements for the proc step.

5. DD override statements must be listed in the order in which they are shown in the proc.

6. DD override statements are only in effect for the duration of the run.

Q: *How are concatenated DD statements in procs overridden?*
A: Overriding concatenated DD statements requires the following:

1. To override only the first DD statement in a concatenation, code only one overriding DD statement.

2. To override all DD statements in a concatenation, code an overriding DD for each concatenated DD statement.

3. The overriding DD statements must be in the same order as the concatenated DD statements.

4. Code a DDname on the first overriding DD statement only. Leave the DDname blank on all following DD statements.

5. To leave a concatenated statement unchanged, code its corresponding overriding DD statement with a blank operand field.

Compiling, Link Editing, and Execution

Q: *What does a mainframe compiler output in the "object deck" and what does the linkage editor do with it?*
A: The compiler outputs the source code into the object deck in a form to be read by the linkage editor. The linkage editor combines the object dataset (object deck) from the compiler with machine language code for input/output and other tasks to create an executable "load module."

Q: *If a program executed attempts to divide a number by zero, do arithmetic on a field that does not contain numeric data, or has some other serious logic error, an abend will occur. What is the "normal" response that MVS would issue?*
A: MVS would issue a "system completion code" that would indicate the nature of the problem, dump the program's memory area, and flush the job from the system. The dump may be used for problem analysis. The dump is printed or stored in a dataset as specified in the //SYSUDUMP DD statement. If //SYSUDUMP is omitted, MVS will provide the completion code value, but not the dump.

Q: *Where must load module(s) reside?*
A: Load module(s) must reside in a Partitioned DataSet (PDS).

Q: *What are some of the common linkage editor options and what do they mean?*
A: Some of the commonly used linkage editor options are:

1. LIST—Lists the linkage editor control statements and is usually specified. Omit the parameter if no listing is desired.

2. MAP—Produces a storage map showing the length and relative locations of all control sections. Default is NOMAP.

3. XREF—Includes MAP plus a cross-reference table of the load module. (MAP and XREF are mutually exclusive.)

4. NOCALL—Cancels the automatic library call mechanism. NOCALL is used for creating subroutine libraries so that the load module contains a single subroutine. CALL is the default.

5. LET—Marks load modules as executable even if minor errors are found. NOLET is the default.

6. PRINT—Allows the messages to be written to a SYSOUT DD statement and it is the default. NOPRINT suppresses the messages.

7. AMODE—Specifies whether the program uses 24- or 31-bit addressing. AMODE ANY specifies both 24- and 31-bit addressing. AMODE 24 requires the program to run below the 16-meg line. The default is established by the compiler and is usually AMODE 24.

8. RMODE—Indicates where the program can reside in virtual storage. RMODE ANY allows the program to reside above the 16-meg line and requires AMODE 31 or AMODE ANY. RMODE 24 requires the program to reside below the 16-meg line. The default is established by the compiler and is usually RMODE 24.

9. TERM—Causes linkage editor diagnostic messages to be written to a SYSTERM DD statement. NOTERM is the default.

Q: *What causes the message 'MODULE HAS BEEN MARKED NOT EXECUTABLE'?*

A: An unresolved external reference often causes the message 'MODULE HAS BEEN MARKED NOT EXECUTABLE'. Although the module is not executable, one may be able to recover by link-editing the control section causing the problem and replacing it in the load module.

Q: *Why would the linkage editor add a member to a load library under the name 'TEMPNAME'?*

A: The linkage editor will add a member to the load library under the name of 'TEMPNAME' when a member of the same name already exists on the library and the disposition on the SYSLMOD statement was coded as DISP=MOD. This indicates a problem and needs to be resolved.

Utilities

Q: *What is an IEBGENER used for?*

A: IEBGENER is a dataset utility used to copy sequential datasets, produce a partitioned dataset or member from a sequential dataset, produce an edited sequential or partitioned dataset, and reblock/change the logical record length of a dataset.

Q: *What is an IEBCOPY used for?*

A: IEBCOPY is a dataset utility used to copy one or more partitioned datasets or to merge partitioned datasets. A partitioned dataset that is copied to a sequential dataset is said to be unloaded. When one or more datasets created by an unload operation are used to re-create a partitioned dataset, it is called a *load operation*. Specific members of a partitioned or unloaded dataset can be selected for, or excluded from, a copy, unload, or load process.

Q: *What is an IEFBR14 used for?*

A: IEFBR14 is used to delete datasets, find datasets, catalog, and uncatalog datasets.

Q: *What is an IEHLIST used for?*

A: IEHLIST is a system utility used to list entries in an OS CVOL, entries in the directory of one or more partitioned datasets, or entries in an indexed or nonindexed volume table of contents (VTOC).

Q: *What is an IEHINITT used for?*

A: IEHINITT is a system utility used to write an IBM volume label onto any number of magnetic tapes mounted on one or more tape units. Each volume label set created by this program contains a standard volume label, an 80-byte dummy header, and a tapemark.

Q: *What is an IEBPTPCH used for?*

A: IEBPTPCH is a dataset utility used to print or punch all, or selected, portions of a sequential or partitioned dataset. Records can be printed or punched to meet either standard specifications or user specifications.

Q: *What is an IEBUPDTE used for?*

A: IEBUPDTE is a dataset utility used to create and update dataset libraries, modify existing partitioned members or sequential datasets, and change the organization of a dataset from sequential to partitioned (or vice versa).

Q: *Which utility can be both used for VSAM and non-VSAM files?*

A: IDCAMS utility is used to handle VSAM as well as non-VSAM files.

Q: *Which parameter is required to copy a dataset using IEBCOPY?*

A: The parameter 'COPY' is required to initiate one or more IEBCOPY copy, unload, or load operations. Any number of operations can follow a single COPY statement, and any number of COPY statements can appear within a single job step.

Q: *What is the parameter 'GENERATE' used for on utility IEBGENER?*

A: The parameter 'GENERATE' for the utility IEBGENER is used when output is to be partitioned, editing is to be performed, or user routines are provided and/or label processing is specified.

Q: *What is the parameter 'MEMBER' used for on utility IEBGENER?*

A: The parameter 'MEMBER' for the utility IEBGENER is used when the output is to be partitioned. One MEMBER statement must be included for each member to be created by IEBGENER. All RECORD statements following a MEMBER statement pertain to the member named in that MEMBER statement.

Q: *What is the parameter 'RECORD' used for on utility IEBGENER?*

A: The parameter 'RECORD' for the utility IEBGENER is used to define a record group and to supply editing information. A record group consists of records that are to be processed identically.

Q: *Which utility uses the 'REPRO' command and what function does it perform?*

A: The utility IDCAMS uses the 'REPRO' command. The REPRO command copies sequential datasets. It performs much the same function as IEBGENER.

Q: *How does one verify that a utility has ended normally?*

A: To verify if a utility has ended normally, one must check the JCL for a return code of zero. Various utilities generate return codes of 0004, 0008, 0012, and higher, in increments of 4, when problems or unusual conditions have been encountered.

Q: *When a utility ends with a nonzero return code, what must be done to resolve the problem?*

A: When a utility ends with a nonzero return code, it is necessary to determine what caused the error. One may start by checking for error messages generated by the utility and look them up on a utility messages manual. Also, the JCL statements and/or control statements should be checked to make sure they were properly coded. Once the error has been identified, it should be fixed and the job resubmitted.

5

MVS for the System Programmer

Paul H. Baneky

Introduction

MVS systems programming encompasses a wide range of information. As far as MVS systems reference questions and answers for passing a technical interview are concerned, an entire book could be written on the subject. Because of the vast amount of detailed information that a system programmer has to know and understand, this chapter should be considered a general introduction to the subject (i.e., covering enough material to pass an interview for a job requiring basic MVS systems information).

An Overview of MVS Internals

Data processing has evolved from serial (single) job processing computers with very limited capacity and resources to a multiprocessor complex capable of processing hundreds of jobs concurrently. The current MVS operating environment can be characterized as a data processing environment that is capable of handling the following:

- Large complex computing
- Multiple processor(s)
- Batch processing
- A large mix of concurrent users

- Teleprocessing applications
- Database processing
- Time-sharing processing
- Nonstop mission critical work

From an "internals" point of view the MVS operating system is divided into three main groups: Supervisor Management, Data Management, and Job Management.

Supervisor Management

MVS Supervisor Management encompasses the following functional areas:

System Resource Management. System Resource Management is involved with:

- Adhering to installation performance specification
- Measuring overall system performance
- Making necessary dynamic adjustments
- Swapping decision making

Program Management. Program Management is concerned with:

- Finding load modules
- Scheduling jobs for execution
- Loading modules into virtual storage

Task Management. Task Management's main functions are:

- Initiate/terminate tasks and subtasks
- Wait and postprocessing
- Enq and Deq processing

Virtual Storage Management. Virtual Storage Management is concerned with:

- Getmain/Freemain processing
- Subpool management
- Creating address space
- Providing the map of virtual storage for each address space

Supervisory Management. Supervisory Management involves:

- Interrupt handling
- Dispatching

- Schedule processing
- Memory-switch routines
- Locking manager
- Exit processing
- Interprocessor communications

  Real Storage Management.   Main functions are:

- Managing page frames
- Page management

  Page stealing

  Page release

  $V = R$ processing

  Timer Management.   Main functions are:

- Date and time processing
- Timing intervals

  Recovery/Termination Management.   Main functions are:

- Functional recovery routine processing
- Abend processing
- Normal task processing

  Auxiliary Storage Management.   Main function is external page storage management.

Data Management

Data Management functions include:

DASD Storage Management.   Main functions are:

- Providing support for the organization, storage, and retrieval of data stored on direct access (DASD) storage devices
- Providing device independence for direct-access storage devices, buffer processing, and I/O record formatting

Input/Output Support.   Main function is scheduling and controlling the transfer of data between storage and input/output devices.

Catalog Management.   Main functions are:

- Locating and updating catalog information used by subsystems and application programs
- Supporting symbolic name references

Access Methods. Main functions are the support of I/O devices (connected to the main frame by I/O channel) and telecommunication data (message) accessing and transfers.

Input/Output Supervisor. Main functions are:

- Initiating I/O operations over the I/O path
- Supporting the IOS interrupt handler which gets control upon the completion of I/O
- Analyzing I/O completion status and returning control to the IOS driver

Virtual Input/Output (VIO). Main functions are:

- Moving data from the channel program buffer to user address space
- Processing read/write operations by means of paging (rather than DASD I/O transfers)

Job Management

Job Management processing includes the following:

Command Processing. Facilitates the processing of commands from a program or console and schedules it for processing.

Reading Jobstream (JCL) into JES. Reads the jobstream (JCL) into the system and queues it to the system spool.

Converting JCL to Internal Text and Build Control Blocks
Initiating Jobs for Execution. Main functions are:

- Requests jobs for execution
- JES2/JES3 selects jobs according to its priority

Allocating Datasets, Temporary Files, and Workspace
Attaching Jobs for Execution (Initiates Work)
Output Processing (JES Output)

- Spools SYSOUT
- Processes end-of-step/job by collecting the output of all job steps and spooling it to disk for printing

Task Termination. Returns to the system all resources allocated to the job step(s).

Terminology

ACR	Alternate CPU Recovery
AIB	Application Interface Block

ALCWA	Allocation Work Area
BUFC	Buffer Control Block
CCA	Catalog Communications Area
CCH	Channel Check Handler
DAFM	Dynamic Allocation Function Map
EDB	Extent Definition Block
EPA	External Parameter Area
JDT	JCL Definition Table
LCT	Linkage Control Table
PCCB	Private Catalog Control Block
RMS	Recovery Management Services
RVT	Recovery Management Vector Table
SIOT	Step Input/Output Table
TCT	SMF Timing Control Table
V = R	Virtual equals Real
V = V	Virtual equals Virtual
VAT	Virtual Address Table

Questions and Answers

Q: *What is a Program Status Word (PSW) and how is it used?*

A: A program status word is an 8-byte control register cooperatively managed by both the MVS system and the hardware. The PSW contains the address of the next instruction the CPU is going to execute.

Q: *What do the letters "MVS" stand for?*

A: Multiple virtual storage.

Q: *Describe the PSW switching mechanism. . . . Is this a hardware or software action?*

A: When an interrupt occurs, the current PSW is stored in a preassigned storage location called the "old PSW." The CPU then fetches a new PSW from a preassigned new PSW storage location. Execution continues using the new PSW. There is an old PSW/new PSW pair for each of the six interrupt types. This is a hardware action.

Q: *Name the six interrupt types for which there are a "pair" of old/new PSWs.*

A: External, program check, machine check, supervisor call, I/O, and restart.

Q: *What is an SVC? Why does MVS use it?*

A: An SVC is a supervisor call. The MVS operating system uses this type of facility in order to bring some uniformity and integrity to access system functions and resources.

Q: *What types of SVCs are there in MVS systems?*

A: There are six types of of SVCs, numbered 1 through 6. Types 1, 2, and 6 reside in the nucleus after IPL and in the SYS1.NUCLEUS dataset before IPL. Types 3, 4, and 5 reside in the Link Pack Area (LPA) after IPL has taken place and in an LPA or LNKLST-eligible dataset.

Q: *What is an SVC 0 and how is it used?*

A: An SVC 0, or Supervisor Call 0, is a machine instruction that causes a machine interrupt and starts the I/O initiation process.

Q: *When would an SVC 6 get issued versus an SVC 8?*

A: An SVC 6 is issued when a LINK is taking place versus a LOAD which involves an SVC 8.

Q: *Name one of the control blocks to which you would go to find the address(es) of other control blocks.*

A: The Communication Vector Table (CVT).

Q: *What is a program request block?*

A: A program request block contains information needed by the system concerning programs. It also includes a save register area.

Q: *How can you find the current location of the CVT?*

A: The address of the CVT can be found at hex location "10."

Q: *In what section of MVS does the CVT reside?*

A: In the nucleus.

Q: *What is the ASCB?*

A: The ASCB is the Address Space Control Block.

Q: *What does the Address Space Control Block contain?*

A: The Address Space Control Block represents the existence of an address space to MVS. The ASCB contains information and pointers needed for address space control.

Q: *Systemwide information about an address space is stored in the ASCB. Where is this "systemwide information" located?*

A: In MVS/SP, systemwide about address space is stored in the SQA (the System Queue Area). In MVS/XA and MVS/ESA, the ESQA is also used.

Q: *Where is user-related address space information stored?*

A: User-related address information is stored in the Addresses Space Extension Block (ASXB).

Q: *What is an ECB and how is it used?*

A: An ECB is an Event Control Block. It is a control block that is used to determine if an event has occurred. By interrogating the ECB status codes, a process can determine if an event has occurred and what its status was.

Q: *Where does MVS get the parameters necessary to utilize itself after the correct nucleus has been loaded?*
A: MVS gets the parameters it needs from the SYS1.PARMLIB dataset.

Q: *Describe JES2.*
A: JES2 (Job Entry Subsystem 2) is the part of MVS that reads, converts, executes, and outputs all jobs received.

Q: *What are the two main JES2 datasets?*
A: The two main JES2 datasets are the spool (i.e., SYS1.HASPACE) and the checkpoint (i.e., SYS1.HASPCKPT) datasets.

Q: *What is the main JES2 control block?*
A: The main JES2 control block is the HCT (Hasp Control Block).

Q: *IOS is said to have two "ends." What are they?*
A: A "front end" and a "back end."

Q: *Describe the responsibilities of the front end and the back end.*
A: The front end schedules, validates, and initiates the I/O operation. The back end responds to the completed I/O operation and initiates postprocessing and error recovery (when required).

Q: *Which IOS control block holds the device and subchannel status?*
A: The IOSB (the I/O Supervisor Block).

Q: *On completion of an I/O operation, what is posted in order to notify the requestor of the completed I/O operation?*
A: The Event Control Block (the ECB) is posted.

Q: *What is the Channel Address Word?*
A: The Channel Address Word or CAW is a fixed location in main memory where the address of the channel program is stored before beginning an I/O operation.

Q: *What is a CCW?*
A: A CCW, or Channel Command Word, is an instruction that is used for a channel to do its I/O operations. One or more channel command words make up a channel program.

Q: *What is a Request Queue Element?*
A: A Request Queue Element, or RQE, is a system resident control block in IOS used by the EXCP processor to initiate an I/O request and monitor its status.

Q: *In a multiprocessing MVS environment, how are programs executed?*
   1. Randomly
   2. Serially (one at a time)
   3. Event scheduled
   4. Concurrently
   5. All of the above
A: Concurrently (4).

Q: *If an FOB has been initiated (started) and swapping has taken place, what are in the "EPS page slots"?*
A: "Page frames" and "inactive pages."

Q: *In MVS, a virtual address space is divided into segments. What is the size of each segment?*
A: In MVS/SP systems, the size of each segment is 64K. In MVS/XA and MVS/ESA, the size of each segments is 1 MB.

Q: *What are the two methods used by MVS to manage real storage?*
A: Paging and swapping.

Q: *What does the Dynamic Address Translation table (the DAT) do?*
A: The DAT translates virtual addresses into real addresses.

Q: *Is dynamic address translation accomplished by hardware or software?*
A: Dynamic address translation is accomplished by the combination of both the hardware feature in an IBM or IBM-compatible machine and MVS system software.

Q: *In MVS, how is virtual storage organized?*
A: Virtual storage is divided into three sections, or areas: a common area, a private area, and a system area.

Q: *Does the common area contain any subareas (i.e., is it further subdivided)?*
A: Yes. The common area contains the System Queue Area (the SQA), the Pageable Link Pack Area (PLPA) and the Common System Area (CSA).

Q: *What "subareas" are contained in the private area?*
A: The Local System Queue Area (LSQA) and the Scheduler Work Area (SWA).

Q: *What does the system area contain?*
A: Nucleus load modules and the nucleus extension.

Q: *What is the System Queue Area (SQA) and how is it used?*
A: The System Queue Area or SQA is a part of the MVS common area. It is used for MVS control blocks which must be fixed in real memory and be globally addressable.

Q: *What is the CSA used for?*
A: The CSA is used for interaddress space communication.

Q: *What does the Common System Area (CSA) contain?*
A: The CSA contains, among other things, data areas used by the system and subpools.

Q: *What is a subpool?*
A: A subpool is a group of logically related variable-size blocks of virtual storage.

Q: *How are subpools identified?*
A: Subpools are identified by a number which can range from 0 to 255.

Q: *Does that mean there are a maximum of 256 4K subpool blocks?*
A: No. Subpools can have multiple 4K blocks of storage.

Q: *What does subpool 252 contain?*
A: Subpool 252 contains reentrant library modules.

Q: *What is an "FBQE" and what is it used for?*
A: An FBQE is a Free Block Queue Element and is used to describe the number of 4K contiguous freespace areas within a given address space.

Q: *How is the external page table used?*
A: The external page table is used to locate an allocated page that is not in main storage.

Q: *What is the prime responsibility of the ASM?*
A: The Auxiliary Storage Manager (ASM) manages the virtual storage that resides on the external page storage. The ASM, working in conjunction with the I/O supervisor (IOS), performs both the paging and swapping operations.

Q: *What does the SRM do?*
A: The System Resource Manager (SRM) manages the use of system resources in keeping with the installations specified performance objectives.

Q: *What is an ICS?*
A: An ICS Installation Control Specification (ICS) defines which work coming into the system will be assigned to which performance groups.

Q: *What are the three system resources controlled by the SRM?*
A: 1. CPU

   2. I/O

   3. Main storage

Q: *What standard MVS facility would you use to check system resource usage?*
A: You would use the Resource Management Facility (RMF).

Q: *If no physical swaps are being performed, what conclusion could you come to about storage commitment?*
A: That real storage is not overcommitted.

Q: *What is an SRB? How many are there and how are they used?*
A: A System Resource Block (SRB) is an enhancement to the Task Control Block (TCB) dispatching mechanism. There are two kinds of SRBs: "global SRBs" and "local SRBs." There is one global SRB queue for the entire system and one local SRB queue for each address space initiated.

Q: *How is a service request defined?*
A: A service request:
1. Is short in duration
2. Deals with specific functions for IOS, ASM, SRM, and the system interrupt handlers
3. Defines and represents a service request as a simplified version of the TCB

Q: *MVS performance measurement and tuning depends on which of the following?*
1. Model and type of spooling unit
2. Measurement tool
3. Scheduled workload
4. Workload being run
A: Workload being run (4).

Q: *There are two very different and separate orientations for computer performance. What are they?*
A: They are:
1. Throughput-oriented, which places the emphasis on processing a workload (various batch jobs)
2. Response-oriented, which places the emphasis on providing rapid and consistent response time

Q: *Given the way an Excp works, what might you do to a dataset to improve an application's responsiveness?*
A: Increase the dataset's block size.

Q: *What is the basic method for solving a performance problem?*
A: 1. Identify which part of performance is not satisfactory.
2. Measure the actual performance.
3. Identify the processing bottleneck.
4. Correct the problem and remove bottleneck.
5. Remeasure performance, modify/correct as required.

Q: *Why would you use storage isolation?*
A: Storage isolation is used to protect the working set size for an application. This protection isolates the working set from page stealing and has a stablizing effect on the application's performance.

Q: *How can the FLPA help to improve overall system performance?*
A: The Fixed-Link Pack Area (FLPA) keeps in real storage the modules you have included in this member of SYS1.PARMLIB. Note that the modules in the "IEAFIX00" are nonpageable for the duration of the IPL. "Extremely high use" reenterable, reusable modules should be included with this member.

Q: *How many fixed-link pack areas are there?*
A: Three: the PLPA, the MLPA, and the FLPA.

Q: *How can the PLPA help in the system performance area?*
A: Since "paging I/O operations" are much faster than a typical program fetch, putting high-use reenterable and serially reusable modules in the PLPA can help in this area.

Q: *What types of SVC routines can be found in the PLPA?*
A: Types 3 and 4 SVC routines.

Q: *What kind of devices should be used for demand paging I/O operations?*
A: Fixed-head devices should be used for demand paging because fixed-head devices provide higher speed and performance than can be obtained from disk.

Q: *What kind of devices should be used for swapping I/O operations?*
A: Nonfixed-head devices should be used for swapping I/O operations. Swap I/O should be given as many channel paths as possible.

Q: *What would be your performance objectives when you are involved with tuning I/O operations?*
A: Good I/O susbsystem performance is based on providing as much concurrency and I/O overlap as possible, as well as reducing the overall I/O service time. This can be accomplished by carefully monitoring all I/O system activity and then configuring channels, control units, individual devices, and by thoughtful dataset placement.

Q: *How would you determine if the current task has any subtasks?*
A: By locating the TCB for the current task and checking the TCBLTC field. If the TCBLTC field contains zeros, then the current task has no subtasks.

Q: *What is the PCCA, and what does it contain?*
A: The Physical Configuration Communication Area (PCCA) contains information about the physical facilities associated with each cpu in the system. For each cpu there is a corresponding PCCA.

Q: *What is an "FLIH" and how is it used?*
A: A FLIH is a First-Level Interrupt Handler. It handles SVC interrupts.

Q: *What is the difference between a first-level and a second-level interrupt handler?*
A: The first-level interrupt handler (FLIH) runs disabled and saves the registers as well as other key system information. The second-level interrupt handler (SLIH) processes/handles an interrupt using nondisabled code.

Q: *On an I/O interrupt, what does the second-level I/O interrupt handler use to see if any interrupts have occurred while it was in control?*
A: The second-level I/O handler uses the Test-Pending Interrupt, TPI.

Q: *What function does a BLDL macro perform?*
A: A BLDL macro calls a program that searches a Partitioned DataSet (PDS).

Q: *In which library are MVS utilities stored?*
A: In SYS1.LINKLIB.

Q: *Name one type of module that is stored in SYS1.NUCLEUS.*
A: System initialization modules.

Q: *Name three members of SYS1.PARMLIB.*
A: IEAIPS00, IEAOPT00, and IEAICS00.

Q: *What function does IEAICS00 perform?*
A: IEAICS00 controls performance groups assignment to user-defined job names.

6
UNIX

Chayim Leib Weiss

The Operating System

Unix as it exists today is an operating system with two major "camps" of development: Unix Systems Laboratories (USL) and the Open Software Foundation (OSF). Unix is an open operating system architecture—"open" meaning that it is not hardware-dependent and appears the same to the end user regardless of hardware platform. This makes Unix attractive to hardware manufacturers. Their desire to port a commercial implementation of Unix for their equipment increases their appeal to the commercial business community, supplying a standard operating system environment.

Hardware platforms range from laptops to mainframes and include everything in between. This is one of the reasons that Unix comes in many different release levels and hardware implementations. Most versions of the operating system, regardless of release version or hardware platform, are closely related in functionality. Therefore, operating in one is similar in functionality to others but may, however, require minor operational adjustments.

The Interview

The Unix operating system is a complex operating environment that provides the user with the tools and utilities for application development. These tools are delivered with the standard operating system. Thus, the candidate is required to have a broad spectrum of talent from shell programming to communications. The purpose of this chapter is to help prepare you for an employment interview. While this chapter is structured to benefit the beginner as well as an experienced person, it does *not* cover coding or programming (with the exception of shell scripts). The question-and-answer format that has been used will allow you to gauge your own experience level as well as show you your Unix "strengths and weaknesses."

Questions and Answers

Q: *What are some of the standard communications facilities shipped with most versions of Unix?*

A: Standard communications facilities can include: TCP/IP, XNS protocol suites, and uucp (Unix-to-Unix Copy) programs. There are different implementations of networking which can include the following protocols: tftp, ftp, telnet, rfs, ppp, nfs (using RPC and XDR), snmp, and smtp. Transmission Control Protocol/Internet Protocol (TCP/IP) includes tcp, udp, ip, icmp, arp, and rarp. Xerox Network System (XNS) can include: echo, rip, pex, spp, error, and idp.

Q: *Describe some of the communications diagnostic tools which would help you troubleshoot your network.*

A: Some utilities which aid in troubleshooting a network include:

netstat	Shows the status of the network
ping	Sends packets to a destination address and tracks the performance of packets round trip
spray	Sends packets (like ping) but, instead of one packet, it sends a burst of packets for greater duration, putting a simulated load on a network component to better test its communications
ifconfig	Can be used to ascertain useful network information as well as to configure the network port
etherfind	Gives network information about all network traffic passing through the network connection

Q: *Describe the communications tools delivered with the operating system that can be used to transfer data from one system to another.*

A: File transfer utilities include ftp, cu (call another Unix system—in some implementations it has a file transfer protocol as part of its utilities such as "take"/"put"), xmodem, ymodem, kermit, and uucp.

Q: *Describe some communication tools that allow for remote execution.*

A: Remote execution can be accomplished using uux (Unix-to-Unix execution), telnet (remote login-rlogin), rsh (remote shell), and rcp (remote copy) for a Unix ethernet subnet.

Q: *List network addressing concepts.*

A: Network addressing involves:

1. 32-bit addressing
2. Net portion-host portion, with the net portion assigned by NIC
3. Class A, B, and C, based on sizes (B = 65,535 hosts)
4. Subnet within a company
5. Netmasks

Q: *Describe some network addressing principles.*

A: The internet address is a 32-bit integer which designates network and host ID. Internet addresses can be divided into Class A, B, and C type networks.

Every host address must be unique; otherwise, hampered network communications would ensue. The internet address is comprised of network, subnet, and workstation. Every IP datagram contains the 32-bit address of the source as well as destination address in the IP header.

Q: *What is a broadcast address?*
A: Broadcast address is a reserved IP address plus broadcast (1s or 0s) in which broadcasts of thirty-two 1s (sometimes called all 1s) are put on the network. Directed broadcast addresses can map broadcasts to hardware. Local network broadcast address (limited broadcast address) can provide a broadcast for a local network regardless of assigned IP addresses. The 32-bit broadcast of all 0s is interpreted to mean local network (if zero) and local host (if zero).

Q: *What is netmasking and why is it used?*
A: Netmasking is a 32-bit designation similar to the address in a format of 255.255.255.255. In this form, netmasking is turned off. When netmasking is turned on, it provides a mechanism which changes the way the network sees the IP address, through a mathematical conversion.

Q: *Can you have multiple internets connected by routers?*
A: Yes.

Q: *Describe the steps for adding a server with an operating system to your TCP/IP network.*
A: The first step is to assign a unique internet address to the workstation. The netmask has to be assigned the same as other devices in that subnet. The physical device has to be attached to the network, and the workstation connected. When attaching the Attachment Unit Interface (AUI), you must make sure that it corresponds with the jumper settings on the unit. (A personal computer can have the jumpers on the card set for either BNC connector—thin ethernet—or transceiver.) Next, the system should be booted. At this point, you should "ping" another workstation or server using its IP address. If the "ping" works properly, the next step would be to change the /etc/hosts, /etc/netmasks, /etc/defaultdomain to include all the necessary information required by the system to recognize the network automatically upon booting. (If this system was a client or diskless workstation in an NIS network, then the "domainname" command can be set appropriately or changed in /etc/defaultdomain and rebooted, which will cause it to connect to its NIS master.)

Q: *Describe how you would attach a serial modem to the system.*
A: Make sure the serial port you have chosen for your modem is recognized at boot time. If you are going to use the line for dial-out, the serial port must be owned by uucp. Connect the modem to the serial port using a straightthrough cable (pins 2 and 3 are not crossed). You must have at least pins 2, 3, 7, 8, and 20 connected. If you intend to use the modem for dial-in, make the following entry in /etc/inittab (for 9600-baud speed):

```
t1a:2:on:/etc/getty -t60 ttyla m
```

If you intend to use the modem for dial-out, make the following entry in /etc/inittab (for 9600-baud speed):

```
t1A:2:off:/etc/getty -t60 tty1A m
```

An entry for the modem must be placed in the devices file (HoneyDanBer) /etc/uucp/devices (/usr/lib/uucp/devices in older Unix versions). On Sun/Os, an entry could be made in the /etc/remote file. This implementation is a BSD implementation of "cu" used by the "tip" command. Both of these files must include the port name (/dev/ttyb) and initialization information for the modem. Once connected to the modem, set the internal modem registers according to requirements. Once established, add information to the /etc/uucp/Systems, /etc/uucp/dialers files to communicate with other systems.

Q: *Describe how you would troubleshoot a modem dial-out session using only uucp.*

A: There are built-in features which provide troubleshooting for a modem connection. System V provides a utility called "Uutry," which shows each step in the initialization and communications of the modem. There is a "debug" level for all uucico utilities using the -d (debug level 1–9) option, which gives similar information.

Q: *What type of security is provided with Unix systems?*

A: Most Unix security installations are "B2" to "C2" level security. The more relaxed security is the "B2" level, which is the security most installations rely on. The most prevalent security implemented on the Unix system is password protection. It is the window of protection that denies unauthorized access to the operating environment. The password field of /etc/password or /etc/shadow is encrypted using a derivative of the DES algorithm.

Q: *What are the "standard Unix shells" and how do they differ?*

A: Most Unix systems have Bourne "/bin/sh" and C-shell "/bin/csh". K-shell is sometimes provided with the operation environment. C shell is an interactive command line shell which allows for the editing of command line execution. Bourne shell, while a noninteractive command line execution shell, is the prime choice of shell script creation.

   A common interactive alternative to the Bourne shell supplied with some systems is the Korne shell (/bin/ksh). It is similar in features and syntax to the Bourne shell and has the interactive features of the C shell, but may vary in functionality on different platforms.

Q: *The following is an often-asked interview question: "Describe the types of shells with which you are familiar, which one you are most used to using, and how proficient you are in the use of these shell commands."*

A: A typical acceptable answer could be: "I happen to have become accustomed to the Bourne shell using early versions of Unix. I then became accustomed to the Korne shell and happen to like it very much. It has an interactive command line editor (which has 'vi' or 'Emac' style command line editing), one that can be custom-set by the user. It has built-in environment variables which allow for a customized environment. Having a number of years' experience using the shell, I have become very accustomed to shell programming. Script writing is almost second nature and I could apply the technique to all phases of systems administration. I have written scripts that perform automatic systems backup during low CPU utilization hours. I have written interactive scripts which help to restore files to the system, scripts which can add or remove a user from the system, and scripts for new system installation."

(*Note:* If you plan to use any of these examples, be prepared to give an example of the script—or bring a copy of a script you have previously written.)

Q: *Where would you find shell scripts that would give you an idea of a system's normal operation?*

A: Many shell scripts can be found in the "/etc" directory. These scripts contain the sequence of commands which are involved in the proper initialization and execution of system startup functions.

Q: *Name two of the better-known versions of Unix that are currently available.*

A: The most predominant versions of Unix today are AT&T System V and Sun O/S.

Q: *What utility would you use to partition a disk for a new processor?*

A: Sun Microsystems (Sun O/S) provides a program called "format." This program can format, partition, repair, and maintain supported disks. Newer versions of AT&T Unix read drive characteristics from the CMOS RAM chip, partition information being defined in the "volume table of contents" ("VTOC") after being created using the "disksetup" utility. Additional disks could be added using the "diskadd" utility.

Q: *Describe the ISO/OSI model.*

A: The ISO/OSI model (International Standards Organization/Open Systems Interconnect) is a seven-layer model which depicts the components of a network in standard terms. The layers are comprised of:

Layer 1 (the physical layer)	Concerns the standards by which a network is physically attached to the network
Layer 2 (the data-link layer)	Provides services to the physical layer
Layer 3 (the network layer)	Provides services for the presentation layer in a connection and connectionless network service
Layer 4 (the transport layer)	Provides reliable end-to-end data transfers in a connection- and connectionless-oriented network
Layer 5 (the session layer)	Processes services provided by the transport layer and provides services to user processes

| Layer 6 (the presentation layer) | Deals with the representation of data as it is being exchanged; also makes the services of the session layer available to the application |
| Layer 7 (the application layer) | Deals with the application |

Q: *Describe how you would add memory to a system.*

A: To add memory to the system, the system first must be "halted," powered off, unplugged, and (where required) switches must be set to prevent electrical charges (from backup battery packs) from discharging impulses. A grounding strap should be worn to prevent static electricity discharge which could result in damage to one or more components. The system can then be opened and the paired (memory cards usually come in matched pairs) boards inserted into the slots according to manufacturer specifications. The system can be closed, powered on, and the new memory can be tested in maintenance mode to make sure it was properly installed. The MBUF kernel parameter should be set to 0 so the number of kernel I/O buffers is determined at boot time, based on the amount of memory installed.

Q: *Describe how you utilize error messages which the operating system generates.*

A: First, it must be determined from where the message is coming—whether from an application, the network, or from the operating system. This often can be determined from the context of the error itself. The "dmesg" command "cats" the "usr/adm/messages" file. System V errors are written to the "/usr/adm/error" file. This can be helpful in tracing problems and patterns of errors as they occur. Once identified, corrective measures can be explored and implemented.

Q: *Describe how you would set up (physically attach) a new serial printer to the system.*

A: The printer must be unpacked and set up according to manufacturer setup instructions. The appropriate cable is attached to the system. The printcap (Sun O/S) must be created to send the proper sequences to the printer. Also, an entry must be made to the termcap to send the same sequences to the printer.

Q: *How would you set up a printer if it were a parallel printer?*

A: To install a parallel printer (on System V):

1. The parallel port should be configured for interrupt vector 7. You must run "mkdev parallel" if you plan to use a port other than the built-in parallel port.

2. Verify that you are connected to the printer correctly: (date ; echo "\f\c") > /dev/lp0.

3. Run "sysadmsh". Interface chosen should be HPLaserJet; device name should be /dev/lp0 and hardwired.

4. From "sysadmsh", enable the printer.

5. From "sysadmsh", let the printer accept requests.

Q: *Describe the built-in utilities for a printer provided with the operating systems.*

A: The standard printer utilities for Sun O/S include "lpc" to administer the printer. This utility lets you start, stop, enable, disable, cancel, and print jobs. The "lpd" (line printer daemon) is run at system boot time and picks up print jobs and directs them to the printer.

The System V utilities include "lpadmin", which controls configuration of printers. The "lpsched" which initializes printer services and runs as a daemon after multiuser mode is initiated.

Q: *You have an ASCII terminal that is connected to a server. The ASCII terminal has stopped working. Describe how you would troubleshoot the device.*

A: An ASCII (dumb) terminal has stopped working. What you should do is:

- Check the brightness.
- Check the power and communication connections.
- Enter the setup mode and verify the terminal configuration settings, which should be 9600 baud, 8 data bits, 1 stop bit, and no parity.
- Enable the port to which the terminal is connected (for example, enable tty005).
- Verify that there is a getty process associated with the terminal port. Enter:

  ```
  ps -t tty005
  ```

- Test the hardware communications by disabling the port and redirecting output to the terminal:

  ```
  echo hello > /dev/tty005
  ```

Q: *You have an X terminal that has stopped working. Describe how you would troubleshoot the device and identify the problem.*

A: The problem resolution would be similar to resolving a problem on an ASCII terminal. The differences involve dealing with the communications network as opposed to a serial connection. Therefore, the network connection must be verified. It must also be ascertained that an "X" application has not caused normal operation to stop. If there is a problem with the application, it can be killed to free the X terminal. If everything checks out as far as network, hardware, and application, the window manager can be killed and a new x admin process respawned on the device to reinitialize it.

Q: *Your system has a bad disk. Describe how you would determine the problem, boot the system, and recover the data.*

A: If a disk other than the system disk is bad, the system could remain in service and an attempt made to repair the disk by using the "fsck", "format", "newfs" (BSD)/"fsck", "diskadd", "mkpart" (System V). The file systems can then be restored, given that an established system of making backup is in place. If the disk is the root partition, the system would have to be booted in maintenance mode from tape loading the operating system into memory. A backup of data and applications can then be restored to the system. If a disk cannot be reinitialized using these methods, the chances are that either the disk or the disk controller are bad. On occasion, the replacement of a disk controller alone can restore the disk to full operation without damage to the data on the file system.

Q: *What is the difference when a system boots single user from multiuser?*

A: A system that boots in single user mode does not supply all the services that it does in multiuser. Single user mode allows only console support of user activities. This ensures that a known state of the system exists. In single user mode the administrator is the only one capable of changing the data on the disks.

Q: *Describe the boot sequence of a BSD type operating environment.*

A: The boot sequence for a BSD system starts on the "restored mode"—meaning Suns ">" or "ok" prompt. The system goes through self-diagnostics, then loads Unix to memory. On Sun systems, an "L1 A" or break signal can bring the system into "restored mode" where selected services can be performed. Next, the system verifies the hardware and checks the state of the disks flags. These flags are set to OK when the system shuts down gracefully. If these flags are set to off (say, by an abnormal shutdown), the system does an "fsck" (file system check) on the disk, repairing any abnormal condition found. Flags are set to OK but the system does not do "sync", then reboots. It goes through the same steps again prior to loading Unix. After the system passes the file system check stage, it starts the services in the /etc directory, the network services, and the "rc.local" file.

Q: *Describe the boot sequence of a System V type operating environment.*

A: The boot sequence of System V system starts in the "restored mode." First, self-diagnostics are performed. Next, "Unix" is loaded to memory and the system verifies the hardware and checks the state of the disks flags. (These flags are set to OK when the system shuts down gracefully.) If these flags are set to off (by an abnormal shutdown), the system does an "fsck" (file system check) on the disk—repairing any abnormal condition found, and flags are set to OK. Next, the system scans the "/etc/inittab" to determine the state to initiate run level. Services are initiated corresponding to run level specified. These processes initialize services consulting the "/etc/rc(run level)" and execute all services in the "/etc/rc(run level).d" subdirectories. Cron, gettys, and printer services are started and login banners are sent to video displays.

Q: *Why would you boot a system in single user mode?*

A: A system booted (BSD) or "init"ed (System V) to single-user mode could be because of the need for operating system maintenance, upgrade or repair, file system maintenance or repair, application installation or communications maintenance, or modification—as well as problem isolation, identification, and resolution.

Q: *Describe the mechanisms of the "cron" command and how it works.*

A: "Cron" is a command whose services are initialized when the system is brought up in multiuser mode. When loaded, it executes commands at specified dates and times. It runs in background as a clock daemon until it is killed either by the "super" user or when the system shuts down or "init"ed in a mode that kills it. The cron daemon wakes up once a minute to see if anything needs to be run. Heavily loaded systems may expect a delay of a few minutes. These commands are specified in a specially formatted file in the "/usr/spool/cron/crontabs" (or "var/spool/cron/crontabs") directory. The file that executes "super" user commands can be found in the root file. Regular users may also submit jobs to "cron" deamon as long as they have "cron" permission.

Q: *You have to set up an "X" terminal environment for a user. Describe what files are needed to customize the user's environment.*

A: The files that are needed are:

.xinitrc	Executes the "run command (rc)" file; contains commands for setting up the environment
.xsession	Executes the desired window manager and initializes applications in the windowing environment
.Xdefaults or .xresources	Resource definitions and configuration file
.twmrc	The initialization file for the "twm" (toms window manager)
.mwmrc	The initialization file for the mwm (motif window manager)

These files control/customize the users windowing environment.

Q: *Describe how an "X" terminal boots on a network.*

A: An "X" terminal on power-up goes through a series of hardware checks. Next, the terminal loads saved configuration information using "rarp" or "bootp" or "tftp". Next, "xdm" (which is running on the server) connects with the "X" terminal. It sets up the "X" environment and puts a login banner on the "X" terminal display, allowing the user to login onto the system.

Q: *Describe how a DOS PC could be added to a network using TCP/IP communications.*

A: First the communications hardware and software are installed and configured. Files are then set up to initialize the communications and software drivers. The internet address and netmask are set for the subnet. The communication commands should then be added to the PC's boot process to activate the resources. Mounts are also initialized allowing the PC to mount disk resources of the Unix server at boot time.

Q: *Name some types of window managers.*

A: A window manager is a means of controlling the "X" windowing environment. The window manager determines the look and feel of the windowing system. It also controls the methods of transferring data between applications. Some window managers include "uwm" (universal window manager), "twm" (toms window manager), "mwm" (motif window manager), "olwm" (openlook window manager), and "awm" (ardent window manager).

Q: *What file(s) would you use to customize the user's operating environment using a window manager?*

A: Either an "rc" file or, if it does not exist in the users HOME directory, a system default "rc" (system.(window manager)rc) file is used. The .(window manager)rc file can be configured to control fonts used, resources, colors, key bindings, actions, and menus.

Q: *If involved with an older version of Unix (pre-System V.4), how would you modify a kernel parameter?*

A: Files containing the parameters could be edited directly or a system administrative utility could be run to modify a kernel parameter.

Q: *Why would you not be required to do this for System V.4 systems?*

A: System V.4 has loadable kernel modules, which means that the old process of recompiling and loading a new Unix kernel is not required.

Q: *What are some possible reasons that a change in the kernel might be required?*

A: A change in a kernel might be required because of a change in operating environment (i.e., an application may be added, additional users may require a change in the kernel, or hardware/communication may be needed). System fine-tuning (to increase performance) could also be a reason for recompiling the kernel.

Q: *What are some of the utilities that can be used to monitor system performance?*

A: The utilities which can effectively monitor system performance can include: ps (process status), pstat (process table status—BSD, Sun O/S), swap (System V), sar (system activity report—System V), and vmstat (virtual memory status—BSD, Sun O/S).

Q: *What is memory paging and swapping?*

A: Paging is the operation of loading and unloading segments of memory. Swap partitions are areas of disk which hold pages of memory.

Q: *How would you increase swap space on your system?*

A: Swap space can be added utilizing the swap command (System V): "swap -a /dev/block_special_device_partition start_value size_in_bytes". The "swap -1" command will list the current swap partitions. To add swap space to a BSD-Sun O/S system, additional steps must be taken. First, an empty file must be created using the "mkfile -empty size_of_file_in_MB file_name". Next, the command "swapon -a file_name" will activate the area of swap.

Q: *What kind of process is the mount command?*

A: The mount command is a process by which resources can be merged into the system's local file tree structure.

Q: *What steps does the operating system take (during boot) to mount file systems?*

A: The mount command is executed as part of the boot-up sequences. When a system boots multiuser, the "/etc/rc.local" (BSD Sun O/S) file or "/etc/dfs/dfstab" (Solaris 2.x), "/etc/rc2" (System V) file is executed—which in turn consults the files in "/etc/rc2.d" (in run-level directory), executing them. Then the "/etc/fstab" (BSD Sun O/S) "/etc/vfstab (System V) entries are consulted, mounting the defined entries.

Q: *Name some of the standard software that is supplied by the operating system that administers printers.*

A: Some standard printer administration utilities include:

SUN O/S—BSD

lpr	Queues print jobs to the printer
lpc	Administration interface to printer commands; includes start, stop, status, down, up, enable, disable
lpd	The printer daemon process
lpq	Lists queued print jobs
lprm	Removes print jobs from the print queue
lpstat	Shows the status of print jobs as well as the status of printers

SYSTEM V

lpadmin	Configures the lp subsystem by defining printers and devices
lpfilter	Used when adding, deleting, changing, or listing filters used with the lp print subsystem
lpforms	Administers forms used with the lp subsystem
lpsched	Runs as a daemon process
lpshut	Gracefully shuts down printer services
lpmove	Moves print requests from a named destination to an alternate destination

Q: *What is "fsck" and when is it used?*

A: The "fsck" command is the "File System Check" command. This utility actively checks and repairs inconsistencies in the file system. In System V, if no file system is designated on the command line, the "/etc/checklist" file is consulted for a list of file systems to check.

Q: *What are the dump and restore commands and when are they used?*

A: The "dump" and "restore" commands are utilities for backing up and restoring data to/from disk (BSD, Sun O/S). (System V has the "ufsdump"/"ufsrestore" and "backup"/"restore".)

Q: *What is the "gettydefs" file and when would you need to modify it?*

A: The "/etc/gettydefs" file (in older versions, /etc/gettytab) is the file where the line definitions for terminals (tty) are written.

Q: *How would you find out the attributes of a serial line, ASCII terminal, or an "X" terminal window?*

A: The command to determine the attributes of a serial line, ASCII (dumb) terminal, or a window on an "X" terminal would be the "stty -a" command. This command lists all the attributes currently available on that terminal.

Q: *Describe how you would automate the backup of the data on your network without operator intervention.*

A: An automated backup of a network facility requires the creation of backup or dump scripts that would be active in the "cron". The backup scripts could use the "cpio", "tar", "dd", or "dump" command.

Q: *Name some of the parameters involved in installation of a third-party vendor software package in a network facility.*

A: The install process requires answers to the following parameters:

1. Location of installation media (floppy, tape, etc.).

2. Where will the application reside on disk?

3. Where will the binary (executable) files reside?

4. Should the initialization scripts be added to the boot-up sequence?

5. Setting up of environment variables.

6. Setting up of users.

Q: *Describe how you would modify the kernel to install a database.*

A: Some products require that a change of the Unix kernel be implemented to include "Shared Memory Segments," "Message Queues," and "Semaphores" attributes. Some Unix operating systems come configured with the default kernel which meets this requirement, while others require that they be modified either manually or by using the administrative facilities supplied with the operating system.

Q: *What is a raw disk partition?*

A: A raw disk partition is a segment of disk that does not have a file system created on it.

Q: *Describe some standard Unix commands used to transfer data from one media to another (physical media).*

A: Some of the standard commands which transfer data to media include:

cpio (copy in/out)	Can be used to transfer data: disk-to-disk, disk-to-tape, tape-to-tape, or tape-to-disk
tar (tape archive)	Transfers disk-to-disk, disk-to-tape, disk-to-file, or tape-to-disk
bar	A variation on the tar command with more options provided with the utility
dd (convert and copy a file)	Allows for the transfer of data between dissimilar systems or media

Q: *Summarize the Network Information Service (NIS).*

A: NIS is a protocol developed by Sun Microsystems. This service provides hardware and software resources across a networked distributed computing environment. The command set related to NIS commands are prefaced by "yp" (i.e., "ypinit", "ypbind", "yppush", "ypset", etc.). Commands are usually located in the "/usr/etc/yp" or "/var/yp" directories.

Q: *What steps are required to add a new user to the system using NIS?*

A: To add a new user to the system using "NIS" you would:
   1. Add the user's name to the group and passwd file to include "home directory" and "shell".
   2. Create the user's login directory and add it to the "automount" tables.
   3. Add and compile this information for "NIS" to pass this new information to the network.
   4. Add to the user's home directory any customizing required for the user environment.

Q: *What is "domainname" command?*

A: "domainname" (Sun O/S BSD) and "dname" (System V) print or define the the domain name for NFS and RFS resource utilization. It is maintained in "/etc/defaultdomain" (Sun O/S BSD) and "/etc/rfs/ <transport> /rfmaster" files.

Q: *How would you add a user under System V Unix?*

A: To add a user in System V, use "sysadmsh", choose "Accounts", "User", and "Create". Enter UserName, optionally "Comments", and answer "no" to ModifyDefaults (unless you want to change options like login group, groups it belongs to, Login shell, Home directory, etc.). When you exit from the window, a series of creation messages are displayed. Finally, "sysadmsh" prompts you as to whether an initial password should be created. Your options are: Now (assign the new account a password), Later (does not assign a password—cannot login), or Blank (assigns an empty password—user is asked to set a password at first login). Last of all, you have to specify whether or not to force the change of the password at first login.

Q: *Describe the process by which a user logs on to the system.*

A: A user logs into the system at a login prompt either on an ASCII (dumb) terminal, an "X" terminal, or via modem connection. In all cases, the login prompt is placed there by a "getty" or "xdm". The user enters his or her login ID and password. These are validated against the "/etc/passwd" or, in the case of NIS, the NIS password file after which the user environment is initiated. The login starts the "shell" which is indicated in the passwd file.

Q: *Describe some cabling methods to physically attach components to a TCP/IP network.*

A: Communications physical attachment can include thick and thin ethernet cable, unshielded twisted pair, wireless, or fiber.

Q: *What are daemons?*

A: Daemons are processes that are run when the system is initialized and continue to run while the system is in operation. Their purpose is to wait in the background until their services are required.

Q: *Give the names of some daemons.*

A: Some examples are: rpc.mountd, nfsd, mountd & biod (NFS daemons), lpd (line printer daemon), rlogind (rlogin and rsh daemon), telnetd (telnet server daemon), routed (network routing daemon), and rwhod (remote who daemon). The most common daemon is probably the cron daemon.

Q: *What is a font?*

A: Fonts are families of typefaces that come in different sizes, weights, and orientations. They are character sets used for windowing displays.

Q: *Describe the standard Unix directory structure and the contents of some of its directories.*

A: The Unix directory structure is a tree structure. Its source is the root file system or the root directory. All other directories branch off the root directory. In the "/etc" directory system, utilities and commands can be found. In the "/bin" and "/usr/bin" directories are system and user commands. In the "/usr/ucb" directory are BSD type user commands. In the /usr/spool directory is the mail, cron, uucp, and spool subsystems. In the "/usr/lib" is the standard Unix library directory. The "/tmp" directory is the area of disk where temporary space is allocated for applications and users.

Q: *What is NFS?*

A: NFS is the Network File System. It is a distributed file system utility which allows for centralized administration of network resources. This implementation is utilized both by System V and Sun O/S and BSD.

Q: *What is RFS?*

A: RFS is the Remote File Sharing. It is a System V implementation of the capabilities of sharing and administering resources among interconnected machines.

Q: *Name some NIS commands and explain what they do.*

A: Some NIS commands include:

ypbind	Daemon responsible for locating the NIS server and maintaining bindings of the domain names to servers
ypinit	Initializes NIS services
ypserv	Daemon that handles all client requests
ypwhich	Returns the server name for which the domain is bound

Q: *What is involved in "systems integration" as it applies to the administration of a Unix operating environment?*

A: There is a broad spectrum of responsibility in the administration of these systems. Involved are network, operating systems and internals, third-party applications, communications protocols and applications, hardware, printing and device drivers, shell script programming, and time management.

Q: *What is the "ipcs" and what does it report?*

A: "ipcs" is both a Unix command and an operating system facility. The "ipcs" module is the "interprocessing communications facility" which controls message queues, shared memory segments, and semaphores. The "ipcs" command reports status and returns information on message queues, shared memory segments, and semaphores.

Q: *What is the automounter and what does it do?*

A: The automounter is a facility which automatically mounts and unmounts NFS resources.

Q: *Name some maps that help integrate automounter functions into the NIS services.*

A: Some of these maps are:

master (auto.master)	Contains the lists of direct mounts and indirect maps directing the automounter where to look for this information
direct (auto.direct)	Defines specific mount points which mount on a single directory and appear as a link to the direct mount point
indirect (auto. <something>)	Maps that have directories associated with them and are defined in the auto.master map

Q: *What does the "exportfs" command do?*

A: The "exportfs" command makes file systems available for mounting by remote hosts. Tables for exported file systems are maintained in "/etc/exports" (Sun O/S BSD). Under System V, the command equivalent for both NFS and RFS resource sharing is the "share" and "shareall" command which maintains tables in "/etc/dfs/(fstypes, sharetab, and dfstab)" files.

7
The AS/400

Daniel Robert Cohen

Introduction

The Application System/400 was announced by IBM on June 21, 1988 as a major improvement to their midrange computer systems product line. Since its inception, many new and updated AS/400 models have made their debut in the marketplace. The high-end AS/400 models of today now rival IBM's mainframe systems for memory capacity, processing power, and speed. It has become popular to companies of all sizes because of its ease of use and adaptability to diverse operating conditions in various business environments.

The AS/400 allows companies who have made investments in other IBM midrange machines (such as the Systems 36 and 38) and associated software to preserve their working software while moving to a new and versatile machine. The AS/400 can be connected to and communicate with most other IBM systems, including the PC.

IBM has implemented Systems Application Architecture (SAA) into the workings of the system. SAA provides a means to develop software products that will run on other IBM systems, such as the System/370 and the PC. In addition, the AS/400 supports a large number of high-level programming languages such as RPG, COBOL, PASCAL, FORTRAN, BASIC, PL/I, REXX, and C.

A hallmark of the AS/400 is its ease of use. All operating features and commands in the system are accessible via menus. Context-sensitive help can be used to guide the user with unfamiliar tasks. On-line educational tutorial programs are available for those who wish to learn more about the system. The AS/400 also boasts a sophisticated self-diagnostic capability as well as complete user support via IBM's 24-hour help hotlines and Electronic Customer Support (ECS). The hardware is more reliable and the operating system more user friendly than earlier IBM midrange systems.

Summary of AS/400 Software

The AS/400 can operate in System/36 or "native" mode. In addition, IBM supplies a software conversion package for those wishing to migrate from System/36 or System/38. Once the migration is complete, the system may run in any of the available operational modes. For those wishing to operate in AS/400 native mode, it is necessary to convert software written on previous systems to be AS/400 compatible.

The AS/400 supports all programming languages that were supported by the Systems/36 and 38. For example, RPG/II and OCL are both available on the AS/400 operating in System/36 mode. RPG/III and CL are both available when operating in System/38 mode or when operating in AS/400 mode but utilizing System/38 object types, compilers, and command processors. The newest and most advanced versions of all languages supported (such as RPG/400 and COBOL/400) are also available in native mode.

The operating system, called OS/400, is based primarily upon the operating system of IBM's midrange System/38, called CPF (Control Program Facility). OS/400 is the interface between the machine, the user, and other programs on the system. It was designed to allow for technological improvements in the underlying machine hardware without affecting software applications that operate under OS/400. IBM has accomplished this through use of a licensed internal code machine instruction set—"layers" which isolate the higher-level AS/400 applications from actual machine implementation. The OS/400 handles interactive, batch, and a vast array of functions that "insulate" the user from underlying operations creating a user-friendly system.

The OS/400 provides the ability to locate, use, and create "objects" on the system. It enables users or programs to send messages within the system or to communicate with other systems. It maintains detailed informational logs concerning all events that take place and performs problem analysis and system diagnostics. The OS/400 provides access to Electronic Customer Support (ECS) and manages data storage, data retrieval, and updates through a relational database structure. The OS/400 provides system security which controls user access to various objects. The OS/400 maintains a huge number of error and informative messages that are automatically sent to the user where appropriate, to assist in problem determination and recovery.

The AS/400 can be connected to a vast array of other computer systems. Some examples are the IBM PC (and IBM PC compatibles), S/370, S/36, S/38, and with all other AS/400 models. It can communicate remotely with other systems using a wide variety of communications protocols such as System Network Architecture (SNA), Distributed Data Management (DDM), Local Area Network (LAN), Advanced Program-to-Program Communications Support (APPC), and Advanced Peer-to-Peer Networking Support (APPN). Most workstation devices and printers can be connected to the system. Unlike older midrange systems, the AS/400 provides for automatic device configuration which defines a new device to the system and makes it usable as soon as it is connected to the AS/400 and switched on.

Terminology

Input inhibited: Refers to the flag that is displayed on the terminal to indicate that the CPU is busy processing the last command inputted from the user. The user cannot enter any information until the input inhibited indicator light goes out.

DDS (Data Description Specifications): A method by which database files are defined and created on the AS/400.

PDM (Program Development Manager): A productivity tool for programmers providing functions such as copying, deleting, scanning, changing, or creating source files.

CPF (Control Program Facility): Refers to the operating system on the S/38. So much of OS/400 is based upon CPF that the two terms are sometimes used interchangeably. Many of the system diagnostic messages sent to the user on the AS/400 will begin with the prefix CPF. As a result, this and messages that begin with other letters are referred to as "CPF messages."

DFU (Data File Utility): A utility which is used to add, change, update, or delete records in a database.

SDA (Screen Design Aid): A utility for creating display files and menus for interactive applications.

QRY (Query): A utility for creating interactive or batch reports.

SEU (Source Entry Utility): A utility for editing programming language source code.

Object: Everything on the AS/400 that is referred to by a specific name, takes up space, and is defined by specific attributes is called an *object*. Some examples of objects are files, libraries, programs, and user profiles.

Library: Essentially an object that holds a directory to other objects.

QSYS: The IBM system library used by the system for its operation.

Library list: A group of libraries which are used by a job while searching for objects needed during processing.

Current library: A concept taken from the System/36 is the library that is always on top of your library list, and is therefore the first library searched when a job is executing. You can change the current library by issuing the CL command CHGCURLIB.

QTEMP: The temporary library that is created for each interactive job and is used to store objects, including files and programs. When the interactive job ends, all of the contents of QTEMP are deleted by the system.

Source type: Refers to the type of programming language that SEU will code in when creating a new source member.

Key, Keylist, or Klist: Refers to a list of keys that is identified by a symbolic name and is used to access a specific record in a file defined with the same set (and order) of key fields.

Select/Omit: Keywords used in DDS to prevent certain records from being a part of the access path. Even though the records exist in the physical file, they may be excluded by select/omit criteria from appearing in the Logical file.

Invocation stack: The list of programs maintained by the system as one program calls another in a series of calls within a single task or job.

User profile: An object that defines how a specified user or group of users may use the system, and their level of authority. A user must have a user profile in order to access the AS/400.

Job description (JOBD): Defines the environment and encompasses such items as which library list the job will use, which JOBQ the job will be placed upon, and which level of priority will be given the job on the JOBQ for running the job. Every user or group of users on the AS/400 is assigned a job description.

Job switch: A group of eight logical indicators that are part of the job definition, and can be set "on" and "off" and passed between programs. They are frequently used to "condition" various functions in an application.

Time-slice: A finite amount of time in which a job is granted system resources while other jobs are queued (or wait in line). After the time-slice is up, the job is briefly queued while another job is given system resources. In this manner, several jobs can run at the same time.

Level check: Can occur when a program that has been created to access a file and the file format has changed *after* the program has been created. The program will fail if run. The error message will say there is a LEVEL CHECK. In order for the program to run, it must be first re-created over the new file format definition, or the file must be changed (or overridden using OVRDBF) with LVLCHK(*NO) specified.

Spooled file: An object that contains data to be printed.

OUTQ (Output Queue): An object that stores many spooled files to be printed in the order in which they occur on the OUTQ.

IPL (Initial Program Load) or IMPL (Initial Microprogram Load): The initial program that is run by OS/400 when the system is turned on. This program checks the integrity of the hardware and prepares the system for normal operation.

Internally described file: A file on disk that is defined directly by the program that uses it and is not necessarily defined by DDS.

Officevision/400: The word processor and business office operations software package available on the AS/400, although it is sold separately.

QINTER: The name of the IBM-supplied subsystem that provides the interactive functioning environment of the system.

PC SUPPORT/400: The program from IBM that allows a PC to be connected to the system and to utilize functions on the AS/400. This program provides AS/400 terminal and printer emulation, file transfer capabilities, and virtual printing (printing PC output on an AS/400 printer), as well as a single user interface for running AS/400 and PC applications.

QBATCH: The IBM-supplied subsystem that provides the environment for programs to execute in batch.

QCTL: The name for the IBM-supplied controlling subsystem which handles system operations.

Handling
the AS/400 Interview

One may expect an oral or a written technical interview, and some places give both. Some interviewers may give you specifications for a small program or subroutine and ask you to code it. Many shops include math questions as part of their test. It is therefore advisable to review your basic algebra. It is important to realize the interviewer could ask a question on any subject pertinent to AS/400 programming. The question could be as simple as, "How do you compile a program?" or as difficult as, "Explain how to implement performance tuning." Although the level of difficulty and type of questions asked may depend upon the particular position being applied for, remember that many interviewers work from a list of questions and answers, all of which they will ask both the very experienced and inexperienced alike. It is therefore crucial for all applicants, no matter how inexperienced, to study as many areas of AS/400 programming as possible.

Many AS/400 installations use RPG. RPG programming on the AS/400 requires detailed knowledge of the RPG language, a solid understanding of DDS, CL programming, and a working knowledge of the OS/400 operating system. It is especially important for RPG programmers to know the C spec op-codes, and how they work. There are also a number of everyday skills essential to all programmers. Some examples are how to use SEU, SDA, PDM, DFU, and QUERY. Obtaining printouts is an everyday event, and the ability to work with spooled files, Outq's, and printer devices is expected. Over the years there have been many changes and enhancements to RPG, CL, DDS, and OS/400, encompassing most areas of the system. One may expect changes to these areas with every new release of OS/400, and very often the interviewer will ask about recent enhancements to the RPG or CL language.

The questions and answers that follow cover topics that could be asked on RPG, CL, and DDS. Although there is no guarantee you will be confronted with any of these questions, a majority concern important concepts and techniques. Furthermore, most of the questions deal directly with concepts that are applicable to virtually any programming environment. If additional detail is required, books and IBM reference manuals are available.

Questions and Answers

Q: *Name the different types of files used on the AS/400.*

A: Files commonly used are physical files, source physical files, logical files, join logical files, display files, printer files, spooled files, and save files.

Q: *How does a field reference file differ from a physical file?*

A: A field reference file is a file in which field definitions and descriptions are stored, while physical files contain the data defined by the field reference file.

Q: *What does UNIQUE mean?*

A: UNIQUE is specified at file level in DDS for a keyed physical or logical file to indicate that records with duplicate keys will not be permitted.

Q: *What is the difference between FIFO and LIFO record retrieval?*

A: FIFO means first in, first out. When more than one record in a file has the same key, these records will be retrieved in the order of their addition to the file. The first added will be the first retrieved, and so on. FIFO is the default assumed for a file that allows duplicate keys.

   LIFO means last in, first out. Records with duplicate keys will be retrieved in the opposite order of their addition to the file. The last record added will be the first retrieved, and so on.

Q: *What is dynamic select?*

A: Dynamic select means: select records at execution time. This is a DDS file-level keyword (DYNSLT) which is used for logical files. When DYNSLT is specified, the system does not perform record selection (or omission) until the file is read by a program. As each record is read, it is checked using select/omit criteria specified in the file definition.

Q: *Explain how dynamic select differs from access path select.*

A: While dynamic selection always occurs when the file is read, access path selection may (but not necessarily) occur before the file is read. The reason is that access path selection is done when maintenance is performed on the files' access path. The time access path maintenance is performed depends upon what type of file maintenance is specified on the Create Logical File command (Immediate, Delay, or Rebuild).

Q: *Name two major differences between a logical file and a physical file.*

A: A physical file may only have one record format. A logical file may have multiple record formats. A physical file contains actual data. A logical file does not contain data, but provides a logical and sequenced view to the data using indexes which "point" to the records in the physical file.

Q: *Name and define the three methods used to maintain the access path of a file.*

A: 1. *Immediate.*   All access paths associated with the file are updated when a change is made to the file, and it makes no difference whether the access paths are opened or closed—they are all updated immediately.

2. *Rebuild.*   With this method, only open access paths are updated when a change is made to the file. Any access paths that are closed at the time the change was made will not be updated. The next time the access path is opened, the access path will be completely rebuilt.

3. *Delay.* When a change is made to a file, the only access paths that are updated are the ones that are open at the time the change is made. Any access paths that are closed at the time the change is made will not be updated until they are opened. The updates are accumulated and merged into the existing access path structure when it is opened. The entire access path is not rebuilt unless the accumulated changes to the access path are more than approximately 25 percent of the entire size of the access path.

Q: *Explain where each method to maintain an access path is best employed, and note a possible disadvantage to each.*

A: 1. When immediate file maintenance is used, the file can be opened quickly because the access path is kept up to date. This method is ideal for files that are used with interactive applications since it is constantly being opened and updated. The drawback to this method is the slower update (or output) operation for a file with several access paths associated since all the access paths are updated whenever a change occurs in any of them.

2. When rebuild file maintenance is used, opening the file will take a long time because the entire access path will be rebuilt if changes occurred while the access path (that is now being opened) was closed. This method is ideal for files used with applications that are run periodically in batch.

The advantage to this method is faster update (or output) operations for a file with several access paths associated. Since none of the closed access paths are updated when a change is made to the file, and only the particular access path now opened will be changed, the update process will occur more quickly. Rebuilding the access path of an entire file can take a long time. It is therefore generally best to avoid rebuild maintenance for a file used by programs called frequently, or where the file is very large. If the file has unique keys, this method cannot be used. If the file is being journaled, this method cannot be used.

3. When delayed file maintenance is used, opening the file will be moderately, but not extremely, quick. The reason for this is that the access path is merged with accumulated changes, but not entirely rebuilt, when opened. This method is ideal for files used with applications run in batch. This method should be used only when there is a fairly small number of changes to be accumulated for the access paths that are closed. This method provides a compromise between the slow update (or output) speed of immediate maintenance, and the slow open of rebuild maintenance.

The disadvantage to this method is an extremely long open will take place if too many access path changes have accumulated since the last open operation. If the number of changes accumulated for the access path exceeds approximately 25 percent of the total size of the access path, then rebuild rather than delay maintenance should be used when the file using the access path is reopened. If the file has unique keys, this method cannot be used.

Q: *What is a join logical file? State three differences between a regular logical file and a join logical file.*

A: A join logical file is a type of logical file that contains fields from two or more physical files and combines them into a single record format.

1. A regular logical file allows for multiple record formats, and a join logical file allows for only one record format.

2. Changes to data in a physical file can be made via a logical file created over the physical. Changes to data in a physical file cannot be made via a join logical file.

3. The record format name in a logical file must be the same as that based on physical file format. The record format name in the join logical file must be different than the record format names in the "based on" files.

Q: *Name the keywords that are essential in defining a join logical file, and explain their use in the definition.*

A: JFILE—This keyword is used at the record level to specify the two or more physical files to be joined. The first physical file name specified will be the primary, and the rest will be secondary.

JOIN—This keyword is optional when only two physical files are being specified in the join, but is essential when there are more than two. It is used to identify which two physical files are being joined by the keywords and specifications that come immediately after this keyword.

JFLD—This keyword must be specified at least one time for each JOIN keyword entered. Two field names are used with this keyword. The first is taken from the primary file, and the second is taken from one of the secondary files. These are called *join fields,* and are used to control how records between the two files are combined.

JREF—This keyword is used at field-definition level to identify which physical file the specified field is from. This may be necessary since a field name included in the join logical file may exist in more than one physical file upon which the join logical is based.

Q: *What will happen if you fail to specify the JDFTVAL keyword in a join logical file?*

A: If the file-level keyword JDFTVAL is not specified, then any primary file record that does not have a matching secondary file record will be dropped from the join. If there is more than one secondary file, then a match must be found to the primary file for each secondary file.

Q: *What is *LIKE DEFN?*

A: The RPG *LIKE figurative constant, when used together with the verb DEFN (on the C spec), enables the programmer to give work fields defined in the RPG program the same attributes (i.e., length and decimal values, if any) as the database fields specified in the DEFN operation. This eliminates the need for the programmer to specify the work field definition, since the compile brings in the database field definition, and gives it to the work field.

In the following example, DTAFLD is defined by a database file, and WRKFLD takes on the same definition as DTAFLD.

		Factor 1	Opcode	Factor 2	Result
Example:	C	*LIKE	DEFN	DTAFLD	WRKFLD

Q: *Why use *LIKE DEFN?*

A: This coding technique eliminates the need to constantly change the programming code when database fields are changed. When the program is recompiled, the new field definitions will automatically be applied to the program work fields.

Q: *What is a Data Area?*

A: A Data Area is an object used to pass information between programs. It consists of a single field (and one record) of data defined as numeric, character, or logical. The contents of a Data Area may be changed by RPG, CL, or directly by the programmer with entry of a CL command. A Data Area may be accessed and changed by any job. The Data Area, along with its contents, remains on the system until it is deleted.

Q: *Give an example of where a Data Area might prove useful?*

A: When an application requires a new and unique customer number to be generated whenever a new customer is added to the Customer Master File, a Data Area may be used to keep track of the last customer number added, so that the program may access the Data Area record, add 1 to it, and use the result as the new customer number (while updating the Data Area with the new number).

Q: *What is a Local Data Area?*

A: A Local Data Area (LDA) is automatically created by the system when a batch or interactive job is initiated. Every job has its own Local Data Area which consists of a single character field of 1024 bytes. An LDA may be accessed and changed by RPG, CL, or directly (via the command entry screen).

When an interactive job initiates a batch job with the SBMJOB command, the contents of the LDA located on the interactive job are copied to the LDA created with the batch job being executed. The contents of an LDA can be passed between programs (or jobs) when placed in a regular Data Area, or placed in a program field, and passed as a parameter from one program to another. When a job ends, the LDA—along with its contents—is deleted.

Q: *How is a Data Area defined and used by RPG?*

A: To define a Data Area in RPG you need to use *NAMVAR DEFN, with the Data Area name in the Result field (on the C spec). An RPG program may read a Data Area via the IN op-code, and may update (or release it if locked) via the OUT op-code. If *LOCK IN is specified, then other programs may not change the Data Area until the current program releases it. It is also possible to read (and lock) a Data Area via the "Data Area Data Structure" defined using UDS on the I spec.

Q: *Name the CL commands to create, retrieve, lock, and change a Data Area.*

A:

CRTDTAARA	Creates a Data Area
DCLDTAARA	Declares a Data Area which enables a CL program to access it
CHGDTAARA	Changes the data in a Data Area
RCVDTAARA	Receives and copies the current value of a Data Area to a CL field with the same name as the Data Area (applies to CLP38)
RTVDTAARA	Retrieves information from the Data Area, and places it in a CL variable
ALCOBJ	May be used to lock a Data Area so that other programs may not update it as long as it is in use by the current program
SNDDTAARA	Copies the data from a CL field to a Data Area

Q: *What does V2R2M0 mean, and what is its significance?*

A: Version 2, Release 2, Modification Level 0. This refers to the version of OS/400 that is operating on the system. Over time, IBM changes and enhances features in OS/400 which affect all facets of how the system operates. It is important to know which version is currently loaded on the system in order to take full advantage of all features available.

Q: *What is a figurative constant? Give some examples.*

A: A figurative constant is a type of literal that derives its definition directly from the program field with which it is associated. Figurative constants are used for field comparisons (such as FLD1 IFEQ *BLANKS), to initialize fields (i.e., MOVE *ZEROS FLD2), and to position pointers when reading a file (i.e., *LOVAL SETLL FILEX). Some examples are: *BLANKS, *ZEROS, *HIVAL, *LOVAL, *ALL'X..',*ON, and *OFF.

Q: *When an RPG program begins execution, is it necessary for the programmer to initialize program fields?*

A: No. RPG automatically initializes all numeric fields to zero, and all character fields to blank.

Q: *What is a record lock?*

A: When a file is defined with "input for update" on the F spec, and a record is read from that file, the program locks the record for update. If a second program has the same file specified as "input for update," and attempts to read the record while it is locked, the read attempt will fail.

Q: *Describe two ways to check for a record lock.*

A: If an indicator is placed in positions 56 and 57 of the Read or Chain operation, it will be set on if the record is locked.

A File Information Data Structure may be defined for the file. This involves an entry on the F spec file continuation line of KINFDS together with a Data Structure name. The Data Structure name specified on the F Spec is then used on the I spec to define the data structure itself. Within the data structure, RPG predefined subfields may be specified. The Data Structure subfield defined with the RPG reserved word *STATUS will contain the error code 01218 if the record is locked.

In the following example, FLD1 is defined as the File Information Data Structure, and the field name STAT1 will contain the error code 01218 if the record the program is chaining to is locked.

Example 1

```
FFILEX UF E K DISK KINFDS FLD1
*
IFLD1 DS
I          *STATUS STAT1
```

This same error status code is also available in the File Feedback Information area when a numeric subfield occupying positions 11 through 15 is defined in the File Information Data Structure. In that case, the predefined subfield *STATUS would be unnecessary.

In the next example, the field name STAT1 will contain the error code 01218 if a record the program is chaining to is locked.

Example 2

```
FFILEX UF E K DISK KINFDS FLD1

IFLD1 DS
I   11  15  STAT1
```

Q: *Name five ways to release a record lock.*

A: 1. An update (or delete) operation will release a record lock.

2. A READ (or CHAIN) operation performed on the file will unlock a record that was locked by a previous READ (or CHAIN) to the file.

3. A SETLL (or SETGT) operation will release a record lock.

4. The RPG operation UNLCK will release a record lock.

5. When an EXCPT operation is performed to the O spec and the file name is specified by itself, without field names, the record lock is released.

Q: *Name three kinds of arrays, and explain how they are loaded.*

A: 1. A Compile Time Array is loaded into the array name specified on the E spec when the program is created (or compiled). The information used to load the array is taken from entries made by the programmer at the bottom of the RPG source code member.

2. A Preexecution Time Array (otherwise known as a Prerun Time Array) is automatically loaded into the array name specified on the E spec when the program is called, but before the program starts processing data. The information used to load the array is taken from a Table or Array file on the system.

3. An Execution Time Array (otherwise known as a Run-Time Array) is loaded into the array name specified on the E spec by the program after it is called, and while it operating. The data used to load the array is determined during program execution.

Q: *How do you WRITE and READ in a single RPG statement? Explain how this works.*

A: EXFMT (Execute Format) is used to first Write, then Read a Display File format. When coding an RPG program to handle a Workstation File (or Display File), EXFMT will write a Display File format to the screen, which will then wait for a response from the user. Upon user response, control returns to the program which will then READ, inputting any screen fields into the program.

Q: *What RPG statement positions a pointer to the beginning of a group of records?*

A: When a key is used together with a SETLL operation on a keyed physical or logical file, the pointer is moved to the beginning of the group of records that are greater than or equal to the key that is specified on the SETLL operation.

Q: *Which RPG statement is used to read a group of records which all have the same key?*

A: The READE and READP operations may be used to read a group of records with the same key.

Q: *Which single RPG Op-Code performs both SETLL and READE?*

A: A CHAIN Op-Code is the equivalent of a SETLL and READE in a single statement, since it uses a key to position the pointer and then to retrieve a specific record.

Q: *How can you add the contents of one array to another array in a single RPG statement?*

A: Use the ADD op-code to add the contents of one array to another.

Q: *What are the main differences between a primary file and a full procedural file?*

A: A primary file is read automatically and sequentially from beginning to end. The order in which the records are read cannot be changed. Only one primary file is allowed per program.

Processing a full procedural file is controlled by op-codes in the C spec. Records may be read and processed in any order. There can be many files specified as full procedural.

Q: *What is structured programming?*

A: Structured programming is a way of coding a program which gives the program an organized structure and makes it easier to understand, maintain, and debug.

Q: *Explain some approaches to creating a structured RPG program.*

A: Place all sets of logic that will be repeated into separate subroutines which may be called when required. Use proper commenting and documentation to describe each function performed by the program. Avoid GOTO statements. Try to have only one read and one update statement per file format used by the program. Use RPG structured programming op-codes.

Q: *Name some RPG op-codes used in structured programming.*

A: DOUxx, DOWxx, IFxx, ANDxx, ORxx, ELSE, ENDxx, CASxx, ITER.

Q: *What is the difference between DOWEQ and DOUEQ RPG op-codes?*

A: DOUxx will execute at least one time, while a DOWxx may never execute because the comparison which determines whether or not to exit the loop takes place at the first statement of the loop.

Q: *What happens if you change a file format, re-create the file, and then run a preexisting program that uses the file?*

A: If Level Check *YES was specified for the file when it was created, the program will abend with a CPF message (CPF4131) that says there is a "File Format Level Check". Level Check *YES is the default used by the system for file creation. If Level Check *NO was specified for the file when it was created, the program may run; however, the program may produce incorrect results.

Q: *In RPG, which statement must have preceded an UPDATE operation, and what will happen if an UPDATE is performed without that prior statement?*

A: A READ or CHAIN operation must precede an UPDATE operation. If an update is done without a Read or Chain, the program will end with the error: "Update issued without prior read or chain".

Q: *What is a subfile?*

A: A subfile is a group of records of the same type that may be written to, modified, and read from a display file. Subfiles are coded in the DDS source file member that defines the display file. A subfile is considered a "relative record" file since it may not be accessed by a key but only by a relative record number.

Q: *How many formats are needed to code a single subfile?*

A: Two record formats are required in the display file DDS to code one subfile.

Q: *What are the names of the subfile format types and the correct order of their coding in DDS?*

A: The Subfile Record Format is coded first. The Subfile Control Record format is coded second. They must be together with no other record format between them.

Q: *What is the minimum number of DDS keywords necessary to code a subfile? Name them.*

A: A minimum of five keywords are necessary to define and display a subfile. They are: (1) The SFL keyword is used on the Subfile Record Format. (2) The SFLCTL keyword with the name of the Subfile Record Format is specified on the Subfile Control Record Format. (3) The SFLDSP keyword is necessary on the Subfile Control Record Format since it causes the subfile records to be displayed. (4) The SFLSIZ is necessary to define the total size of the subfile. (5) The SFLPAG is necessary to define how many subfile records are displayed at a time.

Q: *Explain what "OS/400 control of subfile rolling" means, and the advantages to using it.*

A: When the subfile is loaded with records and then displayed, OS/400 will control rolling through pages of subfile records. When the Roll UP/DOWN keys are pressed, control does not return to the program. Control is given to OS/400 which rolls and redisplays the subfile.

   The speed of rolling is fast when it is controlled by OS/400. This simplifies coding of the RPG programs that load and display subfiles, as well as DDS which defines them. If the beginning or the end of the subfile is reached, OS/400 will automatically display a message saying it is the beginning or end of the subfile.

Q: *Why would one take control over rolling subfile records?*

A: Taking control over a rolling subfile can reduce the time it takes to display a subfile when there are a large number of records in the subfile. By taking control of rolling, it is possible to load and display the subfile a few records at a time. By defining the roll keys in DDS, control is returned to the program when the roll key is pressed. The program can then add and display more records in the subfile or display existing subfile records as necessary.

Q: *Explain how and why SFLNXTCHG is used.*

A: SFLNXTCHG is specified with an indicator on a Subfile Record Format which is defined to allow modification of subfile records by the user. When a user changes subfile records, the RPG op-code READC is used to read all records that were modified in the subfile, which will allow the program to validate them and display any errors found to the user. When this validation is performed, a record in error is updated in the subfile with the SFLNXTCHG indicator turned on. Updating a subfile record with the SFLNXTCHG indicator set on will cause the record to be considered "modified" even though no further changes are made to the record. When the subfile is read again, even though the user did not change that record, the READC op-code will pick the record up again for validation, and redisplay the same error until corrected. This will prevent the user from ignoring any errors made when changing data in a subfile.

Q: *What is a message subfile?*

A: A message subfile is a special file that may contain multiple messages taken from the Program Message Queue and placed in the message subfile for display on the screen.

Q: *Name the essential DDS keywords used to code a message subfile, and describe their function.*

A: SFLMSGRCD—A record-level keyword used on the subfile record format. This keyword identifies the subfile as being a Message Subfile and allows entry of a line number that indicates on which line of the screen the subfile will begin display of its records.

SFLMSGKEY—Field-level keyword used on the subfile record format together with a predefined field name which contains a hidden, four-position character value used as a message reference key to locate and select messages from the Program Message Queue when loading the message subfile.

SFLPGMQ—Field-level keyword used either on the Subfile Record Format or on the Subfile Control Record Format. This keyword is specified together with a predefined field name which contains a hidden, 10-position character value that holds the name of the Program Message Queue used by the system to build the message subfile. When SFLPGMQ is specified on the Subfile Record Format, the messages are added to the subfile from the Program Queue one at a time.

When SFLPGMQ is specified on the Subfile Control Record Format with SFLINZ, the entire message subfile is loaded in a single output operation as it is "initialized" with messages from the program queue name placed in the field defined with the SFLPGMQ keyword.

Q: *When coding a display (or workstation) file, what is the difference between enabling a command key such as CMD-1 using CA01 or CF01?*

A: When the prefix CA is used in defining command key CA01, any data entered on the screen is *not* returned to the program when the command key is pressed. When the prefix CF is used in defining command key CF01, any data entered on the screen *is* returned to the program when the command key is pressed.

Q: *Which DDS keyword is used to generate a plus sign in a subfile, and what is the purpose of the plus sign?*

A: The SFLEND (Subfile End) is a record-level keyword used to generate a plus sign in the lower-right-hand corner of the screen when there are more subfile records to be displayed. If *MORE is specified with the SFLEND keyword, then the screen will display the word MORE . . . on the lower right while paging through the subfile, and BOTTOM when the end of the subfile is reached.

Q: *Why use the OVERLAY keyword?*

A: When you wish to display more than one record format on the screen at the same time, you may use the OVERLAY keyword. If this keyword is not used, all existing formats on the screen will be removed whenever something new is written to any part of the screen. When OVERLAY is used with a record format written to a screen that has other record formats already on display, the only record formats cleared from the screen are the ones that partially (or fully) reside on the same line numbers as the record format now being written; all other formats will remain on the screen.

Q: *How does CLRL work? Compare it to OVERLAY.*

A: Clear Line (CLRL) is a record-level keyword that is used to clear a specific number of lines from the screen before a format is displayed. The Clear Line keyword controls the number of lines cleared. If the SLNO (Starting Line Number) keyword is specified, then the first line number to be cleared is also controlled by Clear Line. Clear Line may cause two record formats to overlap without the first format being cleared entirely. Only those lines being cleared from the first format are deleted from the screen; all other lines from the first format remain. If CLRL(*NO) is specified in a record format written to the screen, no lines in other record formats already on the screen are cleared. This includes existing lines of formats that may overlap with lines from the new format now being written, although individual characters in an overlapped line may be overlayed by characters from the new format being written with CLRL(*NO). In contrast, the OVERLAY keyword does not control the number of lines that are cleared, and does not allow two record formats to overlap. When a record format with OVERLAY specified is being written and any single line of the record format touches any line of the first format already on display, the first format is entirely deleted before the second format is sent to display.

Q: *What is an Open Query file?*

A: Open Query file is a CL command (OPNQRYF) executed which provides a variety of execution time functions on physical or logical files such as Dynamic Record Selection, Dynamic Keyed Access Path, Dynamic Join, and Group Processing. Based upon the criteria specified on the Open Query file command, a temporary access path to the file specified by the OPNQRYF command is created and shared by other programs called after OPNQRYF is initiated.

Q: *Explain how (and when) a file in an RPG program that uses the access path created by an Open Query file should be overridden.*

A: The file used in the RPG program should be overridden to the file name used in the OPNQRYF statement in the CL program with SHARE *YES specified on the override statement. The override statement must come before the OPNQRYF statement in the CL program.

Q: *Why does a file specified in an RPG program that will use the access path created by an Open Query file need to be overridden?*

A: The override with SHARE *YES done in the CL program will provide the RPG file access to the temporary Open Data Path created by the OPNQRYF command. If the override is not done, then the file opened in the RPG program will not use the logical view created by the Open Query file, and the RPG program will read the records according to specifications in the DDS of the Logical file, ignoring the Open Data Path created by the Open Query file.

Q: *Why use a logical file rather than an Open Query?*

A: If the physical file you are working with is very large, creating and using a logical file will allow an application to perform faster than using an open query file. Since access paths created by open query files are temporary, applications that use an access path frequently will be more efficient using a logical file, since the access path will not have to be rebuilt every time the file is open.

Q: *How many files may be defined in a CL program, and what CL command is used for this?*

A: Only one file may be defined using the DCLF statement in a CL program.

Q: *Does the number of files that may be defined in a CL program cause a limit to the number of files that may be referenced by CL commands in the program?*

A: CL commands such as OPNQRYF and OVRDBF may be performed on more than one file in a CL program.

Q: *What single CL command must be used in a CL program to WRITE and READ a display file to a workstation?*

A: The CL command SNDRCVF may be used to write and read a display file record format to the workstation in a CL program.

Q: *Is it possible to set lower limits to a file in a CL program? How could this be done?*

A: There is more than one way to set lower limits in a CL program. One way is to use the POSDBF command with the parameter "File Position" set to *START. Another way is to use the OVRDBF command, which allows you to position the file by a key value, by a relative record number value, or set to *START (which positions to the beginning of the file).

Q: *How may one check for an error in a CL program to prevent the CL from abending should a command fail to execute properly?*

A: Use the CL command MONMSG with the MSGID parameter set to CPF9999. It may be specified at program level by being placed immediately after all declare statements. In that case, an error detected for any CL command in the program is caught and sent to the job log of the job where the CL program is running. A MONMSG command may be placed immediately following a CL command to monitor for a specific error condition. In that case, you need to specify the error id (or list of several error id numbers) of the error you wish to check for. Part of the MONMSG command is the ability to branch to an error routine in the CL program that can handle and possibly resolve the error, rather than merely recording the error to the job log.

Q: *How would you read a file sequentially from beginning to end in a CL program?*

A: In order to read a file from beginning to end sequentially, use the CL command RCVF followed by a GOTO statement (with the CMDLBL parameter specified in the GOTO to branch back), and execute the same command (RCVF) again until an end-of-file condition is detected by a MONMSG command, which will then branch out of the read loop. A command label must be specified prior to the RCVF statement so that the GOTO statement will branch correctly as the file is read again.

Example
```
PGM
DCLF FILE(FILEA)
READAGN:
RCVF
MONMSG MSGID(CPF0864) GOTO CMDLBL(END)
GOTO CMDLBL(READAGN)
END:
ENDPGM
```

Q: *Is it possible for a CL program submitted in batch to determine that it is, in fact, executing as part of a batch job? How would it "know"?*

A: Use the RTVJOBA command to determine whether the environment the CL program is running in is batch or interactive. Define a CL field name using the DCL statement as a single-position character. Specify that field name on the TYPE parameter in the RTVJOBA command. After the RTVJOBA command is executed by the program, check the value of the field. If the value is 0, then it is a batch job. If the value is 1, then it is an interactive job. (*Note:* A great deal of information concerning the executing job is available through the RTVJOBA command.)

Q: *Where in your CL program should you create a work file that you wish to be automatically deleted by the system when the job the CL is running in has concluded?*

A: Create the work file in QTEMP. When the job finishes, any contents of QTEMP are automatically deleted. The reason is that every job is created with a QTEMP library and, when the job concludes, the QTEMP library and all of its contents are deleted by the system.

Q: *If a single job takes up a large percentage of CPU, what can happen?*

A: Other users on the system will be adversely affected in the form of poor system response time and longer running time for batch programs.

Q: *What actions may be taken to prevent a single job from hogging the CPU? Give some examples.*

A: The actions taken to prevent this problem will depend upon what was found to be causing it. For example, if a program error caused a program to go into a continuous loop, the solution is to halt the program. If the problem is caused by an I/O-intensive program, it may be necessary to change the job using the CHGJOB command so that it will use fewer resources. If the problem is caused by an interactive QUERY, it may be possible to solve the problem by submitting the QUERY in batch (and provide a low priority if necessary).

Q: *What could happen if hard disk space usage approaches 100 percent?*

A: If disk space usage reaches a point where buffer and work areas needed for programs to run are not available, the system will terminate abnormally.

Q: *Name two fast ways to duplicate a file.*

A: 1. The CPYF CL command may be used to duplicate a file.

2. The CRTDUPOBJ CL command can be used to duplicate a file.

Both methods may be done interactively or by a submitted batch job.

Q: *Which CL command allows for selective record-copying from one file to another? Describe two or more ways it may be used to select records.*

A: The CPYF command may be used to selectively copy records from one file to another. There are several parameters in this command which allow selective copying:

FROMKEY/TOKEY (Copy from and to Record Key). These two parameters may be specified with key-field values which will cause records within the range of those specific key-field values to be copied.

INCCHAR (Include Records by Character Test). This parameter compares some part (or all) of a character field to a character string value entered on the command. The record will be included or excluded based upon the results of the comparison.

INCREL (Include Records by Field Test). This parameter allows entry of multiple field value tests using IF/AND/OR logic. The CPYF command will test to determine if a field satisfies the conditioning and will include or exclude based upon the results.

Q: *If you were testing a program interactively, and the Input Inhibited light stayed on longer than you thought it should, what action might you take to terminate the program?*

A: System Request, option 2. (Press the SHIFT key and the System Request key and enter the number 2 on the resulting line.)

Q: *If you have a file with a thousand fields and you are writing an RPG program that will update only one or two fields in the file, what is the most efficient manner to code the update and what pitfall is avoided by this method?*

A: When you are updating only one or two fields from a large file, it is most efficient to execute an output operation to the O spec where the file name and the field names to be updated are specified. This method causes RPG to change the contents of only the field names specified on the O spec. An update to two fields takes up far less system resources than an update to a thousand fields.

The possible pitfall avoided with this technique is the incorrect update of fields you never wished to change. A regular RPG UPDATE op-code changes all fields in the record regardless of whether the programmer intended them to be changed. The output operation to the O spec effects a change only to the fields explicitly specified for update on the O spec. All other fields remain as they were before the update, no matter how they were altered by the program.

Q: *If you have a 10,000-page report and you wish to print only the last 10 pages, how can you get the system to print what you want without printing the first 9,990 pages?*

A: Use the CL command CHGSPLFA (Change Spooled File Attribute) to cause a spooled file to begin printing from whatever page you specify on the command. The parameter PAGERANGE allows you to control the number of pages to be printed from the initial page specified.

Q: *There are some cases where you wish to call an RPG program without having to pass parameters, and other cases where you wish to pass parameters to the very same program when you call it. What is the difficulty with this, and how would you resolve it?*

A: If a program is coded to expect parameters, it will abend if it is called without parameters passed. If a program does not expect parameters, it will abend if parameters are passed.

If a program expects parameters to be passed and you do not wish to pass parameters, one solution is to pass the parameters with blanks and zeros, as with an initialization.

If a program expects parameters to be passed but you specifically do not wish to pass parameters in a given situation, you may specify the Program Status Data Structure which is defined on the I spec using SDS (Program Status Data Structure) with the *PARMS keyword and a field name to contain the data. The field name specified together with the *PARMS keyword will contain the number of parameters passed to the program (a three-digit, numeric amount). The code that specifies the parameter list *ENTRY PLIST on the C spec must be conditioned not to execute when the number of parameters passed to the program is zero.

Q: *The report function you are creating will require a large number of different ways to select and sort the information from a specific file. How could one CL program eliminate the need to create many logical files for this function?*

A: A CL program may be coded to receive the selection criteria specified by the user and place that criteria into a CL field which may be used with the Query Select (QRYSLT) parameter on the OPNQRYF statement. The sort sequence requested by the user may also be loaded into a CL field which will be used on the Key Field (KEYFLD) parameter of the Query Select statement. In this manner, any number of sort and select criteria may be included in the report function without having to create a separate logical for each criteria required.

Q: *The file your CL program must access may not exist on the library list of the batch job in which your CL program is running. How would you code the CL to ensure the program will find the file?*

A: Find the library the file is in, using the DSPOBJD command with *ALL specified on the LIBRARY parameter, and an OUTFILE name specified that will contain all the file information generated by this command, including the library where it is located. If more than one record is generated in the OUTFILE, the file exists in more than one library. In that case, you may wish to send an error and notify the person who called the program that there is a problem the program cannot resolve. If a list exists of legitimate libraries where the file may be found, then you may check the library names in the OUTPUT file against this list. When a library name is found that can be used, then that name will be loaded into a CL field name that will be used on the LIBRARY parameter of any CL commands in the program that use the file.

Q: *After a large report was generated and saved on the OUTQ, the files upon which the report was based were changed in the normal course of business. However, the client has decided to extract certain information contained in that report and create a second report based upon this extracted information. How could a program be written to extract data from the first report without using production files?*

A: Find the position on the report where the required information is located. Be certain the highest possible position location has been determined. Create a nonkeyed physical file with one field defined as character. Use the high-end position of the data needed from the report as the field length. Use the CPYSPLF (Copy Spooled File) command to copy the spooled file to the database file you have created. Every record in the file will now contain a single line of the report. Write an RPG program that uses a Data Structure to break the single field in the file into the actual fields to be used for generating the report data. It may be necessary for the RPG to convert character values in the data structure to numeric amounts.

Q: *In a CL program, the date field is divided into four separate parts, each part being an individual two-position numeric field. Without having seen the program, how do you believe the date is broken up? How would you put it together in a single date field using CL statements?*

A: The dates are broken up into century, year, month, and day. It is necessary to convert each of these two-position numeric fields into two-position character fields before they are combined into a single date field. The reason is that the CL commands used to combine fields will work only with character fields. Use the CHGVAR command to move these numeric fields into character fields. The CHGVAR command with the substring parameter (%SST) may be used to combine these fields into a single program variable. The following examples show how to accomplish a date conversion.

The following example will move the numeric date into a character field. The field name &CHARACTER will now hold the same numbers that were in &NUMERIC, but the numbers will be character values.

Example 1

```
CHGVAR VAR(&CHARACTER) VALUE(&NUMERIC)
```

Example 2 shows how CHGVAR is used with the substring function to make the date into a single field. All field names used here are defined as character. The numbers specified with the substring parameter show the starting position of the change, and how many positions will be changed.

Example 2

```
CHGVAR VAR(%SST(&FULLDATE 1 2)) VALUE(&CENTURY)
CHGVAR VAR(%SST(&FULLDATE 3 2)) VALUE(&YEAR)
CHGVAR VAR(%SST(&FULLDATE 5 2)) VALUE(&MONTH)
CHGVAR VAR(%SST(&FULLDATE 7 2)) VALUE(&DAY)
```

It is also possible to combine these four character fields using a single CHGVAR command with the *CAT (Concatenate) function.

Example 3

```
CHGVAR VAR(&FULLDATE) VALUE(&CENTURY *CAT &YEAR +
*CAT &MONTH *CAT &DAY)
```

Q: *Your interactive program has gone into a continuous loop. How would you pinpoint the problem?*

A: There are a number of actions you may take to determine the cause. While the program is looping, you may immediately use System Request 3 with Option 11 in an attempt to find out which statements are being repeated. This option shows the name of the active program, along with the statement currently being executed.

If you know the program will loop before you call it, you may use the debug facility to pinpoint the statements in error. Use the CL command STRDBG to activate the debug function for the program name that is looping. After you have entered debug mode, you may specify which program statements are to be traced and recorded by debug using ADDTRC *ALL, which will trace and record all statements executed as the program is running. Since there is a limit to the number of statements that may be traced, the program will stop executing, no matter what statement is active, when that limit has been reached. At that point, it is possible to press Command 10 to access a command entry screen. On the command entry screen, you can display the trace data to the screen or to a list which may be printed out. Use the CL command DSPTRCDTA to display the trace data. While viewing the trace information, any statement or set of statements that execute repeatedly are probably the cause of the problem. If no statements are found that are incorrectly repeated, then you may do a CLRTRCDTA, which will clear the trace data and allow for the program to continue tracing. If you know the most likely routine to be causing the problem, then you may specify the beginning and ending statements of the routine to be traced on the ADDTRC command, which will cause the program to trace starting from and ending with those specific statements. It is possible to specify program variable names to be included in the trace information. Knowing field values at the time the loop occurred will help you to analyze why the loop happened and how to fix it.

Q: *Is it possible to view the contents of a field through debug before source statements coded by the programmer begin execution? How could this be useful?*

A: It is possible to use the command ADDBKP (Add Breakpoint) to view contents of a program variable when the program is running in debug mode. Immediately before the program executes the statement number specified on the ADDBKP command, the program stops execution and displays the contents of the program field name that was entered with the ADDBKP command. When an RPG program begins execution, there are certain compiler-generated statements which are first executed that are part of the object code and were not actually coded by the programmer. In the following example, the value in the amount field will be displayed by debug when the program is called and before source code statements are executed. If the field AMOUNT is being passed from another program to this program, then using a breakpoint at '.ENTRY' will ensure that we are looking at the value in AMOUNT before it was changed by this program. If the value in AMOUNT is wrong, this technique can help us find which program is at fault.

Example
```
ADDBKP STMT('.ENTRY') PGMVAR(AMOUNT)
```

Q: *You are tracing a program in debug. You get a message that says, "Maximum number of traced statements reached." You decide that you want the program to continue tracing, and you do not wish to exit the program. What would you do?*

A: First press the error reset key to remove the error. Then access a command entry screen from the Debug Display Breakpoint screen you are currently on by pressing Command 10. Then enter the CL command, CHGDBG, with the number of statements you wish to trace specified on the MAXTRC parameter. For example, if the current maximum number of traced statements is 200 and you wish to increase that number to 1000, enter the following command: CHGDBG MAXTRC(1000). Exit the command entry screen using Command 3 (or Command 12) and debug will automatically continue tracing from the point where it previously stopped.

References

1. *RPG/400 Reference Manual* (SC09-1349-01).
2. *RPG/400 User's Guide* (SC09-1348-01).
3. *AS/400 CL Programmers Guide* (SC21-8077-2).
4. *AS/400 DDS Reference Manual* (SX21-9926-0).
5. *AS/400 Database Guide* (SC21-9659-2).

8
OS/2 Release 2.1

Robert Pesner

Introduction

The following topics will be covered in this chapter:

1. Using OS/2 2.1
   a. OS/2 2.1 features
   b. Installing OS/2 2.1
   c. System configuration
   d. Using the WorkPlace Shell
   e. Running DOS and Windows programs
2. Programming OS/2 2.1
   a. OS/2 Kernel Programming
   b. OS/2 Presentation Manager Programming
   c. OS/2 System Object Model Programming

Overview of OS/2 2.1

OS/2 2.1 is the current release of IBM's single-user, multitasking operating system for microcomputers based on chips compatible with the Intel 80386 and above. It is one of the family of IBM operating systems that support IBM's System Application Architecture (SAA). It was designed to address three major problems users face with DOS:

1. Memory constraints imposed by the 1-megabyte addressability limit of the 8086/8088 chips for which DOS was written.

2. Flexibility constraints imposed by DOS's single-tasking design

3. Lack of standardization among the user interfaces of the many applications available for DOS systems

102

It meets these design goals by:

1. Supporting up to 4 gigabytes of physical memory and providing 512 megabytes of virtual memory to applications in a 32-bit flat address space

2. Supporting multiple concurrent OS/2, DOS, and Windows applications using a preemptive, multithreaded, multitasking manager

3. Providing operating system support for a standardized, object-oriented, windows-based, mouse-oriented graphical user interface called the WorkPlace Shell, based on the most current SAA Common User Access (CUA) specifications (CUA 1991).

In the WorkPlace Shell, the screen functions as a desktop on which the user arranges icons. These icons represent objects, unlike OS/2 1.x or Windows, where icons represent minimized running applications. There are several types of objects, including program objects, printer objects, disk drive objects, data file objects, and folders, which can contain other objects, including other folders. Objects can be acted on directly, by double-clicking or dragging them with the mouse, or through a pop-up menu listing the available actions, which is accessed by clicking on the object with the right mouse button.

OS/2 provides a complete set of services to application programs, accessed by a standard subroutine call interface. These services include:

1. I/O services, including disk files and devices such as screen, keyboard, mouse, COM and LPT ports, CD-ROM, etc. Disk files can be shared by multiple applications; multiwrite access can be managed using locking services.

2. Dynamic memory management, including allocation of memory to be shared between multiple applications.

3. Event notification and resource access serialization using semaphores.

4. Interprocess communication, including queues, anonymous pipes, and local and remote-named pipes. Pipes use a programming syntax identical to the file I/O syntax except for pipe creation. Remote-named pipes allow applications to exchange data across LANs and require the support of a network operating system.

5. Process management, including starting sessions, processes and threads, and controlling execution priority. The ability of applications to spin off subroutines (threads) that execute concurrently with the application main routine is one of the most powerful features of OS/2.

6. Window management, including creating windows, displaying text and graphical output, processing mouse and keyboard events, and exchanging information with other applications.

7. System Object Model services, which provide object-oriented programming enhancements to standard procedural programming languages such as C.

OS/2 applications that manage windows are structured as message-processing programs. All input from the keyboard, mouse, and the desktop environment are placed on a queue created by the application as part of its initialization. The main routine of the application usually creates the main application window and then enters a loop in which messages are read off the queue and passed to a subroutine for processing. The subroutine, known as a *window procedure,* is usually structured as a C-type switch block with cases for the messages the program wants to respond to. Other messages are passed back to the environment for default processing.

OS/2 provides a set of predefined window types and associated window procedures. These window types are the control window classes. They can be used in applications to include entry fields, various kinds of buttons, scroll bars, list boxes, etc., in the user interface without having to code the logic to control them. User-defined window types and associated window procedures must be registered as part of application initialization. User-defined window classes can be public, so that other applications can use them as if they were OS/2-provided control window classes.

The System Object Model provides a syntax for creating object-oriented programming objects in procedural languages. A preprocessor converts the OOP statements into native language statements for compilation. It also generates include files for use both in implementing the objects and in writing applications that use the objects. The WorkPlace Shell is written using SOM, which also allows OS/2 application developers to access the objects in the WorkPlace Shell in their own applications. WorkPlace Shell objects can be parent objects of application-defined objects, which thus can inherit complex behavior that follows the CUA 1991 standard.

IBM provides a set of three tools for developing OS/2 2.1 programs:

1. C Set ++—a 32-bit ANSI-compatible C++ compiler.

2. Developer's Toolkit—C and Assembler include files, link libraries, development tools, and sample programs.

3. WorkFrame/2—an integrated development environment.

Other vendors that sell C or C++ compilers that can create OS/2 applications include Borland, Zortech, Watcon, and Metaview.

OS/2 2.1 is the base operating system for a family of IBM products that provide communications, database, and networking facilities. The other products in this family include:

1. OS/2 Network Transport Services/2 1.0—a collection of OS/2 LAN adapter device drivers supporting Token Ring, Ethernet, and PC Network LANs. NTS/2 is based on the Microsoft/3-COM Network Device Interface Specification (NDIS) standard. NDIS facilitates the integration of LAN adapters from multiple vendors and the sharing of LAN adapters by various protocols.

2. Communications Manager/2 1.0—provides connectivity between OS/2 and SNA networks, LANs, X.25 networks, and time-sharing services accessed through modems. It provides 3270, 5250, and asynchronous start-stop terminal emulation and file transfer. It includes a number of application programming interfaces that can be used to develop distributed processing applications.

3. DB2/2 1.0—a 32-bit relational database engine based on the SQL database standard with a prompted query user interface (Query Manager). It also has support for transparent access of remote data in network-connected Database Manager, DB/2, and SQL/DS databases. (Mainframe access requires an additional product: SAA Distributed Database Connection Services/2.)

4. OS/2 LAN Server 3.0—a network operating system providing file, printer, and serial device sharing to OS/2, DOS, Windows, and Macintosh clients. It includes NTS/2, User Profile Management (a security subsystem), and the LAN Support Program, a collection of LAN adapter device drivers for DOS.

5. TCP/IP for OS/2 1.2.1—an implementation of TCP/IP for OS/2, providing the standard set of TCP/IP applications. NFS server and X Windows server are add-on products to the base TCP/IP. It includes NTS/2 (see above).

6. System Performance Monitor/2 2.0—collects, displays, and reports on performance, tuning, and capacity planning information, including a facility to collect data from servers to a central LAN-connected performance repository.

Terminology

Boot Manager: A facility of OS/2 that allows different operating systems, such as OS/2 2.x, OS/2 1.x, and DOS to be installed in different partitions of a hard disk. The operating system to use is chosen from a menu that appears at boot time.

Clipboard: A facility of OS/2 that allows Presentation Manager and/or Windows applications to pass data to each other. Data may be text, graphics, or in an application-dependent format. Applications must be coded to support clipboard data exchange. Clipboard data exchanges occur upon user request and under direct user control.

Command prompt: A window or full-screen session that displays a DOS-like prompt, allowing the user to issue commands. OS/2 2.1 supports multiple simultaneous OS/2 and DOS windowed or full-screen prompts.

Container: A WorkPlace Shell object that contains other objects. It can display its contents as icons, in tree format, or in table format. The most common kind of container is the folder.

Device driver: A program installed in CONFIG.SYS that supports specific hardware (disk drives, printers, CD-ROM drives, etc.). Device drivers are installed with the BASEDEV and DEVICE statements.

Direct manipulation: A basic technique in the WorkPlace Shell user interface. It usually involves either double-clicking on an object to open a view or dragging an object and dropping it on another object, which then processes the dropped object.

Dynamic data exchange (DDE): A programming facility that allows Presentation Manager and/or Windows applications to exchange data. Data may be text, graphics, or in an application-dependent format. Applications must be coded to support DDE. DDE exchanges usually occur upon user request, although applications can invoke them automatically. The exchange itself occurs under application control.

Dynamic Link Library (DLL): A library of subroutines that is not incorporated into an application .EXE file at link time. Instead, a pointer is maintained to the DLL. This allows multiple applications to share one copy of the subroutines at execution time. When the application is loaded, OS/2 checks if the DLL is already loaded (due to a previous application requirement), and loads the DLL only if it is not already resident. If it is, the application's call addresses are simply fixed to point to the already-resident subroutines.

Extended attribute: The DOS file system provides four file attributes: Archive, Read-only, Hidden, and System. These are bit flags that can be either on or off. Extended attributes are an extension to this idea that allows files to have any number of attributes whose values are not limited to on or off. Extended attributes consist of a name of up to 255 characters and a value which may be virtually unlimited in length. Extended attributes on FAT disks are stored in the file 'EA DATA. SF'. Extended attributes on HPFS disks are stored as part of the file object.

File Allocation Table (FAT) file system: A method of storing files on disk partitions. The OS/2 FAT file system is compatible with but not identical to the DOS FAT file system. Disks created by either operating system can be processed by the other. The OS/2 FAT system supports extended attributes, optional disk caching for reads and writes, and optional disk error checking at boot time.

Folder: A container object that forms the basis of the WorkPlace Shell desktop organization. Folders can contain objects, including other folders, leading to a hierarchical folder structure on the desktop analogous to (and supported by) the hierarchical structure of directories and subdirectories on disks.

Hide button: A possible appearance of the "minimize" button in which the small box is made of dotted lines. This implies that when the window is "hidden," no icon indicating that it is active will appear on the desktop.

High-Performance File System (HPFS): A method of storing files on disk partitions. The OS/2 HPFS is incompatible with DOS. It supports very large partitions on very large disks, reduced file fragmentation, reduced seek time, extended attributes, optional disk caching for reads and writes, and optional disk error checking at boot time.

Message: In Presentation Manager programming, a data structure passed as a parameter to a "window procedure" to indicate that some event has occurred which requires application processing.

Minimized window viewer: An application providing a window that can be used to collect icons representing minimized applications.

Multitasking: A facility of OS/2 that allows multiple applications to share the computer's CPU and each application to execute multiple code functions "simultaneously" through CPU time-slicing.

Notebook: A window that appears like a notebook, with multiple pages and tabs separating the pages into sections. It is used most frequently to configure settings for WorkPlace Shell objects. From a Presentation Manager programming point of view, a notebook is a control window; each page is usually created as a modeless dialog box.

Object: The basic entity in the object-oriented WorkPlace Shell user interface. All objects have certain properties in common: they appear as icons somewhere in the desktop folder hierarchy; they can be looked at through views; they can be acted upon through their pop-up menu (click once with the right mouse button); they can be configured using their settings notebook; and they can be directly manipulated.

Page: A 4-kilobyte block of memory that functions as the allocation unit for all memory management. Pages are also swapped in and out of real memory from backing storage on disk to allow for memory overcommitment where total application memory needs are greater than real storage.

Pipe: A programming facility that allows OS/2 and DOS applications to exchange data. Data is passed as messages between a pipe creator (server) and a pipe user (client). Pipe partners can be running on the same machine or can be communicating across a Local Area Network (remote pipes). Except for the server actions to create the pipe and wait for a client to contact it, the data exchange can be carried out using normal programming language file read and write commands. Pipes can be either named or anonymous. Remote pipes are always named.

Process: A collection of computer resources assigned as a unit, including memory blocks, open files and devices, interprocess communications resources, system semaphores, a current disk, a current directory on each disk, and a set of environment variables. There may be more than one application active in a process and each may have more than one thread.

Queue: A programming facility that allows OS/2 applications to exchange data. Data is passed in shared memory blocks. Programming calls specific to queues are used to pass handles to the shared blocks.

Semaphore: A programming facility used for either event signaling or resource access serialization (MUTual EXclusion) between multiple applications. Applications can indicate events by posting an event semaphore, and wait for an event by waiting on an event semaphore. Applications can wait for access to a resource by requesting a mutex semaphore; when they are done using the resource, they indicate this by releasing the mutex semaphore.

Session: A virtual computer in which one or more processes execute. The session includes a virtual screen, keyboard, and mouse, which all processes in the session share.

Shadow: A copy of a WorkPlace Shell object that remains linked to its original. If a change is made to the original (for example, in its settings notebook), the change affects the shadow as well.

Shared memory: A programming facility that allows OS/2 applications to access a common memory block. Usually, OS/2 imposes a strict separation between the memory blocks allocated to applications to prevent bugs in one application from affecting others. Shared memory blocks must be managed by the sharing applications to prevent problems.

Spooling: A facility that allows multiple applications to share printers without getting interspersed output. Each application's output is held on disk in a spool file until the printer is available.

Thread: The actual executing code in an application. OS/2 applications can have more than one thread. All the threads in an application share memory blocks, open devices, and all other process resources except registers and a stack. Each thread has its own register set and its own stack.

Title bar icon: The icon at the upper-left corner of windows that can be used to access the window's object menu. This replaces the System Menu icon in OS/2 1.x and Windows.

Virtual device driver: A device driver designed for a virtual DOS machine that intercepts applications accesses to devices and passes these on to the real device driver.

Virtual DOS machine: A facility of the 80386 chip (and higher) that allows it to emulate an 8086 chip in protected mode. OS/2 2.1 uses this facility to support multiple DOS and Windows applications.

WIN-OS/2: The component of OS/2 that supports Windows applications. OS/2 2.0 supports Windows 2.1 and 3.0 applications in real or standard mode. OS/2 2.1 supports Windows 3.0 and 3.1 applications in standard or enhanced mode.

Window: A rectangle in which an application displays its output. Windows normally have title bars used to move the window, borders used to change its size, minimize (or hide) and maximize buttons, and a title bar icon used for accessing the window's object menu.

Window list: A WorkPlace Shell window that lists the active applications. It appears as a result of hitting Ctl-Esc on the keyboard or by clicking with both mouse buttons simultaneously at an empty spot on the desktop.

Window procedure: A subroutine in a GUI application that handles messages that indicate when events of importance to the applications window have occurred. Window procedures are usually coded as a switch structure on the message type.

Questions and Answers

Q: *What are three important problems with DOS that led to the development of OS/2?*

A: 1. DOS was written for the 8086/8088 chip, which can address only one megabyte of memory. The various mechanisms that allow DOS applications to address more memory require specific coding techniques. OS/2 2.1 can make 512 megabytes of memory available to applications in a flat address space.

2. DOS was written as a single-user, single-tasking operating system, on the assumption that the user would use one application at a time. The various mechanisms for allowing multiple applications to run simultaneously under DOS are essentially kludges. OS/2 2.1 provides a single-user, multitasking environment with a high degree of protection against application bugs affecting other running applications.

3. DOS applications use various user interfaces. OS/2 2.1 provides a consistent look and feel that application developers can adopt to make it easier for users to learn new applications.

Q: *What are the major new features of OS/2 2.x compared to OS/2 1.x?*

A: 1. Use of the 80386 chip's 32-bit flat addressing model

2. Support for running multiple OS/2, DOS, and Windows applications simultaneously

3. The new WorkPlace Shell user interface

Q. *What are the major subsystems of OS/2 2.1?*

A: 1. File and I/O subsystem

2. Memory manager

3. Multitasking manager

4. Presentation manager

Q: *What are the other major members, current releases, and basic functions of IBM's OS/2 product family?*

A: 1. Network Transport Services/2 1.0—OS/2 device drivers for LAN adapters

2. Communications Manager/2 1.0—communications

3. DB2/2 1.0—database management

4. OS/2 LAN Server 3.0—network operating system

5. TCP/IP for OS/2 1.2.1—TCP/IP

6. System Performance Manager/2 2.0—performance and tuning

Q: *What are the major advantages of OS/2 2.1 over DOS for running DOS programs?*

A: 1. The ability to run multiple DOS programs concurrently.

2. If a DOS application has a bug that would cause DOS to hang or crash, only that application will be affected; other applications would be unaffected.

3. The ability to provide more conventional memory for DOS applications than DOS can, and the ability to provide more virtual memory above 1 megabyte than is actually present on the machine.

4. The ability to run different versions and releases of DOS without rebooting.

5. Access to more sophisticated and higher-performing file systems such as OS/2's FAT and HPFS file systems.

Q: *What are the major advantages of OS/2 2.1 over Windows for running Windows programs?*

A: 1. Preemptive multitasking instead of Window's cooperative multitasking

2. The ability to run Windows applications in separate Windows sessions so that an application bug that would hang or crash Windows (and therefore all running Windows applications) would affect only that application

3. The ability to provide more virtual memory above 1 megabyte than is actually present on the machine

4. Access to more sophisticated and higher-performing file systems such as OS/2's FAT and HPFS file systems

Q: *What are extended attributes?*

A: Extended attributes (EAs) are file attributes beyond the traditional DOS file attributes of read-only, archive, hidden, and system. Extended attributes consist of an arbitrary name up to 255 characters and arbitrary data associated with the EA name.

Q: *Where are extended attributes stored?*

A: On FAT-formatted disks, EAs are stored in a hidden system, read-only file called 'EA DATA. SF' in the root directory of the drive containing the associated file. On HPFS-formatted disks, EAs are stored as part of the file object.

Q: *What are the documented minimum requirements for OS/2 2.1?*

A: 1. 80386SX-based PS/2 or AT-compatible computer

2. 4 megabytes of system memory

3. 18 megabytes of hard disk space

4. CGA display adapter

Q: *What is the recommended minimum for an OS/2 user workstation?*
A: 1. Fast 80386-based PS/2 or AT-compatible computer

2. 6 megabytes of system memory

3. 35 megabytes of hard disk space

4. VGA display adapter

5. Mouse

Q: *What are the possible delivery media for installing OS/2 2.1?*
A: 1. Diskettes

2. CD-ROM

3. Network server

Q: *What are the main system configuration files and their functions?*

A:

CONFIG.SYS	Specifies device drivers, tuning parameters, user shells, and environment variables
STARTUP.CMD	Commands executed at system boot time
AUTOEXEC.BAT	Commands executed at creation of DOS sessions
OS2.INI	Desktop configuration and application initialization information
OS2SYS.INI	Printer and font configuration, COM and LPT port configuration, and default screen configuration

Q: *What are the tuning parameters (and their functions) for the multitasking manager?*

A:

TIMESLICE	Maximum time applications can run before being interrupted
PRIORITY	Whether lower-priority applications get a dynamic boost if locked out of the CPU by higher-priority applications
MAXWAIT	How long lower-priority applications can be locked out of the CPU before getting a temporary priority boost
THREADS	Maximum number of tasks in the system

Q: *What are the tuning parameters (and their functions) for the memory manager?*

A:

MEMMAN	Enables or disables system swapping
SWAPPATH	Specifies location of the system swap file

Q: *What are the tuning parameters for the I/O subsystem, and what are their functions?*

A:

BUFFERS	Number of 512-byte buffers for file I/O operations
DISKCACHE	Caching functions for FAT disks
CACHE	Caching functions for HPFS disks

Q: *Which file systems come with OS/2 and what are the main differences between them?*

A: OS/2 comes with the File Allocation Table (FAT) system and the High-Performance File System (HPFS). FAT is compatible with the DOS FAT file system with the addition of supporting extended attributes. HPFS supports long filenames (up to 255 characters), large partitions (up to 2 gigabytes), large disks (up to 512 gigabytes), contiguous file allocation, and strategic directory placement.

Q: *What is an installable file system?*

A: OS/2 supports file systems supplied separately from the operating system. Installable file systems are installed similarly to device drivers, using an IFS=statement in CONFIG.SYS. Each IFS identifies file system devices such as disks that it owns, usually at format time. When an application uses an OS/2 system call to access a device managed by an IFS, OS/2 automatically passes the request to the IFS.

Q: *What IFSs come with OS/2? What are some other products that use IFSs?*

A: The High-Performance File System (HPFS) is an IFS that comes with OS/2, as does an IFS for CD-ROM data disks. LAN Server uses an IFS to remap local device identifiers to network server directories. TCP/IP Network File Sharing uses an IFS to remap local device identifiers to NFS server directories.

Q: *What is the difference between screen icons in OS/2 2.1 and screen icons in OS/2 1.x or Windows?*

A: Icons in OS/2 1.x or Windows represent minimized application windows; in OS/2 2.1 they represent objects that can be acted on.

Q: *What is the general method for acting on WorkPlace Shell objects?*

A: Point at the object with the mouse, click with the right mouse button, and choose the action from the resulting pop-up menu.

Q: *What happens when you double-click on a WorkPlace Shell object?*

A: You get a view of the object in a window. The information in the view will depend on the kind of object and the default view.

Q: *What are the major categories of objects in the WorkPlace Shell?*

A: 1. Program objects

2. Data objects

3. Printer objects

4. Folder objects

5. Drives objects

6. Shredder objects

Q: *How are WorkPlace Shell objects configured?*

A: Each object has a settings notebook that is accessed from the "Open" submenu of the object's pop-up menu.

Q: *What is the difference between a copy of an object and a shadow of an object?*

A: When a change is made to a copy of an object, the original is unchanged. When a change is made to a shadow, the original is also changed.

Q: *How do you make a drag operation a copy? a move? How do you create a shadow?*

A: Hold the control key down while dragging to get a copy; don't hold down any key to get a move. Create a shadow by dragging with both the shift and control keys down, or use the pop-up menu of the original object.

Q: *What kinds of DOS programs do not run under OS/2 2.1?*

A: 1. Timing sensitive applications

   2. Applications that require more than 1000 interrupts per second

   3. Debuggers that attempt to access 80386 hardware

   4. Applications that write to hard disks by physical sector

   5. Applications that access memory above 1 megabyte using the VCPI standard or using nonstandard techniques

   6. Block device drivers

Q: *What kinds of Windows programs do not run under (1) OS/2 2.0 and (2) OS/2 2.1?*

A: 1. OS/2 2.0: Applications that require Windows Enhanced mode

   2. OS/2 2.1: Applications that require the WINMEM32.DLL; applications that require Windows Real mode

Q: *How are DOS applications configured?*

A: Use the DOS Settings dialog box from the Sessions page of the DOS application's Settings notebook.

Q: *What are the main DOS settings that will increase the amount of conventional memory available in a DOS session?*

A: 1. DOS_HIGH loads DOS above 640K.

   2. VIDEO_MODE_RESTRICTION reclaims video buffers.

Q: *Where can DOS mode device drivers be specified and what is the effect of each choice?*

A: 1. In the OS/2 CONFIG.SYS. In this case, the device driver will be available to all DOS and Windows sessions.

   2. In the DOS settings for an icon representing a DOS command prompt, a Windows Full Screen session, or a DOS or Windows application. In this case, the device driver will be available only to programs started using the icon.

Q: *What kinds of memory above 1 megabyte can DOS and Windows applications access, and how much of each kind is available? What is the default amount of each kind assigned to a DOS session?*

A: 1. LIM EMS has 32 megabytes maximum, 2 megabytes default.

   2. LIMA XMS has 16 megabytes maximum, 2 megabytes default.

   3. DPMI has 512 megabytes maximum, 4 megabytes default.

Q: *If a DOS application fails to operate under OS/2 2.1 because it looks for a facility or version number associated with PC-DOS or MS-DOS, what steps can you take?*

A: 1. Use the DOS_VERSION setting to specify the specific version function required.

   2. Use the VM Boot facility to boot an actual DOS.

Q: *What actual versions of DOS can run in an OS/2 virtual DOS machine?*

A: All flavors of DOS, including PC-DOS and MS-DOS starting with version 1.0, and vendor-specific versions of DOS, such as Compaq DOS, and DR-DOS.

Q: *How can you use a DOS block device driver under OS/2 2.1?*

A: Create a DOS session running actual DOS and include the block device driver in the CONFIG.SYS used to boot that session.

Q: *What are the tools required to build an OS/2 2.1 application in C?*

A: 1. Include files for the OS/2 system calls

   2. A compiler that can generate 80386 32-bit code

   3. OS/2 system link libraries

   4. A 32-bit linker

Q: *What conventions are used to make OS/2 system calls? What is the C Set ++ name for these conventions?*

A: 1. All parameters must be passed on the stack.

   2. Parameters are pushed right-to-left.

   3. Parameters are double-word aligned on the stack.

   4. The caller clears the stack.

   5. Any returned value is passed back in the EAX register.

   These are known as the "system" linkage.

Q: *What is the naming convention for OS/2 system calls?*

A: All OS/2 system calls begin with a three-character prefix that identifies the category of call:

Dos	OS/2 kernel functions
Win	Window functions
Gpi	Graphics programming interface functions
Spl	Spooler functions
Prf	Query or write user initialization file functions
Drg	Direct manipulation functions
Dev	Device query or access functions

Q: *When would you use an OS/2 system call in place of a similar language facility (i.e., DosOpen instead of a C fopen)?*

A: When the OS/2 system call provides additional functionality (i.e., the ability to open a file in various share modes).

Q: *What kinds of devices can be opened using DosOpen?*
A: Files, named pipes, and named devices such as COM and LPT ports.

Q: *What are the major options available when opening files?*
A: Access   Read, write, or read-write
   Share mode   Deny read-write, deny write, deny read, or deny none
   Caching   Prevent caching, prevent write caching

Q: *What kinds of caching are supported by the OS/2 file systems?*
A: Both the FAT and HPFS systems support both read caching and write caching ("lazywriting").

Q: *What is the unit of allocation used by the OS/2 memory manager?*
A: All memory allocation requested using OS/2 system calls is done in units of 4K.

Q: *What kinds of shared memory can applications request?*
A: Named shared memory is allocated with a name beginning with \SHAREMEM\ and can be accessed by any other application that knows the name. Unnamed shared memory is allocated without a name. Access to unnamed shared memory is controlled by the shared memory allocator.

Q: *What is the name of the file OS/2 uses to hold memory blocks that have been swapped out of memory? Where is it located?*
A: It's called SWAPPER.DAT; its location is determined by the SWAPPATH parameter in CONFIG.SYS.

Q: *What is a dynamic link library?*
A: A library of subroutines that is not incorporated into an application .EXE file at link time. Instead, a pointer is maintained to the DLL. This allows multiple applications to share one copy of the subroutines at execution time. When the application is loaded, OS/2 checks if the DLL is already loaded (due to a previous application requirement), and loads the DLL only if it is not already resident. If it is, the application's call addresses are simply fixed to point to the already-resident subroutines.

Q: *What kinds of semaphores does OS/2 support?*
A: 1. Event notification semaphores, which are used to allow a routine to wait for or check on an event that another routine manages

   2. Mutual exclusion (mutex) semaphores, which are used to ensure that only one routine has access to a resource at a time

Q: *What kinds of interprocess communication are available to non-PM OS/2 applications?*
A: 1. Anonymous pipes

   2. Named pipes

   3. Queues

   4. Shared memory

   5. Dynamic link libraries

Q: *What kinds of named pipes are there?*

A: 1. Local named pipes, usable only between applications running on the same machine

2. Remote named pipes, usable between applications running on different LAN-connected machines

Q: *How can a DLL be used for interprocess communication?*

A: The DLL can contain a data segment that is shared by all applications that use the DLL.

Q: *Which interprocess communication functions can be used by DOS applications?*

A: DOS applications running on LAN-connected machines can be clients on remote named pipes running on OS/2 servers. DOS applications running under OS/2 can be clients on named pipes supported by OS/2 applications running on the local machine or on LAN-connected machines.

Q: *What are the advantages of a multithreaded design?*

A: 1. Applications can conveniently manage multiple input sources without polling.

2. Applications can divide their work into different priorities.

3. In PM programs, applications can schedule long-running tasks, such as complex printing, while maintaining the responsiveness of the system.

Q: *How are priorities managed in OS/2?*

A: OS/2 supports 128 priorities divided into four priority classes with 32 levels in each. All applications start out with a default priority but can change to any priority without restriction. Each thread in an application can have a different priority.

Q: *How does preemptive multitasking work in OS/2?*

A: Each thread in the system is either running, runnable (i.e., has work to do), or is waiting (i.e., for user input, the completion of a disk I/O request, etc.). The running thread is allowed to execute until one of the following happens:

1. Its time-slice expires. (The default time-slice is 248 milliseconds.)

2. It requests a system service that involves a wait.

3. A higher-priority thread becomes runnable, in which case the running thread is immediately interrupted.

   If a thread's time-slice expires, other threads of equal priority get time-slices in a round-robin manner.

Q: *How can OS/2 prevent high-priority threads that are constantly runnable from locking lower-priority threads out of the CPU?*

A: If the PRIORITY statement in CONFIG.SYS contains the DYNAMIC option (the default), OS/2 will dynamically and temporarily boost the priority of low-priority threads that are locked out of the CPU for more than the number of seconds specified on the MAXWAIT parameter in CONFIG.SYS (the default is 3 seconds). This priority boost will fade out over a time period defined by the second parameter on the TIMESLICE statement in CON-FIG.SYS.

Q: *What is a session?*
A: A session is a group of applications that share a virtual screen, keyboard, and mouse.

Q: *What is the technical definition of a window?*
A: A programming construct that receives messages and acts upon them. The window may or may not be visible on the screen and may or may not display output and accept input from a user. Windows are identified by window handles.

Q: *What is the technical definition of a message?*
A: A message is an element on a message queue associated with an application. It contains several fields, including a message type, the handle of the window it was sent to, two message-specific 32-bit parameters, a timestamp, and the location of the mouse when the message was generated.

Q: *What is a window procedure?*
A: A subroutine that contains the code to process messages sent to windows.

Q: *How are window procedures associated with windows?*
A: When a window is created, it is created as an instance of a window class. A window class defines the general appearance and behavior of windows created as instances of the class. When a window class is registered, its window procedure is specified. The behavior of the window is defined by the way the window procedure processes messages.

Q: *Does a window procedure have to process all possible messages?*
A: No. A window procedure can ignore messages and typically will ignore the majority of messages defined in OS/2. Any messages that are ignored must be passed back to a default window procedure defined in OS/2.

Q: *What are control windows?*
A: Control windows are instances of predefined window classes that are automatically registered in OS/2 and whose window procedures are provided by OS/2. They can be used by any application.

Q: *What are the main categories of control windows?*
A: 1. Standard window components, such as the frame window, title bar, minimize button, maximize button, and menu icon
   2. User input components, such as entry fields, buttons, list boxes, and spin buttons
   3. Application organization tools, such as containers and notebooks

Q: *What are the main categories of messages?*
A: 1. User input messages, including keystroke and mouse events

2. User interface messages, including messages relating to window movement, resizing, and uncovering

3. Messages from other applications

4. Messages from the system, including messages indicating changes in the environment

Q: *What facilities for screen output are provided by PM?*
A: 1. Text output

2. Font choice

3. Graphics primitives outputs, such as lines, curves, circles, ellipses, and polygons

4. Color choices for text, graphics primitives, and window components

5. Device translation, such as between the screen and a printer

Q: *What kinds of fonts are supported in OS/2?*
A: 1. OS/2 format bitmap fonts

2. OS/2 format outline fonts

3. Adobe type 1 outline fonts

Q: *What is Dynamic Data Exchange (DDE)?*
A: Dynamic Data Exchange (DDE) is an additional form of interprocess communication available to PM and Windows applications. It provides a means for applications to exchange data using messages, so that DDE events are processed in the same way as any other events.

Q: *What is window subclassing?*
A: Window subclassing can be used to add function to a control window without having to re-create all the logic provided by the control window. It involves intercepting messages before they are processed by the control window's window procedure. After taking appropriate action, the subclassing window procedure can discard the message or pass it to the original window procedure for normal processing.

Q: *What is a dialog box?*
A: Dialog boxes are complex windows built out of control windows. They are used in contexts that require specific user input, and are one major way that graphical applications dispense with command lines.

Q: *What are menus?*
A: Menus are lists of choices that applications make available to users. There are two main types of windows in PM:

1. Action bar menus, which appear as a horizontal row of choices just below a window's title bar

2. Pop-up menus, which appear as a vertical list of choices, usually when the user clicks the right mouse button over an object

Q: *What are resources?*
A: Resources are PM application components defined outside of the applications source code, in a resource file. The resource file is compiled by the resource compiler as part of the program generation process, and the resulting file is linked into the application .EXE file to create the final executable. The main types of resources are:
1. Menu definitions
2. Accelerator tables
3. Icon definitions
4. Bitmap definitions
5. Dialog box templates

Q: *What is the System Object Model?*
A: System Object Model (SOM) is a facility that adds object-oriented programming facilities to procedural languages, such as C. It provides a syntax for defining object classes—the Object Interface Definition Language (OIDL)—and a preprocessor for converting the OIDL code into procedural language components.

Q: *What are the main inputs and outputs to the SOM preprocessor?*
    Input
        OIDL file
    Outputs
        .C source template for implementing the class
        .C implementation header, an include file for the program implementing the class
        .C public header, an include file for programs using the class

Q: *What are the main uses of SOM in OS/2 programming?*
A: 1. As a general tool for writing object-oriented programs
    2. As a tool for writing programs that use WorkPlace Shell objects

Q: *What is the relationship between SOM and the WorkPlace Shell?*
A: WorkPlace Shell objects are SOM objects. Applications that wish to extend WorkPlace Shell objects as part of the application design can use SOM to create classes that inherit the characteristics and behavior of WorkPlace Shell objects. Since WorkPlace Shell objects are varied and have complex behavior, applications can achieve levels of complexity without having to recode the behavior. Since the WorkPlace Shell closely follows CUA 1991 standards, applications can easily conform to CUA 1991 by using SOM to inherit WorkPlace Shell objects and their behavior.

9

VM—The IBM Virtual Machine Operating System

Jeff Kaplan

Introduction

IBM's Virtual Machine (VM) operating system provides for the ability to run multiple IBM operating systems simultaneously on a single, physical IBM (or compatible) processor complex. The VM operating system controls "virtual machines." A virtual (i.e., simulated) machine is the functional equivalent of a real processor complex. Each virtual machine is controlled by an operating system, with the VM operating system concurrently controlling multiple virtual machines on an actual, physical computer. Many operating systems, like the IBM MVS/ESA operating system, which normally execute on a real computer while controlling all of the resources of the computer, execute successfully within the virtual machine environment. Some operating systems—for example, the IBM Conversational Monitor System (CMS)—can execute only within a virtual machine environment, not on a real computer. CMS provides for interactive services, such as file editing and application program development, within a virtual machine. IBM has successively made available several versions of the VM operating system. The current version, known as the IBM Virtual Machine/Enterprise Systems Architecture (VM/ESA) operating system, is designed to functionally replace all of the previously released VM systems: VM/370, VM/SP, VM/SP HPO, and VM/XA SP.

The primary component of the VM operating system is known as Control Program (CP). The CP component performs the following major functions:

- Provides support for a variety of real machine operating environments such as 370, XA, or ESA processor mode, and single-image, physically partitioned, or LPAR processor operation.

- Provides support for numerous DASD, tape cartridge, communications, and unit record real input-output devices.

- Concurrent operation of multiple virtual machines, each of which is controlled by an operating system. This includes managing the demand paging for allocation of real storage in the real machine to virtual storage in the virtual machines.

- Provides support for intervirtual machine communication services such as the interuser communication vehicle (IUCV).

- Provides services to real machine operators and to executing virtual machines via CP commands and the DIAGNOSE instruction interface.

- Provides protection facilities such that a given virtual machine cannot access or interfere with the real machine CP operation or with another concurrently running virtual machine.

The CMS component of the VM operating system performs the following major functions:

- File management and maintenance such that disk files can be created, modified, copied, and erased. Files may be shared among any number of users. Access to certain types of MVS-formatted and VSE-formatted files is provided for.

- An editing facility, known as the XEDIT editor, provides for a rich set of editing capabilities.

- Program compilation and execution such that application programs written specifically for the CMS environment can be compiled and executed. Certain MVS and VSE application programs, depending on the MVS and VSE services required by those programs, may also be compiled and executed within the CMS environment.

- REXX, the REstructured eXtended eXecutor language, provides a sophisticated procedural command language environment. REXX permits access to CP commands, CMS commands, and other CMS facilities while also acting as a general-purpose programming language.

- Numerous support services, such as tape cartridge access, screen management, debugging facilities, and interuser communication are also provided for.

The Group Control System (GCS) component of the VM operating system is an operating system that is designed to execute only within a virtual machine environment, not on a real computer. GCS provides the environment that supports the facilities necessary to operate an SNA network. GCS interfaces with licensed IBM program products such as VTAM, RSCS, and NETVIEW. GCS also works with

RSCS, which is the VTAM-provided component that permits SNA-connected terminals to logon to the VM Control Program.

The Dump Viewing Facility (DVF) component of the VM operating system is a set of CMS commands that aid operating systems programmers in dump analysis. The current version of the IBM VM operating system is known as IBM Virtual Machine/Enterprise Systems Architecture (VM/ESA) Version 1 Release 2. VM/ESA V1R2 is designed to functionally replace all of the previously released versions of the VM operating system.

Generally, the previous VM operating system versions can be grouped by the real processor mode supported—i.e., System/370 mode, Extended Architecture (XA) mode, or Enterprise Systems Architecture (ESA) mode.

The latest releases of the previously available VM operating system versions that are in general usage are as follows:

- VM/ESA Version 1 Release 1.1
- VM/ESA Version 1 Release 1.0
- VM/XA System Product Release 2.1
- VM/XA System Product Release 2.0
- VM/XA System Product Release 1
- VM/SP and VM/SP HPO Release 6
- VM/SP and VM/SP HPO Release 5

The Employment Interview

An interviewer will normally target specific areas of knowledge based on the general level of experience of the interviewee as follows:

- A novice user should be able to logon to VM and establish a terminal session; be comfortable with the VM environment and mode switching, including switching between the CP, CMS, and XEDIT environments; issue selected CP and CMS commands; perform simple editing of a file; access and manipulate files; access and manipulate the virtual machine's unit record devices; and know how to navigate the HELP facility.

- An intermediate user would be familiar with most of the common CP and CMS commands; write and execute simple REXX programs; be totally comfortable with manipulating files within minidisks and the Shared File System (SFS); be able to work with real and virtual tape devices and unit record devices; be able to fully utilize XEDIT and write simple XEDIT macros; and be able to compile and test application programs under the CMS environment.

- An advanced user would be able to solve technical problems within the XEDIT and REXX environments; be able to utilize selected CP services and facilities, such as the DIAGNOSE and IUCV services; be familiar with the real machine operation; have a rudimentary knowledge of the GCS environment; and be able to customize his or her own CMS working environment.

It is very important to note that certain CP and/or CMS facilities are available only in the newer releases of the VM operating system. Some of the technical questions and answers in the following section are based on knowledge of those newer services.

Questions and Answers

Novice Users

Q: *After you have logged on to VM, you receive a status message indicating "CP READ." What does this mean?*

A: The CP component of the VM operating system is waiting for you to enter a CP command. If the CMS system is not automatically IPLed when you logon, then you may IPL CMS at this time.

Q: *How do you determine which minidisks and directories you currently have accessed within CMS?*

A: The "QUERY ACCESSED" CMS command. The command response indicates the mode letter used to access a given minidisk (if a virtual device address is displayed) or a given directory (if a directory name is displayed).

Q: *I notice that I have two different files with the same filename and filetype on two different minidisks or directories. What problems may occur because of the duplicate filenames?*

A: Some CMS commands (e.g., "EXEC") use the standard CMS search order of "A–Z" and process the first file found with the proper name. Some CMS commands (e.g., "LISTFILE") permit a specification of "*" for the filemode designation and thus will process all files with the indicated filename on all currently accessed minidisks or directories.

Q: *You would like to save a copy of the results of a sequence of CP and CMS commands that you are about to enter. How can you save a console log of your virtual machine console output on your "A" disk?*

A: You may issue the CP command "SPOOL CONSOLE START *" to start console spooling to your own virtual reader. You then may issue a "SPOOL CONSOLE STOP" command to terminate console spooling and make the console log available in your virtual reader. The log must then be stored as a CMS file using the CMS "RECEIVE" command.

Q: *Why would someone access a minidisk or directory as an extension of itself?*

A: Accessing a minidisk or directory as its own extension (i.e., "ACCESS 300 L/L") will normally cause all files in that minidisk or directory to be accessible as read-only, thus preventing accidental modification or deletion of those files.

Q: *I notice that my "A" disk is my 191 minidisk and that I do not have my top directory currently accessed. What can I do to access my directory as my "A" disk?*

A: Your system administrator has determined that you are to have access to minidisk storage, as a default, and to filepool space. You may request that your filepool space be accessed as "A," as your default, if your installation permits this option. Alternatively, the CMS "SET FILEPOOL filepoolid" command will establish the name of your default filepool. The CMS "ACCESS A" command will access your SFS top directory with a filemode of "A."

Q: *I requested "HELP" for a particular CMS command. When I look at the resultant HELP information on the screen, I notice that I received a very minimal description of the command, without any command syntax or parameter description. What can I do to receive a more detailed command description?*

A: You requested the brief HELP option. The PF1 program function key should indicate that you can enter "PF1" to select detailed or ALL HELP. You may immediately request detailed HELP by entering the CMS "HELP" command with the "DETAIL" option (e.g., "HELP CMS commandname DETAIL").

Q: *I had been editing—using XEDIT, a CMS file—for about an hour when there was a power failure and the system "crashed." I realized that I lost my file changes that I made with XEDIT because I did not have enough time to save or file my changes. What could I have done, besides periodically saving my file, that would have "automatically" prevented the loss of my changes?*

A: You should have entered the XEDIT "SET AUTOSAVE" subcommand at the beginning of the edit session or you could place this command in your "PROFILE XEDIT" file. The XEDIT editor will then automatically save your file at a user-requested interval.

Q: *You are in the midst of editing a CMS file when you decide to save the file. Upon saving the file you receive a message stating that the disk or filespace is full and that your file cannot be saved. What should you do?*

A: You can erase or discard a different file from your minidisk or filepool in order to make room for the saving of the file that you are currently editing. You may also, if you have other read-write minidisks available, save your file on one of those minidisks.

Q: *A programmer spooled a file to your virtual reader. When you try to receive this file you are not able to do so successfully. What could be wrong?*

A: Your virtual reader spool class probably does not match the spool class of the spool file sent to your virtual reader by the other user. You should ensure that your virtual reader will accept any reader file by using the universal reader spool class of "*" (e.g., "CP SPOOL READER CLASS *").

Q: *In the process of XEDITing a file I mistakenly entered a command that caused a pending status message to appear (e.g., " 'CC' pending"). How can I clear the pending status condition?*

A: The XEDIT "RESET" subcommand will cancel all pending status conditions.

Q: *I am editing a CMS file and I would like to insert the letter "X" in column 72 on several lines within the file. I type the desired character on those lines in the proper column, but when I depress the enter key, all of the characters disappear, leaving a blank in column 72 on those lines. What could possibly be happening?*

A: You are probably XEDITing a file that, as a default (based on filetype), has a record length and verify value (columns displayed on the screen) greater than the file's truncation value. As an example, unless changed by your installation, suppose that assembler language source files have a record length of 80, a verify value of 72, and a truncation value of 71. This means that on the screen you will be able to view 72 of the 80 columns of each source record. However, because of the truncation value of 71, you will not be permitted to enter data in columns 72 through 80.

Q: *How can a CMS user activate full-screen CMS?*

A: The CMS command "SET FULL SCREEN ON" will activate full-screen CMS.

Q: *Sometimes, I have a need to move or rearrange the windows of my CMS session. What is the procedure for window manipulation?*

A: You must activate the "window management" window ("WM") via the PA1 key within full-screen CMS or the "WINDOW POP WM" command (or the older "POP WINDOW WM").

Q: *I am currently writing several execs that need to share variables among themselves. What should I do?*

A: The CMS "GLOBALV" command sets and retrieves a collection of named variables. The "GLOBALV PUT" command can be used to save the values of one or more variables. The "GLOBALV GET" command can be used to retrieve variables whose values were previously saved.

Q: *I received a certain error message while XEDITing a file. The error message description referred to an XEDIT ring. What exactly is an XEDIT ring?*

A: An XEDIT ring refers to the capability of the XEDIT editor to independently edit multiple files serially. A user can edit, for example, three files, and switch between all three files via the "XEDIT" command.

Q: *A strange problem occurred while I was XEDITing a file. I had issued the following two commands:*

```
SET PROFILE ON LEFT
SET NUM ON
```

I then issued a "delete" prefix command, "D3," on one of the file's lines. However, only one line (not three lines) was deleted. What could be the cause of this error?

A: Commands in the prefix area are decoded left to right and changes in the numbers (with "SET NUM ON") are looked for. If the prefix area contains, for example, "00034" and you type a "D3" command such that the "3" character overlays the "3" character of the prefix area ("00D34"), then your command will not be fully recognized. This problem can be avoided by always typing a blank after your prefix command.

Q: I am trying to XEDIT a file and I have been receiving an error during execution of the XEDIT profile. How should I go about correcting the error in the XEDIT profile?

A: It is best to edit your "PROFILE XEDIT" file by invoking the editor and requesting that a profile not be called during editor initialization:

```
XEDIT PROFILE XEDIT A (NOPROFILE
```

Q: I have two persistent problems whenever I am editing a file. Everytime that I try to use the keyboard insert key to insert additional characters in a line, I receive an "input inhibited" message; I get around the problem by deleting some blanks from the end of the line before performing the insertion. Another problem that I seem to have is that, after typing some characters and then hitting the "enter" key, all of the characters that I had typed move to the left. I do not know what to do to correct these problems.

A: The XEDIT commands "SET FULLREAD ON" and "SET NULLS ON" will together resolve the "left crush" problem, as it is called, and will enable character insertion at the end of a line without having to bother deleting characters or performing an "EOF" command.

Q: I had noticed a file (that I did not recall creating) on my "A" disk. After browsing the file, I noticed that the file had been automatically deleted. What could have happened?

A: Files with a filemode number of three (3) are automatically erased at the end of reading, whether they are on a minidisk or within the SFS system. Such temporary files are typically created as work files by some CMS commands.

Q: The real machine operator attached a tape drive to my virtual machine at virtual address 170; the virtual address should have been 180. What can I do to correct the virtual address without detaching and reattaching the real tape drive?

A: The CP "DEFINE" command permits redefinition of a virtual device address:

```
CP DEF 170 180
```

Q: I am trying to XEDIT a large file and I have been receiving an XEDIT error message indicating that the file is too large. What can I do so that I can edit this particular file?

A: The CP "DEFINE" command permits redefinition of a virtual machine's configuration, including the redefinition of the virtual machine's storage size. The following command, for example, will increase the virtual machine's storage size to 6 MB, thus permitting the editing of larger files. XEDIT retains the complete file in storage while editing.

```
CP DEF STOR 6M
```

Q: *What determines which CP commands a virtual machine user is authorized to issue?*

A: The virtual machine user's CP privilege class determines which CP commands a user is authorized to invoke. Normally, unless modified by your installation, the privilege classes range from "A", for the primary system operator, to "G", for the general user.

Q: *The system administrator has just allocated a new minidisk for my userid. After logging on, I tried to access the new minidisk, but I received an error message. What is probably wrong?*

A: The minidisk is, most likely, not formatted. All CMS minidisks must be formatted by the CMS "FORMAT" command prior to their usage by the CMS file system.

Q: *CMS module files are nonrelocatable. I do not fully understand what the term "nonrelocatable" means.*

A: When CMS modules are generated via the "LOAD" and the "GENMOD" commands, they are set up to execute at a specific location within the CMS system user-free area. The modules are said to be nonrelocatable because of their requirement of being loaded and run at a specific location within storage.

Q: *What is the distinction between guest real storage and guest virtual storage?*

A: The VM operating system handles three different types of storage:

1. The real storage of the physical machine, known as "really" real storage

2. The storage that appears to be real to a guest virtual machine (guest real storage), known as "virtually" real storage

3. The storage that a virtual operating system guest creates for its own usage (guest virtual storage), known as "virtually" virtual storage

Q: *What is the purpose of the IUCV facility?*

A: The CP IUCV facility is a CP service that enables the transfer of data among virtual machines. The IUCV service exists in conjunction with an older type of intermachine communication vehicle known as VMCF.

Q: *I had copied a file from one minidisk to another minidisk. When I issued a "FILELIST" command, the file appeared to occupy 500 blocks on one of my minidisks, but 1000 blocks on my other minidisk. Is this possible?*

A: The number of blocks that a file occupies is expressed in blocks, where the size of the block varies depending on how the minidisk was formatted. Most minidisks are formatted in either 1, 2, or 4K blocks using the CMS "FOR-MAT" command. A file that occupies, for example, x number of 2K blocks on a 2K-formatted minidisk may occupy about $2x$ number of 1K blocks on a 1K-formatted minidisk.

Q: *What is the distinction between the meaning of a filemode number of 0 for SFS files versus a filemode number of 0 for files stored on a minidisk?*

A: The filemode number of 0 for files stored on a minidisk indicates that the file is a private file (i.e., a user with read-only access) to that minidisk and will not be able to access the private file. A Shared File System (SFS) file, with a filemode number of 0, will be treated as if the filemode number is 1. SFS file access is controlled by granting read authority to that file.

Q: *What is one possible way to move (i.e., copy and delete) files from one SFS directory to a different SFS directory?*

A: The CMS "RELOCATE" command can be used to move files among different SFS directories. SFS file aliases and authorities remain unchanged. The command format is as follows:

```
RELOCATE myfilename myfiletype fromdir TO targetdir
```

Q: *I would like to share one of my SFS files with other users, but I update the file for an extended period of time every day. I would also like to make sure that the file is not damaged by other users. What should I do?*

A: You can use the CMS "CREATE LOCK" command to ensure serialization of access to a given SFS file. The command format is as follows:

```
CREATE LOCK myfilename EXCLUSIVE[or UPDATE]
```

Q: *I use the "PEEK" command often. One problem I have is that the command seems to let me "peek" at only a portion of the file queued in my virtual reader. What can I do to always be able to view a complete reader file?*

A: The CMS "DEFAULTS" command may be used to increase the maximum number of records that, as a default, the "PEEK" command will process.

Q: *How can I print out many CMS files and have all those files print together as one large report, without having a CP separator page between the output resulting from each print command?*

A: The CP spooling system "CONT" option can be used to "spool continuous" your virtual printer; this will batch together many little reports:

```
CP SPOOL PRT CONT        (prior to printing)
CP SPOOL PRT CLOSE       (after the "PRINT" command)
```

Q: *What is the distinction between the CP "LOGON" command and the CP "DIAL" command?*

A: The "LOGON" command permits access to the VM system as a virtual machine user. The "DIAL" command accesses a currently logged-on virtual machine as a user of that system.

Q: *I logged on to VM and then, during the IPL of CMS, I noticed that my 191 ("A") disk had been accessed with read access instead of the usual write access. What could be wrong?*

A: The minidisk is probably defined in the CP directory as "MR", meaning that a write link is established unless another user already has write access, in which case a read link is given.

Q: *I was observing a programmer entering CMS commands at a terminal. The programmer entered "AXES 301 B/B" and the result was the accessing of the 301 minidisk. I do not understand how the CMS "ACCESS" command was invoked because the programmer entered "AXES", not "ACCESS". How could this have happened since "AXES" was not the name of an exec?*

A: "AXES" is probably the name of a synonym for the "ACCESS" CMS command. Synonyms can usually be set up by the CMS user. Some installations may have a standard set of synonyms that they provide.

Q: *Certain CP commands that affect the state of the user's virtual machine (e.g., "IPL", "SYSTEM", "ATTN", and "REQUEST") are meant to simulate which capabilities of a real machine?*

A: CP commands (e.g., the "IPL" command) are meant to simulate the operation of a real machine console (i.e., the functions performed via "buttons" on a real machine). "Buttons" are not usually used on a real machine console anymore, but everyone still uses the term.

Q: *I had logged on to VM, IPLed CMS, "SET FULLSCREEN OFF", and was trying to enter a CMS command that referred to a particular CMS file when I began to have problems. This particular file contained an "@" character in the filename of the file. Every time I typed the command and the filename, the command response was "Invalid Filename". I noticed that a character in the filename next to the "@" character was missing. What could have happened?*

A: The "@" character is probably set on as the CP logical character delete symbol. The CP logical escape character (") should precede the "@" character, in order to actually code the "@" character.

Q: *What is the distinction between the "QUERY DASD" command and the "QUERY DISK" command?*

A: The CP "Q DASD" command presents information about all of the virtual DASD currently defined to a given virtual machine. The CMS "Q DISK" command presents the status of all the currently CMS-accessed minidisks or directories. There may be virtual minidisks that are CP-defined to the virtual machine, but not currently accessed in terms of the CMS operating system.

Q: *What problems could result if two or more users link to the same minidisk, "MW"?*

A: If both users are CMS users and have accessed the same minidisk in "R/W" mode, then there is the potential for permanent data loss on that minidisk. CMS does not support multiple users with write access to the same minidisk.

Q: *The response to a 'Q IMPEX' command is 'IMPEX=OFF'. What does this response imply in terms of CMS command processing?*

A: EXEC files must be preceded by the 'EXEC' command in order to be invoked correctly when your CMS session is set to 'IMPEX=OFF'.

Q: *How can a CMS file be punched without a 'READ' header control card?*

A: The CMS 'PUNCH' command with the 'NOHeader' option is used to punch a file without a header control card.

Q: *What is the purpose of the 'COPYFILE', 'FROM', and 'FOR' operands?*

A: The 'COPYFILE', 'FROM', and 'TO' operands are used to copy a portion of a file.

Q: *What is the purpose of the CMS 'NAMES' command?*

A: The CMS 'NAMES' command can be used to maintain a list of other users with whom you may communicate.

Q: *How can a user unpack a CMS file?*

A: A CMS file may be unpacked by either XEDITing the file and saving the file in unpacked format or by using 'COPYFILE' with the 'UNPACK' option.

Q: *What is the purpose of CMS files that have a filemode number of '4'?*

A: CMS files with a filemode number of '4' are files that are in CMS OS simulated dataset format. These files may be accessed by OS macros in programs running under CMS control.

Q: *How are module files created?*

A: CMS module files, which are nonrelocatable executable programs, are created via the CMS 'GENMOD' command.

Q: *What is the purpose of a file with a filetype of 'AMSERV'?*

A: A CMS file with a filetype of 'AMSERV' contains VSAM Access Method Services control statements that are "performed" by the CMS 'AMSERV' command.

Q: *How can you purge a reader file from within the 'PEEK' or 'RDRLIST' screens?*

A: The CMS 'DISCARD' command is used to purge reader files from within the 'PEEK' or the 'RDRLIST' command.

Q: *What does the XEDIT 'AUTOSAVE' subcommand do?*

A: The XEDIT 'AUTOSAVE' subcommand enables the automatic saving of a file after a selected number of changes or additions to a file have been made.

Intermediate/Advanced Users

Q: *My installation has a real 4245 printer, but my virtual machine has a virtual 3211 printer defined. How can I load an 8 LPI FCB into my virtual printer?*

A: You may use the CP "LOADVFCB" command to load an FCB image into your virtual printer (e.g., "CP LOADVFCB vaddress FCB FCB8") where "FCB8" is a VM-provided 8 lines/inch, 68 lines/page FCB image.

Q: *What is the purpose of the CP "TAG" command as related to RSCS?*

A: The CP "TAG" command associates "tag information" with an output spool file. RSCS interprets this information as addressing and control data (i.e., where to transmit a file destined for a remote user).

Q: *How can a user write a program that is able to determine, when executing, that the host operating system is running within a real machine or within a virtual machine?*

A: The "STIDP" machine instruction returns an X"FF" as the version code of the CPUID, if and only if the executing operating system is running within a virtual machine.

Q: *What is the difference between the "IPL 190" and the "IPL CMS" commands?*

A: When an address such as "190" is used as the target of the CP "IPL" command, then that virtual device contains the IPL bootstrap program or the operating system nucleus program to be loaded. When the name of a system (such as "CMS") is used as the target of the CP "IPL" command, then that name represents a named saved system.

Q: *I observed the real machine system operator enter the following CP command: "ATT 120 SYSTEM volser". What is the purpose of this command?*

A: The CP "ATTACH" command can be used by the real machine operator or other authorized users to make a physical DASD volume available to the "system" for minidisk access.

Q: *What is the distinction between the "#CP" command and the "CP command" command?*

A: The "#CP" command causes the virtual machine to enter the CP environment, normally from the virtual machine environment. The "CP command" command causes a single CP command to be executed from the virtual machine environment.

Q: *How can a user acquire information about the macro members or the copy book members of a MACLIB?*

A: The CMS "MACLIST" command lists information about the members of MACLIB file.

Q: *My installation has an exec that is repeatedly called by a number of CMS users. What can be done to improve performance in regard to the use of this exec?*

A: The exec may be loaded into the CMS installation saved segment or may even be loaded into a virtual machine user's storage via the CMS "EXEC-LOAD" command.

Q: *How can certain versions of VM create a virtual machine with more virtual processors than there are real processors within the host processor complex?*

A: A given virtual machine may have more virtual processors than there are physical real processors in the host processor complex because CP dispatches one or more virtual processors on one or more real processors, as required, on a time-sliced basis.

Q: *What benefit does CP virtual reserve/release support provide?*

A: CP virtual reserve/release support enables multiple virtual machines, executing on the same real machine, to share one or more minidisks, provided that all of the virtual machine operating systems in use support real reserve/release.

Q: *If a temporary minidisk is created, after logon, for a given virtual machine, which program should be used to format or initialize the temporary minidisk?*

A: The program that is needed to format or initialize a minidisk is dependent on the host virtual machine operating system in use. MVS, VM, VSE, and CMS either provide their own format programs or have specific initialization requirements.

Q: *What benefit does CP logical device support provide?*

A: The logical device support facility can be used to create multiple, logical 3270-type devices (i.e., a "programmable" display/printer device). The VM Pass-Through program product uses this CP facility to create multiple terminal sessions for a given user.

Q: *What are some of the benefits that a V=R or V=F virtual machine would enjoy?*

A: V=R and V=F virtual machines enjoy several benefits (e.g., nonpaged execution) such that the virtual machine's pages are kept in real storage all of the time, and no CCW translation of virtual-to-real channel program addresses for certain devices.

Q: *How can MVS application programs execute under CMS control?*

A: Certain MVS application programs can execute under CMS control because CMS can simulate the functions of many MVS operating system services, thus providing for the ability to execute MVS user-written programs.

Q: *What must be done by the CMS user to enable the execution of VSE user-written applications?*

A: The execution of user-written VSE applications is made possible by enabling the CMS/DOS environment via the CMS "SET DOS ON" command.

Q: *What service does the programmable operator facility provide?*

A: The programmable operator facility, known as "PROP," provides for the ability to intercept messages destined for a given virtual machine and to act upon those messages.

Q: *What are the primary applications that the GCS operating system supports?*

A: GCS is a virtual machine supervisor that is designed to support VTAM, NETVIEW, RSCS, and other VTAM-based applications that run natively within a virtual machine.

Q: *What kind of dumps can DVF handle?*

A: The Dump Viewing Facility (DVF) can process CP hard/soft dumps, stand-alone CP dumps, CMS, GCS, and various other program product dumps.

Q: *What is the purpose of the CP and CMS National Language Support (NLS)?*

A: The NLS feature provides for message, HELP file, and command support in various languages. Language support (other than the usual mixed-case American English support) must be installed by your installation.

Q: *What is the difference between a CP hard abend and a CP soft abend?*

A: Basically, errors that cannot be isolated to a particular virtual machine and may compromise overall system integrity result in a hard abend; otherwise, a soft abend results.

Q: *Why are some DASD volumes set up as CP-owned volumes and some DASD volumes are not set up this way?*

A: CP-owned volumes contain areas that are required for CP operation of the real machine (e.g., spooling space areas and page space areas). Volumes containing only minidisk space do not have to be marked as CP-owned.

Q: *What is the distinction, from the virtual machine's viewpoint, of dedicating a device to the virtual machine versus attaching the same device to the virtual machine?*

A: There is normally no difference, from the virtual machine's viewpoint, of attaching a device to the virtual machine versus dedicating a device to the virtual machine.

Q: *How can message traffic from a disconnected virtual machine operator's console be saved?*

A: The CP console spooling facility can be used to save the output directed to a disconnected console. Additionally, SCIF can be used to direct a disconnected console's output to another virtual machine.

Q: *What is the purpose of the CP "DEFSYS" command?*

A: The CP "DEFSYS" command creates a skeleton system data file for the purpose of saving a DCSS or NSS. The CP "SAVESEG" command saves a storage area to the defined system data file.

Q: *What are shadow page and segment tables?*

A: Shadow page and segment tables are used by CP to logically map the machine's physical storage to a virtual machine's operating system created virtual storage.

Q: *How does one "run" a VM-provided stand-alone utility (e.g., "DDR") within a virtual machine?*

A: A VM-provided stand-alone utility may be executed by punching the IPL deck to your virtual machine's virtual reader and then "IPLing" the virtual reader.

Q: *Why would a programmer use the CP DIAGNOSE interface?*

A: The CP DIAGNOSE interface, available within the assembly language or the REXX language, provides for access to selected CP services (e.g., the virtual console service that permits execution of CP commands from within a program).

Q: *What could happen if two or more DCSSs are defined, such that they have overlapping virtual storage addresses?*

A: Overlapping DCSS virtual storage addresses may be okay if a single virtual machine never requires the services of more than one of the overlapping DCSS saved segments at a time.

Q: *How can a general user check the status of the system (e.g., the current processor utilization)?*

A: The CP "INDICATE" command enables a general user to check the overall status of the "system" at a specific instant in time (e.g., the processor utilization is reported by the "INDICATE" command).

10
REXX

Jeff Kaplan

Introduction

REXX, the REstructured eXtended eXecutor language of IBM, is a general purpose programming language that has been ported to and adapted for many different environments (e.g., there are versions of the language for the MVS TSO/E, VM/CMS, OS/400, OS/2, and PC/DOS host environments). IBM has designated a subset of the REXX language as the common SAA (Systems Application Architecture) Procedures Language. This means that you can write REXX applications that execute on different platforms (e.g., MVS and OS/2). The REXX language itself is supported by various compilers and interpreters within the framework of the host environments (e.g., within the MVS environment). IBM has made available the IBM Compiler and Library for REXX/370 licensed program product that provides for compiled REXX language support. The MVS TSO/E licensed program product includes the TSO/E Procedures Language MVS/REXX interpreter, which provides for interpreted REXX language support. The TSO/E REXX interpreter together with the REXX language are known as TSOE/REXX. REXX support has also been extended to the PC environment by both IBM and non-IBM vendors.

We will be limiting our discussion to the facilities supported by the IBM TSO/E REXX interpreter and the IBM VM/CMS System Product Interpreter. REXX programs within the MVS and VM host environments are also known as execs.

Main Features of the REXX Language

- A rich set of language constructs and built-in functions that are especially strong in terms of string-processing capabilities

- A relatively sophisticated parsing and pattern-processing capability

- A free-form language syntax

- Minimal data-typing (typeless) and variable declaration requirements
- Host (VM and MVS) interfacing capabilities
- An interactive tracing and debugging facility
- A user-extendable environment

The Employment Interview

An interviewer will normally target specific areas of knowledge based on the general level of experience of the interviewee as follows:

- A novice user should be able to write and execute REXX execs that utilize several built-in functions, perform simple parsing, demonstrate knowledge of control structures, and provide for minimal interfacing with the host (VM or MVS) environment.
- An intermediate user should be comfortable with most of the REXX built-in functions, be able to code sophisticated parsing routines, demonstrate a "good" programming style, and be able to interface with the MVS or VM host environment.
- An advanced user would be able to interface with various program product environments (such as the XEDIT, ISPF, and the ISPF/PDF environments), be familiar with external function packaging, prepare execs that are written for and execute within non-TSO/E address spaces (MVS only), and prepare full applications utilizing REXX only or a mixture of REXX execs and other vehicles.

Questions and Answers

Novice Users

Q: *I am writing a REXX exec and, when I try to run my exec, I receive an error message implying that the system does not seem to "recognize" my exec as a REXX exec. What is probably wrong with my exec?*

A: The MVS TSO/E REXX language processor and the VM/CMS System Product Interpreter both have specific exec coding requirements that enable those language processors to identify your exec properly. The first line of a CMS REXX program must begin with a REXX comment (i.e., "/* ... */"). The first line of a TSO REXX program should begin with a REXX comment with the word "REXX" included within the comment. Your installation may have set up your environment such that in certain cases the foregoing requirements are not necessary. However, it is still a good practice to always place a REXX comment with the word "REXX" embedded in the comment as the first line of your exec.

Q: *I am trying to write a REXX exec that will accept a line of input from the terminal user when the exec is running. What language construct would you use to accomplish this function?*

A: The "PULL" instruction, which is a short form of "PARSE UPPER PULL" or "PARSE PULL", could be used to acquire a line of input from the terminal user. It is important to note that the "PARSE PULL" instruction attempts to parse lines from the data stack first, before attempting to acquire input from the terminal user. "PARSE EXTERNAL" acquires input from the terminal user, bypassing the data stack.

Q: *My REXX program is supposed to check a given variable to see if the variable's current value is one of the days of the week (i.e., "MONDAY", "TUESDAY", etc.). I wrote a long sequence of "IF, Then, Else . . ." clauses. Is there a better way to do this?*

A: You could use the "SELECT" instruction, as follows:

```
"SELECT;"
"WHEN day_of_week = 'MONDAY' then ..."
"WHEN day_of_week = 'TUESDAY' then ..."
...
"END;"
```

You could also perform a similar function as follows:

```
"True = '1';"
"If wordpos(day_of_week, 'MONDAY TUESDAY ...') =
True then ..."
```

Q: *I am performing an arithmetic calculation "9/2" that is giving a result of "4.5". However, I'm interested only in whole numbers without remainders. What can I do to correct the calculation?*

A: You could code "9 % 2" which will return only the integer part of the result. Alternatively, you could use the "TRUNC" function "TRUNC(9/2)".

Q: *I am supposed to check a variable's value to see if it is the letter "Y" or "N". I wrote "If myvar = 'Y' | 'N' then . . .". Now I have some kind of error. What should I do?*

A: The syntax of the "IF" statement is incorrect. You could code the "IF" statement as follows:

```
"If (myvar='Y') " | (myvar='N') then ...".
```

Q: *I am trying to produce a line of output where a dollar amount appears. I wrote the following statement: "SAY '$' amount". "Amount" is a variable containing a number value. Every time I run my exec, the dollar amount appears with a blank between the dollar sign and the amount. What can I do to correct this problem?*

A: The REXX language abuttal operator permits you to code "SAY '$'amount" to achieve the desired output. You could also use the REXX concatenation operator: "SAY '$'""amount".

Q: *My exec has a line that is coded as follows: "SAY pay_amount". Instead of a salary amount appearing when the exec is executed, the word "PAY_AMOUNT" appears as output from the "SAY" statement. What is the problem?*

A: When a variable has never been initialized (i.e., has never been assigned a value), then the default value of the variable (the variable's name) is used (after being converted to uppercase characters).

Q: *I wrote the following code fragment that is not working properly. The program does not seem to perform correctly after entering my "DO" loops and processing some statements:*

```
"DO outerloop ..."
 "DO innerloop ..."
 " If ... = ...  then SIGNAL nextrec;"
 "end DO innerloop"
 "NEXTREC: ..."
"end DO outerloop"
```

A: The "SIGNAL" instruction disrupts the normal flow of execution within an exec, including looping, and thus should be used very carefully (i.e., to perform processing of abnormal situations only).

Q: *I'm executing my REXX program and I think that it's in a loop. What can I do to stop the execution of the exec?*

A: An exec that is looping may normally be terminated in TSO/E by pressing the PA1 key (attention key) and then responding to the received prompt with "HI" (Halt Interpretation), or "HE" (Halt Execution). A runaway CMS exec may be terminated with "HI" command or by entering a CP command such as "#CP IPL...".

Q: *The value of the variable "string1" in my exec is some arbitrarily long character string. I am supposed to find out what the last three characters are. What should I do?*

A: There are a number of ways to solve this problem. We could use the "REVERSE" function as follows:

```
"answer = REVERSE(SUBSTR(REVERSE(string1),1,3))"
```

or we could code the following:

```
"answer = SUBSTR(string1,LENGTH(string1)-2)"
```

Note that we assumed that the input string was always at least three characters in length. A simpler solution would be to use the "RIGHT" function:

```
"answer = RIGHT(string1,3)"
```

Q: *I am writing a REXX exec where one of my variables has a value that is a character string with data in fixed positions; for example, characters 1–9 of the variable value are associated with a data item and characters 10–30 of the value are associated with another data item. How should I break out all of the unique data items from this one long variable value?*

A: The best way would probably be to use the "PARSE VAR" instruction with a numeric positional pattern:

```
"PARSE VAR data_rec item_1 10 item_2 31 ..."
```

Q: *I am reviewing a REXX exec written by a programmer in another department. The programmer told me that this particular exec repeatedly invokes a different exec as either a subroutine or as a function. How can I tell by looking at the calling exec whether the programmer is calling a function or a subroutine?*

A: Typically, a function is invoked as part of an expression within an instruction—e.g., "SAY myfunc(arg1,arg2) 'is the answer';". A subroutine would be called via a REXX "CALL" instruction.

Q: *I am in the midst of writing an exec with a series of "DO" loops embedded within outer "DO" loops. The one problem that I am having is that sometimes in the course of processing within one of the inner loops, I have to exit that inner loop and continue processing within one of the outer loops. How can I do this?*

A: The flow of control can be depicted as follows:

```
"DO outermost=1 ..."
      "DO  middle=1 ..."
            "DO  innermost=1 ..."
            "...If ... then LEAVE middle;"
            "END innermost"
      "END middle"
      "... processing resumes here ..."
"END outermost"
```

Note that when the "LEAVE" instruction is executed from the innermost loop that processing will resume after the "END" statement of the loop containing the control variable indicated on the "LEAVE" instruction. Note that if, instead of the "LEAVE middle" statement, the programmer coded "ITERATE middle" or "ITERATE outermost", the results would be entirely different.

Q: *I would like to write an exec where the caller of my exec specifies a parameter that is coded on the command line after the name of the exec. How can I acquire, within the exec, the argument that the user will type?*

A: Command-line data arguments are normally parsed using the "ARG" instruction, which is the equivalent of using the "PARSE UPPER ARG" instruction.

Q: *I am having a problem with one of the execs that I am currently working on. How can I go about debugging my exec and "see" the values that selected variables have at any point during processing?*

A: The REXX interactive debug facility, which is activated with the "TRACE ?" instruction will probably be the easiest way to handle this situation. The "TRACE ?R" instruction will trace most statements, showing the final results of the traced statement, and will pause after tracing a statement, thus giving the user an opportunity to enter REXX statements that can display the value of any variable. Alternatively, any number of REXX "SAY" instructions could be added to the exec in order to display variable values at selected points during processing.

Q: *How can I determine if a host command (such as a CMS "LISTFILE" or a TSO/E "ALLOCATE" command) which I will be issuing from within my exec has executed successfully?*

A: The REXX special variable "RC" is set to the value of the return code from the last host command issued from within the exec.

Q: *What problems could occur if a host command is not enclosed in quotes— for example, entering the MVS/TSO host command "ALLOCATE DA(MYDSNAME) SHR" or entering the VM/CMS host command "LISTFILE * * A"?*

A: The host command may not execute correctly; for example, due to the missing quotes, host command operands may be interpreted as REXX operators—i.e., "*" or "(".

Q: *What is the difference between a "PARSE ARG" instruction and a "PARSE PULL" instruction?*

A: "PARSE ARG" processes the passed input argument list, while "PARSE PULL" processes data from the external queue or data stack.

Q: *When is it appropriate to use a "NOP" instruction?*

A: "NOP" is a dummy instruction that is typically used after a "THEN", "ELSE", or "OTHERWISE" construct.

Q: *I have noticed that certain REXX programmers use the "ADDRESS environment" instruction within their execs, and that other programmers prefer to use the "ADDRESS environment command_expression" instruction. Is there a distinction between the two forms of the "ADDRESS" REXX instruction?*

A: The "ADDRESS environment" instruction permanently alters the target host command environment for all succeeding host commands. The same command with a given host command specified will target that host command to the indicated host command environment without affecting the target environment for all succeeding host commands.

Q: *The IBM REXX language reference manual states that the "USERID" function is a non-SAA built-in instruction. What, then, is the implication of using this particular function?*

A: The utilization of a given non-SAA facility implies that your program may not be portable between differing environments (e.g., between the MVS environment and the PC-based OS/2 environment).

Q: *What is the difference between an internal REXX function and an external REXX function?*

A: An internal REXX function exists within a given exec and is identified by the internal label corresponding to the function name. An external function may be written in any one of a number of languages, including REXX, and physically exists outside of the calling REXX program.

Q: *I "ran" an exec that contained the following line:*

```
xyz = SUBSTR(abc,4)
```

I expected some kind of error because I mistakenly left off the third parameter of the SUBSTR function. Should I have received an error?

A: When the "SUBSTR" function is invoked, the third passed parameter corresponds to the length of the returned substring. If this parameter is omitted, then the remainder of the input string is returned as the substring.

Q: *I wrote an exec that ended with the following lines:*

```
...
outline = ... ;
SAY outline;
EXIT 0;
/* End of exec
```

I received a syntax error "pointing" to the last line of the exec. I do not understand how this could have happened since the "EXIT" instruction precedes the final comment line. Is the REXX interpreter correct in indicating an error?

A: The "EXIT" instruction does not mark the end of an exec—merely a point at which processing is to terminate. There may be many "EXIT" instructions within a given exec. Thus, the REXX interpreter continues its syntax checking until the physical end of an exec; in this case, it indicates an error because of an incomplete comment.

Q: *What value should the REXX "LENGTH" built-in function return when passed a null character string as an argument?*

A: The null character string is defined to have a length of zero. A blank character is defined to have a length of one.

Q: *How are arrays implemented in the REXX language?*

A: Arrays are implemented using compound symbols (i.e., data.1, data.2, . . . , data.n).

Q: *The following code fragment, upon execution, displayed*

```
"TEST.HELLO".
test = "Hello";
SAY test.test;
```

The response that I had expected was "HELLO.HELLO". Was I wrong in my assumption?

A: Yes. Your assumption was wrong because substitution never occurs in the stem of a compound symbol. This particular variable had never been assigned a value; thus, the default value of the name of the variable, translated to uppercase, was displayed.

Q: *I wrote an exec that used the "EXECIO" command within a loop, reading and processing one record from a file at a time. What is another way that "EXECIO" could be used reading a complete file with one invocation of the "EXECIO" command?*

A: Many REXX program authors prefer to use the "EXECIO" command with stem processing; i.e., EXECIO * DISKR file_ptr (FINIS STEM filedata. ; The variable filedata.1 will contain the first record of the file, filedata.2 will contain the second record of the file, and so on. The variable filedata.0 will contain the number of records read from the file.

Q: *What is the "danger" of using stack services such as "QUEUE", "PUSH", and "PULL" without using commands such as "MAKEBUF" and "DROPBUF"?*

A: "MAKEBUF" and "DROPBUF" protect the caller's stacked data by preserving the caller's buffers from excessive "pulling" by the called program.

Q: *What is the purpose of the period character when used with the "PARSE" instruction?*

A: The period character acts as a dummy placeholder during the parse operation. So, for example, the period will match and ignore a blank-delimited word during simple word parsing.

Q: *Which of the following would have to be written as a user-provided external function: C2X (character to hexadecimal), X2D (hexadecimal to decimal), or B2C (binary to character)?*

A: The "B2C" function is not a normal REXX built-in function and would have to be implemented as a user-provided external function.

Q: *What is an "easy" way to pad a character string with blanks on the left?*

A: The "RIGHT" function performs blank padding on the left, as necessary:

```
RIGHT('ABC',5) gives "bbABC".
```

Q: *What could be the cause of a problem in the following code fragment?*

```
SIGNAL XYZ;
...
DO ... ;
...
XYZ: ... ;
...
END;
```

A: It is not considered good programming practice, and may cause errors in certain cases, to jump (via the "SIGNAL" instruction) into the middle of an iterative loop.

Q: *What is the result of executing a "SAY" instruction without an accompanying expression (i.e., "SAY;")?*

A: The null string is written. This will, of course, appear as a blank output line.

Q: *How can the "ITERATE" instruction be coded within an inner loop such that an outer loop is stepped?*

A: The "ITERATE" instruction may be used in conjunction with a loop control variable name such that stepping of an outer loop control variable occurs when the "ITERATE" instruction is processed:

```
DO I = 1 to ...;
    DO J = 1 to ...;
        ITERATE I;
    END  J;
END I;
```

Q: *Is there a potential problem with the following code fragment?*

```
to_be_done = 'DO i=1 to 4; SAY "HELLO";'
INTERPRET to_be_done;
END i;
```

A: REXX statements that are to be dynamically interpreted must have wholly contained "DO . . . END" constructs. This particular example contained a variable whose value to be interpreted contained a partially completed "DO" construct.

Q: *How can you unassign a variable such that it is as if that variable had never been used within your exec?*

A: The "DROP" instruction can be used to unassign a variable.

Q: *What is the purpose of the "EXPOSE" option of the "PROCEDURE" instruction?*

A: The "EXPOSE" option of the "PROCEDURE" instruction indicates that any reference to the exposed variables is made to the variable environment of the caller. Thus, the caller's variables (those on the expose list) may be referenced by the called procedure.

Q: *When are the "EXIT" and the "RETURN" instructions equivalent, in their effect, within an executing program?*

A: If there are not any active internal functions or subroutines, then the "EXIT" and "RETURN" instructions are equivalent. Thus, if you are coding a main procedure, you may exit or return from your exec.

Q: *When is it "okay" not to code an "OTHERWISE" instruction within a "SELECT . . . END" construct?*

A: The "OTHERWISE" clause is optional if and only if at least one of the "SELECT WHEN" clauses is true all of the time. If control falls through to an "OTHERWISE" clause that is not present, then an error will be indicated.

Q: *How many times will the following loop be performed?*

```
DO INDEX=1 TO 7 BY 2 FOR 2;
    ...
END;
```

A: The number of iterations of the given loop is bounded by the "FOR" clause; hence, the loop will be performed twice.

Q: *What is the purpose of the following statement?*
```
x=XRANGE("A","I")XRANGE("J","R")XRANGE("S","Z");
```
A: The given statement produces a string of 1-byte codes between and including the characters coded. The resultant string contains all of the uppercase English alphabet.

Q: *The "TIME" function "TIME('L')" returns the current time, including microseconds, when invoked. What will be the result of the following two "TIME" invocations?*
```
SAY "The time is" TIME("L") ". The time NOW is" TIME("L") ".";
```
A: Both "TIME" function calls produce exactly the same result because all "DATE" or "TIME" function calls in a single statement, for consistency reasons, return the same result if invoked more than once.

Q: *What will be the result of executing the following instruction sequence?*
```
x = "...";
y = SPACE(x,0);
```
A: The "SPACE" function, with a second operand of zero, will remove all blanks from the input string.

Q: *What is the length of the null string, i.e., x = LENGTH("");?*
A: The null string is, by definition, a character string of length zero.

Q: *What is the result of executing the following instruction?*
```
x = COPIES("...",0);
```
A: The "COPIES" function, with a second operand of zero, will result in a null string.

Q: *What is the sum of the following expression?*
```
x = "1" + 1;
```
A: REXX arithmetic is typeless (i.e., the character "1" and the number 1 are essentially treated the same way). Hence, the result of the given statement is two.

Q: *What is the result of executing the following instructions?*
```
a = 1;
b = 2;
x = ((a)(b))*2;
```
A: The result of the indicated statement is 24. Variables "a" and "b" are concatenated together, forming the number 12.

Q: *If the variable "y" has never been used (i.e., "y" has never been assigned a value), then what is the result of executing the statement x = y?*
A: When a variable that has never been assigned a value is used, then the value of that variable is the name of the variable translated to uppercase. Thus, the variable "x" will be assigned the value "Y".

Q: *What will the expression "2*2**2" evaluate to?*

A: REXX operator order of precedence dictates that exponentiation is performed first; hence, the given expression "2*2**2" evaluates to "2*4" or 16.

Intermediate/Advanced Users

Q: *How can a two-dimensional array be processed using the REXX language?*

A: A two-dimensional array may be processed via compound symbols as follows:

```
DO I = 1 to ...;
    DO J = 1 to ...;
        ... data.I.J ...
    END J;
END I;
```

Q: *I wrote the following REXX code fragment using the "EXECIO" command. What is the purpose of the "DROP" instruction at the end of the code?*

```
"EXECIO * DISKR file_ptr (FINIS STEM file_data.";
...
DROP file_data.;
```

A: The "DROP" instruction, when used in conjunction with a stem variable name, will unassign all of the compound symbol variables that begin with the indicated stem.

Q: *What is the result of running the following exec?*

```
/* Sample REXX exec */
speech. = "HELLO";
SAY speech.speech.speech;
EXIT 0;
```

A: The text "HELLO" is displayed. Since the stem variable "SPEECH." is assigned a value, all instances of all variables that begin with that stem now have the indicated value.

Q: *I wrote a single exec that can be invoked, via different names, such that the exec performs different processing based on the name used to invoke the exec. How is it possible to determine the name from within a given exec that was used to invoke that exec?*

A: The "PARSE SOURCE" instruction returns the name used to invoke a given exec:

```
PARSE SOURCE . . . . . invoking_name . ;
```

Q: *How can the results of a function call be parsed where the function call and the parsing are coded within one statement?*

A: The results of a function call can be parsed with the "PARSE VALUE" instruction:

```
PARSE VALUE a_function_call(...) WITH ... template ... ;
```

Q: *How would you code a function that is recursively invoked?*

A: The function would recurse by invoking itself via the "RETURN" instruction:

```
... = func(x);
 Func: Procedure ... ;

     ...
     Return Func(x_modified);
```

Q: *What is the difference between these two function calls: VALUE('XYZ') and VALUE(XYZ)?*

A: The function call "VALUE('XYZ')" returns the value of the variable "XYZ". The function call "VALUE(XYZ)" returns the value of the variable derived from substituting the value of "XYZ" (i.e., the value of the variable whose name is currently the value of the "XYZ" variable).

Q: *How can you specify a parse pattern where the pattern is variable in nature (i.e., the pattern is not known until execution time)?*

A: The variable containing the variable pattern must have its name enclosed in parentheses within the pattern template:

```
pattern_variable = ... a parse template pattern ...;
PARSE VAR to_be_parsed ... (pattern_variable) ...;
```

Q: *How can the precision to which REXX arithmetic operations are performed be modified?*

A: The "NUMERIC" instruction with the "DIGITS", "FORM", or "FUZZ" operand affects the precision of arithmetic operations.

Q: *What is the purpose of conditions and condition traps?*

A: Condition trapping enables an executing program to process selected events, known as conditions (e.g., command error and syntax error events).

Q: *When is it appropriate to use the REXX special variable "SIGL"?*

A: The value of the special variable "SIGL" is the line number of the clause currently executing when a "SIGNAL" transfer of control takes place. "SIGL" is most useful when used in conjunction with processing "SIGNAL ON SYNTAX" condition events.

Q: *I am currently writing a subroutine exec that will be invoked by a number of different execs that are possibly executing within differing host command environments. How can I determine the environment within which my exec has been invoked?*

A: The "ADDRESS" function returns the name of the current host command environment.

Q: *How can "EXECIO" be used to close a file without performing any read or write I/O operations?*

A: "EXECIO" can be used to close a file without any read-write operations by specifying a number of lines parameter of zero:

```
EXECIO 0 ... (FINIS;
```

Q: *Sometimes I receive a negative return code (e.g., –3) in the special variable "RC" when invoking a host TSO or CMS command. What could be the cause of such an error?*

A: Negative return codes, in many cases, indicate a host command environmental error (e.g., host command not found).

Q: *Normally, REXX will compare equal if two numbers are numerically equal, discounting leading zeros, etc. My application requires two numbers to compare equal if and only if they are identical, including leading zeros. What should I do?*

A: The REXX language supports a variety of strict (identical) operations. The strictly equal operator is "==":

```
IF var_1 == var_2 then do ... (identical case) ... ;
```

Q: *What is the distinction between the "&" and the "&&" logical operators?*

A: The "&" is the AND logical operator. The "&&" is the EXCLUSIVE OR logical operator.

Q: *Sometimes I receive an error message stating that the length of a clause is greater than an implementation-defined restriction (e.g., 500 characters). What kind(s) of mistakes might cause this error message?*

A: This kind of error can be caused by accidentally leaving out the final, terminating quote of a quoted string, or leaving out the end of comment designator ("*/").

Q: *What is the difference between the failure condition and the error condition?*

A: The failure condition is raised when a negative return code is returned from a command; the error condition is indicated when a nonzero, positive return code is returned from a command.

Q: *What function may I use that would enable a negative number to compare equal to a positive number (i.e., the sign of a number is ignored)?*

A: The absolute value function ("ABS") returns the absolute value of a number, thus permitting a negative number to compare equal to a positive number.

Q: *What is the distinction between the "ADDRESS" function and the "SUBCOM" command?*

A: While the "ADDRESS" function returns the name of the current host command environment, the "SUBCOM" command queries the existence of a specified host command environment within the context of the language processor environment that is currently active. As an example, the list of the host command environments that are available from the MVS/TSO language processor environment might be very different than the possible host command environments within the VM/CMS language processor environment.

Q: *The following two lines*

```
SAY "This is the ti",
"me to say goodbye";
```

result in "This is the ti me to say goodbye". I do not understand why the word "time" has a blank in the middle of the word, since I continued the above statement properly.

A: The REXX continuation character, a comma, is physically replaced by a blank during execution. The concatenation operator may be used to correct this problem.

Q: *What is the distinction between the following two code fragments:*

```
CALL xyz ... ;            CALL xyz ... ;

   ...                       ...

xyz: ...                  xyz: PROCEDURE ... ;
```

A: The two examples are actually very different in practice. When a "PROCE-DURE" instruction is used, the variables utilized within the procedure are protected, and will not cause a reference to the calling routine's variables. This, of course, can be deliberately negated by using the "EXPOSE" operand of the "PROCEDURE" instruction.

Q: *Internal labels may specify the same name as a REXX built-in function. For example, I wrote an exec where an internal function that I coded was named "SUBSTR". I then noticed that I could not invoke the "SUBSTR" built-in function any more within this particular exec. How can you notify the REXX interpreter to invoke a built-in function, even though there is a label with the same name as the function, within the given exec?*

A: The specification of a function name in quotes will force the REXX interpreter to treat that function call as a call to the built-in function and not a reference to the user-coded function with the same name.

```
part = 'SUBSTR'(whole,2,3);
```

Q: *How can you determine the number of arguments passed to a given routine?*

A: The function ARG, without any arguments specified, returns the number of arguments passed to a given routine:

```
counter = ARG();
```

Q: *Why would one use a seed with the "RANDOM" function when testing an exec?*

A: When invoking the "RANDOM" function, the specification of a seed guarantees a repeatable sequence of quasi-random numbers being generated. A repeatable sequence of numbers facilitates the process of debugging the program.

Q: *If the "WORDS(arg_string)" function returns a zero, what is then indicated about the passed argument string?*

A: If the "WORDS" function returns a zero, this implies that the passed argument string is either all blank(s) or is the null character string. This function returns the number of blank-delimited words in the argument string.

Q: *I am creating an indeterminate number of compound variables (i.e., data.1, data.2, . . . , data.n). Later on, in an indexed loop, I want to process all of the created variables. The problem that I am having is that I do not keep track of the number of created compound variables. How can I test, within my processing loop, whether or not a given compound variable was created and assigned a value?*

A: When dealing with compound symbols, the "SYMBOL" function can be invaluable. This function will return the string "LIT" if a given variable has never been assigned a value (or was the object of a "DROP" instruction) or the string "VAR" if a given variable is currently in use.

Q: *What action would a "PARSE PULL" instruction without a template perform?*

A: A "PARSE PULL" instruction without a template will, in effect, discard the read string. This technique can be used to ignore queued input or terminal user input.

Q: *What is the purpose of the following "PARSE" instruction?*

```
PARSE VAR string1 . string1;
```

A: This particular "PARSE" instruction will process the value of a variable, deleting the first word of that value and then assigning the shortened string to the same input variable. This will have the same result as the following function call:

```
string1 = DELWORD(string1,1,1);
```

Q: *When would the "VALUE" function normally be used?*

A: The "VALUE" function is used when there is a need to return the value of a variable whose name is dynamically constructed:

```
x='1'; y='2'; z='3';
sample = 'y';
say VALUE(sample);  /* Displays "2" */
```

Q: *What is the distinction between the DO loop conditional phrases "WHILE" and "UNTIL"?*

A: The "WHILE" condition is evaluated at the top of a loop, after the control variable has been stepped. The "UNTIL" condition is evaluated at the bottom of a loop, before the control variable has been stepped.

11

The RS/6000 and AIX

Scott Boyajian

Introduction

The IBM RISC System/6000 was introduced in February 1990. This family of computers, commonly known as the RS/6000, was primarily distinguished from other IBM products by its implementation of AIX, IBM's version of the UNIX operating system, and by its advanced RISC processor technology. Initially targeted for engineering and scientific uses, the RS/6000 has been embraced by the commercial market as well as the technical community. In 1991 and 1992, the RS/6000 was IBM's fastest-growing product family. AIX, or Advanced Interactive Executive, is the RS/6000's UNIX operating system. The original version of UNIX was developed in the late 1960s by AT&T's Bell Laboratories. During the 1970s and 1980s, AT&T freely licensed UNIX to academic institutions and the operating system became popular throughout the research community. Many universities, most notably the University of California at Berkeley and the Massachusetts Institute of Technology, licensed UNIX and developed extensions to it that remain popular today in AIX and in other commercial implementations of the operating system. AIX Version 3 Release 2, the latest release of AIX for the RS/6000, was announced in January 1992.

RISC, which stands for Reduced Instruction Set Computing, is the processor architecture at the heart of the RS/6000. The RISC architecture was pioneered by IBM scientists in the mid-1970s in an effort to boost processor performance. RISC processors execute a set of machine instructions that is smaller and simpler than more traditional advanced processors with their large, complex instruction sets. Reduced instruction complexity allows the processor to operate at high speeds. IBM calls the RS/6000's RISC architecture POWER, which is purportedly short for Performance Optimized with Enhanced RISC.

Today the RS/6000 product family consists of three major lines: desktop, deskside, and rack-mounted. The primary differentiating factor between these lines is expandability in memory, disk storage, and input/output adapters. Within each RS/6000 line are machines with a variety of processor speeds and standard equipment configurations. See Table 11-1, "The RS/6000 Table," for a summary of current RS/6000 models. IBM offers a variety of memory and disk storage expansion options for the RS/6000. Additional optional storage devices include CD-ROM drives and tape drives in 4-mm, 8-mm, ¼-inch, and ½-inch formats. The RS/6000 is commonly configured with the components of a graphics console: keyboard, mouse, color graphics display, and display adapter. A myriad of available communications adapters enable connectivity to various types of local and wide area networks and to hundreds of asynchronous devices.

AIX includes a number of enhancements that make UNIX easier to use. Prominent among these are two software components: InfoExplorer and SMIT, the Systems Management Interface Toolkit. InfoExplorer is used to search a vast library of on-line publications and help information. SMIT provides menus that guide the user through a wide variety of administrative functions. AIX Windows Environment/6000 is a popular software add-on that provides a graphical user interface for AIX.

The AIX operating system includes support for industry-standard TCP/IP communications protocols. Because TCP/IP has been implemented on a vast array of computer systems, it is often a good means of establishing connectivity with an RS/6000. Other software available from IBM for AIX includes support for SNA connectivity to mainframe computers and for Novell Netware server support.

Applications running on the RS/6000 today vary widely. A major United States national laboratory uses a cluster of high-end RS/6000s for computation-intensive basic research. A large financial securities firm is building a network of hundreds of RS/6000s to perform analysis and manage operations at its branches around the

Table 11-1. The RS/6000 Table

Description	POWER processor (MHz)	Standard memory (MB)	Standard disk (MB)	Input/ output slots
POWERstation M20	33	16	0	1
POWERstation/POWERserver 220	33	16	0	2
POWERstation/POWERserver 340	33	16	160	4
POWERstation 355	42	16	400	1
POWERstation/POWERserver 360	50	16	400	4
POWERstation 365	50	16	400	1
POWERstation/POWERserver 370	62.5	32	400	4
POWERstation 375	62.5	32	400	1
POWERstation/POWERserver 530H	33	32	400	7
POWERstation/POWERserver 570	50	32	2000	8
POWERstation/POWERserver 580	62.5	64	2000	8
POWERserver 970B	50	128	4000	8
POWERserver 980B	62.5	128	4000	16

world. Many customers use the RS/6000 for computer-aided design, engineering, and manufacturing. Academic institutions and government agencies make up a large segment of the RS/6000 user base, but business customers are now a growing majority as more commercial applications become available for AIX. Recent corporate trends toward downsizing (moving applications from mainframes to smaller computers) and the adoption of open systems (computers that conform to industrywide standards) have also attracted the business world to the RS/6000.

Terminology

AIX: IBM's second-generation version of the UNIX operating system.

POWER: IBM's second-generation superscalar RISC processor architecture. Stands for Performance Optimized with Enhanced RISC.

RISC: Pronounced like "risk," stands for Reduced Instruction Set Computing, and describes a computer processor architecture pioneered by IBM researcher John Cocke in the mid-1970s and adapted for commercial use by IBM and other computer manufacturers.

UNIX: An operating system first developed by AT&T's Bell Laboratories in the late 1960s which many computer vendors have licensed and adapted.

Questions and Answers

The IBM RISC System/6000 family of computers combines powerful RISC processor technology with AIX, IBM's "industrial-strength" version of the UNIX operating system. Questions the interviewer might ask range from general background on the product line to hardware and software specifics.

Q: *What is IBM's UNIX workstation called?*
A: IBM's UNIX-based RISC product family is called the RISC System/6000, or RS/6000. Although the RS/6000 family includes rack-mounted computers capable of supporting hundreds of users, many RS/6000s are sold as single-user workstations.

Q: *What operating system does the RS/6000 run?*
A: The RS/6000 runs AIX, IBM's version of the UNIX operating system.

Q: *What is the difference between UNIX and AIX?*
A: UNIX is an operating system first developed by AT&T's Bell Laboratories in the late 1960s. Since then, many computer vendors have written versions of UNIX to run on their systems. IBM's name for its version of UNIX is AIX. AIX is UNIX for IBM RS/6000, PS/2, and System/390 computers.

Q: *What is RISC?*
A: RISC, pronounced like "risk," stands for Reduced Instruction Set Computing. It describes a computer processor architecture pioneered by IBM

researcher John Cocke in the mid-1970s and adapted for commercial use by IBM and other computer manufacturers.

Q: *What are the benefits of RISC?*

A: Before the development of RISC, improvements to computer processors often involved increasing instruction-set complexity. Programmers would take advantage of the improvements by writing assembly programs with the complex instruction set. RISC processors use a much smaller number of instructions. With RISC, complex operations often require multiple assembly instructions. Because the processor design is simplified, however, improvements in overall CPU performance are easier to achieve.

Q: *How is RISC implemented in the RS/6000?*

A: The RS/6000 utilizes a second-generation superscalar RISC processor architecture named POWER. The POWER chip set has been enhanced to contain a 32K instruction cache and a 64K data cache at speeds up to 62.5 MHz on the high-end 580 and 980 RS/6000 models. On the entry M20 and 220 RS/6000 models, a single-chip 33-MHz POWER implementation is used.

Q: *Why is the RS/6000's POWER processor architecture referred to as "superscalar"?*

A: The RS/6000's POWER processor architecture was designed to enable more than one operation to execute in every clock cycle. While the actual number of machine instructions to execute in a clock cycle depends on instruction type and execution order, the POWER architecture allows as many as five independent operations to take place at once. Thus, it is considered a superscalar architecture.

Q: *What is the POWER PC?*

A: POWER PC is a single-chip implementation of the POWER architecture. The POWER PC is being jointly developed by IBM, Motorola, and Apple. It is expected to be used in computers built by IBM, Apple, and other companies, beginning in 1994.

Q: *Describe the RS/6000 Model M20.*

A: The RS/6000 Model M20 is a low-cost diskless workstation. The M20 utilizes a 33-MHz single-chip POWER processor in a system unit with an integrated 17-inch color monitor. It comes standard with 16 MB of memory (expandable to 64 MB), integrated SCSI and Ethernet, one Micro Channel input/output slot, Gt1 graphics adapter, keyboard, and mouse. Licenses for AIX/6000 and AIX Windows Environment/6000 are included.

Q: *Describe the RS/6000 "3×5 series": Models 355, 365, and 375.*

A: The RS/6000 3×5 series includes desktop technical workstations bundled with 400-MB internal disk drive (expandable to 2 GB), keyboard, mouse, Gt3i graphics adapter, and 16- or 19-inch display. Models 355, 365, and 375 are built around a POWER processor running at 42, 50, and 62.5 MHz, respectively. They come standard with 16 MB of memory for Models 355 and 365, and 32 MB memory for Model 375 (all models are expandable to 128 MB), integrated SCSI and Ethernet, and two Micro Channel input/output slots (one is used by the Gt3i). Licenses for AIX/6000 and AIX Windows Environment/6000 are included.

Q: *Describe the RS/6000 "3×0 series": Models 340, 360, and 370.*

A: The RS/6000 3×0 series includes desktop workstation servers bundled with 400-MB internal disk drive (expandable to 2 GB). Models 340, 360, and 370 are built around a POWER processor running at 33, 50, and 62.5 MHz, respectively. They come standard with 16 MB of memory for Models 340 and 360, and 32 MB of memory for Model 370 (all models are expandable to 256 MB), integrated SCSI and Ethernet, and four Micro Channel input/output slots.

Q: *What is the purpose of the shell in AIX?*

A: The AIX user's primary method of interaction with the operating system is the shell. The shell serves as the AIX command line and serves as the default means of standard input and output.

Q: *What are shellscripts?*

A: A shellscript is a set of commands written to be interpreted by an AIX shell. Shells often contain basic programming constructs, such as conditional loops, and are frequently used as rudimentary programming environments. Many AIX system operations may be automated by writing shellscripts.

Q: *Name the shells that AIX supports.*

A: AIX supports the Korn shell, the C shell, and the Bourne shell.

Q: *What is the default AIX shell?*

A: The default AIX shell is the Korn shell.

Q: *What high-level programming language compiler is included with the AIX operating system?*

A: IBM bundles a C compiler with the AIX operating system. About 95 percent of the AIX kernel was developed using the C language. Also included with AIX are a system assembler and the capability of writing interpreted shellscripts.

Q: *What programming languages are available for the RS/6000?*

A: In addition to the native AIX C compiler, IBM provides a number of programming languages for the RS/6000, including FORTRAN, C++, COBOL, Pascal, and Ada. A wide variety of programming languages is available for the RS/6000 from independent software vendors.

Q: *What kind of graphical user interface is available on the RS/6000?*

A: IBM sells a version of the industry-standard X Window System called AIX Windows Environment/6000. Included with this package is the AIX Windows Desktop, an icon-based graphical front end to the operating system.

Q: *Are three-dimensional graphics supported on the RS/6000?*

A: The optional 3D feature of the AIX Windows Environment/6000 supports several 3D graphics programming interfaces, including graPHIGS, PEX, and GL. Two families of graphics interfaces for the RS/6000 support 3D graphics: the Gt4 adapter family and the GTO graphics subsystem.

Q: *What size color displays are available for the RS/6000?*

A: IBM sells 16-, 19-, and 23-inch color displays for the RS/6000. The entry model M20 has a built-in 17-inch color display.

Q: *What is the graphics resolution of the RS/6000?*

A: All IBM graphics adapters for the RS/6000 are capable of supporting 1280×1024-pixel resolution.

Q: *How many colors can the RS/6000 display?*

A: All color RS/6000 graphics adapters from IBM support 8-bit color and can display 256 colors. A 24-bit feature available for the GT4 and GTO adapters enables the display of 16.7 million colors.

Q: *What kind of system input/output bus does the RS/6000 use?*

A: The RS/6000 uses the Micro Channel input/output bus. It is an enhanced version of the PS/2 Micro Channel bus. The latest RS/6000 models are equipped with XIO circuitry that doubles the peak Micro Channel data transfer rate to 40 MB/second and to 80 MB/second for Streaming Data Procedure transfers.

Q: *What internal disk storage options are available for desktop RS/6000s?*

A: All current desktop RS/6000 models include integrated SCSI adapter circuitry. The entry model M20 was designed without space allowance for internal disk storage. The model 220 may be configured with one 3½-inch disk drive. All other current desktop RS/6000 models can accommodate up to two internal 3½-inch disk drives. IBM supplies 3½-inch SCSI disk drives in 160-MB, 400-MB, and 1.0-GB capacities.

Q: *What types of tape drives are available for the RS/6000?*

A: IBM offers internal and external SCSI tape drives in several formats, including 8-mm, 4-mm, ¼-inch, and 9-track formats. Third parties supply tape drives for the RS/6000 in these and other formats.

Q: *Name an exclusive feature of AIX/6000 that protects file system integrity in the event of a sudden power loss.*

A: The Journaled File System, or JFS, is a standard feature of AIX. JFS helps protect file system integrity by keeping a log, or journal, of all changes to the file system. Physical file addresses in UNIX are kept track of through use of a set of "metadata" known as the *inode table*. In most other UNIX implementations, it is possible for this metadata to become corrupted in the event of an interruption in power. AIX avoids this problem through use of its Journaled File System.

Q: *What is the current version and release of AIX/6000?*

A: At publication time, Version 3 Release 2 is the current level of AIX/6000.

Q: *What is the purpose of an AIX device driver?*

A: An AIX device driver is software which enables an input/output device to interact with the operating system and with application programs. The device driver serves as a layer between hardware and software, shielding applications and the operating system from details specific to a device's hardware implementation.

Q: *What is InfoExplorer?*

A: InfoExplorer is the standard AIX help system. It provides access to on-line documentation for the operating system and for many AIX extensions and application programs. AIX users may find help information with Info-Explorer by following a hierarchy of menus or by specifying search words.

Q: *What is SMIT?*

A: SMIT, or the Systems Management Interface Toolkit, is a standard AIX component that aids in performing systems administration tasks. For example, SMIT can be used to configure input/output devices, to partition storage space, and to add new users to the system. SMIT is a menu-based front end to many UNIX commands.

Q: *What is an Xstation?*

A: The Xstation, IBM's X terminal product, is a graphical display connected to an RS/6000 via local area network or a serial connection.

Q: *How does an Xstation work?*

A: The Xstation is dependent on a network-connected RS/6000, and its specialized processor is only capable of running graphical user interface code known as the "Xserver." AIX and any application software accessed from an Xstation actually executes on the host RS/6000. An AIX extension called Xstation Manager/6000 is required on the host RS/6000.

Q: *Describe the Xstation Model 150.*

A: The Xstation Model 150 is a high-performance X terminal that can be attached to an Ethernet or Token Ring local area network. It comes equipped with 2 MB of video memory standard and 6 MB of system memory standard (expandable to 22 MB).

Q: *Is the Xstation-RS/6000 connection proprietary?*

A: No, the Xstation Manager/6000 software and the Xstation itself use industry-standard TCP/IP services, including bootp, tftp, and X Windows. It is possible to connect non-IBM X terminals to an RS/6000 and to connect IBM Xstations to non-IBM UNIX workstations.

Q: *Name three types of local area networks supported on the RS/6000.*

A: The RS/6000 supports local area network adapters that enable connectivity to Ethernet, Token Ring, and Fiber Distributed Data Interchange (FDDI) networks.

Q: *What are the functions of AIX NetView/6000?*

A: AIX NetView/6000 is IBM's Simple Network Management Protocol (SNMP) domain network management software for the RS/6000. It is capable of monitoring network-attached TCP/IP devices and is capable of managing network-attached SNMP-enabled devices. The software provides a graphical user interface and an optional bridge for forwarding alerts to mainframe-based NetView.

Q: *What is AIX PC Simulator/6000?*

A: PC Simulator/6000 is an optional AIX extension that allows the user to run many DOS programs in a nonnative, or "simulated," environment.

Q: *What 3270 terminal emulators are available for the AIX/6000?*

A: The tn3270 emulator is a standard component of AIX. It requires the 3270 host system to have TCP/IP. IBM also sells the 3270 Host Connection emulator and SNA Services/6000.

Q: *What is AIX DCE?*

A: AIX DCE is based on the Open Software Foundation's Distributed Computing Environment. DCE is a set of client/server foundation services that enable the development of distributed applications. These distributed applications may function over different types of computers that implement the core set of DCE services.

Q: *What is Encina for AIX/6000?*

A: Encina for AIX/6000 runs on top of AIX DCE and provides a set of tools for development of transactional applications that require high levels of data integrity.

Q: *What is CICS/6000?*

A: CICS is the computer industry's most popular transaction processing system. CICS/6000 is a transaction monitor that runs on top of Encina for AIX/6000. It allows the transfer of skills and applications from existing CICS systems to the RS/6000.

Q: *What is AIX High Availability Cluster Multi-Processing/6000?*

A: AIX High Availability Cluster Multi-Processing/6000, or HACMP/6000, is software that enables a backup RS/6000 application server to automatically take over the clients of a primary RS/6000 application server in the event of a failure.

Q: *How does a "diskless" RS/6000 work?*

A: A diskless RS/6000 workstation has no local storage media. It is completely dependent on a network-attached machine for loading AIX and applications software. Unlike on an X terminal, however, the applications run locally on the diskless machine's processor.

For the next four questions, assume that a company is evaluating the purchase of one or more RS/6000 workstations to perform a set of office applications (e.g., desktop publishing, electronic mail) for a six-person workgroup. The applications require the AIXwindows Environment/6000 graphical user interface.

Q: *Is it necessary to purchase fully functional RS/6000 workstations for all six workers? If not, what are some alternative configurations?*

A: The company could purchase one RS/6000 to function as a nondedicated server. The other five stations could be attached via a local area network. These could be diskless RS/6000 workstations, Xstations, or personal computers with Xserver software.

Q: *What would some pros and cons of diskless RS/6000 workstations be in this setup?*

A: On the pro side, each user would have the performance benefit of having a local RS/6000 processor on his or her desk. Another benefit is the absence of software maintenance overhead required at the remote workstation. On the con side is cost: office applications don't typically use a great deal of processor power, and it may be difficult to justify the expense of five diskless RS/6000 workstations and the requisite five AIX licenses.

Q: *What would some pros and cons of Xstations be in this setup?*

A: On the pro side, Xstations require no software maintenance overhead except for some minor configuration at the server. Typical Xstation cons involve performance bottlenecks because all application software runs on the host workstation. Actual performance in this scenario will depend on characteristics of the selected applications.

Q: *What would some pros and cons of personal computers be in this setup?*

A: On the pro side, personal computers with Xserver software would give the users access to the workstation-based applications and simultaneously provide the capability of running local PC applications. On the con side, performance of PC-based Xservers can vary. Screen resolution on personal computers is usually lower than on their RS/6000 counterparts. This can make running X windows-based applications difficult.

For the next three questions, assume that the following three computers are connected together on an Ethernet:

- A Compaq Deskpro running DOS 5.0 and Windows 3.1
- An IBM PS/2 running Novell Netware 386 Version 3.11
- An IBM RS/6000 running AIX 3.2

The Deskpro uses the Windows IPX driver to access files on the IBM PS/2 but has no access to files on the RS/6000. There are several ways such access could be enabled while maintaining the Deskpro-PS/2 client/server relationship.

Q: *Describe a way to enable Deskpro-RS/6000 file access by adding software only to the Deskpro.*

A: Load a network protocol driver that supports both IPX (for Netware connectivity) and TCP/IP (for AIX connectivity). One popular software package that could help accomplish this is Novell LAN Workplace for DOS. Once the IPX-TCP/IP driver has been installed on the Deskpro, it will be necessary to configure NFS (TCP/IP's remote file-sharing component) on both the Deskpro and the RS/6000.

Q: *Describe a way to enable Deskpro-RS/6000 file access by adding software only to the RS/6000.*

A: Installation of IBM's Netware for AIX/6000 (Netware/6000) program product will enable the RS/6000 to provide file-sharing services via the Deskpro's IPX driver. Once Netware/6000 is installed and configured, the RS/6000 will appear to the Deskpro user as a second Netware file server. In addition to providing file-sharing services, Netware/6000 will allow the Deskpro user to print or initiate a terminal session to the RS/6000.

Q: *Describe a way to enable Deskpro-RS/6000 file access by adding software only to the PS/2.*

A: Installing Novell's NFS Netware Loadable Module (NLM) on the PS/2 will allow the Netware 386 file server to mount AIX file systems residing on the RS/6000. The Deskpro user will be able to log in to the Netware file server and to access these file systems as Netware volumes.

References

1. *Getting Started: Using RISC System/6000,* IBM Corporation, 1992, IBM publication number GC23-2377.

2. Jim Hoskins, *IBM RISC System/6000: A Business Perspective,* John Wiley & Sons, New York City, 1991.

3. IBM publication number GA23-2674.

4. *RISC System/6000 System Overview,* IBM Corporation, 1992, IBM publication number GC23-2406.

12
Oracle

James Fee Langendoen

Introduction

Oracle, a Relational Database Management System (RDBMS), is a product of Oracle Corporation. Oracle is a tightly integrated set of tools and utilities supporting the core database and was introduced to the public in 1979. Oracle provides the functionality to run on dozens of diverse systems, from large IBM mainframes through mini's and Unix systems right down to PCs. Applications which had been written for one hardware platform can be easily ported to Oracle on any of the other supported hardware platforms. In addition, Oracle has made great strides in connectivity issues, so that Oracle running on a VAX can share information with Oracle running on a SUN. In addition, Oracle uses an SQL "superset" of the ANSI standard called SQL*Plus. Since SQL*Plus is based on the ANSI standard, Oracle is able to share information with other ANSI-compliant relational database management systems.

In order to provide a more complete environment, Oracle also provides a "front-end" product called SQL*Forms. SQL*Forms makes it possible to develop the entire application using only the Oracle toolset. SQL*Forms provides a means to create a set of fields and constant text which displays data to the user so that data can be entered or altered in the database tables. It is important to note that it is SQL*Forms that provides the transportability of Oracle applications. SQL*Forms uses a concept known as *triggers* to perform the functions necessary for data manipulation and validation. A trigger is a procedure executed on the occurrence of certain events. Events are categorized into several classes, each capable of performing the procedure specified at the occurrence of the event. For example, a procedure can be executed when entering an SQL*Form; another may be specified to occur upon leaving the form. Each of these triggers is given a name and a level at which it operates. Triggers can be set for: before or after executing a query, insert, update or delete, or user-defined. Developing good trigger logic is necessary for a successful Oracle implementation. To this end, Oracle has developed a further extension to the SQL language, PL/SQL. PL/SQL is a programming language that augments the power of SQL with procedural capabilities. This allows the user to take advantage of procedural constructs such as branching and looping in the creation of the trigger logic for SQL*Forms. Oracle has also developed SQL*Menu, a utility similar in structure to SQL*Forms, which produces menus and menu trees that allow the user to navigate through Oracle applications.

More recently, Oracle has expanded its available toolset to include a Computer-Aided Software Engineering (CASE) tool. It is actually a set of integrated tools, CASE*Designer and CASE*Generator, developed around an Oracle database, CASE*Dictionary. The CASE tool takes a project from early strategy and planning through the analysis phase and into design and construction. The output is an Oracle application in SQL*Forms and SQL*Menu with triggers in place to enforce the integrity constraints expressed by the data model detailed during analysis.

At last count, Oracle was available for about 80 hardware platforms. Rather than listing them, suffice it to say that Oracle is likely to be available for virtually all normal commercial systems.

Oracle's most current DBMS offering is Oracle7.

SQL*Menu and SQL*Net.   SQL*Menu is a developer's tool for creating a hierarchical structure of menus for accessing SQL*Forms applications. In addition to the inherent security of an RDBMS, SQL*Menu allows the developer an additional layer of security by restricting a user's navigation to only those areas of privilege.

SQL*Net is Oracle's networking protocol for addressing the world outside the DBMS. This capability also allows Oracle, in a Netware environment, to communicate in a DecNet environment.

Questions and Answers

Major Features

Q: *Describe Oracle.*

A: Oracle is an integrated set of tools and utilities supporting a core database. The central feature is the database product. The database provides only the back-end services. A front-end or user interface is still required to allow an end user to connect to the database and to manipulate the data. To this end, Oracle uses tools like SQL*Forms, SQL*Plus, PL/SQL, and the PRO* <language> for build applications. The choice of combinations of these tools is used to develop a user interface appropriate to the target environment.

Q: *What type of data manipulation capability does Oracle provide?*

A: Oracle provides SQL*Forms as a means to create fields and text which can be displayed so that data can then be entered or altered. The form interface is developed in SQL*Forms or may be generated from CASE tool with CASE*Generator.

Q: *What other "languages" does Oracle provide?*

A: Oracle provides the PRO* series of language programs, PRO*ADA, PRO*C, PRO*COBOL, PRO*FORTRAN, PRO*PASCAL, and PRO*PL/1.

Q: *What American National Standards Institute (ANSI) standard language does Oracle use?*

A: Oracle's SQL*Plus is based on the ANSI standard SQL language.

Q: *How "portable" are applications developed with Oracle?*

A: Portability, the ability to take an application from one hardware platform and move it to run on another hardware platform without extensive rework, has been a key feature of Oracle. Due to the consistent RDBMS structure, regardless of platform, it is possible to develop a mainframe application on one system and port it to another.

Q: *To which types of hardware platforms is Oracle limited?*

A: (This is a trick question.) The fact is that Oracle supports virtually all major platforms.

Q: *What is Oracle's optimizer?*

A: Oracle's optimizer is the part of the RDBMS kernel which "reads" a query and decides on the best manner of executing the request based on tables and indexes.

Q: *How does Oracle store information?*

A: Oracle stores information in tables. Each table has one or more columns which describe it. (These are the implementation of entities and their attributes.) The data is stored in rows. All Oracle's internal information is stored in tables (information on users, tables, columns, etc.).

Q: *How do you make a table?*

A: Creating a table in Oracle is a process of describing (in SQL*Plus) the information required by Oracle. You would log in to SQL*Plus with your Oracle username/password and issue the CREATE TABLE command followed by the table name. Then you would detail each column name, datatype, and column constraint (e.g., NOT NULL), followed by any table constraint for the column(s) (e.g., UNIQUE, PRIMARY KEY).

Example
```
CREATE TABLE [user.]tablename
    ({column_element | table_constraints}
    [,column_element | table_constraint} ] ...)
```

Q: *How do you delete a table?*

A: The command for deleting a table is DROP TABLE. This also drops all indexes and any GRANTs. Only a DBA may drop another user's table.

Q: *What is needed to make a column?*

A: Creating a column is done either when creating a table or altering a table to add a column. What is necessary (besides any table information) is the column name, the column's datatype (e.g., CHAR, INT, DATE), default (value), and any column constraint (NOT NULL, etc.).

Example

```
column_name datatype [DEFAULT expression] [column_constraint]
```

Q: *What must the DBA do to allow a user the right to create tables?*
A: The user must be granted RESOURCE by the DBA.

Example

GRANT RESOURCE to user identified by password.

Q: *Describe NULL as used by Oracle.*
A: In Oracle a NULL value is unknown, irrelevant, or not meaningful. Any datatype can be of a null value (unless the column_constraint is NOT NULL). It is important to know that NULL in a numeric datatype is not a zero value. Because NULL represents an unknown value, two columns, each having a null value, are not equal to each other. This also means that logical and arithmetic operators do not work with NULL.

Q: *What is the purpose of an index?*
A: An index is primarily used to facilitate the access to large sets of data. By creating an index, the developer assists the RDBMS by minimizing the number of complete table scans. For example, if there is an index on a column LAST_NAME, and a query is entered for a list of last names beginning with the letter "G," the RDBMS would utilize the index's pointers to the necessary row(s) rather than scan the entire table for values which satisfied the query.

Q: *What is deadlock?*
A: A deadlock could occur in the case where two or more processes cannot complete their transaction because each process has locked the resource that the other process needed to complete its processing. Although rare, Oracle detects and resolves deadlocks by rolling back one of the processes.

Q: *What are DML statements?*
A: DML stands for Data Manipulation Language, which is one of three subsets of SQL. The others are DDL (Data Definition Language) and DCL (Data Control Language). Examples of DML commands are SELECT, INSERT, UPDATE, and DELETE.

Q: *What is the purpose of the table DUAL in Oracle?*
A: DUAL is an Oracle worktable with only one row and one column in it. The purpose for its existence is to facilitate some calculations and functions which are not dependent upon the columns in a table. So the query:

```
SELECT user from DUAL;
```

would return the current Username.

Q: *What is ROWID?*

A: ROWID is a pseudo column for a table with the logical address for each row. It is unique within the database and can be used in a SELECT statement or in a WHERE clause but cannot be changed by INSERT, UPDATE, or DELETE.

Q: *What is a synonym and how is it used?*

A: A synonym is another name given to a table or view for which you have access. It is made with the CREATE SYNONYM statement and results in an easier way of referencing the table.

The command looks like:

```
CREATE SYNONYM new_name for owner_name.table_name;
```

Oracle Tools

SQL*Forms

Q: *What kind of development environment is provided by Oracle?*

A: SQL*Forms is the tool used for the development of its forms-based interface. It provides the developer with an environment capable of design layout, entering or modifying trigger logic, compiling, testing, debugging, and generation of forms. This is also the tool used for modifying an existing form. By breaking down a form to its constituent parts, SQL*Forms allows you to navigate through the various parts, such as blocks, fields, and triggers. In this way, logic can be attached at any or all the various levels to make the form respond to the different design needs. (For example, validation, navigation, and security can be built into the form.) The tool (also a form environment) also provides a screen painter for adding text and the positioning of fields.

Q: *What two types of files are used in forms development?*

A: Two of the most important files are the [filename].INP and [filename].FRM files. INP files are analogous to source code in that they contain database information, trigger and procedure logic for a form in a text file. FRM files contain the compiled form.

Q: *Describe the type of information that you would find in an INP file.*

A: An INP file contains all the information necessary to make a form function, but in a character format (unlike the binary FRM file which is executed). An INP file contains the listing of all table usage, fields, globals, procedures, and triggers. The listing is hierarchic in nature, working from the form level down to the block and then field level. If comments have been provided they will be included. All constituent parts of the form are defined. Procedural logic is listed and trigger logic is recorded for each type at each level it occurs. Fields are defined and their constraints listed. Much like source code, the INP file allows you to follow the logic of a form.

Q: *What is a "trigger"?*

A: A trigger is a procedure executed on the occurrence of certain events. Events are categorized into several classes, each capable of performing the procedure specified at the occurrence of the event. For example, a procedure can be executed when entering an SQL*Form; another may be specified to occur upon leaving the form. Each of these triggers is given a name and a level at which it operates. Triggers can be set for before or after executing a query, insert, update or delete, or user-defined. Triggers may also be attached to a key command. An example of this is when a user hits the COMMIT key: the developer can attach logic to be performed prior to or subsequent to the commit.

Q: *At which three "levels" do triggers function?*

A: Triggers can be set to function:

1. At the form level, which means that they are active throughout the entire form

2. At the block level, which means that they will have meaning only within the block for which they are assigned

3. To a specific field, in which case they will be active only in that field

   There is an order of precedence for the levels, in which the more specific trigger has precedence over the more general (i.e., a block trigger takes precedence over a form trigger and a field trigger takes precedence over either a block or form-level trigger).

Q: *What navigational features can triggers provide?*

A: Triggers may be attached to a defined key at any level (form, block, or field). It is useful to be able to add to or redefine a key's function. In this way, for example, a user hitting the KEY-NEXTFIELD key in the last field of a block can be navigated to the first field of the next block without additional keystrokes. Similarly, upon reaching the end of a form, they can be returned to the "top" of the form.

Q: *Which validation procedures can triggers be used for?*

A: A trigger may contain conditional logic so that, upon entering data (or leaving a field, or based upon data types, etc.), the form can monitor the data entry before the attempt is made to commit it. This can prevent a multirecord commit attempt from failing because the database rejects a single item. This conditional logic can enforce items not covered by the field characteristics.

Q: *What is a procedure?*

A: A procedure is a saved set of commands (SQL, PL/SQL, or both) which can be called.

Q: *Why does Oracle use a key's function as a naming convention?*

A: Since Oracle is available on many different platforms, it is far easier to express what the key does than it is to rewrite the function performed for each platform. In this way, a user on a DEC terminal using PF keys has the same abilities as a user on a PC.

Q: *What is Page 0 (zero)?*

A: Page 0 is the address Oracle uses for the nondisplayed fields of a form.

SQL*Forms Application Questions. Refer to Figure 12-1. This is a simple form with seven fields visible and a series of questions as to how to modify (enhance) it. Consider this form to be a quick sketch done by the sales manager who has a basic understanding of Oracle and SQL*Forms. They want a tracking-and-query system for returns of goods sold. Block 1 represents a new table for the system. Returns_Report will need:

- A unique number for each report entered (field 1)
- The salesperson filing the report (field 2)
- The date the report was filed (field 3)
- The type of product complaint (field 4)
- A description of the complaint (field 5)

Block 2 represents the two fields needed from the Product_Information table:

- The product number (field 6)
- The product description (field 7)

Sample COMPLAINT Form

Block #1—Returns__Report

Report Number	Salesperson	Date Filed
Field #1	Field #2	Field #3

Product Complaint

Field #4

Complaint Description

Field #5

Block #2—Product__Information

Product Number involved in Complaint

Field #6

Product Description

Field #7

Figure 12-1. Sample form.

Q: *How would you make field 1 an incrementing number starting at 1000?*

A: You can build the logic necessary or you can create a SEQUENCE. A SEQUENCE command would look like this:

```
CREATE SEQUENCE report_number increment by 1 start with 1000;
```

Q: *Field 2, "Salesperson," should be made to provide the defined scope of current salespeople from which the user can choose without editing. How would you provide that?*

A: The users should be able to pick from a list of values. In order to do this, a table of the values has to be created. The "List of Values" table also provides validation for entries which a user might type in, without first doing a lookup. (*Note:* If the table referred to in a lookup is not the base table for the block, the user cannot update, insert, or delete data in it from this location.)

Q: *Where will the cursor go when the KEY-NEXTFIELD is hit to exit field 5?*

A: The default navigation would return the cursor to the first enterable field of the current block; in this case, that would be field 1.

Q: *What types of constraints might you use in SQL*Forms for field 5, "Complaint Description"?*

A: This field is a description, so it would be of datatype CHAR. The length would be determined by the column width of the base table; however, the display length could be altered to better tailor the form's layout—possibly resulting in a scrollable field. Input would be enabled and, quite possibly, the mandatory attribute. Query would be enabled; however, it is unclear if update should be allowed. Likewise, no mention was made as to whether the field should allow mixed-case or force uppercase entry. This would also be a good time to establish the INPUT and OUTPUT MASK for the date format desired.

Q: *What is the simplest method of having the cursor go from field 5 to field 6?*

A: The navigation between field 5 and field 6 is the same as between block 1 and block 2. To navigate without the user hitting the NEXT-BLOCK key (which is a different keystroke than KEY-NEXTFIELD), the KEY-NEXTFIELD trigger in field 5 has to be modified to perform the NEXT-BLOCK function.

Q: *Describe a way to populate field 3, "Date Filed," with the current date.*

A: The date field may be populated with the system date by giving it a DEFAULT = $$DATE$$. This would allow the field to be editable in the case that the date desired differed from the current date. The date could also be inserted through a trigger which would allow the designer to prevent a user from entering the field and editing the date.

Q: *For what would you use a default WHERE clause with this form?*

A: Since it was stated that this form would be used for both data entry and query, a WHERE clause (and possibly an ORDER BY clause) would allow the designer to specify a subset of information to be retrieved upon query. This is a practical means of tailoring the form to the end-user's needs.

SQL*Reportwriter

Q: *Briefly describe SQL*Reportwriter's function.*

A: SQL*Reportwriter is the environment Oracle developed to handle report writing, formatting, and distribution. The basic program SQLREP is a menu-driven report development tool with a "fill in the blanks" style. The familiar forms type menu structure is used to enable the developer to supply standard report formats for an application. (It also facilitates the modification of existing formats.) Reportwriter provides the means to copy, rename, drop, generate, and execute reports. The output of SQL*Reportwriter is an executable .REP file.

Q: *What does the RUNREP program do?*

A: The RUNREP (run report) program executes an .REP file.

Q: *Describe a method other than SQL*Reportwriter for making a report.*

A: SQL*Plus is commonly used for interactive reports and queries. It is also capable of providing formatting capabilities using the existing Oracle command structure.

SQL*Menu

Q: *Briefly describe the SQL*Menu environment.*

A: The SQL*Menu environment utilizes a menu structure that provides the developer the capability of tying together the various forms which make up an application. Not only does SQL*Menu provide navigation but it also allows the developer to provide different privileges for differing role groups with a set of forms. SQL*Menu utilizes packaged procedures and PL/SQL to provide the developer with the ability to create application menus for a wide variety of situations.

Q: *How do you add a new user to SQL*Menu?*

A: First, enroll the user's Oracle username in SQL*Menu, and then assign the username to a role group.

SQL*Plus

Q: *Briefly describe the purpose of SQL*Plus.*

A: SQL*Plus (the program) is the command-line environment allowing a user access to Oracle through SQL or SQL*Plus (the language) commands. Ad hoc queries may be performed, databases created, modified, or dropped, files run, and a host of other functions performed outside the structure of an application. This is the primary communication medium for interfacing with the RDBMS.

Q: *How is SQL*Plus accessed?*

A: SQL*Plus is accessed by logging on to Oracle with:

```
sqlplus<username><password>
```

Q: *How is the special character % used?*

A: The % sign is used with logical operators as a match for any number of characters, including zero characters (i.e., a wildcard). An example would be:

```
WHERE last_name LIKE 'SMITH%'
```

This command would return 'SMITH', 'SMITHE', 'SMITHERS', etc.

Q: *What is an Oracle subquery?*

A: A subquery (also called the child query) is a query contained within a query. The child query must be executed in order to perform the parent query. The results of a subquery are not displayed, but only serve to allow the parent query to run.

Q: *How would you add a row to a table from the command line?*

A: You can use the INSERT command to insert one or more rows into a table with SQL*Plus. An example would look like this:

```
INSERT INTO table_name
VALUES (a list of data values);
```

When performing this type of insert, the values must be separated with commas, CHAR and DATE values must be enclosed with apostrophes, and the values must be in the same order as the columns appear when performing a SELECT statement.

Q: *How would you empty all the rows in a table without affecting the structure?*

A: The DELETE command with no WHERE clause will delete all rows, that is:

```
DELETE from tablename;
```

Q: *Describe the COMMIT and ROLLBACK commands.*

A: Insertions and other changes to tables are normally not committed until you exit from SQL*Plus (or you execute an ALTER, AUDIT, CONNECT, CREATE, DISCONNECT, DROP, GRANT, NOAUDIT, QUIT, or REVOKE). Until that time, you can see the changes if you query your tables—but other users cannot. At this point, you still have the option of performing a ROLLBACK, or undoing the changes. The COMMIT command forces the changes to the tables. Once the changes are committed, you may no longer undo them with ROLLBACK. They must be undone one at a time and any deletions must be reinserted.

Q: *What does the COUNT function do?*

A: The COUNT function counts nonnull number values, distinct number values, or the number of rows selected by a query. While COUNT does not count NULL values, it will count 0 (zero) values.

Q: *Why would you issue a CONNECT command from SQL*Forms?*

A: You would use the CONNECT command to change a user while already in SQL*Forms. This is useful when there is a difference of privileges involved. An example of this would be:

```
CONNECT username[/password] [@database]
```

CONNECT logs you off of Oracle, commits any pending changes, and then logs on the new username.

Q: *What does the @ sign do in SQL*Forms?*

A: The @ (at) sign is a command-line command for starting a file. It is similar to the START command but does not allow command-line arguments.

Q: *What does ERASE operate on?*

A: The ERASE is a packaged procedure for clearing global variables. An example is:

```
ERASE(global.variable)
```

This will erase the named global variable.

Q: *What does the NVL function do?*

A: The NVL (NULL VALUE SUBSTITUTION) function is used to substitute a true value for any NULL value found. The full command looks like this:

```
NVL(value, substitute)
```

Q: *Which function would you use to add the values in a set of data?*

A: The SUM function is used to sum all values for a group of rows. The full command would be:

```
SUM(value)
```

Languages and Commands

Q: *Describe the substring command "SUBSTR" and explain its use.*

A: The substring command is an SQL command for parsing a segment from a character string. The full command looks like this:

```
SUBSTR(string, start [,count])
```

where string is the character string, start marks the beginning of the function, and count optionally ends the function. If count is not specified, the function continues to the end of the string. An example of this would be fixed-position alphanumeric data elements (ABC1234) in which you wish to segregate the numeric value.

```
SUBSTR('ABC1234', 4) returns the string 1234
```

Q: *Describe the instring command "INSTR" and explain its use.*

A: The instring command is an SQL command for locating the position of a set of characters in a string. This function is also useful when used in conjunction with the SUBSTR function. The command format is:

```
INSTR(string, set [, start [, occurrence] ])
```

where string is the character string, set is the query string, start is the beginning of the function (optional), and occurrence is the number of times the query string appears (optional). An example of this would be finding the position of a segment in a hyphen-delimited string (breaking out a piece of an "intelligent key").

```
INSTR('ABC-1234-022-XYZ', '-', 2)  returns a position of 9
```

Note: 2 refers to the second occurrence of the character '-'.

Q: *Describe the command DECODE and what it does.*

A: The DECODE command is used to bring IF, THEN, ELSE logic to SQL. It tests for the IF value(s) and then applies the THEN value(s) when true, the ELSE value(s) if not. The full command looks like:

```
DECODE (value, IF1, THEN1 [IF2, THEN2,]. . . , ELSE)
```

Q: *What is a pseudo column?*

A: Oracle uses pseudo columns for selecting information that is not an actual column in the table. Examples of this would be USER, UID, SYSDATE, ROWNUM, ROWID, NULL, and LEVEL.

Q: *What is the proper format for the DELETE command?*

A: The DELETE command is an SQL command used to delete all rows (optionally, that satisfy a condition) from a specified table. The full command format is:

```
DELETE FROM [user.] table [@link] [alias] [WHERE condition];
```

(As a side note, Oracle V5 does not reuse the space the deleted rows occupied unless an EXPORT and IMPORT are successfully executed. In Oracle V6 and Oracle7 this space can be reused.)

Q: *Where do you find the LOOP statement in Oracle?*

A: LOOP in Oracle is a PL/SQL statement. It gives the developer the ability to utilize a procedural construct in addition to the set manipulation available through SQL. There are four kinds of LOOPs: (1) the basic LOOP (infinite), (2) the WHILE LOOP, (3) FOR counter, and (4) FOR record IN.

Q: *What is the symbol for concatenation of values and how is it used?*

A: The concatenation symbol is the vertical double bars (||). It is used to join character values into a single string.

```
'XYZ' || 'ZZY'    would result in    'XYZZZY'
```

Q: *Describe EXIT and its functions.*

A: EXIT has two functions in Oracle. In PL/SQL, it is a means of ending a LOOP, and control falls through to the statement following the LOOP. In SQL*Plus, it is the command to end a session and return the user to the operating system (or calling program, menu, etc.).

Q: *What is a BIND VARIABLE?*

A: A BIND VARIABLE is a variable in an SQL statement which must be replaced with an actual value before the statement can be executed.

Q: *What is the purpose of a CLUSTER?*

A: Oracle does not allow a user to specifically locate tables, since that is part of the function of the RDBMS. However, for the purpose of increasing performance, Oracle allows a developer to create a CLUSTER. A CLUSTER provides a means for storing data from different tables in a more easily retrievable format than if the table placement were left to the RDBMS.

Q: *Where is the maintenance release listed?*

A: Oracle places the maintenance release number in the second position of the software version number. For Oracle V6.0.13, the maintenance release is 0.

Q: *What is a time stamp?*

A: A time stamp is the date and time that a row is created or last modified.

Q: *What is a buffer used for in SQL*Plus?*

A: SQL*Plus uses a buffer (an area in computer memory) to allow editing of SQL and SQL*Plus commands.

Q: *Describe how Oracle interfaces with third-generation languages.*

A: Oracle, being a 4GL environment, sometimes must contend with existing 3GL systems. In order to allow this to occur with a minimum of difficulty, Oracle has provided a series of 3GL extensions which allow a precompiler to convert the PRO*<Language> code into a form which may then be compiled. This allows a developer to create user exits and other programs capable of accessing the Oracle database.

Oracle CASE Tools

CASE*Method, CASE*Dictionary, CASE*Designer, CASE*Generator

Q: *Which methodology does CASE*Method support?*

A: CASE*Method supports the Information Engineering methodology.

Q: *Which "Life Cycle" does CASE*Method support?*

A: CASE*Method is based upon the Business System Life Cycle. This is a top-down approach designed to partition the project into specific major stages. A refinement of the original SDLC (System Development Life Cycle), the Business System Life Cycle starts with the Strategy stage before moving into Analysis. The Business System Life Cycle also allows for iteration of tasks rather than the "Waterfall Model" of the original System Development Life Cycle.

Q: *What are the major stages of the Business System Life Cycle used by CASE*Method?*

A: There are seven stages. The first is Strategy which feeds into the second, Analysis. The third is Design, which branches and supplies both Build and User Documentation as fourth and fifth stages. They, in turn, provide the basis for the sixth stage, Transition. The seventh stage is Production.

Q: *What benefit is derived from using these stages?*

A: Any development project consists of a large number of tasks. Success of the project depends on them all being carried out. A methodical approach to breaking the project down into stages, each with clearly defined deliverables, gives greater control over the accomplishment and tracking of those tasks. The Information Engineering methodology is based upon the early stages laying the groundwork for subsequent stages.

Q: *What is the CASE*Dictionary?*

A: The CASE*Dictionary is a multiuser Oracle database designed to function as the central repository for all of the information captured through the Business System Life Cycle. This is similar to a Data Dictionary or Encyclopedia, but rather than simply recording information, CASE*Dictionary is a functioning part of an integrated toolset.

Q: *Describe Oracle's Data Dictionary.*

A: Oracle's Data Dictionary is the central source of information for the RDBMS and all the users. The information is a set of tables owned by the system (and DBAs) which is maintained by Oracle. They contain all information entered about database objects, users, privileges, events, and use. The Data Dictionary is structured to allow a DBA to query the information for system management and maintenance.

Q: *What does the CASE*Dictionary do?*

A: The CASE*Dictionary provides the focus of all the other CASE tools. It is the repository for the information gathered during each stage, passing the information on to subsequent stages. This ability to exchange information among the tools allows for a broader range of completeness and consistency checks. Since the tools integrate with the Dictionary, there is never a synchronization problem and any query will yield the project's most current state. The ability to query the CASE*Dictionary gives a developer control over the progress of a complex project.

Q: *What is CASE*Designer?*

A: CASE*Designer is a set of graphic tools used to provide a designer with the ability to model a project while automatically recording the results in the CASE*Dictionary. These tools include the Dataflow Diagrammer, the Entity Relationship Diagrammer, the Function Hierarchy Diagrammer, and the Matrix Diagrammer.

Q: *What is the Dataflow Diagrammer used for?*

A: The Dataflow Diagrammer is a graphic tool used to model the process side of a project. It is an analytical tool used to model the flow of information between functions. The output provides a nontechnical view of the project suitable for the basis of discussion with the end users.

Q: *What symbols are used for a dataflow diagram and what do they represent?*

A: The Dataflow Diagrammer uses a limited symbol set to model the passing of data. Data may arrive from an external source, but when it does, it is handled or processed. In Oracle's tool a PROCESS is represented by a round-cornered box. The DATAFLOW itself is represented by a directional line (an arrowhead at one end). The place where data is stored is a DATASTORE and is represented by an open-ended rectangle.

Q: *What is the Entity Relationship Diagrammer used for?*

A: The Entity Relationship Diagrammer is a graphic tool used to model the data side of a project. It is an analytical tool used to model the data required by the system. The output provides a view of the project which, when combined with end-user discussion, provides insight into how the users relate data objects to each other. This definition of relationships forms the basis of the underlying business rules of the project. This verification process ensures that the analyst has modeled the system that fulfills the needs of the users.

Q: *What symbols are used for an entity relationship diagram and what do they represent?*

A: The Entity Relationship Diagrammer also uses a limited symbol set to model the things about which information is kept (ENTITIES), which are represented by rectangles. They may be either in the system or considered external entities. Entities are related to other entities by RELATIONSHIPS, an expression of the business rules of the system being modeled. (For example, the statement "A customer must have one and only one account" reflects a one-to-one relationship between customer and account.) A relationship is represented by a line. The line is solid when defining a mandatory relationship and dotted when defining an optional relationship. A relationship line can also have an optional side and a mandatory side. A relationship also expresses the relationship degree (one-to-one, one-to-many, many-to-one, many-to-many) with a single line indicating one and a crowsfoot indicating many.

Q: *What is the Function Hierarchy Diagrammer used for?*

A: The Function Hierarchy Diagrammer is a graphic tool used to model the ordering (hierarchy) of the system's processes, enabling a developer to arrange the functions into meaningful parent/children structures. This in turn helps to lay out a project in a structure which reflects new or redefined functionality.

Q: *What is the Matrix Diagrammer used for?*

A: The Matrix Diagrammer is a general-purpose tool to aid the developer with the interrelationship of different objects in the dictionary. For example, the matrix could be of functions against entities, critical success factors against business functions, program modules to tables, or variants of these and/or other possibilities.

Q: *What is the relationship of the Dataflow Diagrammer to the Functional Hierarchy Diagrammer?*

A: The Dataflow Diagrammer is an early analysis tool which is used to evaluate the essential processes of a system. This may take several iterations combined with user input. That information forms the basis of the function hierarchy and Oracle's CASE tool prepopulates the Function Hierarchy Diagrammer with the processes from the Dataflow Diagrammer.

Q: *What is CASE*Generator?*

A: CASE*Generator is Oracle's 4GL code generator. It takes the information stored in CASE*Dictionary (supplied by CASE*Designer, manually inputted, or a combination of both) and generates the application, module by module. The end result is a functioning product that operates in an SQL*Forms environment, complete with constraints and integrity checks. The generator is capable of also building menu structure and reports.

Q: *What benefits do Oracle's CASE tools offer over traditional development techniques?*

A: There are several benefits, starting with the basic graphic tools. Since the strategy and analysis stages are involved with user interviews, walk-throughs, and discussions, many initial requirements are subject to modification as they are more completely understood. The graphic designer tools allow these changes to be made rapidly, while capturing the underlying information in the CASE*Dictionary. The tool also provides a high degree of error checking, bringing possible problems to the analyst's attention. The tool also helps multiple analysts work on a project with a minimum of redundancy. The central dictionary makes charting progress an easier task with both packaged reports and the ability to perform ad hoc queries. The Generator function saves substantial time over hand-coding the application since it is based on elements in CASE*Dictionary.

Additional Readings

In addition to the Oracle documentation, the following books are recommended:

1. George Koch, *ORACLE, the Complete Reference,* Osborne McGraw-Hill, 1991, ISBN 0-07-881635-1.

2. Richard Barker and Cliff Longman, *CASE*METHOD, Function and Process Modelling,* Addison Wesley, 1992, ISBN 0-201-56525-0.

3. Richard Barker, *CASE*METHOD, Entity Relationship Modelling,* Addison Wesley, 1990.

4. Richard Barker, *CASE*METHOD, Tasks and Deliverables,* Addison Wesley, 1990, ISBN 0-201-41697-2.

13
CICS

Arnie G. Fonseca

Introduction

IBM's Customer Information Control System (CICS) is an on-line teleprocessing system developed by IBM. By providing a sophisticated control and service database/data communication system, the application developer can concentrate on fulfilling specific business needs rather than on communication and internal system details. CICS allows data to be transmitted from the terminal to the host computer, have the data processed, access files/databases, and then have data transmitted back to the terminal. To accomplish that, CICS uses a telecommunication package such as VTAM or TCAM and various file access methods: VSAM, DL/1, DB2, etc.

As of this writing the latest release of CICS/ESA is Release 3.3. Some of the new functionality includes:

1. Expanded features for the system programmer
2. Improved above-the-line storage utilization
3. New options for many CICS commands
4. Improved cross-platform communication facilities

Functionality

CICS provides the following support:

Data Communications
- An interface between the terminals and printers with CICS via a telecommunication access method (TCAM or VTAM)

- Multi-Region Operation (MRO), through which more than one CICS region of a system can communicate
- Intersystem Communication (ISC), through which one CICS region of a system can communicate with other CICS regions in other systems

Application Programming
- Interfaces with programming languages such as COBOL and Assembler
- A command-level translator
- A Screen Definition Facility (SDF)
- An Execution Diagnostic Facility (EDF)
- A command interpreter

Data Handling
- An interface with database access methods such as DB2, DL/1, and VSAM
- An interface with error-checking and reporting facilities

Terminology

CICS has its own language. Some of the language abbreviations of CICS are:

SIT	System Initialization Table
PCT	Program Control Table
PPT	Program Processing Table
TCT	Terminal Control Table
DCT	Destination Control Table
EIP	Execution Interface Program
FCP	File Control Program
ICP	Interval Control Program
KCT	Task Control Program
PCP	Program Control Program
SCP	Storage Control Program
TCA	Task Control Area
TCP	Terminal Control Program
TCTTE	Terminal Control Table Terminal Entry
TDQ	Transient Data Queue
TSQ	Temporary Storage Queue
TWA	Task Work Area
AID	Attention Identifier
CWA	Common Work Area
TCTUA	Terminal Control Terminal User Area

MRO   Multi-Region Operation
QID   Queue Identifier

Questions and Answers

Q: *What is the function of the CICS Translator?*

A: The CICS Translator converts the EXEC CICS commands into call statements for a specific programming language. There are CICS Translators for Assembler, COBOL, and PL/1.

Q: *What does "pseudo-conversational" mean?*

A: The programming technique in which the task will not wait for the end-user replies on the terminal. Terminating the task every time the application needs a response from the user and specifying the next transaction to be started when the end user presses any attention key (Enter, PF1 through PF24, PA1, PA2, Clear) is pseudo-conversational processing.

Q: *How can you start a CICS transaction other than by keying the Transaction ID at the terminal?*

A: ▪ By coding an EXEC CICS START in the application program
  ▪ By coding the trans id and a trigger level on the DCT table
  ▪ By coding the trans id in the EXEC CICS RETURN command
  ▪ By associating an attention key with the Program Control Table
  ▪ By embedding the TRANSID in the first four positions of a screen sent to the terminal
  ▪ By using the Program List Table

Q: *What is the purpose of the Program List Table?*

A: The Program List Table records the set of application programs that will be executed automatically at CICS start-up time.

Q: *What are the differences between an EXEC CICS XCTL and an EXEC CICS START command?*

A: The XCTL command transfers control to another application (having the same Transaction ID), while the START command initiates a new Transaction ID (therefore a new task number). The XCTL continues the task on the same terminal. START can initiate a task on another terminal.

Q: *What are the differences between an EXEC CICS XCTL and an EXEC CICS LINK command?*

A: The XCTL command transfers control to an application program at the same logical level (do not expect to control back), while the LINK command passes control to an application program at the next logical level and expects control back.

Q: *What happens to resources supplied to a transaction when an XCTL command is executed?*

A: With an XCTL, the working storage and the procedure division of the program issuing the XCTL are released. The I/O areas, the GETMAIN areas, and the chained Linkage Section areas (Commarea from a higher level) remain. All existing locks and queues also remain in effect. With a LINK, however, program storage is also saved, since the transaction expects to return and use it again.

Q: *What CICS command do you need to obtain the user logon-id?*

A: You must code EXEC CICS ASSIGN with the OPERID option.

Q: *What is a resident program?*

A: A program or map loaded into the CICS nucleus so that it is kept permanently in main storage and not deleted when CICS goes "short on storage."

Q: *What is some of the information available in the EIB area?*

A: ▪ The cursor position in the map

   ▪ Transaction id

   ▪ Terminal id

   ▪ Task number

   ▪ Length of the communication area

   ▪ Current date and time

   ▪ Attention identifier

Q: *What information can be obtained from the EIBRCODE?*

A: The EIBRCODE tells the application program if the last CICS command was executed successfully and, if not, why not.

Q: *What is the effect of including the TRANSID in the EXEC CICS RETURN command?*

A: The next time the end user presses an attention key, CICS will start the transaction specified in the TRANSID option.

Q: *What is the function of the EXEC CICS HANDLE CONDITION command?*

A: To specify the paragraph or program label to which control is to be passed if the "handled condition" occurs.

Q: *How many conditions can you include in a single HANDLE CONDITION command?*

A: No more than 16 in a single handle condition. If you need more, then you must code another HANDLE CONDITION command.

Q: *What is the EXEC CICS HANDLE ABEND?*

A: It allows the establishing of an exit so cleanup processing can be done in the event of abnormal task termination.

Q: *What is the difference between an EXEC CICS HANDLE CONDITION and an EXEC CICS IGNORE command?*

A: A HANDLE CONDITION command creates a "go-to" environment. An IGNORE command does not create a go-to environment; instead, it gives control back to the next sequential instruction following the command causing the condition. They are opposites.

Q: *What happens when a CICS command contains the NOHANDLE option?*

A: No action is going to be taken for *any* exceptional condition occurring during the execution of this command. The abnormal condition that occurred will be ignored even if an EXEC CICS HANDLE condition exists. It has the same effect as the EXEC CICS IGNORE condition except that it will not cancel the previous HANDLE CONDITION for any other command.

Q: *What happens when a CICS command contains the RESP option?*

A: No action is going to be taken for any exceptional condition occurring during the execution of this command. When an abnormal condition occurs, the CICS response code is a field in the program work area and can be checked later (usually at the next sequential instruction).

Q: *Suppose that an application program uses the HANDLE AID ENTER (main-logic) and the HANDLE CONDITION ERROR(abort-rtn) command. If the program issued a RECEIVE MAP, and a MAPFAIL condition occurred, which process will take control: main-logic or abort-rtn?*

A: Main-logic will receive the control because Handle Aid has priority over Handle Condition.

Q: *When the task suspends all the handle conditions via the PUSH command, how does the task reactivate all the handle conditions?*

A: By coding an EXEC CICS POP HANDLE command.

Q: *What is the difference between the INTO and the SET option in the EXEC CICS RECEIVE MAP command?*

A: The INTO option moves the information in the TIOA into the reserved specified area, while the SET option simply returns the address of the TIOA to the specified BLL cell or "address-of" a linkage section.

Q: *Define the function of the Basic Mapping System (BMS).*

A: BMS allows the application to be device-independent. It translates the formatted data stream, thus enabling the application to reference data by symbolic labels.

Q: *Suppose you have a field in a map named ACCTID, and you want it bright. Explain how can you do this during the execution of the application.*

A: By moving either DHFBMBRY to the ACCTIDA field in the symbolic map (bright only) or DFHBMASB to the ACCTIDA field in the symbolic map (askip bright).

Q: *What are three ways available for a program to position the cursor on the screen?*

A: 1. *Static positioning.* Code the insert cursor (IC) in the DHFMDF BMS macro.

2. *Relative positioning.* Code the CURSOR option with a value relative to zero (position 1,1 is zero).

3. *Symbolic positioning.* Move high values or –1 to the field length in the symbolic map (and code CURSOR on the SEND command).

Q: *Reducing the data traffic is a very important factor in an on-line environment. Explain the difference between the MAPONLY and DATAONLY options in the EXEC CICS SEND MAP.*

A: A vast majority of the maps are defined as input/output. Therefore, to reduce data transmission the first time a map is sent, you should use MAPONLY because this will set up the initial template on screen. After that, the application needs to be sent only the variable data in the symbolic map (DATAONLY).

Q: *What is the Modified Data Tag (MDT)?*

A: The MDT is a 1-bit attribute character of a BMS field. When it is set on, CICS will transmit the data contained in the associated map field.

Q: *Name three ways the Modified Data Tag can be set on.*

A: The Modified Data Tag can be set on:

1. When the user enters data into the field

2. When the application program moves the DFHBMSFSE to the attribute character

3. By defining it in the BMS macro definition

Q: *How do you specify in your program which fields are not to be sent to a map (terminal)?*

A: By filling the fields with low values.

Q: *What happens if neither MAPONLY nor DATAONLY are specified?*

A: The data from the physical map and the data from the symbolic map are merged, causing an increase in the data transmission.

Q: *What is a mapset?*

A: A mapset is a collection of BMS maps link-edited together.

Q: *What is the function of the DFHMDF BMS macro?*

A: The DFHMDF macro defines fields, literal, and characteristics of a field.

Q: *The DFHMDF is a subset (a subdivision) of which BMS macro?*

A: DFHMDF is a BMS macro that is a part of the DHFMDI macro.

Q: *What is the function of the Terminal Control Table (TCT)?*

A: The TCT defines the characteristics of each terminal with which CICS can communicate.

Q: *When an application program issues an EXEC CICS RECEIVE MAP command and there is no data sent back to the application program, what exceptional condition will occur?*

A: A MAPFAIL condition will occur.

Q: *What does it mean when EIBCALEN is equal to zeros?*

A: When the length of the communication area (EIBCALEN) is equal to zeros, it means that no data was passed to the application.

Q: *How can the fact that EIBCALEN is equal to zeros be of use to an application programmer?*

A: When working in a pseudo-conversational mode, EIBCALEN can be checked if it is equal to zero. A programmer can use this condition as a way of determining first-time usage (of the program).

Q: *Which CICS system program is responsible for handling automatic task initialization?*

A: The Transient Data Program (TDP).

Q: *What are some differences between a Temporary Storage Queue (TSQ) and Transient Data Queue (TDQ)?*

A: ■ Temporary Storage Queue names are dynamically defined in the application program, while Temporary Data Queues must first be defined in the DCT (Destination Control Table).

   ■ When a TDQ contains a certain amount of records (trigger level), a CICS transaction can be started automatically. This does not happen when using a TSQ.

   ■ TDQ (extrapartition) may be used by batch application; TSQ cannot be accessed in batch. The Transient Data Queue is actually a QSAM file.

   ■ You may update an existing item in a TSQ. A record in a TDQ cannot be updated.

   ■ Records in TSQ can be read randomly. The TDQ can be read only sequentially.

   ■ Records in Temporary Storage can be read more than once, while records stored in Temporary Data Queues cannot. With TDQs it is "one read" only.

Q: *What will happen if a task issues an EXEC CICS DELETEQ TD against an Extrapartition Transient Data Queue?*

A: An invalid request exceptional condition will occur. The default action is that the task will be terminated.

Q: *In an on-line environment, how can you prevent more than one user from accessing the same Transient Data Queue at the same time?*

A: By issuing an EXEC CICS ENQ against the resource. When processing is completed, a DEQ should be executed.

Q: *Is there any way of releasing a resource previously enqueued by a task other than by issuing an EXEC CICS DEQ command?*

A: You can issue a SYNCPOINT command. You can also RETURN control to CICS, as CICS automatically releases a resource when a task is terminated.

Q: *When an application is invoked via the EXEC CICS START command with the FROM option, how does the application gain access to the common area?*

A: An EXEC CICS RETRIEVE command will access the common area.

Q: *What happens when an EXEC CICS SYNCPOINT is issued?*

A: The Logical Unit of Work (LUW) is terminated. Everything on the Deferred Work Element (DWE) chain is cleaned up. If Dynamic Transaction Backout (DTB) is on, everything is committed. GETMAIN areas are freed. File locks are released. I/O areas and linkage sections are released. Browses are terminated. Working storage is *not* affected.

Q: *What is a Logical Unit of Work?*

A: A Logical Unit of Work is all the processing that takes place between two "sync points."

Q: *The DFHCOMMAREA is used to pass information from one application to another. What are some other ways that this function can be accomplished?*

A: You can also pass information in the following ways:
- By using a Temporary Storage Queue
- By using an intrapartition TDQ
- By using the Task Work Area
- By using TCTUA
- Through a file

Q: *How do you define a Task Work Area?*

A: By defining it in on the PCT (the Program Control Table).

Q: *What is stored in the Temporary Storage Table?*

A: The TST contains the names of the Temporary Storage Queues that are to be recovered in the event of an abend.

Q: *What information do you get when an EXEC ASSIGN STARTCODE is issued?*

A: You will be able to determine if the application was started by: (1) a transient data trigger level (QD), (2) a START command (S, SD), (3) user (U) or terminal input (TD), or (4) Distributed Program Link (D, DS).

Q: *Which CICS command must be issued by the application in order to gain access to the Common Work Area (CWA)?*

A: EXEC CICS ADDRESS with CWA option.

Q: *In which CICS table would you specify the length of the TASK WORK AREA (TWA)?*

A: In the Program Control Table (PCT).

Q: *Explain the function performed by the Program Control Table (PCT)?*

A: The PCT defines the relationship between a transaction and an application program.

Q: *When a data table is loaded into memory using the EXEC LOAD command, how does the application program free that memory when the table is no longer needed?*

A: By coding an EXEC CICS RELEASE command with the program option.

Q: *What is the function of the HOLD option in the EXEC CICS LOAD command?*

A: When a program is loaded from the CICS DFHRPL concatenation library (into main storage), the HOLD option will result in the program remaining in memory after the task terminates. When this option is not specified, main storage is automatically released by CICS.

Q: *Explain the function of the File Control Program (FCP)?*

A: The FCP provides the application program with the ability to read, browse, add, delete, and update records in a file defined in the FCT.

Q: *What is the function of the File Control Table?*

A: It defines the file and contains the characteristics of the dataset.

Q: *If an application has a VSAM/KSDS file READ command with the update option, and it finds that the update is no longer required, how does the application release the exclusive control of the record read?*

A: By executing an EXEC CICS UNLOCK command with the File or Dataset option. A SYNCPOINT will also release the exclusive control.

Q: *What is a deadlock?*

A: Deadlock (also known as a "deadly embrace") occurs when a task is waiting for a resource held by another task which, in turn, is waiting for a resource held by the first task.

Q: *Which CICS program is responsible for the management of the DSA (the Dynamic Storage Area)?*

A: The Storage Control Program (SCP).

Q: *What happens when an application issues an EXEC CICS GETMAIN command to obtain main storage and the SHARED option is specified?*

A: There is no automatic release of the obtained storage at the end of the task which requested it.

Q: *How can an application release main storage acquired by an EXEC CICS GETMAIN command?*

A: By coding an EXEC CICS FREEMAIN command with the data. SYNCPOINT will also release the storage area.

Q: *What is the function of the REQID in the EXEC CICS STARTBR command?*

A: When you have multiple browse operations at the same time on the same file, the REQID must be coded on the READ Next/Prev command to distinguish one browse from the other.

Q: *Which CICS command must the application program issue to terminate a browse?*

A: An EXEC CICS ENDR command. SYNCPOINT also ends the browse.

Q: *What is the function of the EXEC CICS RESETBR command?*

A: To reposition the browse (with VSAM files this can be done just by altering the RIDFLD) and to change the characteristics specified on the STARTBR command without ending the browse.

Q: *When debugging a CICS application, why would you use the CEBR command?*

A: To view the contents of the TSQ or TDQ.

Q: *Mention some of the most common operations you can perform with the CEMT CICS transaction.*

A: Create a new copy of an application program   `CEMT S PR(prgname) NEW`

Close a file from CICS   `CEMT S DA(filename) CLO UNE`

Disable a transaction   `CEMT S TRANS(transid) Dis`

Q: *What is the function of the CEDA transaction?*

A: It is used to perform the Resource Definition On-line operation (RDO). It adds, deletes, and changes table entries.

Q: *What CICS command does the application have to issue to update an existing record in a VSAM/KSDS file?*

A: The EXEC CICS REWRITE command.

Q: *What CICS command does the application have to issue to update an existing record in a TS queue?*

A: The EXEC CICS WRITE command with the rewrite option and the item number.

Q: *What is the purpose of the CICS BIF DEEDIT?*

A: To remove all characters other than digits from an alphanumeric field. Remaining digits will be right-justified and padded with zeros as necessary.

Q: *What is the Base Locator for Linkage (BLL) used for?*

A: The BLL is used to address storage outside of the working-storage section of the application program. A set of BLL cells is also known as the *parameter list*. It is not used (explicitly) in COBOL II, although the BLL cells can be found in the TGT of a COBOL II program.

Q: *Explain the term "transaction routing."*

A: *Transaction routing* is a CICS "mode" of intercommunication which allows a terminal connected to local CICS to execute another transaction owned by a remote CICS.

Q: *Explain the term "function request shipping."*

A: *Function request shipping* is one of the CICS modes of intercommunication which allows an application program in a local CICS to access resources owned by a remote CICS.

Q: *Explain the term "MRO" (Multi-Region Operation).*

A: MRO is the mechanism by which different CICS address spaces within the same CPU can communicate and share resources.

Q: *If, when executing a "READ INTO" command, the length of the actual (variable) length record exceeds the length specified in the LENGTH option, what will happen (if anything)?*

A: You will get a LENGERR.

Q: *When a second READ WITH UPDATE is given against the same file in the same task prior to releasing the file, what will happen?*

A: An INVREQ will take place.

Q: *How could you prevent such an error?*

A: After the first read, and prior to the second read, you could:

1. Issue an UNLOCK.

2. Execute a DELETE.

3. Execute a REWRITE.

4. Execute a SYNCPOINT.

Q: *Name one condition that would result in the inability to execute a backward browse.*

A: If you issue a STARTBR with a generic key, a backward browse will not work.

Q: *You have duplicate keys and you have loaded an alternate index into RIDFLD. What would happen if you issued a READNEXT after switching from a direct retrieval read?*

A: You would get the same record twice.

Q: *You are doing a mass delete using a generic key. What could you do to determine the number of records that have been deleted?*

A: You would use the NUMREC (data area) option with the generic key. Upon completion of the mass delete, the data area would contain a count of the number of records that were deleted.

Q: *How should the data area used with the NUMREC option be defined?*

A: S9(4) COMP.

Q: *Which command will terminate a VSAM mass insert operation?*

A: An UNLOCK command.

Q: *Which command(s) will deblock DAM files?*

A: DEBKEY will deblock by key. DEBREC will deblock by relative record number.

Q: *What could cause you to get an INVREQ when building a logical message to a screen?*

A: You have changed the disposition specified while building a logical message.

Q: *What could cause you to get a MAPFAIL when issuing a RECEIVE MAP command?*

A: You would get a MAPFAIL if no data was transferred from the screen.

Q: *What command would you issue if you wanted to discontinue building a logical message?*

A: You would issue a PURGE MESSAGE command.

Q: *Can you intermix a SEND TEXT and a SEND MAP when building portions of a logical message?*

A: No, you cannot intermix these two commands.

Q: *How do you release page buffers?*

A: By issuing a FREEMAIN command.

Q: *What do you have to do to determine if data was sent (from a screen) from a specific (single) field?*

A: You have to check the MDT for that field.

Q: *Which command would you issue to get data in a task that was started by a START command?*

A: You would issue a RETRIEVE command.

Q: *What would happen if you issued a READNEXT TS command and there were no more data in the queue?*

A: You would get an ITEMERR.

Q: *You have a DL/I file and you want to issue a READPREV. Will it work correctly?*

A: You can issue a READPREV only against a VSAM file.

Q: *Can you issue a BROWSE command in a CICS program that is pseudo-conversational?*

A: Yes, but the BROWSE will terminate at the end of each task in the session—it will not carry over.

Q: *What are the two ways to "set up" a browse starting with the first record in the file?*

A: You can:

1. Set the complete key equal to hex zeros (the default option is GTEQ).

2. You can specify KEYLENGTH(0) and GENERIC options.

Q: *In a VSAM file, when you want to do a mass delete, the file has to be unprotected. How can you specify to the system that a file is unprotected?*

A: In the FCT you set LOG = NO.

Q: *When you are sending your first data screen to the terminal, it is recommended that you specify the ERASE option. Why?*

A: If you do not include the ERASE option, the screen size will be the same as the previous screen size setting . . . and this may not be correct. There may also be material on the screen which would remain if not overlaid by fields of your map.

Q: *Which key, if depressed by the terminal operator, will set the screen size to its default size?*

A: The CLEAR key.

Q: *Does a HANDLE CONDITION command take precedence over a HANDLE AID command?*

A: No, the HANDLE AID takes precedence.

Q: *What does the BMS ROUTE command do?*

A: The ROUTE command initiates the building of a logical message that will be scheduled for delivery to one or more terminals.

Q: *What has happened if you abend with an "APCT"?*

A: The program tried to execute a program that was either:

1. Not defined in the PPT or active RDO group
2. Disabled

Q: *What does the ERASEUP command do?*

A: The ERASEUP command:

1. Clears all MDTs
2. Unlocks the keyboard
3. Erases all unprotected fields
4. Positions the cursor at the first unprotected field

Q: *What will happen if you issue an XCTL or a LINK and the called program cannot be found?*

A: You will get a PGMIDERR.

Q: *What happens to the exception (HANDLE CONDITION, HANDLE ABEND, HANDLE AID) condition settings in a called routine once control has been transferred to the called routine?*

A: Once you are in the called routine, all condition settings are deactivated.

14

IBM's DB2

John Cornetto, Jr.

Introduction

DB2 is the relational database system that runs in an MVS environment. It was developed by IBM and interfaces with SQL. With the use of SQL DB2, databases can be accessed by a wide range of host languages. SQL is the relational database "application language" that interfaces with DB2. Because of its capabilities, SQL and, in turn, DB2 have gained considerable acceptance. Thus, a working knowledge of DB2 increases one's marketability. The questions and answers that follow are intended for those with a working knowledge of DB2 as a "self-test." If you need to brush up, the nearest technical bookstore is your next stop.

Questions and Answers

Q: *What is DB2 (IBM Database 2)?*
A: DB2 is a subsystem of the MVS operating system. It is a Database Management System (DBMS) for that operating system.

Q: *What is an access path?*
A: The path that is used to get to data specified in SQL statements.

Q: *What is an alias?*
A: It is an alternate name that can be used in SQL statements to refer to a table or view in the same or a remote DB2 subsystem.

Q: *Explain what a plan is.*
A: A plan is a DB2 object (produced during the bind process) that associates one or more database request modules with a plan name.

Q: *What is a DB2 bind?*

A: A bind is a process that builds "access paths" to DB2 tables. A bind uses the Database Request Module(s) (DBRM(s)) from the DB2 precompile step as input and produces an application plan. It also checks the user's authority and validates the SQL statements in the DBRM(s).

Q: *What information is used as input to the bind process?*

A: 1. The database request model produced during the precompile

   2. The SYSIBM.SYSSTMT table of the DB2 catalog

Q: *What is meant by the attachment facility?*

A: The attachment facility is an interface between DB2 and TSO, IMS/VS, CICS, or batch address spaces. It allows application programs to access DB2.

Q: *What is meant by AUTO COMMIT?*

A: AUTO COMMIT is a SPUFI option that commits the effects of SQL statements automatically if they are successfully executed.

Q: *What is a base table?*

A: A base table is a "real" table—a table that physically exists in that there are physical stored records.

Q: *What is the function of Buffer Manager?*

A: The Buffer Manager is the DB2 component responsible for physically transferring data between an external medium and (virtual) storage (performs the actual I/O operations). It minimizes the amount of physical I/O actually performed with sophisticated buffering techniques (i.e., read-ahead buffering and look-aside buffering).

Q: *What is a buffer pool?*

A: A buffer pool is main storage that is reserved to satisfy the buffering requirements for one or more tablespaces or indexes, and is made up of either 4K or 32K pages.

Q: *How many buffer pools are there in DB2?*

A: There are four buffer pools: BP0, BP1, BP2, and BP32.

Q: *On the create tablespace, what does the CLOSE parameter do?*

A: CLOSE physically closes the tablespace when no one is working on the object. DB2 (Release 2.3) will logically close tablespaces.

Q: *What is a clustering index?*

A: It is a type index that (1) locates table rows and (2) determines how rows are grouped together in the tablespace.

Q: *What will the COMMIT accomplish?*

A: COMMIT will allow data changes to be permanent. This then permits the data to be accessed by other units of work. When a COMMIT occurs, locks are freed so other applications can reference the just-committed data.

Q: *What is meant by concurrency?*

A: Concurrency is what allows more than one DB2 application process to access the same data at essentially the same time. Problems may occur, such as lost updates, access to uncommitted data, and unrepeatable reads.

Q: *What is cursor stability?*

A: It is cursor stability that "tells" DB2 that database values read by this application are protected only while they are being used. (Changed values are protected until this application reaches a commit point.) As soon as a program moves from one row to another, other programs may read or change the first row.

Q: *What is the function of the Data Manager?*

A: The Data Manager is a DB2 component that manages the physical database(s). It invokes other system components, as necessary, to perform detailed functions such as locking, logging, and physical I/O operations (such as search, retrieval, update, and index maintenance).

Q: *What is a Database Request Module (DBRM)?*

A: A DBRM is a DB2 component created by the DB2 precompiler containing the SQL source statements extracted from the application program. DBRMs are input to the bind process.

Q: *What is a data page?*

A: A data page is a unit of retrievable data, either 4K or 32K (depending on how the table is defined), containing user or catalog information.

Q: *What are data types?*

A: They are attributes of columns, literals, and host variables. The data types are SMALLINT, INTEGER, FLOAT, DECIMAL, CHAR, VARCHAR, DATE, and TIME.

Q: *What is a Declarations Generator (DCLGEN)?*

A: DCLGEN is a facility that is used to generate SQL statements that describe a table or view. These table or view descriptions are then used to check the validity of other SQL statements at precompile time. The table or view declares are used by the DB2I utility DCLGEN to build a host language structure, which is used by the DB2 precompiler to verify that correct column names and data types have been specified in the SQL statement.

Q: *What does DSNDB07 database do?*

A: DSNDB07 is where DB2 does its sorting. It includes DB2's sort workarea and external storage.

Q: *What is meant by dynamic SQL?*

A: Dynamic SQL are SQL statements that are prepared and executed within a program while the program is executing. The SQL source is contained in host variables rather than being "hard coded" into the program. The SQL statement may change from execution to execution.

Q: *What is meant by embedded SQL?*
A: They are SQL statements that are embedded within an application program and are prepared during the program preparation process before the program is executed. After it is prepared, the statement itself does not change (although values of host variables specified within the statement might change).

Q: *What is meant by entity integrity?*
A: Entity integrity is when the primary key is in fact unique and not null.

Q: *What will the EXPLAIN do?*
A: EXPLAIN obtains information (which indexes are used, whether sorting is necessary, which level of locking is applied) about how SQL statements in the DBRM will be executed, inserting this information into the "X".PLAN_ TABLE where "X" is the authorization ID of the owner of the plan.

Q: *What is a foreign key?*
A: A foreign key is a column (or combination of columns) in a table whose values are required to match those of the primary key in some other table.

Q: *What will the FREE command do to a plan?*
A: It will drop (delete) that existing plan.

Q: *What will the GRANT option do?*
A: It will grant privileges to a list of one or more users. If the GRANT option is used in conjunction with the "PUBLIC" option, then all users will be granted privileges. Also, you can grant privileges by objects and types.

Q: *What does the term "grant privileges" mean?*
A: *Grant privileges* means giving access/authority to DB2 users.

Q: *What is a host variable?*
A: This is a data item that is used in an SQL statement to receive a value or to supply a value. It must be preceded by a colon (:) to tell DB2 that the variable is not a column name.

Q: *What is an image copy?*
A: It is an exact reproduction of all or part of a tablespace. DB2 provides utility programs to make full-image copies (to copy the entire tablespace) or incremental image copies to copy only those pages that have been modified since the last image copy.

Q: *What is meant by an index?*
A: An index is a set of row identifiers (RIDs) or pointers that are logically ordered by the values of a column that has been specified as being an index. Indexes provide faster access to data and can enforce uniqueness on the row in a table.

Q: *What is an index key?*
A: It is a column or set of columns in a table used to determine the order of index entries.

Q: *What is meant by an index scan?*
A: When an entire index (or a portion thereof) is scanned to locate rows, we call this an index scan. This type of access can be used, for example, to select all rows of a table in some order and avoid a sort for a query.

Q: *What is meant by indicator variable?*
A: An indicator variable is an integer variable used to show whether its associated host variable has been assigned a null value.

Q: *What is a join?*
A: A join is a relational operation that allows retrieval of data from two or more tables based on matching column values.

Q: *What is meant by locking?*
A: Locking is a process that is used to ensure the integrity of data. It also prevents concurrent users from accessing inconsistent data. The data (row) is locked until a commit is executed to release the updated data.

Q: *What is a "nonleaf" page?*
A: This is a page that contains keys and page numbers of other pages in the index. Nonleaf pages never point to actual data.

Q: *What is meant by null?*
A: This is a special value that indicates the absence of data in a column. This value is indicated by a negative value, usually -1.

Q: *What is an object?*
A: An object is anything that is managed by DB2 (that is, databases, tablespaces, tables, views, indexes, or synonyms), but not the data itself.

Q: *What will the DB2 optimizer do?*
A: The optimizer is a DB2 component that processes SQL statements and selects the access paths.

Q: *What is a page?*
A: This is the unit of storage within a tablespace or indexspace that is accessed by DB2.

Q: *What is a pagespace?*
A: Pagespace refers either to an unpartitioned table, to an index space, or to a single partition of a partitioned table of index space.

Q: *What is a predicate?*
A: A predicate is an element of a search condition that expresses or implies a comparison operation.

Q: *Describe a primary key.*
A: A primary key is a key that is unique, nonnull, and is part of the definition of a table. A table must have a primary key to be defined as a parent.

Q: *What is a recovery log?*

A: A recovery log is a collection of records that describes the sequence of events that occur in DB2. The information is needed for recovery in the event of a failure during execution.

Q: *What is a Resource Control Table (RCT)? Describe its characteristics.*

A: The RCT is a table that is defined to a DB2/CICS region. It contains control characteristics which are assembled via the DSNCRCT macros. The RCT matches the CICS transaction ID to its associated DB2 authorization ID and plan ID (CICS attachment facility).

Q: *Where are plans stored?*

A: Each plan is defined uniquely in the SYSIBM.SYSPLAN table to correspond to the transaction(s) that are to execute that plan.

Q: *Describe referential integrity.*

A: Referential integrity refers to a feature in DB2 that is used to ensure consistency of the data in the database.

Q: *What is meant by a repeatable read?*

A: When an application program executes with repeatable read protection, rows referenced by the program cannot be changed by other programs until the program reaches a commit point.

Q: *What is a row?*

A: A row is a single occurrence of the columns (of data) described by the table definition.

Q: *Describe what a storage group (STOGROUP) is.*

A: A STOGROUP is a named collection of DASD volumes to be used by tablespaces and index spaces of databases. The volumes of a STOGROUP must be of the same device type.

Q: *What is meant by synonym?*

A: A synonym is an alternate name for a table or view which is stored in the SYSIBM.SYSSYNONYMS table.

Q: *Describe what a table is.*

A: A table is a DB2 structure in which column names are used to specify the information that is being stored by row.

Q: *What is a tablespace?*

A: A tablespace is a VSAM dataset which is used to store one or more tables. The physical page can consist of 4K or 32K pages.

Q: *How would you move a tablespace (using STOGROUP) to a different DASD volume allocated to that tablespace?*

A: 1. If the tablespace used is only allocated to that STOGROUP:

   ■ ALTER STOGROUP—add volume (new) delete volume (old)
   ■ REORG TABLESPACE or RECOVER TABLESPACE

2. Create a new stogroup that points to the new volume. ALTER the tablespace and REORG or RECOVER the tablespace.

Q: *What is the format (internal layout) of 'TIMESTAMP'?*
A: This is a seven-part value that consists of a date (yymmdd) and time (hhmmss and microseconds).

Q: *What is a unique index?*
A: An index specified as unique is an index for which no duplicates are allowed.

Q: *What is meant by a unit of recovery?*
A: This is a sequence of operations within a unit of work (i.e., work done between commit points).

Q: *What is a view?*
A: A view is an alternative representation of data contained in one or more tables. A view can include all or some of the columns contained in the table or tables.

Q: *What does a view do?*
A: A view restricts access to specific columns and rows.

Q: *What is a data model?*
A: A data model is a way of representing entities, attributes, and relationships.

Q: *When a transaction issues a commit, to what is the commit writing?*
A: A commit triggers a write to a log record.

Q: *Can DASD types assigned to storage groups be intermixed (i.e., 3350s and 3380s)?*
A: No.

Q: *What type of information is contained on the BSDS?*
A: The BSDS contains information about active and archive logs, their dataset names, and the volumes on which they reside.

Q: *What are the three types of page locks that can be "held"?*
A: Exclusive, update, and share.

Q: *Can DB2 be accessed by TSO users? If yes, which command is used to invoke DB2?*
A: DB2 can be invoked by TSO users by using the DSN RUN command.

Q: *What are the names of the different types of DB2 tablespaces?*
A: Simple, segmented, and partitioned.

Q: *What is the maximum number of partitions allowed in a partitioned tablespace?*
A: The maximum is 64.

Q: *How are write I/Os from the buffer pool executed?*
A: Asynchronously.

Q: *After a table has been recovered, which flag is turned on?*
A: The Copy Pending flag is turned on.

Catalogs

Q: *What is the DB2 catalog?*
A: The DB2 catalog is a set of tables that contain information about all of the DB2 objects (tables, views, plans, etc.).

Q: *In which column of which DB2 catalog would you find the length of the rows for all tables?*
A: In the RECLENGTH column of SYSIBM.SYSTABLES

Q: *What information is held in SYSIBM.SYSCOPY?*
A: The SYSIBM.SYSCOPY table contains information about image copies made of the tablespaces.

Q: *What information is contained in a SYSCOPY "entry"?*
A: Included is the name of the database, the tablespace name, and the image copy type (full, incremental, etc.), as well as the date and time each copy was made.

Q: *What information can you find in SYSIBM.SYSLINKS table?*
A: The SYSIBM.SYSLINKS table contains information about the links between tables created by referential constraints.

Q: *Where would you find information about the type of database authority held by a user?*
A: SYSIBM.SYSDBAUTH.

Q: *Where could you look if you had a question about whether a column has been defined as an index?*
A: This information can be found in SYSIBM.SYSINDEXES.

Q: *Once you create a view, where would information about the view be stored?*
A: When a view is created, system information about the view is stored in SYSIBM.SYSVIEWS.

Utilities

Q: *What will the copy utility do?*
A: The copy utility will create an image copy of a tablespace or a dataset within a tablespace. There are two types of image copies: full and incremental. A full image copy copies all pages in a tablespace or dataset. An incremental image copy copies only pages that have been modified since the last use of the COPY utility.

Q: *What will the LOAD utility do?*

A: The LOAD utility will load data into one or more tables in a tablespace or partition. The LOAD can also replace the contents of a single partition or of an entire tablespace.

Q: *What can the MERGECOPY utility do?*

A: It can merge several incremental copies of a tablespace to make a single incremental copy, and it can merge incremental copies with a full-image copy to make a new full-image copy.

Q: *What will the RECOVER utility do?*

A: This utility recovers data to the current state or a previous state. The largest unit of data recovery is the tablespace; the smallest is a page. Data is recovered from image copies of a tablespace and database log change records.

Q: *What will the REORG utility do?*

A: It will reorganize a tablespace to improve access performance and reorganize indexes so that they are more efficiently clustered.

Q: *What will the REPAIR utility do?*

A: It will repair invalid data with valid data and/or reset status conditions. The data may be your own data or data you would not normally access: space map pages and index entries.

Q: *What will the RUNSTATS utility do?*

A: RUNSTATS will scan tablespaces or indexes gathering information about utilization of space and efficiency of indexes. The information is stored in the DB2 catalog, and is used by the SQL optimizer to select access paths to data during the bind.

Q: *What will the STOSPACE utility do?*

A: This utility updates DB2 catalog columns that tell how much space is allocated for storage groups and related tablespace and indexes.

Q: *While the Copy Pending flag is on, is the tablespace that was just recovered available for use?*

A: No, it is not available.

15
SQL

Michael A. Senatore

Introduction

Structured Query Language (SQL) provides the ability to create and define relational database objects. After these objects are defined, the language permits one to add data to these objects. Once data has been added, one can modify, retrieve, or delete that data. The language provides the capability of changing the created objects as well as removing them altogether. The language also provides the capability of defining what type of authority one might have when accessing the data.

Data Definition Language

As the name implies, there is a group of SQL statements that allows one to define the relational structures that will manage the data placed in them. The "CREATE" statement brings Relational Database Management System (RDMS) objects into existence. The types of objects one can create are Stogroup, Database, Tablespace, Table, Index, View, Synonym, and Alias. The definitions of these objects are as follows:

Stogroup: A storage group is a list of disk volume names to which one can assign a name. One defines the list of disk volumes and assigns the Stogroup name with the Create Stogroup statement.

Database: A database is a logical structure in which tables and indexes are later created. The database is defined and associated with a Stogroup with a Create Database statement.

Tablespace: A tablespace is an area on disk that is allocated and formatted by the Create Tablespace statement.

Table: A table is an organizational structure which is defined in a Create Table statement. In this statement, the data attributes are defined by column, giving each column its own unique name within the table.

Index: An index is used in conjunction with the "Primary Key" parameter of the Create Table statement. It is made with the Create Index statement and provides the duplicate record-checking necessary for a unique key.

View: A view is an alternative perspective of the data present in a database. It is made with the Create View statement and can represent a subset of the columns defined in a table. It can also represent a set of columns combined from more than one table.

Synonym: The Create Synonym statement defines an unqualified name for a table or a view.

Alias: The Create Alias statement defines an alternate qualified name for a table or a view.

After a table is created, additional columns may be added with an Alter Table statement. Any RDMS object that was made with a create statement can be removed with a drop statement.

In order to define RDMS objects, one needs various levels of authority. The following is a list of authority levels that can be granted to a user ID to operate on a designated database.

DBADM	Database administrator authority
DBCTRL	Database control authority
DBMAINT	Database maintenance authority
CREATETS	Create tablespace authority
CREATETAB	Create table authority
DROP	Drop authority on a database or subordinate objects

Data Manipulation Language

There are four SQL data manipulation statements (DML) available: Insert, Select, Update, and Delete. After tables are defined, they are ready to store data. Data is added to tables through the SQL Insert statement. Once data has been inserted into a table, it can be retrieved by the use of the Select statement. Data stored in a table can be modified by executing the SQL Update statement. Data can be deleted from a table by using the SQL Delete statement.

These SQL statements perform RDMS operations that can affect only one row at a time if desired. The same statements can, if required, affect many or all of the rows in a table. It is possible to select one row and insert it into another with one statement. It is also just as easy to select all of the rows from one table and insert all of them into another with a single statement. The same scope of operation applies to the update and delete statements. The scope of operation is controlled by the use of the WHERE clause. The operation will affect only the rows that satisfy the search condition. When no search condition is specified, the entire table is affected.

There are additional language elements available that provide the ability to process the table data while it is being retrieved. In addition, there are a variety of functions that modify the value of the data that is returned in a query. There are column functions that act on all of the values of the selected rows for a specified column and return a single answer. There also are scalar functions that return a specific answer for each row that satisfies the search condition.

As mentioned previously, SQL provides the ability to filter what data is retrieved in a select statement by including the WHERE clause. The WHERE clause specifies a variety of comparisons between two values. The values could be column values or the result of an operation involving more than one column or a constant. The comparison operators are the same as those used in COBOL, with the exception of two additional operators. The first is the IN operator that compares a single value to a set of other values. In other words, the comparison checks to see if the single value has a match in the specified list of values. The other is the LIKE operator, in which you can specify a value string that includes "wildcard" characters in such a manner that you can select rows of a table where column values are similar to the extent you require.

SQL provides four arithmetic operations: addition, subtraction, multiplication, and division. An arithmetic expression may involve any combination of column names or numbers. The arithmetic expression may itself be used as a column name or number in a Select, Insert, Update, or Delete statement.

SQL provides the ability to summarize data as it is retrieved from a table via the GROUP BY clause. In this clause, a set of column names is specified as grouping columns and the retrieved data is summarized by the changing values of those columns.

SQL provides the ability to sort the data retrieved from a table via the ORDER BY clause. In this clause, you can specify one or more sort column names as well as if each sort key is ascending or descending.

SQL also provides the ability to perform set manipulation operations. Using SQL, one can SELECT the intersection of two or more sets of data by coding a JOIN. A JOIN is any SELECT statement that has more than one DBMS object listed in its FROM clause. One can combine different sets of data by using the UNION operator. Other set manipulations can be executed by combining different operators and search conditions.

Questions and Answers

Q: *What RDMS objects are created with the SQL CREATE statement?*

A: The SQL CREATE statements are used to create the following objects:

STOGROUP   A storage group
DATABASE   A logical collection of tables

TABLESPACE	An area that stores tables
TABLE	A data structure organized by a specified columns
INDEX	An alternate path to table data
VIEW	An alternate representation of one or more tables
SYNONYM	An alternate name for local table or view
ALIAS	An alternate name for a table definition which may be local or remote, existent or nonexistent

Q: *What RDMS objects are required before you can create a table?*
A: Before you create a table, you need an existing database and tablespace.

Q: *In what RDMS object does one first list column names?*
A: One first uses the column name in the CREATE TABLE statement.

Q: *What is the syntax for a Create Table statement?*
A: The syntax for a Create Table statement is:

```
CREATE TABLE table-name
        (column name list
        primary key(column name))
        in database-name.tablespace-name.
```

Q: *Can one add columns to a table after it has been defined?*
A: Yes, one can add columns to a table after it has been defined by using the SQL ALTER TABLE statement.

Q: *Where in a table are added columns located?*
A: The new columns are added to the end of the table.

Q: *After a table is defined, can columns be removed?*
A: The only way to remove columns from an existing table involves a migration program that extracts only the desired columns of data, redefining the table without the unwanted columns, then populating the new table. One would have to handle all of the old table's dependents programmatically.

Q: *Which RDMS objects can you change with the SQL ALTER statement?*
A: The SQL ALTER statement can change a table index, a table, a tablespace, or a stogroup.

Q: *What authority is required for one to create a table?*
A: In order to create tables, one needs CREATETAB privileges.

Q: *What is the minimum authority required for one to create a tablespace?*
A: In order to create tablespaces, one needs CREATETS privileges.

Q: *When is it necessary to create a table index?*
A: It is necessary to create a table index whenever you want to enforce the uniqueness of the table's primary key.

Q: *What is a synonym?*
A: A synonym is an unqualified alternative name for a table or view.

Q: *What is a view?*

A: A view is a virtual table that can represent all or part of one or more tables. A view can help simplify data access as well as provide an additional layer of access control.

Q: *Can a view involve more than one table?*

A: A view can present data that is the result of a JOIN or UNION of more than one table.

Q: *What is a foreign key?*

A: A foreign key is the key defined in one table to reference the primary key of a reference table. This foreign key must have the same structure as the reference table's primary key.

Q: *What is referential integrity?*

A: Referential integrity is the automatic enforcement of referential constraints that exist between a reference table and a referencing table. When referential integrity is enforced, the value of a foreign key exists as a primary key value in the reference table. In other words, when referential integrity is enforced, all of the foreign key values in, for example, the "department code" column in an "employee" table exist as primary key values in a "department" table.

Q: *What is the difference between cascade and restrict?*

A: Cascade and restrict are part of the delete rule when specifying the referential constraints between two tables. The "cascade on delete" specification tells the RDMS to delete all dependent rows from the dependent table, while honoring any delete rules that exist in those dependent tables. The restrict rule tells the RDMS to fail the delete request if a dependent row exists. If a table with a cascade-on-delete rule has a dependent row in a table that has its own cascade restrict rule with an existing dependent, the entire delete operation will fail. One can get around this by using the set null on delete so that its dependents may still be satisfied.

Q: *Can you cascade an update of a primary key?*

A: You can change the value of a primary key of a reference table only if it has no dependents.

Q: *What is a remote RDMS object?*

A: A remote RDMS object is one that exists in another subsystem. There may be more than one RDMS subsystem on the same platform. The only local subsystem is the one in which your application runs; all others are remote.

Q: *Can one define remote RDMS objects?*

A: No, one cannot execute an SQL CREATE, ALTER, or GRANT statement on a remote subsystem.

Q: *What can you do with an alias that you cannot do with a synonym?*

A: With an alias, one can retrieve data from remote tables and views. An alias can be used by all who have access to the source tables represented by the alias. An alias can be defined for local or remote objects before they exist. The alias definition remains intact after the object it represents has been dropped. None of this is true for a synonym.

Q: *What is a SELECT statement?*
A: A SELECT statement is an SQL statement that retrieves data from a table or view.

Q: *What is the syntax of a SELECT statement when embedded in a COBOL program?*

A:
```
EXEC SQL
    SELECT    column_name1, column_name2, column_name3
    INTO      host_variable1, host_variable2, host_variable3
    FROM      owner.tablename
    WHERE     condition
END-EXEC
```

Q: *What are column-name qualifiers?*
A: A column-name qualifier could be a table name, a view name, a synonym name, an alias name, or a correlation name.

Q: *Why are column-name qualifiers used?*
A: Column-name qualifiers are used as a table designator to avoid ambiguity when the column names referenced exist in more than one table used in the SQL statement. Column-name qualifiers are also used in correlated references.

Q: *What is a correlation name?*
A: A correlation name is a special type of column designator that connects specific columns in the various levels of a multilevel SQL query.

Q: *How do you define a correlation name?*
A: A correlation name can be defined in the FROM clause of a query and in the first clause of an UPDATE or DELETE statement.

Q: *What is a subquery?*
A: A subquery is a query that is written as part of another query's WHERE clause. For example:

```
SELECT column_name1, column_name2
FROM    table_a
WHERE   column_name3 < ( select avg(column_name3)
                         from table_a
                         where column_name4 = 'constant')
```

Q: *What is a correlated subquery?*
A: A correlated subquery is one that has a correlation name as a table or view designator in the FROM clause of the outer query and the same correlation name as a qualifier of a search condition in the WHERE clause of the subquery. For example:

```
SELECT column_name1, column_name2
FROM    table_a x1
WHERE   column_name3 <
      ( select avg(column_name3
        from table_a
        where column_name4 = x1.column_name4)
```

Q: *How does the processing of a correlated subquery differ from a noncorrelated subquery?*

A: The subquery in a correlated subquery is reevaluated for every row of the table or view named in the outer query, while the subquery of a noncorrelated subquery is evaluated only once.

Q: *What is a results table?*

A: A results table is the product of a query against one or more tables or views (i.e., it is the place that holds the results of a query).

Q: *What is a cursor?*

A: A cursor is a named control structure used to make a set of rows available to a program.

Q: *What is the syntax required for the creation of a cursor?*

A: EXEC SQL
```
   DECLARE cursor-name cursor for
      SELECT column1, column2 . . .
      FROM table_name
      WHERE column1 = search-condition . . .
   END-EXEC.
```

Q: *When is the results table for the query in a DECLARE CURSOR statement created?*

A: The results table for a query specified in a DECLARE CURSOR statement of a cursor is created during the execution of the OPEN CURSOR statement.

Q: *What is a read-only cursor?*

A: A read-only cursor is one in which the result table was created by a query containing one of the following:
  - a DISTINCT keyword
  - a UNION operator
  - a column or scalar function
  - a GROUP BY clause
  - an ORDER BY clause
  - a HAVING clause
  - a read-only view in the FROM clause
  - a FROM clause identifying more than one table or view

Q: *How do you bring data from the result table into your program?*

A: Data is brought into a program's working storage area from a results table by issuing a FETCH cursor-name statement.

Q: *What is a host variable?*
A: A host variable is a variable referenced by embedded SQL.

Q: *What is the SQL error you receive when you try to fetch data from a cursor after it has run out of data?*
A: Trying to fetch data from an empty or exhausted cursor returns an SQL error code of 100.

Q: *What is the SQLCA?*
A: The SQLCA is the SQL communication made up of a series of variables that are updated after each SQL statement is executed.

Q: *How and where is the SQLCA specified in a COBOL program?*
A: The SQLCA must be specified in the Working Storage Section of a COBOL program by an SQL INCLUDE statement.

Q: *After an SQL statement is executed, what does a positive value in the SQLCODE variable indicate?*
A: A positive value in the SQLCODE indicates a successful execution, but with an exception condition.

Q: *After an SQL statement is executed, what does a negative value in the SQLCODE variable indicate?*
A: A negative value indicates that the SQL statement did not execute due to an error condition.

Q: *What is the main difference between static SQL and dynamic SQL?*
A: The main difference between dynamic and static SQL is that in dynamic SQL, the SQL statements can be changed, prepared, and bound by the program while it is running. Static SQL statements are prepared and bound prior to execution.

Q: *When must SQLDA (SQL descriptor area) be specified in a COBOL program?*
A: An SQLDA cannot be specified in a COBOL program.

Q: *What is a JOIN?*
A: A JOIN is a relational operation in which data is retrieved from a combination of two or more tables or views based on matching values within the specified column names of each table.

Q: *How do you code a JOIN of three tables that share the same column names?*
A: The columns names in the Select clause need to be qualified by the table or view name they belong to and could be coded as follows:
```
EXEC SQL
   SELECT table1.column1, table2.column1, table3.column1,
          table1.column2, table2.column2, table3.column2
   FROM   table1, table2, table3
END-EXEC
```

Ambiguity could also be avoided by using correlation variables as follows:

```
EXEC SQL
   SELECT a.column1, b.column1, c.column1,
          a.column2, b.column2, c.column2
   FROM   table1 a, table2 b, table3 c
END-EXEC
```

In this manner, the correlation variables (A, B, and C) match the column names with their tables.

Q: *What kind of function is the SUBSTR function and what does it do?*

A: The SUBSTR function is a scalar function. It breaks up a character or graphic string according to the substr argument list as follows:

```
SUBSTR(column-name1, starting character position, length)
```

Q: *What are column functions?*

A: Column functions are features of SQL that allow you to calculate a single value derived from one or more values found in the specified column.

Q: *What column functions are available in SQL and what do they do?*

A: The column functions and descriptions are as follows:

AVG	Returns the average value of the named column
COUNT	Returns the number of rows in the result of the query
DISTINCT	Returns only one occurrence of each value from the specified column
MAX	Returns the maximum value of the specified column of the results table generated by a query
MIN	Returns the minimum value of the specified column of the results table generated by a query
SUM	Returns the sum of the values of the specified column of the results table generated by a query

Q: *What kind of averages can you calculate with the AVG function?*

A: The only type of average you can calculate with the AVG column function is the mean average, which is calculated by dividing the sum of all values by the count of values.

Q: *What is the effect of the GROUP BY clause on column functions?*

A: The column function will calculate its result based on the individual groups created by the GROUP BY specification. In other words, if 500 groups were created by a GROUP BY clause, there would be 500 individual results—one for each group.

Q: *What's wrong with the following query?*

```
EXEC SQL
   SELECT column1, column2, avg(column3), column4
   FROM   table-a
   GROUP  by column1, column2, column3
END-EXEC
```

A: The grouping columns specified in the GROUP BY clause are inconsistent with the columns in the SELECT clause. *All* of the columns in the SELECT clause must appear as a grouping column unless they are being manipulated by a function. This example could be corrected as follows:

```
EXEC SQL
  SELECT  column1, column2, AVG(column3), column4
  FROM    table-a
  GROUP BY column1, column2, column4
END-EXEC
```

Q: *What is a predicate?*

A: A predicate is the SQL language element that specifies a condition about a value or set of values that may be true, false, or unknown.

Q: *What are the different types of predicates?*

A: In SQL, the predicate types are: Basic predicates, a Quantified predicate, the Null predicate, the In predicate, the Between predicate, the Like predicate, and the Exists predicate. These predicate types can be preceded by a "NOT" to reverse their meaning.

Q: *What are the Basic predicates?*

A: The Basic predicates are:

=	Equal
¬=, <>	Not equal
<	Less than
>	Greater than
<=	Less than or equal
>=	Greater than or equal
¬<	Not less than
¬>	Not greater than

Q: *Can the table named in the From clause of a Delete statement containing a subquery be the same table referenced by the subquery?*

A: No. In a Delete statement with a subquery, the outer query and the subquery must reference different tables.

Q: *What's wrong with this query?*

```
EXEC SQL
  SELECT AVG(COUNT (employee_id))
  FROM  emptable
  WHERE salary > 20000.00
  GROUP BY dept
END-EXEC
```

A: Assuming that all of the columns named exist in the EMPTABLE table, what is wrong is that you cannot nest a column function within a column function.

Q: *What are the valid possibilities for nesting functions?*

A: There are three valid ways to nest functions:

- Column functions within Scalar functions
- Scalar functions within Column functions
- Scalar functions within Scalar functions

Q: *What arithmetic operators can one apply to Date or Time data types?*

A: The only arithmetic operations one can apply to Date or Time data types are addition and subtraction.

Q: *Where and when is the HAVING clause used and what does it do?*

A: The HAVING clause is coded after the GROUP BY clause in a query that is summarizing results by one or more grouping columns. The HAVING clause behaves the same as the WHERE clause except that it is used to specify the conditions each returned group must satisfy. If one row in the group fails the conditions of the HAVING clause, the entire group is not returned as part of the result.

Q: *How can you sort the output of a query in the order of the results of an expression in the Select clause?*

A: Use the ORDER BY clause and refer to the expression by its position in the list of columns named in the SELECT clause. For example:

```
EXEC SQL
   SELECT column1, column2, column3, (column1 - column3),
          column4, column5
     FROM   table-a
     ORDER BY 4
END-EXEC
```

Q: *How can you combine the results of two or more SELECT statements?*

A: One can combine the results of two or more SELECT statements by using the UNION or UNION ALL keyword. These keywords cause the results of each SELECT statement to be combined as a single result table.

Q: *Why would you use the UNION keyword instead of a Join?*

A: A Join depends on the common values of the columns named in a search condition. If there are no common values in two tables (for the specified search columns), there would be no way to combine data from two tables that did not have a common range of values. For example, if employee data was stored in separate district tables, and the districts did not share employees (have the same employee in more than one district), it would be impossible to Join the tables by employee ID. In this situation, in order to retrieve all of the employees from three districts, you would have to code a UNION of the three tables as follows:

```
EXEC SQL
   SELECT empid, empname, salary
     FROM   district1-tab
```

```
    UNION
    SELECT empid, empname, salary
       FROM   district2-tab
    UNION
    SELECT empid, empname, salary
       FROM   district3-tab
END-EXEC
```

Q: *What is the difference between UNION and UNION ALL?*

A: During the merge of the multiple result (one for each table in the union), the UNION keyword causes the duplicate rows to be removed from the final result. The UNION ALL keyword is processed so that all of the duplicate result rows remain in the merged result table.

Q: *If you want to sort the output of a query that consists of the union of more than one table, where do you place the ORDER BY clause and how do you reference the sort columns?*

A: In a union of multiple tables, the ORDER BY clause is coded in the last SELECT statement. The sort columns are referenced by the integer that represents their position in the list of column names found in the Select clause.

Q: *Can the select statements in a union have subqueries?*

A: Yes. The results of any valid SELECT statement may be merged with the results of another.

Q: *Can a subquery have a UNION keyword?*

A: No. Only outer-level queries can use the UNION or UNION ALL keyword.

Q: *If you have four similar tables combined by the UNION keyword, how can you tell which table a result row came from?*

A: Place a different constant at the end of the column list in the SELECT clause of each SELECT statement in the union. The merged result will have this constant present to indicate which SELECT statement and therefore from which table the row came. Look at the following example:

```
EXEC SQL
  SELECT col1, col2, col3, 'table1'
     FROM table1
  UNION
  SELECT col1, col2, col3, 'table2'
     FROM table2
END-EXEC
```

The final result rows will have a 'TABLE1' or 'TABLE2' constant to tell you which table they came from.

Q: *When is the WHERE CURRENT OF clause used?*

A: The WHERE CURRENT OF clause is used in cursor processing in order to execute an UPDATE or DELETE statement. When a result table row is brought into the program's working storage by a FETCH statement, the cursor position remains on that row until the next FETCH statement or until the cursor is closed. During this time, the cursor position could be used to update or delete the row from the table named in the DECLARE CURSOR statement.

Q: *What clause must you code into the DECLARE CURSOR statement if you later wish to use the UPDATE WHERE CURRENT OF clause?*

A: In order to use the UPDATE WHERE CURRENT OF clause during cursor processing, you must code a FOR UPDATE OF clause listing all of the columns you wish to update. Review the following example:

```
EXEC SQL
   DECLARE cursor-name CURSOR FOR
      SELECT col1, col2, col3,
      FROM table01
      FOR UPDATE OF col1, col3
END-EXEC
```

Q: *How do you make sure that the changes made to a table become permanent?*

A: Issue an SQL COMMIT statement.

Q: *What is a Unit of Recovery?*

A: A Unit of Recovery is the amount of processing in a program that is recoverable (i.e., can be undone). A Unit of Recovery ends and a new unit begins whenever a ROLLBACK or a COMMIT is issued.

Q: *What effect does a COMMIT or ROLLBACK have of any or all of the open cursors that are being processed?*

A: As soon as a ROLLBACK or COMMIT is issued, all of the open cursors are immediately closed. When this happens, all cursor positions are lost.

Q: *If you want to continue processing the same cursor from the last position before the last COMMIT, what could you do?*

A: Construct your cursor so that it uses the unique sort key (use the ORDER BY clause) of the result table being processed as a value compared by a "greater than" predicate. Before the first DECLARE CURSOR statement is issued, set this host variable to zero so that your cursor will be positioned at the first possible row of the result table. As you fetch data from the cursor, you will automatically be keeping track of your position in the result table. After the COMMIT, simply reopen your cursor and you will be positioned as desired.

Q: *What does the "*" mean when in a SELECT statement?*

A: The asterisk allows you to select "ALL COLUMNS" from the table named in the SELECT statement without having to name the columns explicitly.

Q: *Why is it a bad practice to use the SELECT * in static SQL?*

A: The reason to avoid the SELECT * in static SQL is because database requests are validated at precompile time. If the table definitions for the tables used in a static program change (i.e., columns are added) all of the "INTO" clauses for those changed tables will become invalid, causing the programs to end abnormally. If you list all of the table column names explicitly, column additions will not affect the static programs.

Q: *What is a STOGROUP?*
A: A STOGROUP is a named object that lists the DASD volumes that are designated to store DB2 data.

Q: *Where is the isolation level specified?*
A: Isolation level is specified in the BIND or REBIND statement.

Q: *What is the difference between Cursor Stability and Repeatable Read?*
A: With the isolation level set to Cursor Stability during read-only processing, a page lock is held all the while an applications cursor is positioned on it. As soon as the cursor acquires a lock on the next required page (i.e., the cursor is positioned on a different page of data), the previous page lock is released. With the isolation level set to Repeatable Read, all of the pages of data selected by the DECLARE CURSOR statement are locked until the next explicit or implicit commit.

Q: *What is the difference between a Smallint and an Integer?*
A: A Smallint data type is 2 bytes long and has a range from –32768 to +32767. An Integer is 4 bytes long and stores numeric data ranging from –2147483648 to +2147483647.

Q: *What is a solution table?*
A: A solution table is a temporary table made to store the result of an SQL query. This is another name for a results table.

Q: *What is a recursive reference?*
A: A recursive reference is the act of referring to a single table more than one time from a single SQL QUERY.

Q: *Can a UNION and a JOIN be used in the same select statement?*
A: No. The UNION keyword cannot be placed within a SELECT statement. A UNION keyword is used to combine two or more SELECT statements.

Q: *What does the LIKE search condition allow you to do?*
A: It allows you to select table rows based on a comparison of partial strings.

Q: *What is the difference between a "%" and a "_" when used with the LIKE keyword?*
A: A "_" represents a single unknown character, while a "%" represents from 0 to many characters.

Q: *How do you select the lowest value from a numeric column?*
A: Use the MIN column function.

Q: *How do you get a string representation of a signed decimal number?*
A: Use the DIGITS scalar function.

Q: *What is Authority and is it needed all of the time?*

A: Authority is the privilege level required to access data from an RDMS and is required at all times. If you have no privileges, you cannot access the data.

Q: *What SQL statement defines a foreign key?*

A: A foreign key is defined in the CREATE TABLE statement or in an ALTER TABLE statement.

Q: *Why would you want to use a synonym?*

A: A synonym is used for convenience. When a synonym is created for a table, that table can be accessed by all privileged user IDs without having to use the Authorization ID as a qualifier.

Q: *What type of table lock is used when updating a table?*

A: Before the application can change data in a table it must acquire an exclusive lock on the page on which the changing data resides.

Q: *What is the minimum lock level instituted for an inquiry?*

A: The minimum lock level is a SHARE lock.

Q: *When is the Delete command restricted?*

A: When the user does not have Delete privileges on the specified table or if there is a referential integrity constraint enforced for a dependent foreign key.

Q: *What is the difference between a searched update and a positioned update?*

A: A searched update can update one or more rows of data depending of whether the rows satisfy the search conditions written into the update statement. A positioned update updates the single row pointed to by the cursor named in the update statement.

Q: *Can you use a positioned update when the cursor is pointing to a results table made of data from more than one table?*

A: No. A positioned update cannot operate on a read-only cursor, such as one where the results table is made with a JOIN.

Q: *How can you work through a results table in reverse order?*

A: You cannot. However, you can specify the sort key as descending in the ORDER BY clause.

Q: *Can you remove a column of data from a table without dropping the table?*

A: No. You can, however, create a view and omit the column from the view.

Q: *What happens to the table data on a volume when the volume is removed from a STOGROUP with the ALTER STOGROUP statement?*

A: Nothing. The data remains available, as before. The volume, however, will not be used the next time DASD is allocated for that STOGROUP.

Q: *What happens to the table data when the primary index of that table is dropped?*

A: Nothing. Only the index space is dropped.

Q: *What is the WHENEVER SQL statement used for?*

A: The WHENEVER statement is used to specify the HOST LANGUAGE statement to execute every time the specified exception condition exists.

Q: *What exception conditions can be trapped by the WHENEVER statement?*

A: NOT FOUND, SQLERROR, and SQLWARNING.

Q: *How do you control the scope of a WHENEVER statement?*

A: The scope of a WHENEVER statement is controlled by its placement in the listing, *not* by its execution order.

References

1. IBM Database Version 2 Release 2 Library
   - *SQL User's Guide,* SC26-4376-0
   - *Application Programming and SQL Guide,* SC26-4377-1
   - *SQL Reference,* SC26-4380-1
2. C. J. Date, *A Guide to the SQL Standard,* Addison Wesley, 1987.

16
IDMS

Paul King

Introduction

IDMS is an acronym that stands for Integrated Database Management System. It was written by the programming staff at the B.F. Goodrich Rubber Company in the late 1960s shortly after General Electric left the mainframe manufacturing field. IDMS is based on the GE database system called IDS: Integrated Data Store. That system was based on database organization ideas put forth in the late 1950s and early 1960s by Charles Bachman, who later went on to develop the Bachman reengineering products. Much of what one finds in the database portion of IDMS is a loose conversion from the original General Electric system.

IDMS was purchased from B.F. Goodrich in the early 1970s by Cullinane Database Systems, Inc. During the next two decades they added many features and products, including: the IDMS/Central Version multisession database manager; the IDD data dictionary, Online Query; the IDMS/DC teleprocessing monitor; and ADS/Online, a fourth-generation application development system. IDMS was sold to Computer Associates in the late 1980s and has since been enhanced by them to include full SQL relational database capabilities.

Terminology

ADS/Batch: A batch version of ADS/Online.

ADS/O, ADS/Online, Application Development System Online: A fourth-generation application program development and execution system that runs in the IDMS Central Version environment. It is accessed using IDMS/DC or IDMS/UCF. A batch version, ADS/Batch, is available, though less common.

Area lock: The first page in every IDMS area has a lock bit. This bit is tested to determine if an area is already open for update elsewhere.

ASF, Automatic System Facility: An attempt to add a user-friendly mechanism for generating simple table-oriented ADS/O applications without defining customized OLM maps or writing, testing, and debugging customized ADS/O executable DIALOG PROCESS code.

BCF, Batch Command Facility: A batch implementation of the Online Command Facility available in IDMS Release 12.0.

CALC, Location Mode CALC: One of four different modes available to store IDMS database records. For Location Mode CALC, a symbolic key field must be specified.

Catalog, IDMS System Catalog: A dictionary system database added to IDMS in Release 12.0. It contains the definition of IDMS/SQL databases: tables, columns, areas, indexes, constraints, etc. The system catalog also contains one or more DMCL and DBTABLE (database name table) definitions.

Central Version, CV, IDMS Central Version, IDMS/CV:

1. Central Version is the name for one of two IDMS application program operating MODES. The other is LOCAL MODE. In Central Version MODE a database access command is routed from the processing program's region through an SVC to a centralized copy of IDMS executing in its own region.

2. The Central Version of IDMS contains a multiprocessing, multitasking executive that simultaneously handles multiple concurrent IDMS requests from diverse sources. IDMS/CV has a record-locking mechanism to prevent two update requests from simultaneously modifying the same database record.

Central Version Number, IDMS/CV ID number: The number, usually from 1 to 9, used to identify a particular IDMS Central Version while it is running in an operating system region. Since IDMS requires only one SVC for all CVs that may be running, using a CV number keeps requests for services for different CVs from becoming confused.

DBNAME, Database Name:

1. An IDMS database may be given a name up to eight characters long. An IDMS database application program may use this name to request access to one of several existing versions or copies of the same database.

2. Before Release 12.0, a named list of subschema mappings that could be used at execution time to associate or BIND a run-unit to one of several possible SCHEMAs and, hence, the proper one of several, probably similar, databases.

DBNODE, Database Node, NODENAME: The eight-character name given to a Central Version within a network of Central Versions.

DDL, Data Definition Language: The language used to define an IDMS database: files, areas, records, and sets. The syntax resembles COBOL. The DDL source statements describing an entire IDMS database definition is coded into a named entity called the Schema. DDL source statements describing the part of a database accessible to an application program are coded into a named entity called the Subschema. Schema and Subschema DDL source is compiled by the Schema and Subschema compilers and, if found error free, is stored in the IDMS Integrated Data Dictionary (IDD).

DDDL, Data Dictionary Definition Language: The language used to describe record, element, program, map, module, system, user, task, line, terminal, and other entities to the IDMS Integrated Data Dictionary.

DDS, Distributed Database System: A product that enhances IDMS by tying multiple central versions together in a network. Each central version called a *node* is referenced by its unique node name, DBNODE.

DIALOG, ADS/Online DIALOG: An ADS/Online program. A typical DIALOG consists of:

1. ADS/O source code in a module called the *premap* process
2. ADS/O source code in one or more *response* processes

DMCL, Device Media Control Language: The language once used to define the IDMS database buffer pools, journals, and IDMS Areas available to IDMS database programs. It was replaced by BCF/OCF in Release 12.0.

DMCL Module, DMCL Load Module: The load module created when the object code output from the DMCL compiler or BCF/OCF is link-edited into a load library. The DMCL module contains the run-time definition of IDMS Areas, buffer pools, journals, and operating system files.

DML, Data Manipulation Language: The high-level language a programmer usually uses to code database operations into an IDMS program. Primary data manipulation verbs are: STORE, MODIFY, ERASE, OBTAIN, CONNECT, and DISCONNECT.

Escape, ESCAPE/TOTAL: An IDMS product that emulates the TOTAL database management system from Cincom Systems. It permits the conversion of TOTAL databases into IDMS while preserving the investment in TOTAL applications programs and programming talent. Escape provides a utility that converts the TOTAL DBD into an equivalent IDMS Schema, a utility that loads a TOTAL database into an equivalent IDMS database, and a run-time Application Program Interface duplicating the API within TOTAL for use by the TOTAL programs.

IDMS, Integrated Database Management System: A family of related database products consisting of, but not limited to, IDMS/DB, CULPRIT (short for Column Print, a third-generation report-generating tool enhanced to operate with IDMS/DB), and IDMS/CV (originally called CAMP—Central Access Monitor Program).

Integrated indexing: The enhancement to IDMS in Release 10.0 that supports traditional B-tree indexing within the IDMS DBMS itself. It replaces the SPF, a cumbersome indexing mechanism.

Location mode: Refers to the four different ways or modes IDMS can use to store database records: CALC, VIA, DIRECT, and VSAM.

Log, IDMS/CV Log: A special unjournaled IDMS database file used by IDMS/CV only. CV records session messages, statistics, tasks, and system dumps on the Log.

Page group: An extremely large database may require more than the 16-million-plus database pages to contain all of the data records. Such a database must be broken or segmented into smaller chunks. Each less-than-16-million-page "chunk" is called a *page group*.

Protocol: A named template used by the DML preprocessor to generate the native language call to the IDMS run-time subroutine.

Run-unit: A recoverable unit of work performed by an IDMS database program. A run-unit starts with successful completion of an IDMS BIND and ends with a successful FINISH. If there is a failure before the successful FINISH, the database may be recovered by backing out all of the pages with a process called *rollback*.

Subschema: The named dictionary entity listing the Schema Areas, Records, and IDMS Sets available to a database program.

SYSCTL, SYSCTL file: The default name of the file used by an IDMS/CV to communicate important information to an IDMS batch program, CICS, or other region attempting to use the central version services. That information includes the IDMS SVC number, the IDMS/CV ID number, default DBNAME, DBNODE, DICTNAME, and DICTNODE.

SYSIDMS, SYSIDMS file: The name of a new batch application program file for Release 12.0 used to feed options to the batch IDMS run-time system. Options include: CV/Local mode, Journal/Nojournal, DMCL name, DBNAME, DBNODE, DICTNAME, DICTNODE, TRACE ON/OFF, etc.

VIA, Location Mode VIA: When a DBA wants to cluster SET MEMBER records near its owner, he or she uses Location Mode VIA. When asked to store a VIA record, IDMS attempts to store the record on the same page as the record's SET OWNER.

Questions and Answers

Q: *What is the difference between an OBTAIN and a GET?*
A: GET commands IDMS to move the data contents of a database record from the IDMS buffer pool into a program's working storage. The record must first have been retrieved by IDMS. FIND does that. OBTAIN simply performs the FIND and the GET in one operation.

Q: *What does an OBTAIN ANY do?*
A: This is so obscure that it is almost a trick question. OBTAIN ANY is simply another way to say OBTAIN CALC.

Q: *What does OBTAIN DUPLICATE do?*
A: OBTAIN DUPLICATE pertains to CALC records only when defined with duplicates allowed. Once a program OBTAINS a CALC record, OBTAIN DUPLICATE will retrieve the first duplicate.

Q: *What does the IF SET EMPTY IDMS command do?*
A: It checks the current owner of the specified set to see if there are any member records.

Q: *What does the IF SET MEMBER IDMS command do?*

A: It checks the current member of the specified set in the command to see if it participates in the set or not.

Q: *Looking at it from a programmer's point of view, what do you like most about IDMS?*

A: Some DBMSs require commands to be coded directly in CALL program statements. One must then debug them one call at a time. IDMS allows one to write database commands using program statements similar to the native language, be it COBOL or PL/I, so coding it is easier. IDMS also provides a precompiler that checks the whole program for syntax and semantics, validating all of the IDMS code in one pass before testing starts.

Q: *What is the difference between a CV batch and a DC batch program?*

A: A CV batch program only uses regular IDMS databases. A DC batch program is an IDMS batch program that can use additional IDMS/DC functions including the Scratch and Queue facilities.

Q: *What method can be employed during system and program design to avoid database record deadlocks?*

A: Make a list of all the records in the Schema. Place the records in a sequence designed to minimize record-locking bottlenecks. When writing programs, always lock the database records in the sequence in which they appear on the list.

Q: *How can you avoid having to check the IDMS error-status field after every IDMS DML command?*

A: Write the program using an autostatus protocol.

Q: *How does an IDMS application program communicate with the IDMS DBMS?*

A: It communicates by calling the IDMS Application Program Interface using standard subroutine linkage and passing parameters. For some IDMS commands, the program must move a value into one or more fields within the Subschema Control Block. For example, the DIRECT-DBKEY field must be set prior to STORE of a DIRECT record.

Q: *How does IDMS communicate with an application program?*

A: IDMS has several avenues. Exceptional condition codes are usually sent back in the ERROR-STATUS or LR-STATUS field of the Subschema Control Block. ERROR-SET, ERROR-RECORD, and ERROR-AREA fields may communicate the name of an object in error. The contents of IDMS records are returned to a program in the IDMS record data structures (01 levels) within the DATA DIVISION. Of course, if IDMS hits very great difficulty and can't proceed, it will simply abort the program setting the user abend code.

Q: *What is an Area sweep?*

A: When a program reads all of the pages within an Area in sequence from first to last, that is called an *Area sweep.*

Q: *Describe the IDMS statements that a simple program would contain if its whole purpose were to STORE a CUSTOMER record in an IDMS database.*

A: The program must be coded to:

1. Specify the name of the Subschema it will use. Optionally, it may also specify the Schema name and version, database name, database node, dictionary name, and dictionary node.

2. COPY from the dictionary the record definition for the CUSTOMER record. This places the record 01 level definition in working storage.

3. BIND the RUN-UNIT to establish the run-time connection to IDMS.

4. READY for UPDATE the IDMS Area in which the CUSTOMER record is stored.

5. Once the CUSTOMER record data fields are populated, issue the STORE CUSTOMER command.

6. Check ERROR-STATUS for zeros.

7. Issue FINISH to commit the CUSTOMER record to the database file. The ERROR-STATUS field must also be checked after the BIND, READY, and FINISH to make sure they also worked.

Q: *Why doesn't the program check the ERROR-STATUS after the Subschema define and COPY?*

A: Those are checked by the IDMS precompiler with appropriate action taken at that time. They cause no actions at program execution time.

Q: *What is the SYSIDMS file used for?*

A: SYSIDMS is a new file in the Release 12.0 batch IDMS interface. It is used to activate numerous run-time options such as local versus central version mode, journaling versus No-journaling, DMCL name, DBNAME, and so forth.

Q: *How can one avoid adding a SYSIDMS file to all of their batch jobs when running in Release 12.0 or later?*

A: That may not be possible. If you want to take advantage of some of the special run-time options, such as database tracing or QSAM support, a SYSIDMS file is needed to input the option parameter cards. However, if there are no special requirements, using IDMSDMCL for the batch DMCL will make the SYSIDMS file unnecessary.

Q: *What is QSAM support and why is it used?*

A: For non-VSAM database files, IDMS uses BDAM to access database pages. With BDAM, IDMS must wait while a read is in progress. However, when doing an Area sweep, QSAM can be used instead. With QSAM support, the processing for one database page overlaps reading of the next page in an Area. This serves to reduce the program elapsed time.

Q: *What common database programming mistake do beginners make when coding the Area sweep of owner records combined with set processing of each owner's members?*

A: They don't reestablish area currency on the proper owner occurrence prior to OBTAIN NEXT WITHIN AREA.

Q: *How do you improve performance of a batch job that will read every record in one Area if it's running in local mode?*

A: In Release 10.2, link-edit the IDMSQSAM driver into the program. In Release 12.0, put the QSAM option in the SYSIDMS file.

Q: *When searching for several member records in succession by symbolic key on a chained sorted set, how can you prevent IDMS from starting each search from the beginning of the set?*

A: Sort the search symbolic keys in the same sequence as the member records in the set and specify the CURRENT option on the OBTAIN NEXT RECORD IN SET USING command.

Q: *How does IDMS know when an Area is locked?*

A: When IDMS readies an Area for update, it sets the lock bit on the first page in the Area to 1. Prior to doing that, it checks the lock bit value. If it is 1, IDMS knows it can't proceed because someone else has put the Area into update. If it is 0, IDMS knows the Area is available for update.

Q: *How does IDMS know if a record is locked?*

A: Record locks are kept inside of the Central Version (CV) only. CV locks a record by putting the record's DB-Key into the list of locked records. Any DB-Key in the list identifies a record as being locked.

Q: *Regarding the attributes of IDMS sets, explain what Mandatory, Optional, Automatic, and Manual mean.*

A: Automatic and Manual define the actions IDMS takes when storing a member record on a set. Automatic means the record is automatically connected to the set. Manual means that it is not. Connection, in that case, must be done with a CONNECT IDMS command. Mandatory and Optional define the actions a program may command for a record already connected to a set. Optional indicates that the record may be removed from the set by a DISCONNECT in an update program. One could say: "Continued participation in the set is optional." Mandatory indicates that disconnection is not allowed. One would say: "Continued participation in the set is mandatory." Then, only erasing the record will remove it from the set.

Q: *What is a logically deleted record?*

A: A logically deleted record occurs when IDMS cannot completely delete all of a database record one tells it to ERASE. This occurs only when erasing a record that is a member of a chain set with no PRIOR pointers and when the run-unit has not established any currency on the prior record in the set. When erasing a member record, IDMS always requires access to the set's

PRIOR record so that its NEXT pointer can be modified to point past the record being erased. If IDMS can't do that, then at least the data portion of the database record is removed. But the record prefix containing all set pointers must remain to keep the chain intact.

Q: *How can logically deleted records be avoided?*
A: The easiest way is to always specify PRIOR pointers for every chained set. For a set without prior pointers, always establish set currency on the member record prior to the one being erased immediately before the erasure.

Q: *How can logically deleted records be dealt with?*
A: One can simply leave them there, not dealing with them at all. IDMS will also ignore them, although they do take up space and add overhead to internal set processing. One can write an update program that reads each owner and then each member of each problem set, setting up the conditions that allow the logically deleted record to be removed. One can run the IDMSDUMP utility with the LDEL option, followed by the IDMSLDEL utility. Perhaps the best action is to restructure the set(s) that have logically deleted records to include PRIOR pointers. Unfortunately, since restructure cannot process a database containing logically deleted records, they still have to be cleaned up first.

Q: *What happens when a program ERASES a record from an IDMS database?*
A: IDMS attempts to disconnect the record from each set in which it participates. If that is successful, the record is effectively erased when IDMS sets its line index to null. If the record was the highest-numbered record on the page, the line index is returned to the unused area on the page instead. If IDMS cannot disconnect the record from every set, then the data portion is released and just the prefix remains. It is marked as a logically deleted record.

Q: *Does IDMS free the space on a page taken up by a record when it is erased?*
A: Yes and no. When IDMS erases a record, the free space on the page is increased by the proper amount, but the space is not available for reuse. Free storage on a page remains fragmented and dormant until IDMS can no longer satisfy a store record request from the unused storage area toward the back of the page. At that point, all database records already on the page are shifted as far as possible to the front, squeezing all free, fragmented storage back into the unused area.

Q: *When a program performs an Area sweep using OBTAIN NEXT WITHIN AREA for a CALC record, in what sequence will the records be retrieved?*
A: Randomly, assuming the CALC algorithm has successfully stored them randomly.

Q: *How could a program process CALC records in sequence by CALC key value?*
A: One approach would be to define an index on the CALC key field and retrieve all of the records by the index, starting at the beginning of the index.

It is usually faster, however, to perform an Area sweep of the CALC records using IDMS QSAM support, building SORTIN work records from just those fields that are needed. Sorting SORTIN by the CALC key will put the records in proper order.

Q: *What are the four types of currency?*
A: Area, Set, Record, and Run-unit.

Q: *What are the four set currencies or pointers that may be used by IDMS in Set processing?*
A: Current of Set, Next in Set, Prior in Set, and Owner of Set.

Q: *What is the difference between local and central version mode?*
A: Programs using local mode usually run quicker and more efficiently. There is no overhead from extra SVC calls, and journaling is not required. Also, a local mode program may use a local DMCL with customized buffer pools. On the negative side, updating in local mode requires exclusive use of the database. Central version supports shared database update capability to many batch and on-line programs simultaneously. CV journaling provides automatic recovery from both program and system failures.

Q: *What is the SYSCTL file?*
A: The SYSCTL file is a file that is initialized by IDMS central version at start-up time. It is used as a program to communicate with CV. A program may sign on to a particular central version by virtue of the fact that its JCL contains a SYSCTL file that points to the data set initialized by the desired CV.

Q: *What is in the SYSCTL file?*
A: The IDMS/CV start-up puts into the SYSCTL file: the CV SVC number, CV ID number, the CV NODE name, and default DBNAME.

Q: *Who uses the information in the SYSCTL file?*
A: The IDMS interface uses it. The interface is linked into a batch program or loaded into a teleprocessing monitor like CICS. Some or all of this is used by the IDMS application program interface to communicate with a central version.

Q: *Is there any way to avoid using a SYSCTL file?*
A: You could hard-code the information into an object module called IDMSOPTI and link that into each program. That, however, surrenders the flexibility SYSCTL affords.

Q: *Why would anyone ever want to use IDMSOPTI?*
A: Someone may want to avoid having a SYSCTL JCL statement. Or there may be a desire to force every program to use central version mode. One can use IDMSOPTI to force programs to use a particular database name or node.

Q: *What's the difference between IDMS batch and IDMS local?*
A: Batch and local are actually two different attributes of a program. So comparing them may be difficult. Batch refers to a program scheduled by the

operating system. This is in contrast to an on-line program that is scheduled by a teleprocessing monitor. Local refers to one of two modes in
which an IDMS batch program may run. The other mode is called central
version.

Q: *What is the UPSI byte and what will IDMS use it for? (This may come up
in an interview at a DOS/VSE site.)*

A: That's the old User Programmable Switch Indicator. It provided a way for
DOS running on the System 360 to simulate the switches on the front of the
IBM 1401 computers. The DOS UPSI JCL card used to be the only way a
DOS application program could inform the IDMS interface that it wanted to
run in CV mode. Adding support for a SYSCTL file to the DOS version
of IDMS made the UPSI card pretty much obsolete as far as IDMS was
concerned.

Q: *When is batch local mode preferable to batch CV?*

A: When there is a desire for greater efficiency or operating independence.
Local mode avoids the overhead of CV by reducing the SVC calls and
avoiding some potential bottlenecks, like CV journaling. Local mode
programs are often faster, but not always. On a heavily loaded system,
where CV has a very high priority and the batch job has a very low priority, the job may run quicker using CV since all database I/O would be
scheduled from the higher-priority region. Local mode also affords independence from the CV environment. A local program may utilize a customized DMCL for improved buffer pool configuration and a dedicated
journal file to eliminate any bottleneck caused by journal activity from
other programs.

Q: *What are the different parts of an ADS on-line DIALOG?*

A: A DIALOG is composed of an OLM map containing terminal screen definitions and related records (unless it is a mapless DIALOG); premap and
response processes containing executable code, work, and database records
containing data fields; plus other definitional items such as subschema and
database name, DIALOG type (mainline or not), and the like.

Q: *What's the best way to design ADS/O DIALOGS so as to minimize the
amount of storage allocated in the storage pool across pseudo converses?*

A: The ADS/O DIALOGS should be designed in a two-level configuration. The
top level could be called a screen handler. It would do all simple input validation and syntax checking. If the DIALOG found no errors, the first-level
DIALOG would call the second level. The second level would contain all
database access logic. Once it completed the database function it would
return control to the first-level DIALOG with an indication of success or failure. When constructed this way, storage consumed by database record
buffers is freed on return from the second-level DIALOG. That way, the
only storage held in memory across pseudo converse is that which would be
associated with the dialogue map.

Q: *What is the difference between a LINK, an INVOKE, and a TRANSFER?*

A: A LINK calls a lower-level DIALOG. Record currencies are passed. On return, execution resumes at the next ADS/O statement. Record currencies are passed back. An INVOKE calls a lower-level DIALOG. Record currencies are passed. On return, execution resumes at the premap process or the map-out in the calling DIALOG. A TRANSFER calls a DIALOG on the same level. Record currencies are not passed. Execution is not returned to the calling DIALOG.

Q: *What does a RETURN CONTINUE do?*

A: A RETURN CONTINUE returns control to the first command in the premap process of the DIALOG receiving control.

Q: *What ADS/O command is used only to send a message?*

A: DISPLAY.

Q: *How do you perform a numeric test on a field in ADS/O?*

A: IF field MATCHED '#####'. The number of #'s should equal the length of the field you are testing.

Q: *What does EXIT do?*

A: EXIT terminates a WHILE command.

Q: *How do you determine if the operator modified any fields on the screen?*

A: IF field CHANGED or IF field ERASED.

Q: *What is the syntax for loop control in ADS/O?*

A:
```
WHILE condition REPEAT.
   ADS/O statement.
   ADS/O statement.
END.
```

Q: *Does ADS/O support nested subroutines (i.e., a subroutine defined within another subroutine)?*

A: No.

Q: *What is the main difference between scratch records and queue records?*

A: Scratch records disappear when central version terminates. Queue records may remain in the system for a specified period of time before they are purged. Also, storing records on a queue may be set to trigger a task to process them.

Q: *Describe in general terms the steps needed to define an on-line mapping map.*

A: 1. Define the work records (if any) to be attached to the map using IDD.

   2. Enter OLM and complete initial map definition, including the map name, version, type, and associated database or work records.

   3. Proceed to full-screen definition and paint the literals and data fields as they are to appear at run time.

4. Complete the second definition pass going field by field through the screen specifying field attributes.

5. When all is done, perform the map generate. This reads the map definition and builds the map load module for use at run time.

Q: *When building an OLM map, what will be the default cursor position?*
A: It will be set to the first unprotected field.

Q: *Can one override this?*
A: Yes, on the map definition format screen, put the cursor on the desired field and hit PFK 6.

Q: *In on-line mapping, what is the difference between an EDIT table and a CODE table?*
A: An EDIT table associated with a map field is used by OLM at run time to automatically table lookup and validate data keyed in by a terminal operator. A CODE table is used to both validate codes and translate them into their associated values. A typical EDIT table might include all valid customer types for a customer application. A CODE table may be used to translate the two-character state abbreviation into the full state name.

Q: *What is the difference between loosely coupled and tightly coupled edit and code tables?*
A: In OLM, a tightly coupled table is linked right into the map load module. A loosely coupled table is linked separately and referred to by name at run time. When you change and regenerate a loosely coupled table, the change is reflected the next time the table is loaded. Changes to a tightly coupled table don't take effect until the map is regenerated.

Q: *What is the IDMSOPTI module used for?*
A: The IDMSOPTI module is an object module that may be link-edited into the load module of a batch application program. The purpose of the OPTI module is to specify various options that may be associated with a run-unit. These options may force CV or local mode. They may specify the name of the SYSCTL data file, the name of the database, and the name of the database node that the run-unit will use.

Q: *What IDMS utility would be used to repair an IDMS database?*
A: IDMSDBAN (database analysis) isolates many types of database corruption. And IDMSPFIX, also called PFIX or Page Fix, would be employed to effect actual repairs on the database pages.

Q: *What's the difference between a FILE and an AREA?*
A: A FILE is an operating system entity used to access DASD storage, among other things. An AREA is an IDMS entity used by applications programs to access IDMS database records. They are very similar in concept, but one is an operating system creation and the other belongs to IDMS.

Q: *Can you be more specific about any relationship between them, since they are so similar?*

A: The relationship between an IDMS AREA and a FILE can be very direct, since each page within an IDMS database is stored on one fixed-length operating system FILE record. In other words, database pages map directly to file records or blocks.

Q: *Then why aren't AREAs simply called FILEs?*

A: While a FILE can, and often does, contain all of one and only one IDMS AREA, that is not a requirement. A large area may be spread across many files, or parts of files. On the other hand, a file may contain several, or parts of several, AREAs. So there can be a many-to-many relationship between files and areas. In general, AREAs are laid out across operating system files and the files are laid out across DASD devices in a way that attempts to optimize run-time performance and recoverability from program, system, or hardware failure.

Q: *What has happened when CV, during system start-up, leaves all the areas of one database offline?*

A: Most likely those areas are locked. They are locked because some other CV or local batch job is running and has locked them. The more ominous possibility is that a CV or batch job that had locked them has failed, leaving them locked. Another more insidious possibility is that they were restored from a database backup that was taken while someone else had them locked.

Q: *What do you do about it?*

A: Wait until the local batch job is finished and, if appropriate, vary them online manually. If another CV has them locked, then find out who is scheduling two CVs against one database at the same time. If no CV or batch job can be found on the system, or any other system sharing the DASD, then you are looking at some type of earlier failure. The CV you are starting was probably not the prior failure. If it had failed, warmstart would have corrected the problems. Look for the local-mode batch job that failed. If a bad backup was restored, then you are in a traditional recovery situation which may require another restore and roll-forward.

Q: *How must the Schema and DMCL (or just the DMCL in Release 12.0) be set up to support copying of one "small" database to another?*

A: All areas in both databases must have identical area-to-file mapping, identical page ranges and page sizes, records and sets.

Q: *If the "small" databases don't have identical page sizes and ranges, how could you still copy one to the other?*

A: Run Unload from one, Initialize and Reload into the other. It shouldn't take very long on small databases.

Q: *What is the most likely cause for CV to hang up?*
A: Either log full or all journals full.

Q: *What do you do for an unrecoverable I/O error on a database file?*
A: 1. Quiesce the Area and, if CV is using it, also quiesce CV.

   2. Deallocate the bad file.

   3. Reallocate the file on a good DASD pack.

   4. Restore the file from the last good backup. Note the Area can't have been locked when it was backed up.

   5. Assemble all of the journal tapes from the backup to the point of failure.

   6. Roll forward the one broken file to the point of failure.

   7. Roll back any run-units in flight at the time of the error.

Q: *What if some of the journals are unusable?*
A: Then you can't properly recover.

Q: *What are your options?*
A: Restore the database and rerun all of the updates that have occurred since the last restore.

Q: *How do you recover from an unrecoverable I/O error on a journal file?*
A: It depends when it occurs. If it occurs during journal archive, the safest thing to do would be immediately to execute a normal shutdown and back up the entire system. While that is running, reallocate the bad journal to another device and reinitialize all of them.

Q: *What if the journal I/O error occurs within CV?*
A: When IDMS/CV gets an I/O error on a journal during normal operations, it recovers by immediately switching to the next journal and stops using the broken one.

Q: *Describe the steps DBA would take to properly add a 2-byte field to the symbolic key of a CALC record.*
A: 1. Restructure the record adding the 2-byte field.

   2. Unload/reload the area so IDMS can recast the CALC record's placement based on the new, longer symbolic key.

Q: *What steps will a DBA take to convert a chain-sorted set to an indexed-sorted set?*
A: Perform an unload/reload, changing the definition of the set in the reload schema to indexed.

Q: *How would you do that on an area too large to make unload/reload practical?*
A: Restructure the record, adding the indexed-sorted set definition with the manual attribute. Write a program to read each set owner. For each owner, read the members in the chain-sorted set. For each member, issue a CONNECT on the indexed set. Finally, when that is all done, restructure again to remove the chain set pointers.

Q: *What is the name of the database name table in Release 10.2, and what determines its version number?*

A: The name is IDMSDBTB. It is given a version number matching the system number that contains its definition.

Q: *Where is it stored and how is it accessed?*

A: In Release 10.2, it is stored in the load area used by the dictionary containing its definition. It is accessed by CV, which loads it from that load area. It is accessed in local mode from a load library, after punching the IDMSDBTB object and link-editing it into a step library.

Q: *Any changes to that in Release 12.0?*

A: Yes, lots. In Release 12.0 the database name table becomes an entity in its own right, called DBTABLE. DBTABLE definitions are stored by the command facility in the new Release 12.0 catalog load area. The name is given by a DBA.

Q: *How can a many-to-many relationship be implemented within an IDMS database design?*

A: Place a record type, called a junction record, between the two records for which the many-to-many relationship is desired. Make the new record a member of two sets, with each record in the many-to-many relationship owning one of the sets.

Q: *What is a subschema and what are some of the things it contains?*

A: A subschema specifies a proper subset of the areas, records, data elements, and sets from one IDMS Schema definition. Default and allowable usage modes may be specified for Areas. Allowable commands may be specified for records and sets. Optionally, a subschema may contain one or more LRF logical records and all associated LRF DML code. The subschema load module contains a time stamp of when it was GENERATED. In Release 10.2 and earlier, it may contain the name of a DMCL it will use in local mode.

Q: *When would an index be used in a database design?*

A: An index would be placed on a record field, or fields, when there is a requirement for partial key retrieval. If retrieval will always be by full symbolic key, then defining another CALC record with that key and tying it to the target record with a chain set would be more efficient.

17
VSAM

George W. Harrison

Introduction

VSAM (Virtual Storage Access Method) was produced by IBM as a replacement for ISAM. VSAM supports functions similar to those of ISAM, but provides better performance. While other access methods were device-dependent, each requiring a separate utility, VSAM supports four dataset operations—key-sequenced, entry-sequenced, relative-record, and linear—and requires only one utility. VSAM is a component of both IBM's VSE and MVS operating systems, thus allowing dataset portability between operating systems.

Questions and Answers

Terminology and Concepts

Q: *Name some of the differences between CA and CI.*

A: CI, Control Interval, is the unit of transfer between virtual storage and DASD. The size of a control interval must be a multiple of 512 when less than or equal to 8192. If the size is larger than 8192, it must be a multiple of 2048.

　　CA, Control Area, is auxiliary storage that is reserved by VSAM to hold or receive control intervals. The minimum size of a control area is two control intervals. The maximum size is one cylinder.

Q: *How do you specify the amount of CI available to a file?*

A: The amount of control interval space available to a file is specified in the FREESPACE (FSPC) parameter of the DEFINE command.

Q: *How do you specify the amount of CA available to a file?*

A: The amount of control interval space available to a file is also specified in the FREESPACE (FSPC) parameter of the DEFINE command. The amount of FREESPACE specified must be large enough for at least one control interval.

Note: The FREESPACE parameter is specified as FSPC (X Y)—where X is the percentage of the control interval to be left empty, and Y is the percentage of the control area to be left empty after a key-sequenced file is initially loaded.

Q: *If, for example, FSPC (100 100) were specified, does that mean that both the control intervals and control areas would be left empty because 100 percent of both the control interval and the control areas are specified to be empty?*

A: No, they would not be left empty. One record would be written for each control interval, and one control interval would be written for each control area.

Q: *Can you run out of CA and/or CI?*

A: Yes. When you run out of freespace, there would be no space available to add a new record.

Q: *If you can run out of CA or CI, how do you know it has happened?*

A: When you try to add a new record, a message would inform you that this has happened.

Q: *If you do run out of CA or CI, what should you do about it?*

A: You have to reorganize the file. Reorganizing a file involves copying the file (building a backup) onto another area or media (tape), deleting the file you want to reorganize, redefining the file (allocating more space, freespace, etc.), and reloading the file.

Q: *When reorganizing a file, do you have to sort the backup copy of the file prior to reloading it?*

A: If you are using IDCAMS, you do not have to sort the records.

Q: *What types of datasets are supported by VSAM?*

A: The types of datasets supported by VSAM are KSDS (key-sequenced), ESDS (entry-sequenced), RRDS (relative-record), and LDS (linear).

Q: *What is the difference in the way an application would access a relative-record dataset and a linear dataset?*

A: Records in a relative-record dataset are accessed by relative-record number, a sequential position of the record in relation to the first record in the dataset. Linear dataset records are accessed sequentially, in the same way as an entry-sequenced dataset.

Q: *How are records stored in each type of data file supported by VSAM?*

A: A key-sequenced dataset is ordered by key and is accessed by an index.

An entry-sequenced dataset has to have its data stored sequentially. Records can be added only at the end of the dataset.

Data stored in relative-record datasets are stored in "slots." Data is accessed by record number.

Data stored in linear datasets are stored sequentially, similar to the way records are stored in an entry-sequenced dataset, except that control fields used by the other access methods are not present.

Q: *Can you access variable-length blocked records using VSAM?*
A: Yes.

Q: *What is a cluster?*
A: A cluster is a VSAM-defined structure and consists of data and, if the access requires a key, index components.

Q: *Where would you use the UPGRADE parameter and what function does it perform?*
A: UPGRADE is an option that can be specified when defining an alternate index. Whenever you update the base cluster, if you have specified UPGRADE, the alternate indexes dataset will also be (automatically) updated.

Q: *What is the function performed by a VSAM "ALTER"?*
A: A VSAM "ALTER" allows modification of the characteristics of a dataset.

Q: *Name the different kinds of catalogs that are accessable to a VSAM user.*
A: A VSAM user can access a VSAM master catalog as well as user catalogs.

Q: *What is the CRA?*
A: The CRA is the Catalog Recovery Area.

Q: *How do you define a CRA?*
A: A CRA is automatically created if "RECOVERABLE" parameter is specified when the VSAM master or user catalog is defined.

Q: *What is a VSAM model?*
A: A VSAM model provides different default values than the system defaults provided by the DEFINE command.

Q: *Is it advisable to use a VSAM model?*
A: It is not recommended to use VSAM models. Once created, they tend to be used by programmers without thought being given to individual dataset requirements.

Q: *Where, why, and when do you use the ERASE option when deleting a dataset?*
A: The ERASE option fills the data component of a cluster or an alternate index with binary zeros, thus erasing all previously written data. It is not recommended to use this option because it is not needed for security. In addition, it is time-consuming.

Alternate Indexes

Q: *What is an alternate index?*

A: An alternate index is an additional way of accessing key-sequenced data record stored in a base cluster.

Q: *What is a path?*

A: A path is a set of linkages that connect alternate indexes to a base cluster.

Q: *What is a path used for?*

A: A path is used by VSAM to access a record in a base cluster by means of an alternate index.

Q: *When would you use an alternate index?*

A: An alternate index would be used whenever it is necessary to access data by more than one means.

Q: *Do alternate indexes have to be unique?*

A: No, alternate indexes do not have to be unique.

Q: *Can you build an alternate index for an ESDS?*

A: Yes, they can be built for KSDS as well as for ESDS.

Q: *How would you specify an alternate index (i.e., what steps do you have to execute)?*

A: To allocate an alternate index you have to:

1. Define the alternate index and relate it to its base cluster.
2. Define the path which will allow access to the base cluster via the alternate index.
3. Build the alternate index.

Q: *How do you determine the record size of an alternate index?*

A: This question is best answered by using an example.

A key-sequenced employee dataset (file) with a key of social security number needs to be accessed by department number. To access this dataset by department, department number has to be specified as an alternate index. Since each department contains more than one employee, the alternate index is nonunique. The minimum record size must account for 5 bytes of control information plus the length of the base cluster key. The maximum record must account for the control information plus the length of the alternate key plus the length of the base cluster key for each allowable prime key.

In this example, the record key length of the base cluster is 9 bytes, the department number is 4 bytes, and each department has a maximum of 200 employees.

```
RECORD SIZE = 5 + KEY LENGTH OF THE ALTERNATE INDEX + (KEY
    LENGTH OF THE PRIME KEY * THE NUMBER OF NONUNIQUE PRIME
    KEYS)

MINIMUM RECORD SIZE = 5 + 4 + (9 * 1) = 9 + 9 = 18
MAXIMUM RECORD SIZE = 5 + 4 + (9 * 200) = 9 + 1800 = 1809
```

The record length of this alternate index would then be specified in the define of the alternate index as:

```
RECORDSIZE (18 1809)
```

VSAM Spaces

Q: *What is the difference between a user catalog and a master catalog?*

A: There can be only one master catalog per system, but there can be an unlimited number of user catalogs. Each user catalog has an entry in the master catalog with a connecting pointer.

Q: *What is the difference between a unique dataset and a suballocated dataset?*

A: VSAM uses two types of dataspaces: suballocatable and unique. A suballocatable dataspace can contain one or more datasets, while a unique dataspace can contain only one dataset. A dataset in a suballocated dataspace is a suballocated dataset, while a dataset in a unique dataspace is a unique dataset.

Q: *Under what conditions would you want to define a dataset as being a suballocated dataset?*

A: Under most cases, a dataset would be defined as suballocated. A dataset must be suballocated if the REUSE option is used.

Q: *How can you check how much freespace (unused space) is available for future additions in an ESDS?*

A: The freespace available for future additions to an ESDS can be obtained by checking the FREESPC-BYTES entry in the data component portion of a LISTCAT listing.

Q: *How can you check how much freespace is available for future additions in a KSDS?*

A: The technique used for determining the amount of freespace for an ESDS can also be used for a KSDS.

Q: *What are some of the more important types of information that can be obtained from a LISTCAT?*

A: Some of the information that can be obtained from a LISTCAT:

- The names of the associated entries: data component, index component, and/or alternate index clusters
- KEYLEN—the length of the primary key
- RKP—the relative key position in the record (starting with byte 0)

- AVGLRECL—the minimum record length
- MAXLRECL—the maximum record length

Q: *Where can you find LASTCC and MAXCC entries?*
A: The LASTCC and MAXCC entries can be found on the output produced by the execution of the IDCAMS program.

Q: *What does LASTCC contain?*
A: The LASTCC contains the condition code that resulted from the immediately preceding/executed function command.

Q: *What does MAXCC contain?*
A: MAXCC contains the highest condition code that resulted from the previous functional command stream.

Q: *What is the meaning of condition code "8"?*
A: Condition code of "8" means that major functions were bypassed even though the function to be executed was completed. For example, an entry specified to be deleted could not be found.

AMS—Access Method Services

Q: *What is AMS?*
A: AMS stands for Access Method Services. It is an IBM-provided service program that is used to create and maintain datasets.

Q: *How are the services supplied (by AMS) invoked?*
A: Access Method Services are invoked by execution of the IDCAMS program.

Q: *Name five AMS commands and tell what each is used for.*
A: ALTER   Changes the attributes of a previously defined VSAM object
   DEFINE   Defines a VSAM object (catalogs and clusters)
   DELETE   Deletes a VSAM object
   LISTCAT   Lists information contained in a VSAM catalog
   REPRO   Copies, converts, merges, and reorganizes catalogs and datasets

Q: *Can you use AMS to build a generation dataset?*
A: Yes, you can.

Q: *Which command could you use to build a generation dataset (in AMS)?*
A: A GDG can be built by using the DEFINE GDG command.

Q: *What function does the SHAREOPTIONS perform?*
A: SHAREOPTIONS provides data integrity. SHAREOPTIONS is specified in the DEFINE command.

Q: *What is the format of the SHAREOPTIONS command?*
A: The format is

```
SHAREOPTIONS (CROSS-REGION | CROSS-SYSTEM)
```

Q: *What parameters are valid with SHAREOPTIONS?*

A: CROSS-REGION can have values 1 through 4. CROSS-SYSTEM options can have a value of only 3 or 4.

Q: *When would you use each of the SHAREOPTIONS options?*

A: CROSS-REGION: You would use the CROSS-REGION options as follows:

1. When the dataset can be opened by only one user for writing and many users for reading. Read and write integrity (VSAM) will ensure that these rules are adhered to and that someone with read access cannot update records.

2. This option is the same as option 1 except that only write integrity is provided. Read integrity must be provided by the user, as no controls are provided to prevent a user from reading a record that is being updated (by another user).

3. The dataset can be opened by multiple users for updating and reading. Read and write integrity must be provided by the user.

4. This option provides the same level of read-write integrity as option 3. The difference is that VSAM will not allow a control area (CA) split. Instead, VSAM provides a new buffer for each direct-access request (for space).

    CROSS-SYSTEM: CROSS-SYSTEM option 3 is the same as CROSS-REGION option 3, and CROSS-SYSTEM option 4 is the same as CROSS-REGION option 4.

Q: *What function does the UPGRADE option do?*

A: UPGRADE allows an alternate index to be updated at the same time as the base cluster is being updated.

Q: *What is a reusable dataset?*

A: A reusable dataset is one that can be reloaded without using the Access Method Services command DELETE/DEFINE before reloading the dataset. In addition, the REUSE option must be specified when the dataset is defined and also when reloading with the REPRO command.

Q: *What is the sequence set?*

A: The sequence set is the lowest-level index that is built (and updated) by AMS.

Q: *What function is performed by the IMBED parameter?*

A: The IMBED option places the sequence set with the data component. The sequence set for each control area is written on the first track of the control area as many times as will fit. This reduces rotational delay and increases the amount of disk storage needed for the dataset.

Q: *What function is performed by the REPLICATE parameter?*

A: The REPLICATE option writes the sequence set for each CA as many times as will fit on the first track of the CA area. If the IMBED option has been specified, the sequence set is replicated whether or not REPLICATE has been specified.

Q: *Can you build a PDS using AMS facilities?*
A: A PDS cannot be built using AMS.

Q: *What utility is used to load a VSAM dataset?*
A: REPRO is used to load a VSAM dataset.

Q: *Does data have to be sorted prior to loading a VSAM file?*
A: REPRO, while loading a dataset, does a current (record ready to be loaded) record key compare to the key of the last record that has just been loaded. As out-of-sequence conditions are treated as errors, the dataset being loaded has to be in sequence.

Q: *What utilities can be used to back up a KSDS file?*
A: EXPORT or REPRO can be used.

Miscellaneous VSAM

Q: *What can happen if you have an error condition in the master catalog?*
A: If there is an error condition in, or involving, the master catalog, access can be denied to datasets and user catalogs.

Q: *What can happen if you have an error condition in a user catalog?*
A: An error condition in the user catalog can deny access to datasets.

Q: *How can you check the status of the master catalog?*
A: Run a LISTCAT.

Q: *How can you check the status of a user catalog?*
A: Run a LISTCAT.

Q: *Name two different procedures for fixing a problem in the master or user catalog.*
A: 1. A backup copy of a nonrecoverable catalog can be reloaded using REPRO.
   2. The EXPORTCRA command can be used to retrieve catalog information from the Catalog Recovery Area (CRA).

Q: *What is a feedback code?*
A: A feedback code is the return code passed from VSAM to the processing program.

Q: *What is the meaning of a feedback code of 08?*
A: A feedback code of 08 indicates a logical error.

Q: *What is AMP and when would you use it?*
A: AMP is a JCL Access Method Services parameter and is used to override VSAM default parameters. AMP is usually invoked when an improvement in performance is desired.

Q: *What is the AMP parameter BUFNI used for?*
A: BUFNI is used to specify the number of index buffers.

Q: *In AMP, what is BUFND used for?*
A: BUFND is used to specify the number of data buffers.

Q: *What is the AMP parameter BUFSP used for?*
A: BUFSP is used to specify the amount of virtual storage. Virtual storage is used to open a VSAM dataset.

Q: *Where do you specify your BUFNI and your BUFND options?*
A: In the DD statement (MVS).

Q: *What kind of password protection (if any) is available in VSAM?*
A: Password protection can be defined for clusters as well as for data and index components.

Q: *Name and describe the various levels of password protection.*
A: There are four levels of password protection.
   1. MASTER PASSWORD—Master password protection allows all operations—read, add, update, and delete—for the dataset, its index(es), and its catalog entry.
   2. CONTROL INTERVAL PASSWORD—Control interval password protection allows users to read and write entire control intervals. This is usually not made available for general use.
   3. UPDATE PASSWORD—Update password protection allows records to be retrieved, updated, deleted, and added.
   4. READ PASSWORD—Read password protection allows read access only.

Q: *What is the purpose of the VERIFY command?*
A: The VERIFY command is used to compare the end-of-file information (high-used RBA) in the VSAM catalog with the actual end of file. If these indicators are not in agreement, the end-of-file information in the catalog is corrected.

Q: *Where and when would you use the VERIFY command?*
A: Files are verified at the OPEN, so it is rare that a VERIFY will actually be executed. Error messages will indicate when a VERIFY should be performed.

18

IMS DB—DL/I

Julian T. Glyck

Introduction

IMS (Information Management System) is IBM's hierarchical database product. For many years, IMS was the most popular database for IBM mainframes. IMS consists of two components: DB, or Database and DC, or Data Communications. The DB component is concerned with the actual manipulation of IMS databases, while the DC component is a teleprocessing package which utilizes IMS calls and structures. Due to the overwhelming preference for CICS over IMS DC in the industry, the teleprocessing "part" of IMS (DC) has not made the impact it otherwise would have. This chapter focuses only on the DB component of IMS.

IMS organizes groups of related information into databases. Each database is further subdivided into segment types. IMS segment types are organized into hierarchic levels. At the top level is the root segment type. A given database can have one and only one root segment type. Segment types directly underneath the root segment type are said to be "children" of the root segment type. Conversely, the root segment type is the "parent" of those segment types. Each child segment type, in turn, can be the parent of one or more child segment types. IMS databases can have a maximum of 255 segment types and 15 levels (much more than you are ever likely to see), and a virtually unlimited number of segment types within each level. Each segment type can have zero, one, or many segments associated with a particular root record. Database segments can be accessed directly, via keys, or indirectly, by navigating through the database until the desired segment is accessed. Not every segment type needs to have a key associated with it. When the database is being designed, a decision has to be made as to whether a particular segment type will have a key associated with it and whether to allow segments with duplicate keys.

Terminology and Concepts

DL/I (Data Language/I) is the *language* used to manipulate IMS databases. You can either access DL/I directly, through the Call-Level Interface (Call 'CBLTDLI'), or indirectly, via the High-Level Interface (EXEC DL/I). With the Call-Level Interface, your program calls the DL/I program, 'CBLTDLI', to access and/or manipulate IMS databases. The value of the parameters passed informs 'CBLTDLI' as to what action the programmer wishes it to perform. In the High-Level Interface, instructions are given via EXEC DL/I commands. These commands are converted to calls to the High-Level Programming Interface via a preprocessor. The High-Level Interface was developed subsequent to the Call-Level Interface as a way of simplifying the DL/I interface for IMS programmers. Because of this, it has become the preferred way of accessing IMS databases. From the job interview point of view, you should still be familiar with the Call-Level Interface because there are still many DP shops which do not use the High-Level Interface. In addition, there are a significant number of programs which were written prior to the development of the High-Level Interface.

DBDs, PSBs, and ACBs

IMS controls the structure of, and access to, its databases via DBDs (Data Base Definitions), PSBs (Program Specification Blocks), and ACBs (Access Control Blocks). DBDs, PSBs, and ACBs are generally not the responsibility of the application programmer, but you need to know why they are needed and how they can affect your program. IMS databases are defined in a Data Base Definition (DBD). DBDs contain such information as the segment types, their place in the hierarchy (what the parent segment type is), and the segment keys (if any).

Program Specification Blocks (PSBs) contain information about how a specific program is to access one or more IMS databases. Each PSB consists of one or more Program Communication Blocks (PCBs). PCBs contain information as to which segments in a database can be accessed, what the program is allowed to do with those segments (insert, replace, etc.), and how the database is to be accessed (primary or alternate indexes). If the program is accessing more than one database, the PSB will contain a separate PCB for each database. In addition, a PSB may contain more than one PCB for a single database. This can occur if the program needs to access the same database in more than one way, or if the program needs to maintain position in more than one place in the same database.

Access Control Blocks (ACBs) are generated by IMS as an expansion of information contained in the PSB in order to speed access to the applicable DBDs. It is the ACB, rather than the PSB, that IMS uses when running your application program. In batch programs, ACBs can either be "GEN"ed ahead of time, or at execution time, depending on the JCL used to invoke the program. The advantage of building the ACB at execution time is that you are assured of the latest changes to the PSB and DBD(s) being incorporated into the ACB. The disadvantage is the overhead of building the ACB every time you run the program. In CICS, you have no such choice; the ACBs must be built ahead of time, as it is wasteful to build an ACB every time you execute an on-line transaction.

DL/I Calls

DL/I calls can be subdivided into retrieval calls, update calls, and miscellaneous calls.

The retrieval calls are as follows:

GU (Get Unique)	Gets the first segment which matches the qualifiers specified in the call
GN (Get Next)	Gets the next segment in hierarchic order which matches the qualifiers in the call
GNP (Get Next Within Parent)	Gets the next segment under the current parent which matches the qualifiers specified in the call
GHU (Get Hold Unique)	Same as GU, but locks the segment for subsequent update (DLET or REPL)
GHN (Get Hold Next)	Same as GN, but locks the segment for subsequent update (DLET or REPL)
GHNP (Get Hold Next Within Parent)	Same as GNP, but locks the segment for subsequent update (DLET or REPL)

Update Calls

ISRT	To insert a segment in the database
REPL	To replace an existing segment with new data (the key to the segment cannot be changed, and a previous "Get Hold" command must be issued)
DLET	To delete an existing segment from the database (a previous "Get Hold" command must have been issued)

Miscellaneous Calls

CHKP	To take a "checkpoint" or commit updates to the database before the program terminates
XRST	To restore database position after a checkpoint has been taken
PCB	To schedule a PSB in an on-line program
TERM	To terminate a PSB in an on-line program

In general, DL/I acts on one segment at a time. GU and GHU are used either for random processing or to establish position in the database, while GN, GHN, GNP, and GHNP are used for sequential processing.

SSAs

SSAs (Segment Search Arguments) are the means by which the Call-Level Interface communicates to IMS the specific segment(s) you wish to access or update. SSAs have the following format:

```
SegmentName*CommandCodes(Fieldname Rel.Oper. Value)
```

Segment Name refers to the segment type being either retrieved, updated, or specified as part of the access path to the segment type being retrieved/updated.

Command Codes refer to special codes which alter the normal way in which IMS processes a call. (Command codes are described in a separate section.)

Field Name refers to the key field or search field within the segment that is being used to qualify the segment.

Relational Operator refers to the comparison that is to be made between the field name and value. Relational operators are as follows:

EQ	Equal
GT	Greater than
LT	Less than
GE	Greater than or equal
LE	Less than or equal
NE	Not equal

Value refers to the value the field name is being compared against. SSAs can be qualified or unqualified. An unqualified SSA contains only the segment name for the segment type being retrieved. Unqualified SSAs will retrieve the first (GU processing) or next (GN processing) segment of that type. Qualified SSAs will cause the call to retrieve only the segments of that segment type that meet the qualification criteria. A single DL/I call can have multiple SSAs to describe the access path at each level within the hierarchy.

Command Codes

Command codes are optional codes which are embedded in SSAs to alter the normal way in which IMS processes a call. Command codes are as follows:

C (Concatenated key)	Allows you to define the access path to the desired segment in a single SSA, with the keys to the segments along the path concatenated into one large key.
D (Path call)	Allows more than one segment along the access path to be retrieved/updated at once. (Ordinarily, only the lowest-level segment in the path is retrieved.) A "D" must be placed in the SSA of every segment in the path you wish to retrieve. The results are placed in one concatenated I/O area.

F (First)	Locates the first segment that satisfies the SSA. (This code is significant only for Get Next processing, since a Get Unique behaves this way normally.)
L (Last)	Forces IMS to find the last segment which satisfies the SSA.
N	Indicates which segments you retrieved with a path call you don't want IMS to replace.
Q	Locks a segment for your program's exclusive use.
U	Specifies that current database position at that level is not allowed to be changed by the call.
V	Specifies that current database position at that level and all levels above are not allowed to be changed by the call.
"Null" (command code)	Used as a placeholder in SSAs so that command codes can be inserted or removed from SSAs without having to define separate SSAs in working storage.

DL/I Call Formats

The format for an IMS call via the command-level interface is as follows:

```
CALL 'CBLTDLI' USING Function
          DB-PCB
          IO-AREA
          SSA(s).
```

Function refers to one of the previously described DL/I calls. DB-PCB refers to the PCB for the database being accessed, as defined in the LINKAGE SECTION of your program.

IO-AREA refers to an area in working storage which contains the space for the database segment which IMS is to retrieve into or update from.

SSA(s), as described previously, specify the access path IMS is to take to retrieve or update the correct segment. Not every call needs every parameter. For example, SSAs are not required on a REPL or DLET call (since the access path has already been specified on the previous "Get Hold" call).

The format for an IMS call via the High-Level Interface is as follows:

```
EXEC DL/I Function
  USING DB-PCB
  SEGMENT(Segment Type)
  WHERE(Expression)
  INTO/FROM(I-O Area)
  Special Options
END-EXEC.
```

Function refers to one of the preceding DL/I calls.

DB-PCB refers to the PCB for the database being accessed, as defined in the LINKAGE SECTION of your program.

Segment Type refers to any segment type(s) you wish to access or specify as part of the access path.

Expression refers to the means by which you communicate to IMS the specific segment(s) you wish to access or update. In general, the expression format is identical to the call-level SSA format, with the exception that neither the segment name nor command codes are specified in the expression (since they are specified elsewhere in the call).

Special Options include many of the call-level command codes:

First (equivalent to command code F)

Last (equivalent to command code L)

Current (equivalent to command code V)

Keys (equivalent to command code C)

What IMS Returns
to Your Program

In addition to retrieving desired segments into the I-O Area specified by your call, IMS returns status information about the call. For the High-Level Interface, this information is returned in the DL/I Interface Block (DIB). In the Call-Level Interface, this information is returned in the PCB mask for the database being accessed. The fields in the DIB are as follows:

Translator Version	A two-character code identifying the version of the DIB format being used (for documentation and troubleshooting).
Status Code	A two-character code indicating whether the call was successful and, if not, why not. These return codes should be checked by your program after each call. (The section which follows tells you some of the codes which you should commit to memory.)
Segment Name	Name of the lowest-level segment along the hierarchic path for which the call was successful.
Segment Level	Indicates the lowest hierarchical level for which the call was successful.
Key Feedback Length	Indicates the length of the concatenated key to the retrieved segment. If you want to see the actual key, you must specify the KEYFEEDBACK option on the call, and reserve an area in working storage large enough to accommodate the key.

The fields in the PCB mask are as follows:

Database Name	Name of database being retrieved
Segment Level	Same as for High Level
Status Code	Same as for High Level
Processing Options	Four-character code indicating all the functions this PSB can perform: G(GET),I(ISRT),R(REPL),D(DLET)
Segment Name	Same as for high-level
Key Feedback Length	Same as for high-level
Key Feedback Area	The actual concatenated key to the lowest-level segment retrieved

Status Codes

As described earlier, IMS returns a status code after each call. While there are some 50-odd return codes, here are the codes you are most likely to be asked about (in approximate order of importance):

Spaces	Successful return.
GE	Unable to find a segment that will satisfy the call (most common on a "GU" with a qualified SSA).
GB	End of database reached without satisfying a GN call (analogous to an "End of File" condition when reading a sequential file).
II	Tried to insert a segment that already exists on the database.
GA, GK	In satisfying a "Get Next" call, IMS returned a different segment type. (*Note:* this is not necessarily an error.)
DA	A REPL was issued where the key field was modified by the program. (This is not allowed in IMS.)
DJ	A DLET or REPL was issued without issuing a previous successful "Get" (High-Level Interface) or "Get Hold" (Call-Level Interface) command.

What to Expect at the Interview

The interviewer will generally want to verify that you know the following:

- DL/I command syntax (the High-Level Interface, the Call-Level Interface, or both)
- IMS calls, the IMS return codes, and what else IMS returns to the program
- A general understanding of DBDs, PSBs, PCBs, ACBs, command codes, and SSAs
- An understanding of how IMS works under CICS (if the interviewer expects you to write CICS programs)

All of these topics are covered in the questions which follow. In addition, interviewers often look for something intangible: that you are an experienced IMS programmer and didn't get all your knowledge from a book. While no book can replace years of experience, many questions which pertain to "real life" situations are contained in the questions and answers that follow. If, at an interview, you come across a question which was not covered in this book or your own experience, *don't panic.* Nobody has personally encountered every possible IMS capability in a business setting. Trust that your overall mastery of IMS concepts will be demonstrated by your answers to other questions. If the brief answers do not fully explain the topic, for additional information I would suggest reviewing the topic in either the IBM manuals or a book dedicated to IMS-DL/I concepts.

Questions and Answers

Q: *What are the parameters needed for an IMS call (Command-Level Interface)?*

A:
```
Call 'CBLTDLI' USING function
                 DB-PCB
                 IO-AREA
                 SSA(s).
```

Q: *Do you always need every parameter? Which ones don't you need, and why?*
A: No. You don't need SSAs on a DLET, REPL, or unqualified GU.

Q: *What are the parameters needed for an EXEC DL/I command?*

A:
```
EXEC DL/I function
         USING DB-PCB
         SEGMENT(Segment Type)
         WHERE(Expression)
         INTO/FROM(I-O Area)
         Special Options
END-EXEC.
```

Q: *What is the return code you get after a successful IMS call?*
A: Spaces.

Q: *What is the return code you get after an unsuccessful ISRT?*
A: II.

Q: *What two return codes could you get on an unsuccessful "Get" (GU, GN, GNP) call?*
A: GE (not found) or GB (end of database reached).

Q: *(Follow-up to previous question.) Why would you get one versus another?*
A: A GE is commonly received when doing a qualified GU call for a record that does not exist. A GB is commonly received when doing a GN call where there are no more segments of the type requested.

Q: *What is the difference between a PSB and a PCB?*
A: A PSB (Program Specification Block) contains all the access paths of all the databases a program can access. A PCB (Program Communication Block)

contains a single access path to a single database. (A PSB contains one or more PCBs.)

Q: *Is there any return code other than spaces that still might indicate a successful retrieval of data on a "Get" call?*

A: Return codes of GA or GK indicate a change in segment type retrieved, which is OK if that is what you intended.

Q: *Let's say you needed to update segments in the database, but didn't know if the segments already existed. If the segment existed, you were to update the existing segment. If it didn't exist, you were to create the segment. Name two ways to accomplish this in IMS.*

A: 1. Do GHU. If you get return code GE, ISRT the segment. Otherwise, REPL the segment.

   2. Try to ISRT. If you get return code II, do GHU followed by REPL.

Q: *(Follow-up to previous question.) Which would you choose and why?*

A: If you're pretty sure the segment exists, use technique 1; otherwise, use technique 2.

Q: *How would you retrieve more than one segment along the hierarchic path to the lowest-level segment?*

A: Use Path Call (command code of D).

Q: *What is parentage? Why is it important?*

A: Parentage is a pointer to the segment retrieved after a successful GU or GN call. It is important because subsequent GNP calls use the parentage pointer to retrieve all segments of the type requested that belong to that parent.

Q: *What is the difference between maintaining database position and maintaining parentage?*

A: Parentage is affected only by successful GU and GN calls. Also, certain command codes can affect parentage, but not position.

Q: *Is it sufficient to check the IMS return code after a call in a CICS program?*

A: No. The UIBRCODE must be checked first. A value other than low values indicates a problem with the CICS to DL/I interface, in which case the return code would be meaningless.

Q: *Is database position maintained between tasks in a pseudo-conversational CICS program?*

A: No.

Q: *(Follow-up to previous question.) How do you get around this problem?*

A: Make the program conversational (generally a bad idea). A better idea is to store the concatenated key to the segment between tasks, and retrieve the previously accessed segment upon reentry into the program.

Q: *How would you access an IMS database segment via a secondary index?*

A: Via a PCB set up for secondary index access. The syntax is exactly the same as for a primary key read. Only the key name is different.

Q: *Can you access a segment via a primary and a secondary index in the same program?*

A: Yes, you can. You need two PCBs: one for the primary index access and one for the secondary index access.

Q: *Can you maintain more than one position in the same database at the same time? How?*

A: Yes. With multiple PCBs for a single database.

Q: *How does IMS know that the PSB you are using is the correct one for the program?*

A: It doesn't. IMS does not stop you from using another program's PSB in your program—but the program may fail if it wasn't set up for the databases and access paths your program needs.

Q: *What is the difference between a DBD and a PSB?*

A: A DBD (Database Definition) describes the characteristics of a particular database (the segment types, primary key, search fields, etc.). A PSB (Program Specification Block) describes how a particular program views the databases it accesses, which segments it has access to, which index can be used for access, whether Replace or Insert is allowed on a particular segment, etc.

Q: *If a batch program aborts or is terminated before completion, what happens to the IMS updates you have already made?*

A: They are lost.

Q: *(Follow-up to previous question.) How can you prevent this from happening?*

A: Your program can take checkpoints (IMS CHKP call) which will commit all the updates prior to the checkpoint.

Q: *Is it advisable to use checkpoints in a CICS program? If not, why not?*

A: No. A checkpoint will not update CICS's dynamic log (for dynamic transaction backout), and CICS and IMS will be out of sync.

Q: *(Follow-up to previous question.) What should you use instead?*

A: Issue a CICS SYNCPOINT command.

Q: *What is the difference between GN calls with no SSAs, an unqualified SSA, and a qualified SSA?*

A: GN calls with no SSAs will successively retrieve every segment in the database in hierarchic sequence. GN calls with an unqualified SSA will successively retrieve every segment of a particular segment type. GN calls with a qualified SSA will successively retrieve only those segments of a particular segment type that meet the qualifying criteria.

Q: *What happens if you end a CICS program without terminating the PSB? If so, why bother to terminate the PSB at all?*

A: The PSB will automatically terminate when the task ends. If you have a long-running task, you may want to free up IMS resources before the task ends.

Q: *What is an ACB?*

A: The ACB (Access Control Block) is an expansion of information from the PSB. It is used to enable IMS to access the information it needs from the DBD more quickly.

Q: *Is the ACB built before a batch program is run?*

A: Not usually. Generally, the ACB is built at execution time by IMS before the batch program runs. However, the ACB can be prebuilt by the DBA before execution time—but slightly different JCL must be used to execute the program.

Q: *How does a CICS program gain access to the ACB?*

A: When you schedule a PSB (IMS function "PCB"), you are actually accessing the ACB.

Q: *What do you have to do to your program when the program's PSB is changed?*

A: Nothing, unless the change directly affects what you are doing in the program (secondary index access, etc.).

Q: *Can you use fully qualified SSAs with a GN call?*

A: Yes.

Q: *(Follow-up to previous question.) What is the difference between this and a GU call with fully qualified SSAs?*

A: A GU call will always position you at the first segment which matches the qualification, whereas successive GN calls will position you to the next matching segment.

Q: *Can you "back up" in an IMS database?*

A: No. You must use either a GU or a GN with a command code of F (First) to go to the first entry of the segment type, and then use successive GN commands to get to the segment you want.

Q: *Are duplicate keys allowed in an IMS database?*

A: Yes.

Q: *(Follow-up to previous question.) If so, how do you access the segment you want?*

A: If you know the segment you want is the first or last duplicate, you can use command codes of F (First) or L (Last) to retrieve the segment you want. If not, you must access the duplicates via successive GN calls.

Q: *What is an IO-PCB?*

A: An IO-PCB is used in IMS/DC programs (not discussed here) and to establish checkpoints in batch programs (via the CHKP call). If it exists in the PSB, it is always the first PCB.

Q: *(Follow-up to previous question.) How do you restore database position after a checkpoint is taken?*

A: Via an XRST call (checkpoint restart).

Q: *What information does IMS return in the DL/I Interface Block (High-Level Interface)?*

A: Translator version, status code, segment name, segment level, key feedback length.

Q: *What information does IMS return in the PCB mask (Call-Level Interface)?*

A: Database name, segment level, status code, processing options, (DL/I reserved area), segment name, key feedback length, key feedback area.

Q: *If you use a concatenated key to restore position, will it also restore parentage? Why should this matter?*

A: No. It matters because a subsequent GNP call may fail or give unexpected results.

Q: *How would you retrieve the last segment under a particular parent segment?*

A: Use a GNP call with a command code of L (Last).

Q: *How do you establish accessibility to IMS databases in a CICS program?*

A: 1. Schedule the PSB (use "PCB" call).

2. Move UIBPCBAL to 01 level in LINKAGE SECTION containing as many S9(08) COMP fields as the PSB has PCBs.

3. Move PCB addresses (from the individual COMP fields described in item 2) to their appropriate BLL cells.

Q: *What does it mean when you get a return code of AM on an ISRT call? How would you solve this problem?*

A: It means that the PSB does not give the programmer permission to perform the ISRT. The problem can be solved either by using another PSB that does have the necessary authority or by getting the DBA to give the PSB a processing option of "I" on the segment.

Q: *What is the difference between a GN and a GNP call?*

A: A GN is a general-purpose retrieval call which can be used for a variety of successive accesses depending on the SSAs and command codes used. A GNP is a special-purpose retrieval call which is used to retrieve successive segments after position on a "parent" segment has been established by a "GU" or "GN" call. (GNP calls do not affect parentage.)

Q: *What must you do before issuing an REPL or DLET request?*

A: You must first successfully retrieve and lock the segment(s) with a "Get Hold" call (GHU, GHN, GHNP). (*Note:* with the High-Level Interface, a "Get" call [GU, GN, GNP] is acceptable.)

Q: *What does a processing option of "A" in a PCB mean?*

A: It means that the PCB will allow the program to perform all of the basic I/O operations (Get, Insert, Replace, Delete).

Q: *What happens when you try to replace key data in a segment? How do you get around this problem?*

A: The call fails (with a return code of "DA"). You get around this problem by first deleting the original segment, and then reinserting it with the new key value.

Q: *What is a logical relationship?*

A: A logical relationship is one in which a segment from one database is related to another. If properly set up in the DBD and PSB, a program can access the segment in the other database as if it were a dependent segment of the current database.

Q: *What is the difference between a unidirectional and bidirectional logical relationship?*

A: A unidirectional logical relationship is one in which a logical relationship exists only between database A and database B. A bidirectional logical relationship is one in which a logical relationship exists between database B and database A as well.

Q: *Must every IMS database have a primary key to its root segment?*

A: Yes.

Q: *In what order are nonkeyed segments stored on the database?*

A: The order varies, depending on the Insert rules defined in the DBD. Options are First (place the most recent ISRT first), Last (place the most recent ISRT last), or Here (place the ISRT where the database is currently positioned).

Q: *Does IMS support variable-length segments? How? Why is this feature rarely used?*

A: Yes. A 2-byte binary field containing the length of the segment is placed at the beginning of the segment (the application program must maintain this field on update). This feature is rarely used because IMS handles repeating groups by allowing multiple segments and segment types. Only data that is truly variable in nature (such as comments or other text strings) would be candidates for variable-length segments.

Q: *What happens if the I/O area specified in the call does not match the length of the segment as defined in the DBD?*

A: Data could either be lost (on ISRT or REPL) or it could overlay other data in your program (on retrieval). You will *not* get a bad status code from IMS.

Q: *Does a GNP call affect parentage?*

A: No.

Q: *What is a load PSB?*

A: A load PSB is a PSB used for the purpose of loading an empty database.

Q: *Can you perform any call except ISRT with a load PSB?*

A: No.

Q: *Can you use a load PSB against a database that already has some records in it?*
A: No.

Q: *What happens if you issue a "Get Hold" command, but no subsequent DLET or REPL?*
A: Nothing. (It is not a problem as far as IMS is concerned.)

Q: *What happens if you issue an IMS call in between a "Get Hold" command and a DLET or REPL?*
A: The DLET or REPL will fail as if the "Get Hold" command had never been issued.

Q: *Does the High-Level Programming Interface require a "Get Hold" before a DLET or REPL? If not, how is it done?*
A: No. Any "Get" command that positions the database at the desired segment is acceptable.

Q: *What is a search field?*
A: A search field is a nonkeyed field which is used in your SSA to restrict the segments that will satisfy the call.

Q: *How are search fields defined?*
A: Any field which is defined in the DBD is automatically a search field.

Q: *Can search expressions be combined with index expressions or other search expressions? If yes, how?*
A: Yes. One expression can follow another, with the ampersand (&) connecting the two expressions.

Q: *Why is it important to be careful when using search fields?*
A: Since search fields are nonkeyed, they can be inefficient. (This is a particular concern in on-line programs.) Also, the records may not be retrieved in the order in which you need them (i.e., if you use a ">" operator, you may not get the segments in size order).

Q: *Can you turn a database "upside down" (access a low-level segment as if it were the root)? How? How do you access the new "root"?*
A: Yes. You need a secondary index to the low-level segment: a DBD which defines a "logical database" where the parent segment is the "logical child" of a "physical child" segment, and a PCB which provides access to this logical database. The application programmer can access the logical database exactly as if it were a regular database.

Q: *If a SEARCH field is converted to a secondary index, what changes, if any, need to be made to the application program?*
A: The SSA must be changed to access the key field rather than the search field.

Q: *Can an index be accessed directly? How? Why would you want to do this?*
A: Yes. By setting up a PCB to go after the index DBD. Accessing the index only is much quicker if all you need is a count of segments or a list of keys.

Q: *Where is the database positioned after a DLET request?*

A: At the segment following the deleted segment.

Q: *What are the tradeoffs involved in adding a secondary index versus using a search field?*

A: A search field requires less processing time on update and takes up less space. A secondary index provides faster retrieval (in most cases).

19
Client/Server Networks

David Dodge

Introduction

Like many relatively new terms in the computer industry, Client/Server means different things to different people. Generally, however, Client/Server is understood to mean a computer system that consists of the following elements:

- One or more intelligent workstations, personal computers, or portable devices that function as "clients" by requesting services from another system or system component

- One or more platforms (e.g., personal computers, minicomputers, or mainframe hosts) that function as a "server" by providing processing, database, and communication services to clients

- The networking infrastructure and software that links them all

From an end-user viewpoint, Client/Server computing usually means being able to access a range of data, applications, computing power, printing, and other services from a single workstation—without having to know which machine or component of the system is actually providing the requested service. This capability or characteristic is referred to as *transparency* of location.

The Client/Server Environment: An Overview

Many types of computer platforms can be used as the architectural building blocks in a Client/Server system. A typical client platform might be an Intel 286-, 386-, or 486-based microcomputer. It could also be an Apple MacIntosh or a Reduced Instruction Set Computing (RISC) workstation such as a Sun SPARC or an IBM RS/6000. The client could even be a portable computing notebook or slate, a hand-held computer, or a personal information aid. Servers can be virtually any platform as well. The more typical would be a 386 or 486 PC, a RISC-based server, a minicomputer, or a mainframe. As a file server, any of these platforms would supply file records to a requesting client workstation. The client would then further sort the data. Most servers, though, function today as multitasking database servers.

Servers act as the heart of a Client/Server system. A newer generation of server platforms, sometimes referred to as *superservers,* has been introduced in order to meet the increased demands on the server hardware. A superserver will generally be a high-end workstation with optimized performance, expanded memory, improved fault tolerance, enhanced security, greater scalability (add-on) capabilities, and more substantial remote diagnostic and system administration features.

Operating Systems

In a distributed Client/Server computing environment, an operating system provides both base services and extended services to clients and users. The base services typically include the following capabilities:

- *Preemptive multitasking.*   The operating system allots fixed time slots for each task to execute and automatically handles all task switching.

- *Task prioritization and synchronization.*   The operating system executes tasks based on their priority and then ensures that concurrently running tasks don't interfere with each other when sharing resources.

- *Interprocess communications.*   The operating system enables communications to share and exchange data within a single machine or across machine boundaries.

- *Locking and integrity.*   The operating system safeguards data integrity by temporarily locking other process tasks out of a file or record while it is being used or changed. This must be done without significant degradations in performance.

Extended services are usually added through modular software that is "layered" on top of the operating system's base services. Extended services are frequently adopted into standard base services after they become more common among competing operating systems. Extended services can include the following:

- *Communications protocols.*   Permit communications among platforms from different vendors.

- *Database management system links.*   Allow users to identify and locate resources and system services.

- *System management services.*   Help users configure the system and monitor its use.

- *Network operating system facilities.* Provide access to printers and other peripheral devices on a network.

- *Object-oriented services and protocols.* Allow data objects, images, and graphics to be stored, transferred, and exchanged. Many of these services are being developed and refined in newer operating system releases.

Network Operating Systems

A network operating system (NOS) is the software program that makes it possible for computers to communicate with one another over a network and to share resources. The NOS enables a user to access a database, use a printer, or use another computer's applications as if they resided on his or her workstation. The more robust LAN operating systems such as Banyan's VINES, Novell's NetWare, and Microsoft's LAN Manager were structured more like minicomputer or Unix operating systems from the outset. Since their server software mediates simultaneous requests for network resources and runs multiple programs at one time, they are considered to be multiuser, multitasking systems. Although a server can also function as an individual workstation with some LAN operating systems or special versions, larger networks are usually not configured this way. Novell NetWare and Banyan VINES actually require a dedicated server.

Another advantage of the more robust, multitasking LAN operating systems is that they usually offer additional features and tools for managing the network. System administrators also normally want software that provides enhanced security, print spooling, network administration capabilities, diagnostic support, improved memory management, and greater fault tolerance when purchasing these systems. The selection of a LAN operating system is normally made based on these characteristics and on whether the organization wants to dedicate a workstation to the server role.

Application Programming Languages

Over the last few years various database access tools and user-query products have emerged. These tools tend to simplify aspects of using a DBMS, and they generally preclude the need to develop custom programs to retrieve limited sets of data from the database. Most complex information systems requirements, however, still mandate the development of custom applications or the use of off-the-shelf software packages. These programs are written in one or more programming languages. These languages can be grouped into three general classes: procedural languages, SQL-based languages, and object-oriented languages.

Most programming languages are considered to be procedural languages. This means the code is written as a series of procedures, with each procedure performing some task that contributes to the use of the application. Procedures to update data and to re-sort the data would be examples. The common third-generation languages (3GLs) such as COBOL, FORTRAN, Pascal, C, and BASIC are all procedural programming languages. In his guide to Client/Server databases, Joe Salemi also states that programming languages that are unique to particular products or DBMSs are often called fourth-generation languages (4GLs). Examples include Microsoft's Visual BASIC language and the Paradox Application Language (PAL) used with Paradox. These procedural languages can be extended and linked to databases and other systems using Application Program Interfaces (APIs). An API is a set of precoded functions or procedural calls usually provided with a product or made available in a software library that can be coupled to an application or database.

SQL-based languages use the Structural Query Language (SQL) as their foundation. SQL was designed as a language intended to provide access to relational DBMSs. However, there is no mandatory requirement that a relational database must understand SQL, and SQL can be used to access a nonrelational DBMS. While SQL is generally considered an important standard that helped foster the transition to Client/Server, no one should assume that all SQL-based languages are compatible with one another. There are a variety of SQL-based languages in use today, each providing extensions or additional capabilities to the basic SQL specifications. Developers should therefore be cautious when selecting the languages and products they will use to build applications.

Object-Oriented Programming (OOP) languages are relatively new, and they require a very different approach to building application software. Rather than performing a series of procedures, OOP languages call for events or actions to be taken on objects such as a "customer," or a photographic image, or an "employee." Examples of such languages include C++ and SmallTalk. Several of the application development tools on the market today employ object-oriented languages and approaches. Other tools that up to now have used procedural or SQL-based languages have recently incorporated many of the object-oriented programming techniques and features. This blending can be expected to continue as vendors seek to optimize the strengths of the various languages and techniques.

Application Development and Data Access Tools

To many people it is the front-end application software and graphical user interface environments that have made Client/Server computing so alluring. To discuss the topic with greater clarity, these tools can be divided into three major groups based on their primary uses and limitations. These groups are: (1) desktop extension software, (2) application development tools, and (3) data access and query tools.

Desktop extension software products are essentially programs that add functionality to existing commercial database or application products such as Lotus 1-2-3 and dBase. The extension products make PC DBMSs and applications easier to use by providing access to servers or other databases, creating forms and reports, supporting development of ad hoc queries and data extracts, and populating spreadsheet packages with server-based data. The shortcomings of these tools include the fact that they are often tied to specific applications or DBMS products, and that they can impose a performance penalty on the workstation because of the data translations they must make. These tools can also require additional workstation processing power and memory.

Application development tools are software products used to build customized, workstation-based, Client/Server applications. Some of these tools simply put a graphical front end on existing mainframe host applications without changing the "back-end logic," an activity referred to as "facelifting." Facelifting is usually a measure that yields only a small subset of the benefits of true Client/Server computing.

Other development tools are intended to support construction of complete Client/Server applications. These products use proprietary procedural or object-oriented 4GL programming languages to develop applications that have a graphical user interface and that support SQL queries to multiple back-end DBMSs. Professional developers with programming experience are the target users for most of these tools, although generally only a few days of training are needed before an individual can become competent with such a product. Most of the tools are designed to work in a "Windows" environment, and they enable the injection of multimedia, image, and other technologies into new applications.

Data access and query tools are most often intended for use by people who are not professional programmers. These tools support creation of database queries and the development of customized reports and forms. Some tools also support integration of data from multiple, disparate sources and are often characterized as Executive Information System (EIS) shells. Such tools are very good for users who need to retrieve data but do not need to change it.

In summary, it is worth pointing out that many of the application development and data access tools available today actually overlap the groups into which they were put for this discussion. The overlaps are increasing because vendors continue to add features and functions with each new version or release of their products. As a result, it is becoming harder to categorize them. The key, therefore, to selecting the right tool is to establish a set of criteria that helps you evaluate various products in an objective fashion, rather than simply following someone else's grouping scheme.

Terminology

A partial mastery of some of the terminology and buzzwords associated with Client/Server computing will improve any technical interview as long as such terms aren't used to hide a lack of knowledge. A handful of the most frequently encountered terms and phrases that haven't as yet been introduced in this chapter are defined as follows:

Cooperative processing: Cooperative processing describes how a computer processing job is shared among two or more computing platforms. It implies that the processing workload is divided up in the most efficient fashion. This term and the term *distributed processing* are frequently used as synonyms for Client/Server computing.

Distributed processing: Distributed processing refers to computer processing carried out in different locations (i.e., geographically dispersed) on independent computer platforms connected by a network. The aim here is also the most efficient use of computing resources by dedicating each computer processing unit (CPU) to the task for which it is best suited.

Downsizing: Downsizing can imply full replacement of a mainframe host environment with networks and workstations. It definitely means off-loading significant processing workload or applications from the host, and deferring or avoiding altogether the purchase of additional host-based MIPS.

Interoperability: Interoperability refers to the cooperative operation of software programs that reside on dissimilar computer systems. It implies the ready exchange of data and functionality.

Open systems: Open system describes a computer system or major component that has its interface services and formats designed to enable application software built for it to interoperate with other applications on local or remote systems, and to be ported or moved to a range of other systems with minimal changes.

Topology: A topology is the layout or blueprint of a network. A logical topology describes how data and signals travel over the network to its stations—i.e., sequentially or in a broadcast. A physical topology describes how the cables or wires are laid out to connect the nodes—i.e., a star or daisy chain.

Questions and Answers

The questions and answers in this chapter have been broken into major headings designed to classify subject material for easy access by the reader.

Client/Server Strategy Issues

Q: *How do you provide business justification for transitioning to Client/Server computing?*

A: The best business justification can differ from organization to organization. Normally, though, the expense and effort associated with the transition to Client/Server computing is expressed in terms of:

- Achieving better price/performance from computer platforms
- Reducing the costs of procuring computer hardware; reducing training or maintenance costs over time
- Achieving greater interoperability and portability among applications
- Improving a company's competitive posture through productivity, reduced cycle time, faster responses to market changes, etc.

Q: *How should you approach identifying the "end users" of a system and what do you need to know from them?*

A: You need to look for both the "primary" user of a system, such as a customer service representative or a salesperson, and any "secondary" users, such as a supervisor or an executive. An executive, of course, can be a primary user. Check an organization chart, understand where the information flows, and look outside the boundaries of the organization to identify potential users, such as suppliers or customers. Each user will have his or her own expectations and needs. Ask about the types of data they want, formatting and reporting requirements, how they want to interact with the system (e.g., keyboard, mouse, light pen, touch screen), who they communicate with, and the system speed and capacity they must have. These are only a few examples of what you need to know from each type of end user.

Q: *Why is it important to understand whether you are building either an on-line transaction processing system or a decision support system (DSS)?*

A: Many of the characteristics of an OLTP system and a decision support system are different. For example, an OLTP system typically requires high performance and greater availability. A DSS usually requires greater flexibility, has fewer users, and its database values are more static. Their respective response time requirements are often different. An OLTP usually processes individual records and transactions, while a DSS more frequently looks at groups of records.

Q: *Identify some of the ways an application can be placed or distributed between a client workstation and a server.*

A: An application ordinarily has several components, including the user interface, its presentation management services, its business logic, and database logic. Any of these software components can reside on the client workstation, including a subset of the database management system services itself. The server would generally provide the DBMS services, and could house any of the other software components if required to improve processing efficiency.

Q: *What are some of the rules of thumb that can be used to decide where to place the data in a Client/Server-based system?*

A: Data should normally be placed as close to the primary users as possible, while still protecting data security and data integrity. If important data is likely to be lost on individual workstations because of problems such as LAN instability or lack of user training, then it is better to keep the data on a server. Typically, data should be stored at the lowest point in the architecture that satisfies sharing requirements, timeliness/performance needs, capacity as well as update and access requirements, and issues of ownership/security. The requirements of the business rather than the needs of individual users should predominate if conflict occurs.

Q: *Name some of the areas in which technical alternatives should be considered when designing or implementing a Client/Server system.*

A: Alternative technologies, standards, methodologies, and techniques should be reviewed when building a Client/Server system to ensure the optimum is selected. Other areas in which technical alternatives need to be considered would include data and processing placement, user interface, component configuration, transport/communications media requirements, and conversion approaches.

Q: *What are some of the data management and control issues you encounter when building a Client/Server system?*

A: The management and control of data is only one aspect of Client/Server systems management, but a critical one. Some of the issues encountered in this area include:

- Data security and copy control
- "Ownership" of data
- Read versus update rights
- Data definitions and key standardization
- Data archiving strategy and media
- Data distribution and synchronization
- Refreshment or update strategy
- Time-stamping techniques

Q: *When migrating from a host-based environment to a Client/Server architecture what are some of the issues that must be anticipated?*

A: Migration from a mainframe host environment to Client/Server computing can mean a big change in technology and in other areas. Some of these other issues or areas that need to be anticipated would include the political shifts that might take place as more people have access to data, changes in training requirements, and changes in relationships with external organizations or customers. Workflow management, business processes, and internal organizational relationships could also be altered as Client/Server technology provides additional analytic capabilities, faster computing, and greater opportunity for productivity improvements.

Q: *How do technology and training requirements change when an organization adopts a Client/Server strategy?*

A: Client/Server computing will demand new skills and different types of training for an organization's end users, system developers, and the information systems maintenance staff because of new design and development techniques such as data and process modeling, prototyping, windows design flow, human engineering factors, and distributed design considerations. New technology skills must also be cultivated in areas such as the use of application development tools, local area network management, system and application integration, and coding skills in languages like C and SQL.

Q: *What are some key changes that take place in the roles and responsibilities of a company's Information Systems (I/S) department when the company adopts Client/Server computing?*

A: Ordinarily the Information Systems department will have to become more a source of standards and system support than purely a development and maintenance organization. Users will look to the I/S department to provide policies, technology recommendations, management of the network infrastructure, data management, and other aspects of systems management. The I/S department often will need to shift more toward responsibilities like system and software procurement, electronic software distribution and update, help desk-type operations, software licensing, and data archiving.

Client/Server
Application Design

Q: *What is a JAD session and how does it apply to Client/Server?*

A: A Joint Application Design (JAD) session is a set of activities carried out jointly by systems analysts and designers and the end users of an application. These activities are focused on defining or refining the requirements for an application, how it will be used, the data needs of the users, and how the system should function. JAD sessions are but one way to gather requirements for Client/Server applications. The sessions are normally held with small groups of end users and led by a facilitator or systems analyst.

Q: *Explain why you would prototype an application or employ rapid application development techniques.*

A: Prototyping is a technique of interactively defining and refining end user application requirements by building portions of a proposed application system. In parallel, the developers demonstrate their work to the users to determine if their needs and vision are being satisfied by the somewhat superficial elements of the system they are seeing take shape. Rapid application development involves segmenting an application into smaller units or parts so that each one can be developed and put into operation much more quickly than conventional development techniques permit.

Q: *What is meant by business process reengineering and what is its relationship to Client/Server computing?*

A: Business process reengineering describes the effort associated with examining current business activities and processes used within an organization to determine if better working methods can be adopted to meet the organization's objectives. It involves a review of the rationale behind the work, the logic of information flows, the logic of who participates and in what sequence, and the consideration of alternatives for improvement. Business process reengineering often should precede or parallel development of a Client/Server application because of the opportunities for improvement that are inherent in the architecture, the technology, and the integration capabilities Client/Server computing provides.

Q: *How does object-oriented design differ from more conventional techniques?*

A: Object-oriented design focuses on identifying discrete entities called objects that have a data structure and a behavior that permits or involves operations of various types. In other words, software procedures are designed and built around objects. In more conventional structured analysis and design, the emphasis is placed on identifying and decomposing the functions a system should perform and the data it should provide to a user. Object-oriented design is more complex, but the software built using this technique is considered to be more robust and less fragile. It is argued that if functions and requirements change, objects are easier to revise than is software and a data design built around those functions. Current evidence tends to support this view, but too few object-oriented systems have been built and tested to convince everyone.

Q: *What are the characteristics of a good application design methodology?*
A: A good application development methodology is one that:

- Encompasses the entire development life cycle, from requirements definition through system maintenance
- Is modular so that it allows entry and exit at various points
- Allows the developer to select structured analysis, object-oriented, information engineering, prototyping, or any other technique that is best for the task
- Addresses the unique challenges of building Client/Server systems that have both distributed data and applications
- Includes iterative planning and strategy refinement to deal with issues such as systems management, documentation and training requirements, cultural and organizational implications, configuration management, software changes and upgrades, as well as operations and support

Q: *What is the role of data modeling in Client/Server application design?*
A: Data modeling is a technique for depicting business information needs and the rules associated with data usage. When employing structured analysis or information engineering design techniques, data modeling is a critical step in defining the scope of an application, defining the views of data that users can obtain, determining how the data from multiple sources can be integrated, and developing the structure of the database itself. When designing a Client/Server application, a data model will also be important as you determine whether to distribute or centralize data and where to locate the data on the network.

Q: *What is third normal form?*
A: Normalization of data refers to a process of organizing and structuring data so that you have no redundancies or inconsistencies. Normalization is a modeling and refinement technique achieved in steps. First normal form, the first step, involves eliminating groups of "repeating" data elements. Second normal form involves aligning each portion of the data with its associated key or unique identifier. Third normal form involves removing data attributes or elements that depend on attributes other than the key. Some people like to say that in the third normal form, attributes must depend on "the key, the whole key, and nothing but the key."

Q: *What is a Context Diagram, as used in application design and process modeling?*

A: A Context Diagram is a single bubble-like drawing used in process modeling (data-flow diagramming) techniques. It depicts the scope of the system (also called its *domain*) and shows the data flows that move in and out of the system at their most abstract level.

Q: *When designing a decision support system application, what should be modeled first: the processes or the data?*

A: Ordinarily, it is better to model the data first when designing a Decision Support System (DSS). The data will be more stable and predictable than decision support processes. DSS processes can often depend on what questions are being asked and the analytic processing that will be required to answer them. Ad hoc queries and processes, for example, can depend on who the questioner is. If the data are modeled and the database contains all the basic data types useful to analysts, then nearly all queries will be satisfied even though never modeled or anticipated. This is a generalization and not an iron-clad rule.

Q: *What is a remote procedure call?*

A: A remote procedure call is an element of an application program that transfers control and data to another part of the program. A Remote Procedure Call (RPC) is used to transfer control and data across a network. When an RPC is executed, the calling program is temporarily suspended while a set of parameters is transferred to another network node. It is there that the procedure is carried out. When the procedure is complete, the results are sent back to the original station where the calling program continues its operation. Remote procedure calls are important mechanisms in distributed transaction processing.

Q: *Explain what is meant by the term "two-phase commit."*

A: Two-phase commit refers to the two message-passing phases of a transaction processing event. The first phase occurs when a coordinating node sends a message to subordinate nodes on a network to determine if all required work has been completed. If so, the transactional updates are temporarily recorded in nonvolatile storage. The second phase message is sent when the coordinating node determines whether to abort the transaction or permanently commit the update to stable storage.

Q: *What is the definition of DCE (Distributed Computing Environment)?*

A: The Distributed Computing Environment (DCE) is an open systems standard published by the Open Software Foundation. It describes an integrated set of technologies that are intended to promote interoperability (i.e., make it easier to develop, use, and maintain applications in a heterogeneous distributed environment). DCE identifies specific technologies to support remote procedures calls, distributed naming services, distributed file services, time-stamping and synchronization, network security, and thread APIs.

Q: *What is an API and how is it used?*

A: An Application Program Interface (API) is a set of program functions or a specification for them that provides the capability for applications to interact with network operating systems, DBMSs, or other application software. In other words, the API is used to link applications to other software components or database management system services.

Q: *What is the difference between "Upper CASE" and "Lower CASE" tools?*

A: Upper CASE tools are those that provide support for the "upper half" (planning, analysis, and high-level design) portions of a system development life cycle. Lower CASE tools support the "lower half" of the development life cycle—i.e., detailed design and construction (code generation).

Q: *What is the purpose of a dictionary or repository when designing a Client/ Server application?*

A: A data dictionary or a repository is used to store and access information about data, programs, and objects. These tools can be helpful in designing complex Client/Server applications and databases by supporting data modeling, data definition, access path definition, software configuration and change management, use of software standards, and project management. Several of the most recent releases or versions of application development tools have incorporated dictionary and repository functions.

Client/Server Application Development

Q: *What are some of the criteria you would use to evaluate and compare various application development tools?*

A: Because of differences in features, support, technical environments, and price, it is important to develop a set of criteria with which you can compare and evaluate application development tools to select the best one for a project. The criteria you use might include the following:

Quality of SQL support

Data import/export capabilities

Quality of technical support

Quality of documentation

Capabilities to import images/multimedia

Cost of run-time modules

Operating systems supported

DBMSs supported

Network operating systems supported

Object-oriented features

Adaptability to prototyping

Total price per developer/per end user

Q: *What is meant by an Application Development Environment (ADE)?*

A: An Application Development Environment (ADE) refers to a set of software capabilities that effectively merge upper CASE, project management, application development tool, and repository functions into an integrated suite of tools. The more advanced ADEs that are now emerging will provide a consistent user interface for all tools, along with on-line methodology and project management assistance, testing and debugging capabilities, object-oriented development tools, and repository functions that also support an index of reusable objects.

Q: *What are some of the strengths or advantages of products that "extend" the capabilities of familiar desktop applications such as Lotus 1-2-3?*

A: Desktop extension software products can help end users integrate existing PC databases into graphical Client/Server applications. These products may also be easier to learn and cost less than more complete application development tools. Additionally, desktop extension products tend to be extremely versatile, have good documentation, and require less workstation RAM than other development tools.

Q: *Why do "windows" applications and graphical user interfaces represent a new way of thinking for programmers?*

A: More conventional mainframe and midrange system applications are oriented toward predetermined usage patterns. Programmers know that end users will have to access the main menu, go through a series of well-laid-out steps "screen by screen," and complete one transaction or analysis before another is begun. On the other hand, with "windows" applications and graphical user interfaces, end users are no longer so restricted. A user can begin one application in the middle of another, or take any of a dozen or more routes to build and execute a query. An end user can also retrieve or input data from multiple sources on a network. Today's programmers must anticipate virtually anything an end user might want to do or might accidentally do. This means a new way of thinking about programming, and it means more complex challenges for programmers to build in safeguards, on-line help, and branching dialog logic.

Q: *What is referential integrity?*

A: Referential integrity refers to an operating principle of the Relational Database Model. It is an aspect of data integrity that predetermines how the database management system should react when an end user attempts to delete a database record on which other records depend. Good referential integrity features will not permit a user to inadvertently orphan data records this way.

Q: *What is a "multithreaded" application?*

A: The term *thread* describes a process within an application that performs a specific step or task. A single-threaded application does one thing at a time, while a multithreaded application performs multiple tasks simultaneously.

Multithreaded applications, for example, can update a database, display a series of graphics, and print a report all at the same time.

Q: *In graphical user interface terminology, what is a "combo box" and what is a "radio button"?*

A: A "combo box" is a combined data field and scrollable list box. The item that is currently selected in the list box automatically appears in the data field. The rest of the list box is displayed only upon demand by the user. This way it takes up less screen space. A "radio button" is a boolean switch used to provide settings where only one of a group of options can be selected at one time.

Q: *What is meant by the term or acronym CUA?*

A: The Common User Access (CUA) interface standard is a derivative of IBM's Systems Application Architecture. It is intended to provide users with a consistent view of the applications they employ. The standard addresses how window layouts should appear on the user's screen, how action bars and pull-down menus operate, how push buttons work, how information is displayed within a window, how fields are formatted, how items are selected from the screen, how the cursor operates, and many other presentation techniques that users often take for granted.

Q: *How does the term "animate" relate to Client/Server application development?*

A: Animate generally refers to the feature of an application development tool that allows you to follow along in an outline and see each line of application code highlighted as it runs. This feature is useful to see if everything is working the way the developer intended.

Q: *Explain how a DLL is used.*

A: A Dynamic Link Library (DLL) is a group (or library) of software functions/procedures that are compiled and stored outside the main body of an application program. The DLL is accessed and executed at certain points in the application, either automatically or by user choice. A DLL is typically used to add special functions to software, such as providing imaging capabilities, performing special statistical procedures, or exporting data to graphics packages. Some application development tools are sold with DLLs to make it unnecessary to develop such code.

Client/Server Databases

Q: *Describe the key advantages provided by a Client/Server database.*

A: A key advantage of a Client/Server database is the ability to locate the data in the most advantageous place for large numbers of users. Most of the important advantages of a Client/Server system result from splitting the computer processing between the client platform and the database server. One such advantage is that the workstation needs only the power and speed to be able to run the front-end software, thereby extending the life of less capable PCs that don't have the memory and processing horsepower required to operate a complex DBMS. Client/Server databases also help reduce the amount of data transferred over the network, sending only the results sets rather than an entire file.

Q: *What is the starting point for determining whether you should use either a Client/Server database management system or a stand-alone PC DBMS?*

A: The most significant question to be asked at the outset is whether you require simultaneous multiuser access. If you don't, then select a stand-alone PC DBMS. If you do, then you're likely to need a server-based DBMS.

Q: *Explain the difference between dynamic SQL and embedded SQL.*

A: Stand-alone SQL used for interactive queries of a database is commonly called *dynamic* SQL. If the SQL is contained inside an application written in a procedural programming language, it is usually referred to as *embedded* SQL.

Q: *What are some of the advantages and disadvantages of using the Microsoft SQL Server DBMS?*

A: In its current release, the Microsoft SQL Server DBMS provides adequate performance and capacity for a reasonable price. It supports Microsoft's LAN Manager, IBM's LAN Server, and Novell's NetWare. The most significant advantage of SQL Server, however, is the large number of application development tools and other third-party products with which it interfaces. The disadvantages of Microsoft's SQL Server include the fact that it is not as fast as the Sybase NLM version and that it is still based on older OS/2 code. Microsoft has not updated SQL Server to operate with OS/2.X even though its performance and preemptive multitasking capabilities make it a good platform for server DBMSs. A newer version of SQL Server will probably be based on Microsoft's Windows/NT product.

Q: *What are some of the advantages and disadvantages of using Gupta Technologies' SQLBase DBMS?*

A: Gupta Technologies' SQLBase is the least expensive of all high-profile Client/Server DBMSs. It is a widely accepted product that operates with the DOS, OS/2, or NetWare on the database server, and Microsoft's LAN Manager, IBM's LAN Server, Novell's NetWare, or Banyan's VINES on the LAN server. It is also highly scalable and is reputed to have excellent performance. Its most significant disadvantages are the amount of RAM its communication driver requires on the client platform and the relatively small number of application development tools and other third-party products with which SQLBase is compatible.

Q: *Explain some of the pluses and minuses of using a Unix-server DBMS.*

A: A high-end Unix system can support several times the number of database users that most PC Client/Server DBMSs can handle. Greater speed on a

Unix RISC platform is another advantage. A Unix-server DBMS also supports various forms of advanced multiprocessing and has better security features than PC-based DBMSs. On the minus side, Unix-based DBMSs are usually harder to learn and more difficult to use. There are fewer experts around, and Unix-based DBMSs are more expensive than PC DBMSs. Finally, Unix-based DBMSs need a more powerful, robust, and expensive platform on which to run.

Q: *What is IBM's DRDA?*

A: The Distributed Relational Database Architecture (DRDA) is IBM's standard for promoting multivendor database interoperability. DRDA handles SQL interoperability across heterogeneous database servers (i.e., similar operating systems, networks, and hardware platforms). Oracle, Novell, Sybase, and Gupta Technologies have all announced their intention to support DRDA.

Q: *What is a simple definition of the term* data domain?

A: A data domain is an allowable set of values for a specific data element in a particular field or table column.

Q: *How does disk mirroring provide database integrity?*

A: Disk mirroring provides database integrity by ensuring that data is automatically written to (recorded on) two or more storage devices so that it can be recovered even if you suffer media failure in one copy or device. Sometimes disk mirroring is accomplished by writing to a duplicate database on another platform; sometimes it is done on another portion of the same hard disk.

Q: *What is a BLOB?*

A: Binary Large Objects (BLOBs) are large binary files of data ranging up to 2 gigabytes or so in size. A BLOB can be an image, a video, a voice track, a graphic, a document, or a database snapshot that is treated as a single object by the system or application.

Local Area Network (LAN) Design

Q: *What are the advantages offered by each of the two basic physical LAN topologies?*

A: Under the daisy chain topology, the cable is run along the shortest path between each network node. The result is that this topology uses far less cable. This topology also does not require special power or space for a wiring hub. The star topology has each node connected via a central wiring hub, usually located in a wiring closet. This topology's primary advantage is survivability. Even if the cable between the hub and any one station is lost, the rest of the network will remain operating. With the star topology, it is easier to install, maintain, and change node locations.

Q: *What is the purpose of a network interface card (sometimes called an adapter card)?*

A: A network interface card is a printed circuit board required by each computer on the LAN. These cards take the serial signals off the network cables and move them into a parallel data stream inside the PCs. The cards also change the data from parallel back to serial and amplify the signals so they can travel the required distance over the network. Network interface cards also perform the media access control function.

Q: *Name the three standard protocols for LAN cabling and media access control.*

A: The three standard protocols for LAN cabling and media access control are Ethernet, ARC net, and Token-Ring.

Q: *When deciding which LAN cabling to use, how would you differentiate shielded twisted-pair, coaxial, and fiber-optic cable?*

A: Shielded twisted-pair cables provide protection against most electromagnetic interference, but they are relatively expensive. This type of cabling is also bulky and often requires custom installation. Coaxial cable costs less, is easier to install, and has similar resistance to electromagnetic noise. A caution with coaxial cable, though, is that you must be careful to select high-quality cable with the right impedance for the right protocol. Fiber-optic cable is more expensive than coaxial or shielded twisted-pair, but it permits signals to travel greater distances without repeaters. Fiber-optic cable is more secure and is much more reliable because it does not pick up electrical signals and impulses.

Q: *Describe the OSI model and its relevance to Client/Server computing.*

A: The Open Systems Interconnection (OSI) model has seven layers that describe standards by which computers can communicate with one another. These standards, ranging from physical cabling to presentation environments and application programs, provide the basis for integrating many of the Client/Server products available today. The OSI model also provides a reference framework for developing and evaluating communications protocols used in networks.

Q: *What is TCP/IP?*

A: Protocols are essentially rules for exchanging and interpreting data transferred over a network. The elements of a protocol typically specify the format in which data is to be sent, the signal strength to be used, an information structure for handling the data, the sequence in which the data should be sent, and the proper speed for transmitting it. The Transmission Control Protocol (TCP) and the Internet Protocol (IP) are two U.S. Department of Defense-specified protocols that have been adopted by many companies worldwide. The TCP/IP software protocols provide a standard set of communication parameters that help facilitate data exchange among dissimilar computer platforms.

Q: *What is the NetBIOS interface?*

A: NetBIOS (Network Basis Input/Output System) is a software program or protocol originally developed by IBM and Sytek to link a network operating system with a particular type of network interface card. This software program, now modified and used by many companies, operates at the OSI session and transport layers. It provides the interface between a computer and other resources on the network. In this regard, it functions much like the TCP/IP protocols. In fact, the Internet Protocol portion of TCP/IP encompasses the NetBIOS interface.

Q: *Explain how "polling" works in LAN environment.*

A: Polling involves the sequential, but extremely rapid, inquiry of each device on a network to see if it wants to transmit a signal.

Q: *What is Carrier Sense Multiple Access (CSMA)?*

A: A network interface card helps control access to network communications media. One method of executing this function is the listen-before-transmitting technique, commonly designated CSMA (Carrier Sense Multiple Access). This technique actually has the system operate like a two-way CB radio or walkie-talkie. Any station on the network must listen before it transmits a signal. If the station does not sense the carrier or transmission of another station on the network, then it is free to send its own signal. The CSMA technique is often combined with an additional method of dealing with transmission conflicts—i.e., the situation where two stations listen and detect no signal, then simultaneously transmit their own message. This additional method is referred to as Collision Detection (CD). Collision detection avoids two signals being sent at the same time, or if they are, it mediates between them.

Q: *What is the function of a bridge?*

A: A bridge is a hardware and software device that is used to link local area networks. It extends the network and helps to segment the message traffic that passes over the media. Hardware bridges forward traffic from one network to another only if the messages are properly addressed to devices or nodes on the other LAN.

Q: *How would you differentiate among the major LAN operating systems from Banyan, Novell, and Microsoft?*

A: New releases of network operating systems continue to deliver more advanced functions and features to users. Thus, any function/feature differentiation among major NOS products will be valid for only a limited time. Selecting among major operating systems should be based on specific criteria reflecting the needs of the organization. Criteria commonly of significance should include: performance, throughput, capacity, number of simultaneous users supported, server RAM usage as well as survivability and fault tolerance, and support of distributed processing.

Q: *Why is IEEE 802 important to a LAN design specialist?*

A: The Institute of Electrical and Electronics Engineers (IEEE) established a general committee to develop standards for network physical topology and cabling. These standards address the various protocols that are used in the physical and data-link layers of the OSI model. The two PC LAN standards of particular importance are 802.3 and 802.5. Standard 802.3 represents many Ethernet characteristics, while 802.5 describes the Token-Ring architecture.

Q: *What is a NetWare Loadable Module (NLM)?*

A: A NetWare Loadable Module (NLM) is a software application that runs in a server under Novell's NetWare 3.X. NLMs are produced by various companies to allow the server to provide functions that would normally reside on other network devices.

Q: *How does a multitasking network operating system environment often differ from a peer-to-peer network?*

A: A peer-to-peer network allows any PC on the network to share resources such as printers and files. A peer-to-peer network server often acts as both a server and a PC workstation. In a multitasking network operating system environment, on the other hand, the server would not generally support both server software and normal PC applications. The requirements of multitasking typically demand a dedicated server.

Q: *What is the purpose of a gateway?*

A: A gateway is a device that typically links PC networks to host machines, such as a minicomputer or mainframe, or larger packet-switching networks. A gateway provides linkage at the OSI session layer and permits different protocols to communicate with each other.

Network Management and Administration

Q: *Identify some of the key functions or areas that network management addresses.*

A: Most commentators agree that network management includes:

Fault management	Detecting and isolating system problems
Configuration management	Monitoring and changing network connections, equipment, and software
Asset management	Tracking the inventory of network components (i.e., cable, hardware, and software)

Security management	Safeguarding against unauthorized access to network resources or components
Performance management	Monitoring and controlling access to and/or use of network resources to maintain adequate levels of responsiveness.

Q: *How does accounting and financial management relate to network management?*

A: For purposes of accurate billing, growth justification, and operating budget viability, it is important to know which customers or users are employing the network and which ones send and receive the greatest amount of traffic. These questions can be answered by monitoring connection times, number and size of messages, sender and receiver addresses, and user IDs.

Q: *What is the advantage of monitoring and controlling a network from the wiring hub?*

A: Since all LAN traffic goes through the wiring hub, it is easier to monitor and report on network activity from this point. The hub has a central view of every network node that allows better data collection and more effective control of the devices at each node.

Q: *What is the Simple Network Management Protocol (SNMP)?*

A: The Simple Network Management Protocol (SNMP) is a Department of Defense-originated network reporting and control framework that provides a structure for formatting, transmitting, and collecting information about devices operating on a network. SNMP works well and is used in many large networks today. The network management products that incorporate the SNMP structure are inexpensive and do not require a lot of CPU power or computer memory. However, variant configurations of the basic structure and lack of good security features are considered SNMP weaknesses.

Q: *Why is it important to monitor LAN performance and analyze operating statistics?*

A: Performance measurements and LAN operating statistics can help managers and administrators detect early indicators of problems, plan for network growth, justify staff and budgets, and build a base of data for comparing LAN efficiency and performance.

Q: *In the context of network management, what is an "agent"?*

A: An agent is a set of programs that collects network management information in a network element or a node, performs an appropriate level of management, and then forwards relevant information to a higher-level collection point or network manager.

Q: *Describe several objectives of good security management.*
A: Good security management objectives include the following:

- Verifying and authenticating user identification
- Controlling access to network resources so that only authorized individuals can use them
- Providing secure communications
- Protecting data from unauthorized changes

Q: *What capabilities are provided by a LAN traffic counter?*
A: A LAN traffic counter is a software product that runs on a network station to provide the capability to view which nodes are active, to determine the volume of network activity, and to detect when transmissions errors across the network occur.

Q: *What does a LAN protocol analyzer do?*
A: A network message is wrapped in leading and trailing data fields formatted by the appropriate protocols. If communications are disrupted, analyzing a message's sending and receiving addresses can help determine the source or nature of the problem. A protocol analyzer is used to decode protocol-configured communication packets so that they can be read.

Q: *What are the benefits of using LAN metering software?*
A: LAN metering programs help provide information concerning how the network applications are being used. They can also be used to control the number of simultaneous users of each application and to establish improved LAN security.

References

1. Gerald Hopple, *State of the Art in Decision Support Systems*, QED, Wellesley, Mass., 1989.
2. Frank J. Derfler, Jr., *Guide to Connectivity*, Ziff-Davis Press, Emeryville, Calif., 1991.
3. Stan Schatt, *Understanding Local Area Networks*, 2d ed., Howard W. Sams & Co., Carmel, Ind., 1990.
4. Joe Salemi, *Guide to Client/Server Databases*, Ziff-Davis Press, Emeryville, Calif., 1993.
5. Steve Guengerich, *Downsizing Information Systems*, Sams Publishing, Prentice-Hall, Englewood Cliffs, N.J., 1992.

20

Networks and Network Administration

John H. Lister

Introduction

Since its inception in the early 1970s, IBM's Systems Network Architecture suite of programs and protocols (SNA) has had an immense impact on computer networking and data communications. SNA introduced the concepts of abstraction and virtualization to networks. Instead of an application program having specialized code to support all the different devices that could connect to it and the links to which they were attached, the program could deal in a standard manner with an abstract representation of the devices. The management of the network connectivity and the physical devices was the responsibility of a specific network management and control program, the Virtual Telecommunications Access Method (VTAM) with management of the links and the remote devices being delegated to the Network Control Program (NCP) running in an outboard communications front-end processor (originally a 3705 Communications Controller, currently a 3745). Enhancements to SNA have permitted the growth of large networks supporting many applications residing on multiple processors with access available from any device connected anywhere in the network. The SNA Network Interconnection (SNI) architecture permits internetwork connectivity while maintaining separate network architectures, conventions, and management responsibilities.

The current software environment that is the basis for the technical questions and answers in this chapter includes: ACF/VTAM Version 3.4.1 for MVS/ESA, ACF/NCP Version 5.4.1, ACF/SSP Version 3.6, NetView Version 2.2, and NetView Performance Monitor Version 1.6.

Questions and Answers

This section is designed to explore a candidate's knowledge of SNA architecture, message formats, and protocols.

Q: *What is a session?*
A: A session is a logical connection between two SNA entities.

Q: *What means are used by SNA to regulate traffic flow through the network?*
A: SNA uses message *pacing* in order to regulate information flow in the network, to prevent network congestion, and to prevent buffer overflow at a logical unit. SNA supports two independent pacing mechanisms: *session pacing* and *virtual route pacing.*

Q: *How do these two pacing mechanisms differ?*
A: Virtual route pacing regulates the flow of messages, on behalf of all sessions, between the subarea nodes of a network. Session pacing controls the flow of messages between logical units on a specific session to avoid buffer overflows and loss of information on that session.

Q: *How does session pacing control the flow of data?*
A: Session pacing controls the flow of data by dividing the traffic in a given direction on a session into *pacing windows,* a specific number of message units. This number may be predefined for a session, or may vary, depending on the capabilities of the nodes supporting the session endpoints. When one session partner starts to send the message units associated with a pacing window, it turns on the pacing request bit in the request header of the message unit. The session partner may then send up to the pacing window numbers of message units to the other partner before it must wait for a pacing response. The receiving session partner determines when to send a pacing response, which can depend on processing rates and buffer availability.

Q: *How is a session established between two logical units?*
A: The fundamental message flow that establishes an SNA session is the sending of the BIND request from the logical unit that is originating the session to the logical unit that is the target of the session request. The session is activated when the target logical unit responds positively to the bind.

Q: *How are the parameters for a session determined?*
A: The BIND request which is used to establish the session carries the session parameters, such as the message sizes in each direction, the optional SNA services that will be used and the LU type. Optionally, the BIND request can carry user data.

VTAM

This section focuses on the other aspects of VTAM: customizing and tuning VTAM, defining the network, and VTAM problem-determination tools.

Q: *How is an SNA network defined to VTAM?*

A: Each of the components of an SNA network is defined in a member of a partitioned dataset SYS1.VTAMLIST. For NCPs, VTAM also uses the Resource Resolution Table (RRT), in SYS1.VTAMLIB, to map logical unit names to network addresses.

Q: *Name some of the resources in VTAMLIST.*

A: Some of the VTAMLIST resources include: VTAM start parameters, VTAM configuration lists, route definitions, application major nodes, local non-SNA and local SNA major nodes, cross-domain resource manager major nodes, adjacent SSCP major nodes, cross-domain resource major nodes, and switched physical unit major nodes.

Q: *How can a node in an SNA network be activated automatically at VTAM initialization?*

A: The configuration member ATCCON00 contains a list of members in VTAMLIST that should be processed by VTAM on start-up. Each member is processed and the major node it represents is added to VTAM's in-storage table of network elements. At this stage the node is *defined* to VTAM. If the node has ISTATUS=ACTIV specified, either explicitly or by inheritance from a higher-level node, VTAM will queue an activation request for the node when higher-level nodes in the path have been activated.

Q: *How does an application interface with VTAM?*

A: An application is defined to VTAM by means of its entry (its ACB name) in VTAMLIST.

Q: *How is the connection made between VTAM and the ACB in storage?*

A: The application program issues the operating system OPEN with the ACB as one of the arguments. This results in a supervisor call machine instruction (SVC 19) which routes control to the operating system. The operating system OPEN routines inspect and validate the control block and determine that it is a VTAM ACB, then pass the request to VTAM. VTAM inspects the control block and makes a correlation between the ACB name and the application name in an active application major node. If it can find a match, VTAM opens the ACB (changes various fields in the ACB to reflect its open status) and inserts the addresses of other control blocks and routines that the application program will need in order to be able to communicate with VTAM.

Q: *How does an application program make requests to VTAM?*

A: An application program issues assembly language macros such as SEND and RECEIVE, with a Request Parameter List (RPL) as an argument, which gives VTAM details of the request to be performed.

Q: *How does VTAM inform an application program of the completion of a request or of an external event?*

A: There are two notification methods that an application program can use. The first is to pass to VTAM in a request the address of an exit routine which will be called when a given request has completed. The second is to pass the address of an Event Control Block (ECB) which will be posted when the event is complete.

Q: *Where does VTAM store messages in transit through the network?*

A: VTAM maintains a set of *buffer pools* (fixed-length areas of storage used to hold control blocks or data in transit through the network). The location of the buffer pools varies according to the operating system and VTAM release level. In MVS/ESA, most of the buffers are in Extended Common Storage (ECSA).

Q: *How can a systems programmer control the sizes of the buffer pools?*

A: The VTAM start options member ATCSTR00 contains the specifications for the VTAM buffer pools. For each of the pools, the systems programmer specifies the size of each buffer, the number of buffers that VTAM is to build at initialization time, and the parameters that VTAM will use to determine when to expand and contract the buffer pools according to changes in the network load.

Q: *What are some of the considerations in choosing the buffer pool parameters?*

A: The goal of choosing the buffer pool sizes is to provide maximum throughput with minimum overhead. Choosing larger buffer pools minimizes the number of times that VTAM has to request virtual storage from the operating system, but costs more in allocated virtual storage. Choosing small values for the expansion and contraction points can result in a considerable overhead because VTAM is constantly acquiring and releasing buffer pool storage from the operating system.

Q: *How would a systems programmer determine VTAM's buffer usage?*

A: The VTAM command D NET,BFRUSE issued from an operator or NetView console displays the current number of buffers from each pool in use, the number of buffers currently in the pool, and the maximum usage of each pool, together with the total storage VTAM has allocated in both its private region and the common area.

Q: *What is the maximum number of sessions that an application program can support?*

A: It depends on the resources available in the system. Each active session consumes a few hundred bytes of control blocks, both in the private area and common storage, to describe the session to both VTAM and the application program. Both the application and VTAM require buffers to support traffic on the session. Processor resources limit the total amount of traffic that an application can support so that, for example, a CICS application could support several thousand sessions, each of which had relatively light traffic (one to two messages per session per minute). Conversely, VM could support only a limited number of highly active users, each of whom consumed a significant amount of processor cycles.

Q: *Which tuning parameters should be considered for an application that is expected to support a large number of sessions?*

A: When an application program LU is defined to VTAM, the EAS parameter on the APPL definition statement specifies an estimate of the number of concurrent sessions the application will have with other logical units—either other programs or devices. VTAM uses this operand to determine how it will allocate storage for the control blocks representing these sessions. Coding a large number causes VTAM to preallocate storage from the common area for a hash table which it uses to store the session representations. This allows fast lookup of session information. If the EAS value is coded significantly smaller than the number of sessions that are established, VTAM will not refuse to establish the additional sessions, but the search time for session information will be increased as VTAM must search a number of separately linked tables. Conversely, if an application will have only a few simultaneous sessions (TSO and NetView applications are specific examples of this application category), then EAS=1 should be coded in order to save system common storage.

Q: *How is the logon string that a user types at a terminal converted into a session initiation request by VTAM?*

A: The user's logon character string, which is usually a keyword naming the application with which the user is requesting a session, is translated to a formal session request by the VTAM component Unformatted Systems Services (USS).

Q: *How does VTAM determine which session parameters to use in starting a session?*

A: VTAM uses a *Logmode* or Logmode entry in a table to specify the session parameters. The session initiation request (through the Logmode parameter) supplies or defaults a Logmode name which is searched in the table.

Q: *How does VTAM determine which network route to use for a session?*

A: VTAM's resolution of a session request results in the Bind parameters and the Class of Service (COS) information being obtained from the Logmode entry. VTAM uses the COS name from the Logmode to index its Class of Service table (Costab) which lists the virtual routes and traffic priorities that are to be used by this session.

Q: *What entries in the COS table are required?*

A: The entry ISTVTCOS is used by VTAM for SSCP-to-SSCP and SSCP-to-PU sessions and is required. A blank COS entry was required for communications with older versions of SNA networks; however, it is strongly recommended as a "default" for sessions where no explicit COS name is specified in the Logmode entry.

Q: *In a multidomain (or multinetwork) environment, where are the Logmode and COS name entries resolved?*

A: The Logmode entry is resolved from the Modetab associated with the secondary LU. This supplies a COS entry, which is supplied as a name to the SSCP which owns the primary LU. This SSCP then uses its own Costab to resolve the name into a network route. The fact that the COS name is supplied from one domain and resolved to a route in another means that a significant amount of coordination is required between the network systems programmers responsible for the two domains.

Q: *How many Class of Service tables does VTAM support?*

A: Each VTAM supports one COS table per network. In a multinetwork environment, the COS tables to be used in adjacent networks are specified in the NCP.

Q: *How does a systems programmer prepare a Class of Service table for a network?*

A: The source for a Class of Service table is a series of assembly language macros, shown in the following example:

```
ISTSDCOS COSTAB
ISTVTCOS COS    VR=((0,2),(1,2),(2,2),(3,2),(4,2),(5,2),(6,2),(7,2))
BATCH    COS    VR=((0,0),(1,0),(2,0),(3,0),(4,0),(5,0),(6,0),(7,0))
         COS    VR=((0,0),(1,0),(2,0),(3,0),(4,0),(5,0),(6,0),(7,0))
         COSEND
         END    ISTSDCOS
```

The example shows the required COS name ISTVTCOS used by VTAM for SSCP sessions, which allows the use of virtual routes 0 through 7 at transmission priority 2. If virtual route 0 is available, it is used; then virtual route 1, through all the routes in the list. The batch entry BATCH uses the same virtual routes, in the same order, but at transmission priority 0. The third entry is the recommended blank entry, which resolves to the same set of virtual routes as the BATCH entry. The source is assembled using macros supplied with VTAM. The object code is link-edited into a load module which is placed in VTAMLIB. For a single network environment, the COS table has a standard name: ISTSDCOS. In a multinetwork environment, the COS table for VTAM's native network is ISTSDCOS. COS tables for adjacent networks can have any names, which must match the names specified in the network definitions in the NCPs.

Q: *How does a terminal LU establish a session to an application program in the same domain?*

A: An outline of a session start flow is as follows: The user at the terminal LU sends a character-coded request to VTAM requesting the session. VTAM's USS routines translate the character-coded request into an INITSELF RU. The INITSELF is sent to VTAM's SSCP service. VTAM's SSCP service sends a CINIT request to the application's LU. The application inspects the session request and sends a BIND to the terminal LU. The terminal LU responds to the BIND. The application then sends an SESST request to VTAM's SSCP to notify it of the session start.

NCP

IBM's Network Control Program (NCP) is the second most important component in an SNA network and comprises a dedicated operating system as well as specific hardware management routines and a description of the network topology which it supports. This section examines some of the technical issues surrounding NCP and its generation.

Q: *How can definition items be defaulted in an NCP?*
A: It is possible to specify a parameter for a lower-level node (in the hierarchy) in a higher-level node. The parameter is then applied to all lower-level nodes in a "sift-down" effect. For example, the DLOGMOD (default Log-mode) parameter applies to an LU. If it is specified on a LINE macro, it will be applied to all LUs on that line that do not have a DLOGMOD parameter specifically supplied for them.

Q: *How can a network administrator arrange for a terminal to be logged-on automatically to an application at network start-up?*
A: If the LOGAPPL parameter is supplied in an LU definition, VTAM will automatically queue a session initiation request to the destination application on behalf of the LU at the time that the LU is activated.

Q: *What mechanisms does NCP use to minimize network disruption in the event of VTAM failure?*
A: Each dependent resource in an NCP is owned by an SSCP, which is responsible for resource activation and session management services. Should the SSCP which owns a resource fail, then the NCP starts Automatic Network Shutdown (ANS) procedures for the resource. The parameter ANS on the NCP PU macro defining the resource determines the NCP action. If ANS=STOP is coded (or inherited), NCP stops all communications with the resource, and any sessions with LUs that the resource supports are terminated. If ANS=CONTINUE or ANS=CONT is coded, NCP continues communications with the resource.

Q: *In the event of ANS, what happens to sessions with dependent LUs?*
A: A session that is already established will continue, and the dependent LU will still be able to communicate with its session partner, provided that the failure that caused the ANS did not disrupt the partner LU or any of the components in the session path.

Q: *How can resources be defined dynamically to an NCP?*

A: NCP Dynamic Reconfiguration supports the addition and deletion of link-attached resources in an active NCP. Network systems programmers prepare Dynamic Reconfiguration source decks, which are filed in VTAMLIST, instructing VTAM which resources are to be changed.

Q: *What definitions in the NCP source must be included to prepare for NCP Dynamic Reconfiguration?*

A: The NCP must be generated with sufficient spare control blocks to accommodate the additional devices. The PUDRPOOL macro specifies the number of spare PU definitions that the NCP will support; the LUDRPOOL macro specifies the number of spare LU definitions that the NCP will support. In addition, each line that may have devices added to it must have the MAXPU parameter specified to allow for the additional devices. If logical units are to be added to an existing PU, the PU must have the MAXLU parameter specified on its definition.

SDLC

Q: *How is an SDLC link activated?*

A: The two link stations on an SDLC link establish communications when one partner sends the Set Normal Response Mode (SNRM) command and receives an acknowledgment. This starts the communications, establishes the frame-numbering scheme, and determines the primary and secondary roles on the link.

Q: *How are the primary and secondary roles determined on an SDLC link?*

A: It depends on the type of node. If one of the link stations is associated with a type 4 node and one with a type 2.X node, the type 4 node is always the primary. If the link stations are both type 4 nodes or both type 2.1 nodes (a type 2.0 node can communicate only with a type 4 or 5 node), then the Exchange Identification (XID) sequence is used to establish primary and secondary roles.

Q: *How many devices can be connected to an SDLC link?*

A: Only one device can attach to an SDLC link in primary mode. There can, however, be up to 253 secondary mode devices using the SDLC multipoint link protocol.

Q: *What is the maximum frame size that can be supported on an SDLC link?*

A: It depends on the link stations at each end of the link and the size of their buffers. Frame sizes of 4096 bytes between type 4 nodes are not uncommon.

Q: *How does an SDLC link station recover from a transmission error?*

A: When a station on an SDLC link receives a frame in error (detected by the lack of a frame checksum or a checksum in error), the frame is discarded.

The sequence numbering of the frames and the acknowledgment of frames by number means that link stations can discover that frames have been received out of sequence and request retransmission.

Token-Ring

Q: *What is the maximum number of devices that a single Token-Ring can support?*

A: The theoretical maximum number of devices on a Token-Ring network is 260. However, this maximum is rarely reached in practice because of electrical restrictions on the total length of cable in the ring and the number of concentrators.

Q: *What are the types of addresses used in a Token-Ring network?*

A: 1. Locally and universally addressed individual station addresses

2. Group broadcast and functional group addresses

Q: *What are the differences between the individual and group addresses?*

A: Individual addresses describe a single station on a Token-Ring and may be the source or destination addresses of Token-Ring frames. Group addresses are used to describe functions, rather than individual stations. A group address is used only as a destination address.

Q: *What considerations are there for choosing locally administered addresses versus universally administered addresses?*

A: Universally administered addresses are managed by the IEEE and are guaranteed to be unique worldwide. For those adapters which support universally administered addresses, the adapter's address is in read-only memory on the adapter and cannot be changed. This means that if an adapter fails, its replacement will have a different universally administered address, which may impact network management schemes. Universally administered addresses do not support any structured assignment which allows identification of the location of a Token-Ring station from its address.

Q: *What procedure does a Token-Ring adapter perform in order to start communications on a ring?*

A: The adapter first of all tests its lobe cable by sending a series of lobe test frames from the adapter to the MSAU, without attaching to the ring. The adapter then connects to the ring and monitors the ring traffic to determine whether it is the first station on the ring. The adapter sends a duplicate address test frame onto the ring to verify that another station with the same individual address is not already on the ring. The adapter waits until the active monitor initiates neighbor notification for the ring, identifies its Nearest Active Upstream Neighbor (NAUN), and identifies itself to its downstream neighbor. The adapter then sends a request initialization frame to the ring parameter server functional address, and uses the response to initialize itself. If there is no ring parameter server, the station uses default values.

Q: *What is the normal procedure for information transmission around a Token-Ring?*

A: A station that has information which it wishes to transmit waits until it receives a token. At that point, it converts the token into a frame (by setting a bit in the Access Control field) and transmits the frame, with destination and source addresses, routing information (if necessary), and the frame data. The frame information is repeated by all the stations on the Token-Ring. When it reaches its destination, the Token-Ring adapter in the station recognizes its address, copies the frame information from the ring into its buffers, and sets the Address Recognized and Frame Copied bits in the Frame Status field. The frame is transmitted around the ring until it reaches the originating station, which removes it from the ring and transmits a token, allowing another station to transmit.

Q: *Token-Rings have been described as "fair." Why is this?*

A: Token-Rings are deterministic, that is, each station can transmit at most one frame before relinquishing control of the token. This means that no one station can gain control of the ring at the expense of other stations.

Q: *What is a beaconing condition?*

A: A beaconing condition exists when a ring station discovers a hard failure in the ring which prevents the ring from functioning correctly. When this situation occurs, the station which discovers the error starts to transmit beacon frames continuously until the problem is resolved or the station removes itself from the ring.

Q: *How does a Token-Ring attempt to recover from a beaconing condition?*

A: When a station on a ring enters the beacon transmit mode, other stations repeat the frame. The frame will eventually arrive at the transmitter's NAUN. When the beaconing station's NAUN copies eight beacon frames, it removes itself from the ring. The station then begins to reattach itself, using the standard lobe attachment tests and duplicate address tests. If these succeed, the station remains reattached to the ring and waits for the beacon condition to terminate. If the ring does not recover after a specified period (the architected timer T(beacon_transmit)), the beaconing station assumes that its NAUN has completed its self-test and has reattached, and that the fault lies with the beaconing station itself. This station therefore removes itself from the ring and goes through the reinsertion attachment tests described here.

Q: *How does a Token-Ring node learn the address of its upstream neighbor?*

A: Every 7 seconds, the active monitor initiates the neighbor notification process on a Token-Ring. It broadcasts an Active Monitor Present frame to all ring stations on its ring the next time it receives a token. The first station which receives this frame copies the information in the frame, including the source address, which is the NAUN address for this station, and sets the Address Recognized and Frame Copied bits in the Frame Status field. Other stations on the ring repeat the frame, but do not take action because they do not require the address information in the frame. When a token is next available, the station which received the Active Monitor Present frame transmits a Standby Monitor Present frame, broadcast to all stations on the ring. The downstream neighbor of this station copies the frame, recognizes that this is its NAUN, and sets the Address Recognized and Frame Copied bits in the Frame Status field. Other stations on the ring ignore this frame, as they are not the downstream neighbor of the transmitter. In turn, all the remaining stations on the ring receive a Standby Monitor Present frame without the Address Recognized and Frame Copied bits set, use this information to update their NAUN information, and transmit a further Standby Monitor Present until the Active Monitor receives a Standby Monitor Present frame, which completes the sequence.

Q: *What are the contents of the Routing Information field?*

A: The Routing Information field comprises the Routing Control field, followed by up to eight 2-byte route designators, which define a ring number (12 bits) and a bridge number (4 bits) through which the frame should travel from its source to its destination.

Q: *How is the Routing Information field built?*

A: The Routing Information field is built during route discovery. As bridges forward-broadcast frames that are used by a ring station requesting a connection with another station, they add the ring number and bridge number to the routing information field, so that when a frame reaches its destination, it has a complete route built from its source, which the destination station can use to return a response.

Q: *How does a Token-Ring node determine the location of another node?*

A: A Token-Ring node which wishes to establish a connection with another node first transmits a TEST or XID frame to its destination on the same ring. If the destination station is on the same ring, then the connection can be established. If the destination station is not on the same ring, then the source station transmits a frame to the destination address with a Routing Information field requesting broadcast to all rings. Bridges forward the frame, which eventually is received at the destination.

Q: *How does a Token-Ring station establish a connection with another node?*

A: After a Token-Ring station has established the location of its partner node, it initiates connection by using an XID frame to negotiate primary and secondary station roles. The primary sends a Set Asynchronous Balanced Mode Extended (SABME) frame to activate the logical connection between the two stations. The secondary acknowledges the frame by sending an Unnumbered Acknowledgment (UA) frame. Finally, the primary sends the first data transmission a Receive Ready (RR) frame to confirm the data transfer mode.

Q: *What are the functions of the active monitor?*

A: The active monitor provides monitoring of the transmission of tokens and information around the ring. It is responsible for maintaining the master clock, which times all information transmission on the ring. It is responsible for resolving error conditions on the ring and for initiating neighbor notification periodically on the ring.

Network Routing

SNA routing, with its three-layer structure, is one of the more difficult concepts that a network systems programmer has to face. Judicious choice of network routes and alternatives, however, is crucial in maintaining network performance, reliability, and availability. This section explores routing concepts and the mechanics of route generation.

Q: *How is routing supported in an SNA subarea network?*

A: SNA routing uses the concepts of subareas to provide routing services, providing the abstraction of "link connections" between individual subareas.

Q: *How is a transmission group made up?*

A: A transmission group comprises one or a number of links of various types between two subareas. Links can be channel connections (a transmission group can comprise only a single channel connection), SDLC links (a transmission group can support multiple physical links), and Token-Ring logical connections (a transmission group supports only a single Token-Ring logical connection).

Q: *What is the difference between an explicit route and a virtual route?*

A: Explicit routes are defined between an origin subarea and a destination subarea over the transmission groups and intermediate subareas which connect them. The explicit route is identified by the origin subarea, the destination subarea, the number of the explicit route which connects the two subareas, and the number of the reverse explicit route, not necessarily the same, which describes the route in the opposite direction.

A virtual route is a logical connection between two SNA subarea nodes, which is defined over a particular explicit route. Virtual route services provide transmission priorities over the underlying explicit route, flow control through virtual-route pacing mechanisms, and data integrity through sequence number checking of individual Path Information Units (PIUs) over the virtual route.

Q: *How are routing tables generated?*

A: Routing tables can be generated by an automated generation tool, such as IBM's Network Design Aid (NetDA).

Q: *Where are network routes defined?*

A: Network routes are stored in VTAMLIST. They are activated to describe the network to VTAM at initialization time. Network routes are included as part of the NCP source deck and assembled into control blocks as part of the network definition process.

Q: *How many routing tables do VTAM and NCP support?*

A: VTAM supports one set of routing tables since it only participates directly in one network. An NCP has a set of routes defined for each of the networks to which it is connected.

Q: *How is routing accomplished in a multinetwork environment?*

A: Network routes are entirely contained within a single network. The gateway NCPs, which are responsible for the interface between two networks, also provide virtual route termination services. NCP translates the session routing from the virtual routes and subarea numbers used in one network to those in another whenever an information frame crosses the network boundary.

Q: *How does the SNA architecture identify networks?*

A: Each SNA network is assigned a unique eight-character name by its network administrator. The name is defined to all Type 4, 5, and 2.1 nodes within the network. For VTAM, the network name is specified by the NETID parameter in the VTAM start list member ATCSTR00. For NCP, the native network name is specified using the NETID parameter of the BUILD macro. In earlier releases of VTAM and NCP, naming the network was necessary only if the network supported cross-network sessions. In current releases, the network name is required.

Q: *Can two networks share the same name?*

A: Two networks which are connected to each other via SNI must have unique names. Most names are chosen arbitrarily by the network administrators to represent the organization which they support.

Q: *How is connectivity possible between separately managed SNA networks?*

A: The extensions to SNA, known as SNA Network Interconnection (SNI), permit application sessions between logical units in two or more separate networks.

Q: *How are other network connections defined to VTAM?*

A: VTAM defines the names and the networks of other SSCPs with which it will communicate in a cross-domain resource manager major node, which is filed in VTAMLIST and activated to VTAM.

Q: *What is the function of the GWPATH definition?*

A: Following is a typical definition of a foreign-network SSCP which defines ONETVTM in network OTHERNET:

```
          VBUILD  TYPE=CDRM
          NETWORK NETID=OTHERNET
ONETVTM CDRM    CDRSC=OPT,CDRDYN=YES,ISTATUS=ACTIVE
          GWPATH  SUBAREA=2,ELEMENT=19,                        X
                  ADJNET=NULLNET1,                             X
                  ADJNETSA=6,                                  X
                  ADJNETEL=2
```

The GWPATH macro following the CDRM macro specifies the representation of ONETVTM in the adjacent network NULLNET1. The SUBAREA parameter defines the gateway NCP which is used to access the CDRM. The ADJNETSA and ADJNETEL parameters define the subarea and element address of this CDRM in the adjacent network. These parameters must correspond to a GWNAU macro in the NCP, which is used to correlate the address transformation information.

Q: *Where are the boundaries between networks?*
A: Network boundaries always reside in NCPs, called *gateway* NCPs.

Q: *How does a network systems programmer define resources in another network?*
A: Resources in other networks are defined using Cross-Domain Resource (CDRSC) major nodes in VTAM. For resource in other networks, the NETID parameter is coded, defining the network in which the resource resides.

Q: *Why would an installation wish to specify the owner of a foreign-network resource?*
A: Primarily for security reasons. Specifying the SSCP which owns a network resource together with the VFYOWNER=YES parameter as in:

```
          VBUILD   TYPE=CDRSC
          NETWORK  NETID=OTHERNET
 OTHCDRS  CDRSC    CDRM=SOMESSCP,VFYOWNER=YES...
```

where SOMESSCP owns OTHCDRS in network OTHERNET, means that sessions cannot be established unless this information is correct. This prevents other resources with the same name from attempting to establish cross-network sessions.

Q: *If the SSCP owner of a foreign-network resource changes, how can the network operator correct this problem?*
A: The owner of a CDRSC can be changed by issuing the MODIFY CDRM command. In the foregoing example, to change the owner of CDRSC OTHCDRS to SSCPTWO, the network operator would issue the command MODIFY NET,CDRM=SSCPTWO,ID=OTHCDRS.

Q: *How does VTAM determine where to forward a session request for a logical unit in another network?*
A: VTAM uses the SSCPs which are specified in an adjacent SSCP list when trying to find a destination logical unit for a session request. Adjacent SSCP lists are VTAM major nodes which are filed in VTAMLIST, and activated on network start-up, or by the network operator.

Q: *What order does VTAM use in searching the adjacent SSCP list?*
A: The order depends on the VTAM start option SSCPORD in the VTAM start member ATCSTR00 of VTAMLIST. If SSCPORD=NO is specified, VTAM searches the table in the order in which the entries were defined. If SSCPORD=YES is specified, VTAM searches the table in the following order:

1. The SSCP that owns the resource (if this is known)
2. The SSCP(s) for which the most recent session-initiation attempt succeeded (if any)
3. The SSCPs for which no session-initiation attempt has been made
4. The SSCPs for which the last session initiation attempt failed

Q: *How would a network operator determine the adjacent SSCP list for a foreign network?*

A: A network operator can use the DISPLAY ADJSSCPS command to show the adjacent SSCP list for a specific network.

Q: *What are the limitations on the number of cross-network sessions?*

A: There are no intrinsic limits in the SNA architecture for the number of cross-network sessions. However, each cross-network session requires storage to represent it in the gateway NCP(s).

Network Administration

NetView

NetView is IBM's strategic network management subsystem: a complex monitoring, analysis, and automation facility.

Q: *What are the major components of NetView?*

A: The major components of NetView are the Command Facility; the Hardware Monitor (formerly the Network Problem Determination Aid, or NPDA); the Session Monitor (formerly the Network Logical Data Manager, or NLDM); and the Status Monitor.

Q: *How does NetView interface with VTAM for command processing?*

A: NetView interfaces with VTAM by opening an ACB defined to VTAM as the primary *program operator*. An application with program operator authority can send commands to VTAM and retrieve the output, using the SENDCMD and RCVCMD macros.

Q: *How can a network systems programmer arrange for automatic execution of commands?*

A: The NetView AT and EVERY commands allow scheduling of NetView, VTAM, and other commands or command lists (Clists) at specified intervals and times of the day. By combining the AT, EVERY, and other Clist support commands, it is possible for a network systems programmer to develop a custom schedule for command execution.

Q: *How can NetView be programmed to react to a network event?*

A: Every VTAM and MVS message starts with an identifier which defines the format and content of the message. NetView has a *message table*, which allows a network systems programmer to associate a command list with a message identifier. The command list receives the entire text of the message, and can parse it to determine the resource(s) which are affected by the event which generated the message, and then take the appropriate action.

Q: *What are the functions of the hardware monitor?*

A: The hardware monitor collects and displays statistical information and error reports (*alerts*) from network-attached and host-attached devices. It also writes records derived from this information to the SMF log.

Q: *How does the hardware monitor receive data from the network?*

A: Each network device which is owned by a VTAM sends error and statistical information on its SSCP-PU session. For example, a 3174 establishment controller can report an error with a coaxial connection to an attached terminal to VTAM.

Q: *A user complains that a printer is printing slowly. How could you determine the cause of the problem?*

A: The exact methodology of problem determination depends on the information found during diagnosis. However, the following are some specific items which can be checked: Resource utilization of the application which is driving the printer—is this a network problem? Is the application not providing the data fast enough to the network? Link utilization of the facilities in the transmission path to the device—is another session consuming a disproportionate amount of the available bandwidth? Is there a large number of temporary errors on the link(s) in the transmission path which impacts throughput and performance?

Q: *How would a network systems programmer determine the number of errors on a line?*

A: NCP maintains traffic and error counters for each of the links which it connects. At intervals, it forwards this information to VTAM on the NCP's SSCP-PU session. VTAM, in turn, forwards the statistics to the NetView hardware monitor (NPDA) where it is filed in the NPDA database. The information may be retrieved with the command NPDA TOT ST N *lname*, which requests a display of all the statistics records associated with the line.

NPM

The NetView Performance Monitor (NPM) provides monitoring, statistical, analytical, and accounting functions for mainframe-based SNA networks, and is an essential tool for network systems programmers in understanding the traffic flow through a network and its performance characteristics.

Q: *What are the functions of the NetView Performance Monitor (NPM)?*

A: Collection, display, and archiving of network performance information, session information, network and session accounting information, response time information, local area network data, and filtering of information recorded on the Systems Management Facilities (SMF) log.

Q: *How does NPM collect data?*

A: NPM uses hardware and software facilities in the 37X5 communications controllers and NCP to collect utilization, link, and accounting statistics.

Q: *How does NPM collect data from an NCP?*

A: NPM uses a virtual line group defined in the NCP, with the parameter NPASRC=YES. This line group has a single line, with a single PU and at least one LU in it. NPM retrieves data from the NCP by means of a session with the NPA LU.

Q: *What are the steps involved in preparing an NCP for data collection?*

A: 1. Add the NPM library to the JCL for the Network Definition Facility (NDF) so that NPM can be included as part of the NCP load module.

2. Add the parameter NPA=YES to the BUILD macro and, optionally, the SESSAC, GWSESAC, PUNAME, and MAXTP parameters, if accounting data collection and transmission priority performance data collection are required.

3. Specify NPACOLL=YES for each of the resources for which NPM data collection is desired.

4. Specify the SPEED parameter on lines, so that NPM can calculate the line utilization.

5. Define the NPALU line group to NCP.

6. File the NCP definition and generate the NCP.

Q: *How does NPM collect response-time data?*

A: NPM collects response-time data by monitoring messages as they pass through VTAM buffers: incoming from a terminal device, outbound to a terminal, and the final acknowledgment from the terminal.

Q: *How does NPM collect Token-Ring data?*

A: NPM collects Token-Ring data by retrieving it from IBM LAN manager. The LAN manager maintains Token-Ring sessions with bridges, and can collect traffic and error statistics from them.

SSP and the Systems Generation Process

This section deals with some of the mechanics of converting network definitions into programs and loading them into communications controllers using IBM's systems support programs.

Q: *What are the services provided by the Systems Support Programs (SSP)?*

A: The Systems Support Programs (SSP) provide services to:

1. Generate a network control program from source definition.
2. Load a network control program into a 37X5 communications controller.
3. Dump a communications controller.
4. Dump the Maintenance and Operator Subsystem (MOSS) and network scanners in a communications controller.
5. Format communications controller, MOSS, and scanner dumps.

Q: *How would a network systems programmer prepare an NCP definition for inclusion in an SNA network?*

A: In order to prepare an NCP definition for an SNA network the following steps must be performed:

1. Generate or modify a set of NCP source definitions using a program editor.
2. Submit the definitions to the Network Definition Facility (NDF) for generation of an NCP load module, an NCP expanded source (NEWDEFN), a Resource Resolution Table (RRT), and an output listing.
3. Verify the output of the NDF.
4. File the resulting NEWDEFN source in VTAMLIST, and the NCP load module and RRT in VTAMLIB.

Q: *What are the processes performed by the Network Definition Facility?*

A: The Network Definition Facility performs the following:

1. It reads the NCP definition source and validates the definition statements and parameters.
2. It builds the NEWDEFN output if the NEWDEFN keyword is coded on the NDF OPTIONS keyword.
3. It generates NCP assembler language source code for the resources coded in the NCP source.
4. It invokes the NCP tables 1 and 2 assemblies, which read the assembly language source code definitions produced earlier, and generate object code for the NCP control blocks.
5. It generates linkage editor control statements.
6. It invokes the linkage editor to combine the object code defining the NCP control blocks with IBM NCP code modules to produce the NCP load module and RRT.
7. It produces an output listing giving details of the results of the individual steps.

Q: *How can an NCP be loaded into a 37X5 communications controller?*

A: If the communications controller is channel-attached to a System/370 processor, two methods are available: (1) VTAM VARY NET,ACT,LOAD=YES command, and (2) use of the SSP independent loader IFLOAD.

Q: *How is an NCP load module transferred to a Token-Ring-attached Communications Controller?*

A: In order to transfer a load module to a Token-Ring-attached Communications Controller, it must first have an active NCP running. To install the initial NCP into a Token-Ring Controller, a small NCP module containing a minimum set of definitions is prepared and generated using the NDF process. This load module is transferred to the hard disk of a local (or SDLC link-attached) 3745 controller using the VTAM MODIFY NET,LOAD command. Using MOSS commands on the 3745 console, the information is copied to the 3745 floppy disk.

The 3745 floppy disk is transported to the remote 3745 location, where MOSS commands are used to transfer it to the hard disk, load it, and activate it. VTAM can then establish communications with and ownership of the NCP in the remote 3745. VTAM MODIFY NET,LOAD commands are then used to transfer a full NCP over the communication path from the host VTAMLIB to the hard disk of the remote 3745, at which point it can be loaded into the 3745's main storage.

21

Object-Oriented
Analysis (OOA) and
Programming (OOP)

Candice Zarr

Object Technology
for Businesses

For many years, object-oriented technology has had a tremendous amount of success in the development of real-time software for scientific and communications applications. Object technology in these areas has already demonstrated potential for higher productivity through the use of reusable components. As a result, object technology is making inroads into commercial business systems. There are outstanding organizations that have successfully made the transition to object technology. They have achieved enviable levels of quality and productivity.

Object-Oriented Analysis and Programming represent a new approach to traditional/functional approaches. Most business systems developers and managers, are familiar with functional, or procedurally oriented, ways of designing and developing systems. CASE, for example, is an adaptation of these procedural approaches. But there are also new activities and techniques for carrying out structured analysis and design. Object technology is one of them and requires an entirely new way of thinking about development. There is no equivalent for existing, structured, functionally or data-oriented system design in the object-oriented paradigm. They are incompatible.

Though the advantages of object-oriented analysis and programming are many, there are distinctly different ways of describing the business problem and the solution that must be mastered. There are entirely new programming languages and development environments. In the first part of this chapter we will be discussing some of these topics briefly. More detailed information will be found in the questions and answers that follow.

Object Methodologies

Like their traditional brethren, object methodologies rarely cover the needs of the entire system's life cycle. Some concentrate on the analysis of the business requirements; others deal more with the infrastructure design strategy. A sign of the youth of this technology is the large number of methodologies which address the analysis and design of new systems. Much less frequently addressed are techniques for analysis and design of enhancements to existing software, or reuse and library management.

While it would be possible to use object analysis and design techniques for developing a traditional, procedurally oriented system, the converse is not true. Methodologies for analysis, design, and development of object systems are very different from traditional approaches. While the goals of the various object methodologies are the same—to produce an efficient, easily extendable system quickly—some are better suited for some projects than others. There are methods which are event-oriented, and those that more closely resemble data-oriented, transaction-driven methods like information engineering. Others are better for first-timers and simpler systems. Each methodology uses its own notation standards. There are automated CASE tools for drawing these specific notations and for storing design information, but they tend to be less functionally developed than their traditional, structured methodology counterparts. Some methodologies have plastic templates for hand-drawing their notation.

Analysis Methods

Unlike the traditional approaches that involve interviewing and transcribing or interviewing and modeling, object-oriented analysis methods are concerned with identifying candidate objects, object behaviors, and cooperation between objects. Object analysis is often conducted in informal settings with small (one to five people), knowledgeable groups of business and IS professionals discussing and refining their definition of system components at a high level. Object analysis is described as "middle-out" as opposed to "bottom-up" or "top-down" traditional approaches. Using appropriate toolsets, prototypes can be used to provide a very rapid definition of end-user requirements. The following are some popular analysis methods:

- Shlaer/Mellor is oriented toward information modeling.
- Coad/Yourdon is popular because this approach is very accessible for the novice.
- Rebecca Wirffs-Brock's "Responsibility-Driven Design," while actually a design method, contains components for analysis which proponents feel is straightforward, natural, and promotes the communication of ideas and team interaction.

Design Methods

Design takes the system components, the objects, and their prescribed behaviors and defines the physical implementations these components will take. Designers may identify existing objects for reuse within the new system. Objects and their behaviors may be combined with other objects to form more generic, reusable, abstract classes. Object subsystem designs (for large projects) are integrated. Object system design promotes an iterative, prototyping approach which facilitates changes and refinements, unlike traditional approaches, in which the entire system is developed based on an agreed set of specifications. Iterative prototyping allows for greater flexibility in designing user interfaces, object behavior and collusion, and for early-on performance testing. Through reuse, there are opportunities for higher-level code quality and a reduced need for testing.

One of the most widely accepted design approaches is Booch, with its well-known "cloud" modeling notation. Booch's approach has been described as "design a little, code a little, test a little, and review a little." It is a cyclic, iterative approach which works well when managed well. Rumbaugh's design method is a more data-intensive approach, which will seem more accessible to those familiar with information engineering and data modeling techniques. Again, Wirffs-Brock is also considered a different approach which models objects with their behaviors and their collaborations. Proponents of Wirffs-Brock feel that it facilitates communication with nontechnicians, as it is easy for them to apply these concepts to the business problem.

The techniques that are used for abstracting objects into classes vary. How class definition takes place and how classes are named is subjective, based upon the development team's perception of the business problem at hand. These decisions will have the effect of either facilitating or hampering the potential reuse of the object. Berard's methodology is a comprehensive, cyclic-iterative approach and includes analysis, design, and testing approaches and implementation procedures, along with techniques for tightly controlled project management.

Object Programming

The most popular languages currently are C++ and SmallTalk, although there are several others which are used successfully: ENFIN, Objective C, Actor, and Eiffel are just a few. There are major differences in hybrid versus "pure" languages. C++ is a hybrid—it's an extension of the procedural C language. When compiled, C++ goes through a preprocessor which produces C code. Depending upon the brand of C++ employed, you will have more or fewer application development tools to help you to test and debug your source code. C++ is also much closer to the machine. That level of detail provides for very tight control over your code, but it can also introduce more bugs and make debugging more difficult.

With any hybrid language, programmers can continue to write procedural code. There is no way to ensure that the object features of the language are being completely employed. This sometimes happens when C programmers are retrained in C++. Like any of us, given a task with a time frame, we tend to solve problems in ways we know will work, rather than searching for and trying out new techniques. SmallTalk advocates point out that in their language, it is not possible (or at least extremely difficult) to write procedural code. The pure object orientation of SmallTalk ensures that systems get the full benefit of object technology. SmallTalk development environments also tend to be more robust—integrating libraries, browsers, debuggers, and editors (although the C++ vendors are catching up). SmallTalk may be either dynamically compiled or interpreted, which places some performance restrictions on applications.

Object Databases

Object databases are developed to provide persistent data for object applications. This ability to store information beyond the life of an object session is part of the impetus that is fueling the growth of object orientation in the commercial world. For application developers familiar with relational database technology (or its predecessors—hierarchical and network databases), there are certain features that they've come to expect.

Working within the framework of expected features, database and application design is greatly simplified. Relational databases contain functionality which ensures that the data is always (or nearly always) available. There are recovery facilities that ensure that data is recovered quickly and in a consistent state after a system failure. Transaction management makes it appear as though each user of the database is the only user. Data updates are conducted so that each user is always presented with a consistent view of the data in an environment where there may be numerous updates, against many resources, being performed concurrently.

Relational databases also take over many of the responsibilities for maintaining integrity in the database. Once resource relationships are defined to the database, the programmer does not need to code logic to maintain these pointers; the RDBMS maintains consistency. RDBMS query language is based upon SQL (Structured Query Language), so skills in developing applications for one RDBMS are fairly transportable to other RDBMS. Transaction management, concurrence, integrity, and standard query languages are features which support the tabularized-data paradigm of RDBMs. Currently, these are only partially and inconsistently addressed by object database systems.

Object database technology provides functions which are not available in the traditional database paradigms. Object databases support long transactions—the type of processing which may change the state of an entire database over a period of weeks or months. Features which support long transactions allow the transaction to be suspended, stored, and subsequently restarted. Some ODBM products also support work-group development and versioning. ODBM interfaces to OO languages are vendor-specific—closely linked with specific OO program language vendors. Some, like GEMSTONE, offer an entire application development platform.

Questions and Answers

The questions and answers that follow include definitions as well as OOA and OOP concepts and usage.

Q: *What is an object?*
A: An object is a computational entity that knows something and knows how to do something with what it knows. What it knows is contained in its encapsulated data. What it knows how to do is represented by its interface.

Q: *What is encapsulated data?*
A: Data that can only be accessed through an interface is said to be encapsulated. (Unencapsulated data can be accessed by direct reference—i.e., by its name.)

Q: *What is an interface?*
A: In the context of the answers to the previous questions, an interface is a collection of names of services that an object can perform along with a specification of the parameters that each of these services allows or requires. These names are bound, at some point, to methods that provide an implementation of the services.

Q: *What is a method?*
A: A method is the implementation of an object service. It contains the detailed computer instructions for providing the service in support of an item in the object's interface.

Q: *What is a class?*
A: A class is the definition of an object. It specifies the data elements and data formats that combine to reflect what an object "knows." A class also specifies the services that each object created from the class can be expected to perform. The collection of all these services is the object's interface, and represents what the object "knows how to do."

Q: *What is the relationship between a class and an object?*
A: A class specifies the data and methods that operate on the data for each object that results from this specification. The class definition also has some methods of its own that know how to create new objects.

Q: *What does it mean to send a message?*
A: Sending a message is the standard way to invoke an object. The message requests a specific service to be performed by the object and is often accompanied by additional information in the form of parameters. An object typically responds to a message by producing a result.

Q: *Summarize the major difference between C++ and SmallTalk.*
A: C++ is a language in which all relationships (bindings) are determined at the time of compilation. In particular, type checking is done at this time. SmallTalk, on the other hand, determines these relationships and checks for

type at execution time. Also, in SmallTalk, there are no intrinsic values that are not objects. SmallTalk also is accompanied by a development and run-time environment as well as a standard class library.

Q: *Discuss the difference between single and multiple inheritance. Why would you choose one over the other?*
A: Single inheritance implies that each class has at most one parent in the class hierarchy, while there can be multiple parents in the multiple inheritance class hierarchy. Some feel that the "real world" is more naturally modeled by the multiple inheritance model.

Q: *What is a method? What is the relationship between methods and messages?*
A: Methods represent the "intelligence" of an object. They know how to access data and produce the appropriate results in response to specific messages that are sent to the object. When a message is sent to an object, the run-time system is responsible for choosing which method responds to that message. The method could be one defined by the class as part of the object's interface, or it could be in the interface of one of the object's parents in the class hierarchy.

Q: *How can you tell if an object model is correct?*
A: There is no absolute way of testing for correctness other than determining whether the model accurately reflects its real-world counterpart.

Q: *What is a class library?*
A: The library containing the set of class definitions along with their inheritance relationships is called a class library.

Q: *What is a class hierarchy browser?*
A: A class hierarchy browser is part of the development environment for developing OO applications. Typically, it has the ability to examine existing class definitions for the purpose of subclassing, copying, or modifying these definitions. In most OO systems, the debugging of the OO application can be triggered from the class hierarchy browser.

Q: *What does CRC design mean?*
A: This is an OO design technique that involves assignment of classes, responsibilities, and collaborations in order to model a real-world enterprise.

Q: *Discuss the relationship between designer, analyst, and programmer on an OO team.*
A: The analyst works with the client of the application to develop a systematic understanding of a problem to be solved by automation. The designer works from this analysis to lay out the class's responsibilities and collaborations that can be implemented by the programmer to complete the solution.

Q: *Distinguish a class variable from an instance variable.*
A: Class variables are those used within the class definition itself (as opposed to instance variables which are distinct for each instance of the class).

Q: *What does the term* virtual class *mean?*

A: In C++ a virtual class is one that is not implemented directly, but is instead implemented by its subclasses. Virtual classes are needed to implement polymorphism in C++.

Q: *What is an OO database?*

A: An OO database stores objects whose lifetime spans the run-units which create and/or use them. These objects are typically shared across applications within an enterprise.

Q: *What is the term used for the situation when the result obtained from sending a message depends on the object to which the message was sent?*

A: Polymorphism.

Q: *Why are GUIs commonly programmed using object technology?*

A: GUIs are populated with graphical objects which must respond to user-generated events such as mouse clicks. Object technology is based on events and event-handling as the means by which objects collaborate. It is thus a natural for implementing GUIs.

Q: *List three components of object technology.*

A: There are certainly more than three components in object technology, but here are the ones probably thought of most commonly:

  1. An OO programming language
  2. A class library that extends the language
  3. A development environment that facilitates use of the language

Q: *What does the term* event-driven *mean?*

A: Applications whose components respond to external stimuli ("events") are called event-driven. Most simulations of real-world activity are done with this technique. Also, GUIs are almost entirely driven by events such as keys being pressed or the mouse being clicked.

Q: *List three techniques for reengineering an existing program so that it is object-oriented.*

A: 1. "Wrappering" is a technique that puts a thin shell around an existing program. This shell ("wrapper") receives incoming messages and routes them to the appropriate internal procedure within the application. This technique allows the application to participate with other parts that have engineered with object technology, but is not a permanent solution, since the real benefits of OO design can be realized only when the application has been completely redone using OO design methodology.

  2. Using a reengineering tool, the potential objects within an application are brought to the attention of the "reengineer," and assistance is provided in overcoming some of the routine, detailed work involved in defining the class definitions for the new objects.

3. A "magic tool" that takes an existing application and produces a corresponding OO application. To date, no such tools have been successfully demonstrated, and the viability of this approach has not been proven.

Q: *Why is object technology suitable for Client/Server applications?*
A: The object model is based on the ability to send and receive messages in an asynchronous and recursive manner. This is the same model needed to support Client/Server applications. Thus, object technology is a natural fit for Client/Server applications.

Q: *How does object technology lead to reusability?*
A: The class hierarchy provided by most OO development environments contains classes whose methods are designed for reuse. These classes typically encapsulate the complex parts of the application. The classes can be either directly reused or can be specialized for a particular use through subclassing.

Q: *What is the theoretical basis for the claim that object technology produces more easily maintained applications?*
A: The objects in the object model are intended to directly reflect the objects in the problem domain. Thus, if one understands the problem domain, the OO application, with proper design, explains itself and is easier to maintain.

Q: *Discuss briefly the history of Object Technology (OT).*
A: Object technology is rooted in the approach to solving real-world problems by simulating these problems on a computer. Originally, this work was done by mathematicians using mathematic modeling tools such as queueing theory. In 1967, the SIMULA programming language brought the world of simulation to the computer, making it much easier to create these models. Borrowing on this approach, Alan Kay at Xerox Parc invented the SmallTalk language that was centered completely around objects, and was thus called the first "pure" object-oriented language. Kay also invented the notion of class hierarchies, based on his background in classification theory in the field of biology. This work took on added importance with the introduction of iconic interfaces used first in the Xerox Star computer. These interfaces have since grown to be the rapidly developing and generally accepted graphic user interfaces used on the Apple MacIntosh and PC-compatible computers running DOS, OS/2, and UNIX operating systems. Those who are expert in object technology believe that much larger application areas (especially those targeted for distributed, Client/Server, or peer-to-peer environments) are best served by being reengineered to the object-oriented paradigm.

Q: *Distinguish between an interface and a class definition.*
A: An interface is the external protocol presented to clients of a class of objects. It is carefully designed so as not to change. The class definition contains not only this interface definition, but also the implementation that supports the

interface. This implementation is free to change as long as the interface remains constant. Since the interface is essential to type-checking at time of compilation, it is useful for language supporting strong type-checking to have interface definitions that can be separated from the class definition. In this way, separately compiled clients of a class can be checked to make sure objects are referenced in the proper manner.

Q: *Describe static and dynamic binding.*
A: Static binding takes place at the time of compilation; dynamic binding takes place at run time. It is difficult to support polymorphism with static binding.

Q: *What is a garbage collector?*
A: When an object is no longer referenced by another object, then it is necessary to reclaim the system resource (typically, storage that has been previously acquired) needed to support it. A garbage collector periodically scans the active object space for objects no longer being referenced and releases the system resources for any such objects.

Q: *What are the advantages and disadvantages of garbage collection?*
A: *Advantages:*   This automatic process relieves the application programmer from the duties of freeing objects that are no longer needed. This represents a substantial savings in the amount of detailed, low-level programming that the programmer must do.

Disadvantages: The garbage collection process is typically not under control of the application. This can lead to unpredictable delays in processing. In SmallTalk this manifests itself in the form of a vacuum cleaner icon appearing on the screen from time to time, indicating that garbage collection is taking place. This is sometimes quite annoying to the end user of the application.

Q: *Discuss the life cycle of an object.*
A: Objects, like their real-world counterparts, have a life cycle in which they are born, mature, grow old, and die. In the case of objects, an object is created, initialized, remains in a "last-used" state, is finalized, and then destroyed. Finalization is the point in the life cycle at which an object has the opportunity to clean up things, knowing that it is about to die. It's like writing its last will and testament. More seriously, it involves closing files, releasing locks, and abandoning any other resource to which it has laid claim during its existence. When the object is destroyed, any references to it are no longer valid. It is important that no such reference remain; otherwise, dangling references might occur, as they sometimes do in C++ when destruction is not done properly.

Q: *What does "genericity" mean?*
A: Genericity deals with the ability to define modules with generic (i.e., non-type-specific) parameters. These parameters can later be specified to generate a family of modules whose main distinguishing feature is their actual

parameter types. This is very similar to the template feature in C++. Thus, one has a generic module, 'Display(T)', where T can be replaced with a specific type, such as circle or square, with T being replaced everywhere in the generic module with the actual parameter type.

Q: *What does subclass mean?*

A: To create a subclass means to specialize an existing class for some specific purpose. What you are really saying when you create a subclass is that the parent class is not exactly what is needed. The subclass need only specify how it is to be treated differently from its parent.

Q: *Discuss the difference between a method and a subroutine.*

A: Methods and subroutines are very similar. They both "know a secret" about some specific and sometimes quite complex process. However, methods are designed to be inherited or overridden. If they are inherited, there is zero work on the part of the OO programmer required to exploit the method's functionality. That is, a message that binds to an inherited method requires no new definition by the implementor. If a method is overridden, it is usually the case that some additional functionality is introduced in the overriding method; then the remainder of the functionality is inherited. Subroutines, by contrast, have no such capability. If a subroutine is not quite right, then either the source code must be copied and modified (if it is available) or some means of intercepting calls to it and possibly modifying its results must be introduced. This leads to a Rube Goldberg solution that causes later maintenance problems.

Q: *Can you have global variables in an OO application?*

A: Yes, but the locality of reference can be carefully controlled. This is typically done with class variables. A class variable is accessible by all instances of the class by sending messages to the class definition (or by direct reference, depending on the policy of the OO language). An example would be a class variable containing an interest rate. This rate would be accessed by all instances of a bank account class containing the variable.

Q: *What is a derived class?*

A: A class derived from another, more abstract, class is called a derived class. For example, a CheckingAccount is derived from the more abstract class, BankAccount, which might be, in turn, derived from the even more abstract class, Account.

Q: *What is the difference between a class and a type?*

A: A type is the specification of an interface; a class is the complete implementation, together with the interface. A type may have many different implementations.

Q: *How can object technology be used to extend a programming language?*

A: The classes defined using object technology are really language extensions. They extend the range of types that the language can reference along with operations ("methods") that give intelligence to the types. For example, a bank account is likely to be imbued with intelligence to display itself and to accept a message to withdraw funds from itself. Every class that is defined enriches the language in some way.

Q: *Distinguish between abstract data type and intrinsic data type.*
A: Abstract data types permit reference to objects in the problem domain; intrinsic data types are all about mapping data items to computer storage. An example of an abstract data type is a propeller; an example of an intrinsic type is a packed decimal value.

Q: *What is a member function?*
A: This comes from C++; it means the same thing as "method." It comes from the usage: a function that is a member of a class definition.

Q: *How old is OT?*
A: Approximately 25 years old. It started in 1967 with SIMULA.

Q: *What is considered by most to be the first OO programming language?*
A: SIMULA.

Q: *What is a persistent object?*
A: An object whose lifetime exceeds the run-unit in which it was created is called persistent.

Q: *What is an embedded system?*
A: Embedded systems are those which are a part of a tool, like an oscilloscope or an intelligent robot. Object technology has been used quite successfully in this environment.

Q: *Can object technology be used in an embedded system?*
A: It has been ... most notably by Object Technology International with their proprietary version of SmallTalk that can run in a very space- and processor-constrained environment.

Q: *Describe a compound object.*
A: Most objects contain references to other objects and are, therefore, compound (also called *complex*). This is another way of reuse in an object system. It is done by taking advantage of a preexisting collection of cataloged objects which can be reused as components of a newly defined object. *Example:* a clock is composed of gears and springs and dials and hands. Each of these might be objects whose class has already been defined.

Q: *What does object collaboration mean?*
A: This is how objects work together to produce the automated solution to a business problem (or any of a large variety of problems that have solutions in the real world, but not in a computerized environment). Objects collaborate by sending one another messages. The receiving object may in turn send messages to other objects to fulfill its responsibility but, ultimately, it

must produce a result which it returns to the object which sent the original message.

Q: *How does object-oriented design lend itself to distributed application design?*

A: OO design is based on a model of computing in which events are triggered by messages. In this model, an object must always be prepared to respond to a message—even when it is already in the process of responding to the message. This is very similar to the model needed for distributed application design, where components of the application may be deployed across a hierarchy of processors and communicate with one another by sending messages. OO design, therefore, provides a good basis for application distribution. It is like drawing perforated boundaries in the application indicating where the application can be broken apart in order to be distributed.

Q: *What is the Object Management Group (OMG)? What are its main goals?*

A: The OMG is a consortium of hardware manufacturers and software vendors who are committed to promoting the OO model of computing. Its main goals are to provide a framework or infrastructure in which class definitions can be shared across languages and objects can collaborate, even when they are objects that were created in different language environments. The Common Object Request Broker Architecture (CORBA) is a product of OMG and lays the groundwork for this kind of leveraging and sharing. It addresses the issue of distribution across a network of processors.

Q: *Which programming languages best support rapid prototyping and incremental development?*

A: Languages that feature incremental compilation and dynamic binding are best suited for rapid prototyping and incremental development. This is because changes can be introduced without requiring massive recompilation and relink editing. These languages typically defer type-checking until execution, and dynamically load methods as they are required. SmallTalk, Objective-C, and OO COBOL are examples of this type of language.

Q: *What are intrinsic data types in SmallTalk?*

A: Intrinsic data types are those that focus on the mapping of data to computer storage and those that place restrictions on the type of operation that can be done on data elements. These are familiar to those who have programmed in third-generation languages such as COBOL and FORTRAN. Examples are FIXED, FLOAT, PACKED DECIMAL. There are no intrinsic data types in SmallTalk. There are only objects which are, in turn, instances of class definitions that reflect data types typically in the problem domain rather than data types that belong to the solution domain. That is, the data types have to do with the problem to be modeled rather than being concerned about laying out bits in computer memory. An example that is often given to illustrate this is as follows: In SmallTalk, to perform the addition 1 + 1, the "+" message is sent to the object 1 accompanied by another instance of 1 as a parameter. One pleasant side effect of this is that neat constructs like heterogenous collections of objects can hold anything in SmallTalk. There are no restrictions like saying that collections can hold abstract data types but not intrinsic data types.

Q: *Why would one choose to use an Object-Oriented Database (OODB)?*

A: Let's be clear about what an OODB is and does. An OODB is a place where persistent objects are managed. A persistent object is one whose lifetime spans units of execution. That is, an object may be created by an application and still be required on subsequent executions of that same (or perhaps another) application. The OODB is the place where the object lives between these executions. An OODB performs all the same services that other database management systems perform: sharing, locking, and committing across an enterprise, as well as services such as backup and restore. The main difference is that an OODB is active (the procedures are stored with the data), while other DBMSs are passive (only the data values are stored). Another distinguishing feature of OODBMS is that references to other objects are stored as well as simple data values. Back to the original question, an OODBMS becomes necessary when an enterprise commits to object technology and needs to share its objects across individual departments within the enterprise.

Q: *How can object-oriented database management systems and relational database management systems coexist?*

A: One way is for the OODBMS to have a way to access the RDBMS when necessary to produce simple object instances—instances that do not reference other object instances. This "side-door" approach allows a single model of data to be maintained. This is an advantage to the OO programmer, since it reduces the complexity of the applications he or she develops. Another way is to define classes whose encapsulated data are the rows of a relational table and whose methods are the stored procedures that access the table. The first approach is preferable, since the complexity of accessing relational tables is contained within the OODBMS and does not have to be addressed by the application developer.

Q: *What is ANSI? ISO? Why are they important for object technology?*

A: ANSI is the American National Standards Institute. ISO is the International Standards Organization. Without such organizations the computer industry and object technology would be chaotic, with no control over language development, class libraries, database interfaces, etc.

Q: *What does concurrent object environment mean?*

A: There are two interpretations of the phrase, "concurrent environment," depending on the point of view of the speaker. From the object modelist's point of view it means that an object can send multiple messages to receiving objects without waiting for a response from the first receiver. From an OO database point of view, it means that shared objects in the database can be concurrently accessed by multiple object spaces.

Q: *What does conformance mean in an OO context?*

A: In a typed OO environment, it means that one object can be used in place of another, as long as their types conform. This usually means that the surrogate object has all the services of the one it's being used in place of—plus, perhaps, some additional ones.

Q: *What is SOM? What is its role in IBM's OO strategy?*

A: SOM is System Object Model. It is an IBM implementation of the OMG Common Object Request Broker Architecture. It contains an Interface Definition Language which permits class hierarchies to be defined without being concerned about implementation details. Its role in IBM's OO strategy is to supply a single object model that all of its languages must support. SOM also contains a variety of object engine mechanisms. Object engines are the base-level support for OO. These engines do resolution of names and object identifiers during execution of an object space.

Q: *What does remote procedure call mean? How does it play a role in OT?*

A: A remote procedure call is like any other procedure call, except the called procedure may be located on another processor. In the context of object technology, it could be the underlying mechanism for transmitting messages, even when the receiver is not located in the local object space. This allows for an object space to become distributed across processors or a hierarchy of processors.

Q: *What has been the main use of OT to date?*

A: Graphic User Interface (GUI) development has been the most visible way that object technology has been used to date. In fact, to many, object orientation and GUI development are synonymous.

Q: *Has OT been used successfully in large-scale commercial applications?*

A: Only in a few instances, to date, has object technology been deployed on an enterprisewide basis. The reasons for this are many, but perhaps the most important is that a very high level of commitment within the enterprise must be made before object technology has a chance to succeed. Also of considerable importance is the fact that most enterprises have "legacy" applications whose continued use would be dependent on reengineering them for use in an object-oriented setting.

Q: *Distinguish between deep copy and shallow copy as these terms are used in OT.*

A: A shallow copy is one that produces an exact copy of a given object instance. If that object instance contains references to other objects, a shallow copy reproduces the object references, but not the object instances to which they refer. A deep copy, on the other hand, copies not only a given object instance, but also all the objects (not just the references, but the objects themselves) to which the instance refers, either directly or indirectly.

Q: *Distinguish between object, object instance, and instance.*

A: These terms are used interchangeably in object technology—they mean the same thing.

Q: *Distinguish between class method and instance method.*

A: A class method (sometimes called *factory method*) is one that is associated with the class, rather than with instances of the class. It usually has to do with producing new instances of the class. By contrast, an instance method is a part of the set of services that every instance of the class is expected to have. For example, every instance of the class OrderClerk might be expected to have a service called placeOrder, while the OrderClerk class might be expected to have a service called createNewClerk. In this example, place-Order would be an instance method, while createNewClerk would be a class method.

Q: *Discuss the importance of reentrancy in an object environment.*

A: Object environments are, typically, event-driven. This means that objects must be able to respond to external events—even when they are already processing such an event. In order to do this, they must have a reentrant base of support. Reentrancy allows a process to be suspended ("stacked") temporarily in order to process a more recent event. Recursion is also necessary for an object environment, as methods must be shared, and it is entirely possible for a method to send a message to itself either directly or indirectly.

Q: *List five elements of the OT infrastructure.*

A: Language, development environment, class library, training, and OO database management system.

Q: *Describe the mentoring approach to OO training.*

A: To have a mentor means to have someone to whom you can turn for advice and leadership. This technique is often used in OO training. A group of people is chosen who have both the technical and interpersonal skills to become mentors. They are then given special "mentor" training. After this training, they return to their environments to help others in the organization learn the OO approach to design, analysis, and programming.

Q: *Name five OO programming languages. Identify those that support dynamic binding and those that support static binding.*

A: SmallTalk, C++, Eiffel, Objective-C, OO COBOL. Each supports some form of dynamic binding. C++, Objective-C, and OO COBOL also support static binding.

Q: *What are pre- and postconditions in EIFFEL?*

A: These are conditions that must exist before (preconditions) and after (postconditions) the successful execution of a method.

Q: *Does C++ support error handling? How?*

A: C++ allows an object to be "thrown" when an exception needs to be raised. This object is "caught" by a method that has been declared to handle the particular exception. The object that is thrown and caught has encapsulated information regarding the exception.

Q: *What are the principal things that must be changed to introduce OO to an existing 3GL?*

A: The language, the execution environment, and the development environment.

Q: *What work is being done to add OO features to COBOL?*

A: The ANSI X3J4.1 committee is completing a technical report recommending a set of features to be added to the COBOL language to support OO programming. Micro Focus has developed an OO programming capability for its COBOL environment that includes extensions to the OO execution environment as well as a new OO development environment.

Q: *What does legacy code mean?*

A: Legacy code is code that was written some time previously that has typically been used for production work for some time, and which has typically had several programmers assigned to maintain and extend it over its lifetime. These programmers have inherited this code as their "legacy."

Q: *Why is OT important for emerging technologies such as multimedia and virtual reality?*

A: Because of its ability to contain complexity through encapsulation, object technology is ideal for environments like multimedia and virtual reality, as these systems tend to be quite complex.

22
QMF

Michael J. Talbot

Introduction

IBM's Query Management Facility provides an effective method of constructing and executing queries directly against the DB2 relational database. It also has report formatting and printing capabilities. In addition to functioning on the MVS/XA or MVS/ESA operating platform, QMF also operates in the VM-based SQL/DS database system. It is functionally equivalent to that version which runs under DB2, notwithstanding file conventions and other differences intrinsic to the VM environment. QMF provides a powerful tool for processing dynamic SQL requests against the DB2 database. QMF can also run as a conversational program under CICS. QMF supports the dynamic preparation of any kind of SQL statement, from a simple query with equal predicates to a complex request involving subqueries, column functions, and special sorting requirements. In addition, database definition (DDL) and database control (DCL) statements can be submitted via QMF. QMF supports two additional interfaces: the *command interface*, which operates from within an existing QMF session, and the *SAA callable interface*, which allows direct queries from within 3GL or REXX application programs.

Principal Functions and Features

- The QMF table editor which provides a powerful tool for updating and/or inserting data into existing DB2 tables.

- QMF bridge and modeling commands, such as ISPF, DRAW, EXTRACT, LAYOUT, IRM, and so forth.

- The DISPLAY CHART command which can be used to invoke the Interactive Chart Utility (ICU) feature of PGF under GDDM. The ICU can present data in various graphical forms, such as pie, bar, histogram, and other such formats.

- QMF objects such as procedures, forms, and queries that can be transferred between systems using the EXPORT and IMPORT functions.

Version 3 Release 1.1

The latest general availability release, Version 3 Release 1.1, was distributed during the second half of 1992 as a full-function Remote-Unit-of-Work (RUW) application capable of exploiting the distributed database features delivered by DRDA and DB2 V2.3. This additional functionality includes support for the enhanced CONNECT command, new global variables, remote connection from CICS, and display of current location name.

QMF as a DB2 application consists of eight tables in a single control database (DSQDBCTL). There may also be other DB2 tables found within a QMF environment, such as sample tables and user-defined tables created through use of the SAVE DATA command. Three of the eight QMF control tables are known as object tables, and these entities are used to store information about "saved" forms, queries, and procedures. In older releases of the QMF product, these stored elements were referred to as *items,* but more recent versions of QMF refer to three kinds of *objects:* the query object, the form object, and the data object. The form object in combination with the data object produces the report or chart.

Terminology

Bridge: A number of QMF bridging commands exist to facilitate the invocation of other important services, such as ISPF, DXT, IRM, and so forth.

Chart: A graphical report which utilizes GDDM/PGF services.

Command: One of many QMF single-word verbs which can invoke various native services and functions.

Export/Import: QMF services allow the movement of QMF objects between systems and even CPUs. These commands invoke MVS QSAM and BSAM functions to copy the various QMF object types.

Form: The form object consists of numerous customized panels which govern the appearance of a QMF report.

Procedure: A collection of QMF commands, including possibly REXX and TSO statements and calls to other services. A QMF procedure can be saved in the control database for later reference.

Profile: Every QMF user must establish initial values for a number of profile variables which, in turn, govern the characteristics of the session.

Prompted query: Refers to a query language for entry-level users of QMF. This facility extends the general prompt philosophy of QMF, whereby functions and commands can be easily established via prompting menus.

Query: A single SQL statement, usually a SELECT with predicate which can be saved in the QMF object database if desired.

Questions and Answers

This section will focus on QMF topics in four major categories: interactive functions, batch QMF, report-writing capabilities, and extended features. In addition, two general types of questions are included in the set: definitional and problem solving.

Q: *What does the LAYOUT command do?*

A: The LAYOUT command permits the testing of a customized form without having to retrieve data via a query. QMF will internally generate several rows of dummy data, and the resultant sample report allows the developer to evaluate specific editing and text-handling options. Care must be taken to ensure that the proper number of columns are maintained in the form, as indicated by the associated query statement. LAYOUT can operate either on the current form in temporary storage, or on any form saved in the QMF control database.

Q: *When you enter QMF interactively, what is the name of the screen that is initially displayed?*

A: The standard invocation of QMF establishes session parameters and then presents the user with an initial screen called the Home panel. This panel contains a large QMF LOGO, several references to IBM copyright and trademark information, and, in the case of V3.1.1, the currently connected location name.

Q: *In the TSO environment, how does QMF connect to the DB2 database?*

A: The QMF product utilizes a low-level attachment mechanism referred to as the Call Attach Facility (CAF). With CAF, thread creation and management are accomplished through the use of assembler macro statements such as CONNECT, OPEN, DISCONNECT, and so forth. This attachment process is completely under the control of QMF system software, and the QMF user is not responsible for its creation or performance.

Q: *I need to delete old queries and forms belonging to a former member of staff. How can I do that cleanup?*

A: QMF contains an internal security mechanism which characterizes saved objects as either shareable or private. In the case of forms, queries, or procs which have been saved with the SHARE=YES option, they can be displayed by issuing the DISPLAY xxx (OWNER=command. Unfortunately, the sharing of QMF objects does not include the ability to ERASE objects belonging to another. The preferred way to delete old objects from the QMF database falls into two categories:

1. Issue the SET CURRENT SQLID statement, specifying the owner in question. This requires secondary authid support, or SYSADM privilege. Then issue the QMF LIST command on various object types, followed by ERASE in the action column.

2. With SYSADM or at least DBADM on DSQDBCTL, issue SQL statements via QMF or SPUFI to delete rows from the three 'OBJECT' tables, as follows:

```
DELETE FROM Q.OBJECT_DIRECTORY WHERE OWNER = 'ownerid'
DELETE FROM Q.OBJECT_REMARKS   WHERE OWNER = 'ownerid'
DELETE FROM Q.OBJECT_DATA      WHERE OWNER = 'ownerid'
```

Q: *Which command produces an immediate termination of a QMF session?*

A: The EXIT command will cause an immediate termination of a QMF session, regardless of the panel or procedure from which it is entered.

Q: *Is there any referential integrity defined between the three 'OBJECT' tables in QMF?*

A: QMF does not make use of DB2 RI in its management of data content in the object control tables. Referential integrity is handled in the application, and this assumes that QMF-provided facilities such as SAVE, ERASE, DISPLAY, and so forth are employed to manage user-defined object definitions.

Q: *A batch process invokes a QMF procedure which produces a result table. Is there any way for this batch process to access the data directly?*

A: The result table produced and fetched into QMF storage cannot be directly accessed by other programs or processes. However, several additional QMF steps can be defined to make this data available. Once the data has been fetched by QMF, it can be exported to an MVS dataset using the EXPORT DATA function. It is also possible to save the data into an application table via the SAVE DATA command. At a later (more convenient) time, this table could be unloaded into a dataset using the EXPORT TABLE facility of QMF.

Q: *What is the DPRE command, and what does it do?*

A: The DPRE command is actually a synonym which invokes a QMF-provided application. This application dynamically allocates a temporary output file containing a QMF report as it would appear in an actual DSQPRINT output. DPRE places the user in browse mode of this dataset, and this facility provides an easy way to visually verify those report-formatting parameters which primarily affect the printed appearance of a report.

Q: *A QMF batch job has suddenly stopped working. What kinds of debugging facilities does QMF provide to assist in error analysis?*

A: One of the parameters which can be set either at initialization or via the SET PROFILE command is the TRACE option. Normally, tracing will be set to NONE once a process has been tested and implemented. Other possible values for TRACE include L1, which records all QMF messages, and L2, which writes all L1 messages and also captures information describing each executing command. These trace records are sent to a print file called DSQDEBUG. If this file has not been allocated, trace data cannot be made available. Note that an initialization parameter called DSQSDBUG can also determine the kind of default tracing which is in effect while a QMF session is being established. For batch mode, this is always L2. It is also possible to enable other kinds of tracing, such as "A" or "U" tracing which are implemented from within an application. In addition, the QMF MESSAGE facility can be used effectively to trace the flow of a complex procedure by interspersing application messages as part of an audit trail.

Q: *In the production environment, how can we prevent users from creating tables via the SAVE DATA command?*

A: Standard QMF installation enables the SAVE DATA function by establishing a "public" tablespace in which anyone can create tables. This privilege can just as easily be disabled in a production system. The ability to successfully SAVE DATA requires a few basic DB2 privileges, including the use of an existing tablespace or the ability to create an implicit one in a given database, and the capability to create tables in that database.

Q: *What is the QMF interrupt handler, and how can we invoke it from a CICS transaction?*

A: The query manager provides several different mechanisms for intercepting and/or canceling errant or long-running queries. One major component of QMF, the resource governor, specifically addresses this kind of capability. A much simpler facility is provided by the QMF interrupt handler. During an interactive session, an executing QMF query can be interrupted by hitting the PA1 or ATTN key, depending on the type of terminal connection on the network. When the interrupt handler gets control, a Prompt panel is presented which asks the user to cancel or continue with the current process. In both cases, the TSO STAX facility is invoked as part of this mechanism. Unfortunately, a similar facility is not available for QMF running under CICS. For QMF under CICS, the interrupt handler does not operate.

Q: *Where would you use the SHOW SQL function?*

A: When a user develops a request for data using prompted query dialogs, the fully completed query panel contains applications-specific object names without any generic SQL verbs and other predicate constructs. The SHOW SQL command will direct QMF to construct an equivalent SQL statement, which is then displayed in a pop-up SQL window.

Q: *When QMF creates a default form, character and numeric data normally adhere to different justify rules. Is there any way to modify these rules?*

A: The FORM.COLUMN panel supports a function called Specify Alignment which permits modifications to the display of column data as left- or right-justified or centered. This alignment can also be separately specified for the column headings.

Q: *What would be the simplest way to clear or erase an SQL query which currently resides in QMF storage?*

A: The QMF RESET command operates on the five different object types which can be found in separate temporary storage areas in QMF. These types are:

query, proc, form, profile, and data. The RESET QUERY command will delete the current query from storage and will also display an empty query panel to the user.

Q: *What do EXP, DIS, and PR have in common?*

A: QMF permits the abbreviation of commands to a few significant letters. The basic rule is that the abbreviated form must correspond uniquely with the full command. EXPORT, DISPLAY, and PRINT are such examples. Although command short forms are quite convenient during interactive sessions, it is not always recommended to incorporate large numbers of abbreviated commands in complex QMF processes. One of the concerns here is that a future command may conflict with locally developed short forms.

Q: *The DPRE command is useful when developing QMF batch reports. What differences between displayed and printed reports does this facility attempt to reconcile?*

A: As mentioned previously, DPRE is quite useful when it becomes necessary to verify the look of a report as it would appear on paper. The fundamental difference between displayed and printed reports relates to the number of pages presented. While a displayed report basically contains one large scrollable page, the printed report will typically contain multiple pages. As a result, the displayed report will contain a single page heading and footing, while DPRE will show heading/footing sections on each page.

Q: *Is QMF a command within QMF? If so, what does it do?*

A: In addition to providing an extensive library of functional commands, QMF also permits the creation and incorporation of customized commands through a facility referred to as *command synonyms*. When a command is issued in QMF, the command synonym table associated with the user session is searched first, followed by a scan of the standard QMF command library. Although it is not generally recommended, it is certainly possible to define a synonym which duplicates an existing (native) QMF command. In such situations, the QMF command called 'QMF', when placed in front of a desired native command (e.g., QMF LIST), ensures that only the native command library will be searched during command processing.

Q: *An end user wants to access a specialized set of QMF synonyms. What steps are required to make this happen?*

A: The ability to build and to access command synonyms is an important and powerful capability within QMF. This question assumes that the application-specific synonym table has been defined and loaded with the appropriate command names and action verbs. An end user can issue the DIS PROFILE command, but *cannot* see the column data which indicates an associated command synonym table. In order for an end user to gain access to the desired synonyms, his or her profile must be updated to reflect the synonym table name in a column called SYNONYMS. This can be accomplished in a couple of ways:

- Request the QMF administrator to update Q.PROFILES, adding the desired synonym table name where CREATOR = 'userid'.
- End users who have been granted update column access to a view of Q.PROFILES which presents only one row based on the CREATOR = USER predicate will make their own changes.

Of the two, the latter approach represents a more end-user-oriented solution.

Q: *How would you generate a list of tables belonging to your ID at a remote location?*

A: The LIST command provides a very useful way to display those QMF and/or DB2 objects which have been created and saved under your ID. Specifically, the LIST TABLES command can develop a list of DB2 table names which exists at the currently connected location with your primary authid as OWNER. There are actually two ways to develop such a list at a remote database server environment:

1. Issue the LIST TABLES LOCATION='location-name' from within a local query session. This will establish a DB2-DB2 distributed unit of work (DUW) session based on three-part names. The data will be fetched and presented back to the local QMF session.

2. Issue the CONNECT command (V3.1.1) pointing to the desired remote subsystem. Follow that with a simple LIST TABLES command. This will essentially establish a remote unit of work (RUW) query session, and the LIST command will be processed at the remote system as a local query request.

Q: *What does the slash (/) accomplish in a database list action field?*

A: The display panel which accompanies the output from a LIST command includes an action column, and from within that column a number of different QMF commands can be issued. Commands such as RUN, EXPORT, PRINT, ERASE, and DISPLAY are just some examples of the kinds of commands which can be entered. It is also possible to represent the fully qualified database object by a simple place holder or slash (/), thereby saving keystrokes in commands which involve multiple parameters. For those familiar with the all-powerful option 3.4 under ISPF, the use of / as a substitution parameter serves a similar function in QMF.

Q: *When generating a report, what form is associated with the PRINT REPORT command?*

A: QMF will always generate a default form when displaying data which has been fetched as a result of an SQL query. The user can modify the form content through use of the various FORM panels, and the modified report can be immediately displayed without having to reexecute the original query. The PRINT REPORT command will match the data object with the form object currently found in memory, and the resulting report will be printed. It is possible to override the current form found in storage by including an explicit reference to a form saved in the database.

Q: *When you enter a question mark (?) on the command line, what should you expect?*

A: QMF remembers previous commands entered from the command line, and the user can display these in reverse sequence by entering the RETRIEVE (or RET) command. The question mark (?) is an acceptable substitute for the RETRIEVE command.

Q: *What is the LRECL of a dataset containing exported SQL queries and procs?*

A: The EXPORT facility of QMF basically invokes MVS services to copy QMF objects to external datasets. The logical record length (LRECL) of exported queries and procs is 79 bytes. Other QMF object types have different DCB characteristics when exported.

Q: *In an application written to utilize the QMF command interface, which command should be included to ensure that selected prompts are presented to the on-line user?*

A: The command interface facility of QMF provides an application development environment which makes use of several specialized commands and facilities. The INTERACT (INT) command can be included with any standard QMF command (e.g., INT DIS) when issued from within an ISPF application which invokes the command interface (DSQCCI). This will ensure that confirmation prompts will be generated back to the user as if a direct interactive session were underway.

Q: *What does it mean to IMPORT a table?*

A: The IMPORT facility of QMF provides a mechanism for bringing database objects into the current QMF environment. IMPORT TABLE extends this capability by facilitating the creation of a new table or the modification of data in an existing DB2 table. Importing a table actually invokes several functions:

- DB2 data and table definition information is copied from an external dataset. Typically, this dataset was created via a QMF EXPORT TABLE command issued on some other QMF system.
- An implicit SAVE DATA command is issued which, in turn, generates an SQL CREATE TABLE statement for a new table, assuming that one does not already exist with that name.
- If the table already exists, an option to replace the current data content or to append to the end of file can be selected through use of the 'Action' parameter.

Q: *What is the SHOW command?*

A: The SHOW command can depict the contents of the various temporary storage areas within QMF. It can be used to navigate between object panels while in an interactive session. It can also present a list of global variables via the SHOW GLOBAL command. The SHOW command without any qualifiers will display a single prompt panel containing all possible SHOW objects.

Q: *What is the difference between SHOW and DISPLAY?*

A: While the SHOW command presents object panels (and their contents) and global variables, the DISPLAY command can actually display database objects which have been saved in the QMF control database. In addition, DISPLAY will present an object panel and the current contents of storage for that object if a database object is not explicitly named. In that instance, both SHOW and DISPLAY perform equivalent functions.

Q: *In a production report, a column has started showing a string of asterisks rather than a numeric value. What does this signify?*

A: Numeric data which is formatted through use of a QMF form will be characterized by a particular edit and usage code, column width, alignment, and offset value. As application data ages, it is normal for its distribution characteristics to change. A developer must always take into account the potential impact that aging business data might have on predefined report forms. Whenever numeric data in a report exceeds the column width as defined in the form, asterisks will be displayed in place of numbers.

Q: *What is a QMF FORM?*

A: A FORM is one of the fundamental objects in a QMF application. A QMF FORM consists of several different kinds of QMF panels which have been customized to produce a final report. The various form panel definitions are normally saved in the QMF database, and the interaction of these various panels with relational data which has been fetched into QMF storage is what generates the final result.

Q: *Describe the use of BREAK in a FORM object.*

A: In a report, it is quite typical to display dependent values associated with some quantity which is held constant over a range of detail. Any column can be established as a break column, which simply means that each time the value in that column changes, a new break is encountered. In order to make effective use of BREAK functions in QMF, it is assumed that query data will at least be ordered (sorted) by the break columns. The use of BREAK on any column is indicated by placing 'BREAK' in the usage field of the column in question.

Q: *How many levels of BREAK does QMF support?*

A: QMF supports a total of six break functions in a single report. This means that there are six separate break panels available under FORM management, and these panels are known as 'F.B*n*', where *n* varies from 1 to 6.

Q: *What does the CHECK command do?*

A: QMF provides a facility called CHECK which is designed to verify the syntactical and logical correctness of form definitions on any of the many form panels associated with an application. CHECK will search for errors, starting with the form panel which was last displayed, and will post an ERROR message on all panels which are not valid. By correcting the error on the panel which is currently shown, followed by another CHECK command, the next error panel will be displayed for similar action.

Q: *What is a QMF profile?*

A: Every QMF session, whether it be interactive or batch, direct or via the command or callable interface, must invoke an initialization process which attempts to establish the default values for a set of variables which, in turn, impact numerous functions within QMF. The values of the various profile variables are derived from a system table called Q.PROFILES. This table contains 15 data elements associated with each individual user, along with systemwide default values provided by a user called SYSTEM. In addition, the QMF SET PROFILE command can be issued once a session has been established, and many (but not all) of the active profile variable values can be modified.

Q: *What is the difference between open and closed enrollment in QMF?*

A: As mentioned earlier, every QMF session must establish initial profile variable values before processing can begin. The order of search for a row in the profile table is as follows: SELECT * WHERE CREATOR = USER; if none, then SELECT * WHERE CREATOR = 'SYSTEM'. In the case of OPEN enrollment, a user called SYSTEM is defined in the Q.PROFILES table, and every new user will derive default session values from that row, provided an entry has not already been created on his or her behalf. Closed enrollment means that the SYSTEM user is *not* present, and for a user who has not been predefined in Q.PROFILE, session initialization will fail.

Q: *How many panels make up the FORM object type?*

A: The FORM object actually consists of a total of 14 different types of panels. These panels include MAIN, COLUMN, PAGE, BREAK (6), CONDITION, FINAL, DETAIL, OPTION, and CALC. When we manipulate a form, we are affecting elements in this set of panels which is collectively known as a FORM. Certain QMF commands, such as IMPORT and EXPORT, operate only on the entire set of panels in a FORM.

Q: *In addition to IMPORT, is there any other way to bring a query into a QMF session?*

A: Assuming that QMF has been started as an ISPF dialog application, the QMF EDIT QUERY command will invoke either the PDF full-screen editor, or a similar tool of your choosing. Once in an edit session, it is a simple matter to copy SQL query code into working storage using the extended copy facilities of the PDF editor. After ending out of the edit session, the QMF query panel will again be displayed with the results of the edit process in storage. This query can then be saved through use of the QMF SAVE facility.

Q: *What is involved in saving customized objects in QMF?*

A: The ability to create and then save customized objects such as queries, procs, and forms in QMF is an inherent capability of the product. No special security is required to be able to issue the SAVE QUERY, SAVE PROC, or SAVE FORM commands. QMF as a DB2 application automatically inserts and/or updates rows in the QMF control database on behalf of a user when these commands are issued. When the save command is issued for an object name which already exists in the database, QMF may prompt for a confirmation to replace the old object, depending on whether the CONFIRM profile value is set to YES or NO.

Q: *What are usage codes in QMF?*

A: An important feature of FORM customization involves the ability to associate special usage codes with specific columns. There are a total of 25 different types of usage codes, including the following general categories:

- Twelve BREAK codes, B1-B6 and BX1-BX6; the BX*n* codes exclude the break column from the display.

- Thirteen aggregation codes, all of which are valid for numeric data, while only five of these are valid for DATE/TIME datatypes. Examples here include MAX, COUNT, SUM, PCT, and so forth.

- Other special usage codes, such as GROUP, ACROSS, OMIT, and CALCid. Only one ACROSS is honored in a report. GROUP assumes that data has been ordered on the associated column. OMIT will delete the column and its data from all reporting aspects.

Q: *What happens when the number of columns in a form is less than the number of columns of data presented via a query?*

A: The number of columns in a form (excluding derived columns) must equal the number of columns requested in a query. Any difference will result in an incompatibility which appears only when the data and form are brought together. In addition, edit and usage codes in the form must match the data types involved in the query. The CHECK facility of QMF does not detect these types of errors. In these situations, QMF will display the form panel which contains the incompatibility, and a message is generated which briefly describes the error.

Q: *A canned procedure has completely stopped working due to some kind of mismatch between data and form columns. How could such a thing happen?*

A: Good coding practice suggests that column names should always be explicitly referenced in a SELECT statement, whether the statement is contained in a 3GL program or dynamically submitted from within a QMF procedure. In the event that an application table structure is altered to include additional columns, the SELECT * FROM . . . statement will immediately produce a failed procedure in QMF.

Q: *What is the ICU and how is it used in QMF?*

A: The Interactive Chart Utility (ICU) is a component of PGF, the Presentation Graphics Facility feature of GDDM. The Graphical Data Display Manager (GDDM) is a major host software product which is required by QMF in the generation of certain kinds of panels. The ICU/PGF is an optional feature which supports the creation of graphical reports based on summarized numeric data. The DISPLAY CHART command automatically invokes the ICU for further manipulation of graphical form content. A number of standard chart types are supported, including bar, pie, histogram, and so forth.

Q: *Describe the basic mechanisms associated with printing a QMF report.*
A: The PRINT REPORT command in QMF functions in one of two distinct ways. The user profile includes a variable which contains the name of a destination printer. If that value is all blanks, the report is sent to a file called DSQPRINT. Typically, this output is directed to a system printer, such as a 3800 laser system. If the printer variable is set to a real (nonblank) name, QMF assumes that a GDDM nickname is being provided, and ADMPRINT services are called to produce the report.

Q: *Can you request a report to be printed when QMF is running under CICS?*
A: The PRINT REPORT command is supported within the CICS environment, but there are some differences in the way this facility behaves in contrast to the TSO version of the command. Within CICS, a QMF report must be directed to either a transient data queue or to temporary storage (main or auxiliary). Both the queue type and queue name can be specified as part of the print command. By default, a report will be directed to an auxiliary storage queue name which consists of the string 'DSQP' concatenated with the terminal name. The actual report must be printed utilizing CICS services.

Q: *What does the ISPF command do in QMF?*
A: The ISPF command is actually a command synonym which produces a bridge to ISPF from within a QMF session. Once in ISPF, all the standard dialog services are available to the developer. Exiting the ISPF session returns the user to the QMF panel from which the original command was entered. For this facility to work, QMF must be started as an ISPF application under TSO. This also means that ISPF is not available under CICS.

Q: *Is it possible to customize any of the QMF panels?*
A: The bottom two lines of most QMF panels can be customized through the use of a function-key table. Both the text and the underlying definitions can be tailored for each primary and secondary panel, and all specifications must appear in a single PFKey table. The association between a user session and a particular function-key table is accomplished via an entry in the QMF profile table. This linkage must be established prior to starting the QMF session.

Q: *Describe the general structure of a function-key table.*
A: A customized function-key table contains four columns: panel, entry_type, number, and PF_setting. The panel value corresponds either to a primary panel such as QUERY or REPORT, or to a secondary or pop-up panel. The

entry type and number correspond to a label (L type) or a key identification (K type). The PF_setting contains either the explanatory text or the actual QMF command to be run. If a K row is left blank, the corresponding function key is deactivated. If an L row is left blank, the first or second line at the panel bottom is blanked out.

Q: *In a DB2 system which has the USA type as the default DATE format, what EDIT code would provide the most compatible presentation of DATE data?*

A: QMF supplies a number of standard EDIT codes which must be included on a FORM definition, and these codes generally correspond to the common data types found in DB2. For character data, for example, there are several Cxx edit codes available. Similarly, date and time data types can and should be formatted through the use of special date/time edit codes. All date and time codes start with T, followed by D for date and T for time data. The particular code TDM/ means date data, month first, separated by a /. This code corresponds closely with the DB2 USA format for date data.

Q: *For aesthetic reasons, a developer would like to eliminate the "timeron" value presented during query processing. Is there any way to modify the Database Status panel or its contents?*

A: We spoke earlier about customizing QMF panels through the use of function-key tables. There are a few panels which cannot be modified in this way, and these include the Table Editor and Database Status panels. It is possible, however, to modify the contents of the Database Status panel by disabling the expected cost message which QMF automatically generates for each query. This can be accomplished quite easily by changing the value of a global variable called DSQDC_COST_EST from 1 to 0. This could be done as part of a start-up procedure which might include the following command as one of its statements:

```
'SET GLOBAL (DSQDC_COST_EST = 0'.
```

Q: *What kind of information is determined in the FORM.PAGE panel?*

A: The FORM.PAGE (or F.PA) panel is used to develop heading and footing text. These text blocks will appear on each report page according to the alignment and other spacing rules associated with each block. It is possible to have only header or footer, as well as both text fields, on a single report page. A number of substitution variables can be utilized to customize the exact statements being generated.

Q: *A customized form includes two break columns, one of which is CHAR(24) and the second of which is LONG VARCHAR. Why does the form appear in error, and why do neither break columns appear to the left as depicted in some examples?*

A: Two separate issues are actually touched upon here. It is not legitimate to break on a LONG VARCHAR column, and that will always generate an error message in QMF. When a valid break column is displayed in a report, an option to automatically reorder the columns must be set in order for break columns to appear on the left. In FORM.OPTION, the appropriate option (J in V3.1.1) must be set to YES.

Q: *What is the EXTRACT command?*

A: The EXTRACT facility actually invokes an ISPF-based bridging command which starts an end-user Data Extract (DXT) session. This interface permits an on-line QMF user to select and move application data from predefined source files into DB2 tables through the use of standard DXT mechanisms. The value of this bridging interface is principally demonstrated in an information center environment.

Q: *What is the function of the QMF spill file?*

A: An SQL query will typically produce an answer set of rows which satisfies the predicate logic coded in the statement. QMF will issue FETCH statements on behalf of the on-line user to bring a certain number of data rows into a temporary storage area reserved for data. When the amount of data retrieved exceeds the amount of storage space available, QMF will externalize the data to a spill file known as DSQSPILL. In the CICS environment, spill file data is directed to auxiliary temporary storage. In both cases, the current DATA object resides in, and is accessed via, this combination of virtual memory and external hardware storage mechanisms.

Q: *In a QMF system which employs closed enrollment, a particular user cannot establish a session even though a row exists in the profile table where CREATOR = USER. What might be wrong?*

A: In a closed-enrollment QMF implementation, a profile table row must exist for each user and the desired run-time environment. A profile row for CREATOR = SMITH and a value of 'CICS' in the ENVIRONMENT column would preclude that person from starting a session under TSO. In addition, the TRANSLATION column in a base QMF installation must always contain the value of 'ENGLISH'. If some other value is reflected in that column, QMF ignores the entire row regardless of what else is stored in the various columns.

Q: *Which default editor is called in the EDIT TABLE command?*

A: The QMF table editor provides a sophisticated and essentially stand-alone facility for editing DB2 table data. This tool is started by issuing the EDIT TABLE command from within a QMF session, and the processing algorithms associated with this facility are unique to QMF. There are no external editing components involved in the edit table facility, and a significant number of panels and execution modules are shipped with QMF to enable this function.

Q: *Where are customized chart forms saved within a QMF session?*

A: The QMF product supports the creation and customization of graphical reports through the use of interfaces to several host GDDM components. It is possible to create a custom form which is intended for use with graphical or chart reports. These chart forms are not saved in the normal QMF object tables. Instead, they are written to an external dataset which is allocated to a special file known as DSQUCFRM.

Q: *What is the difference between SAVE IMMEDIATE and SAVE END when using the QMF table editor?*

A: The QMF table editor can be started in one of two modes: ADD or CHANGE. ADD mode is used for the insertion of new data rows, while CHANGE mode supports all other types of access to a DB2 table. In either mode, the SAVE attribute is set at editor initialization time to a value of "end" or "immediate." With SAVE IMMEDIATE, additions, changes, and deletions to the database are processed at the end of each transaction. Note that save immediate in CHANGE mode requires database support for a cursor with hold, such as is provided in DB2 V2.3. The SAVE END attribute defers any actual changes to the database until the END command is issued in the editor session. SAVE END also permits the cancellation of interim changes via the CANCEL (PF12) key.

Q: *Does the QMF governor offer any control for queries running under CICS?*

A: The QMF governor can measure and limit several different categories of resources, depending upon the environment in which the user is working. There are actually two separate IBM-provided QMF governors—one for the TSO environment and one for the CICS implementation. Governor controls based upon CPU time are available only in the TSO environment, while both TSO and CICS governor prompting can be triggered by the number of rows fetched. The ROWLIMIT definition will force a cancellation of a QMF transaction running in a CICS region.

Q: *Can a query which has been EXPORTED under TSO be IMPORTED into a QMF/CICS environment?*

A: The EXPORT/IMPORT facilities of QMF function in a basically equivalent way, whether in TSO or CICS. Assuming that the releases of QMF are compatible, a query can be exported under TSO in one QMF/DB2 system and IMPORTED directly into QMF running under CICS in another DB2 subsystem. It should be noted that TSO and CICS users who access the same QMF/DB2 system do not need to perform these EXPORT/IMPORT operations; all saved QMF objects are immediately available, subject only to the restrictions imposed by the SHARE parameter.

Q: *An on-line TSO user has received an incomplete data prompt. What does the condition signify, and what can be done about it?*

A: The current DATA object in QMF is completed by retrieving rows of data based on SQL query predicates and limited by the DSQSIROW initialization parameter. The DATA object resides in temporary storage and possibly in external storage on DASD. When the DATA object exceeds the available virtual and auxiliary storage space, an incomplete data prompt may occur when certain QMF commands are issued. When this occurs, the prompt condition requires one of two possible responses: (1) cancel the command or (2) clear the data object via the RESET DATA command.

Q: *What is a national language feature of QMF?*

A: The base installation of QMF establishes what is referred to as an *English-language session environment.* A national language feature implements a multilingual QMF environment by installing additional panel, message, and code support for a second language (e.g., German, French). Each non-English-language element is installed as a separate NLF feature. The profile entry for every user must specify which primary language is invoked on session initialization.

Q: *Does QMF maintain any kind of log for errors which are encountered by users?*

A: Most types of user errors, including GDDM errors and other panel or QMF object-handling error conditions, produce messages which are presented via a HELP screen in an interactive session. In addition, QMF records many of these errors in a DB2 table which is part of the QMF application. The Q.ERROR_LOG table includes creator and time-stamp information, as well as complete message text associated with each event. From time to time, the administrator must delete old entries, since QMF never deletes rows from its ERROR_LOG table. Note that errors associated with session initialization will not appear in this table.

Q: *Is it possible to access data in a remote DB2 system from a local QMF/CICS session?*

A: The distributed database support provided by DB2 V2.3 includes both remote-unit-of-work (RUW) and distributed-unit-of-work (DUW) functionality. In either implementation, two-phase commit across remote connections is not permitted. Subject to that restriction, it is possible to access remote data on a read-only basis from within a local CICS/QMF session.

Q: *What happens when a user spill file is too small?*

A: The DATA object in QMF is completed when all rows are fetched from the database. As mentioned earlier, these rows are kept in storage and are written to an external spill file when memory requirements are exceeded. It is possible to fetch more data than the spill file can accommodate, and when that occurs, an insufficient storage condition occurs. QMF will continue to work, but response may be degraded in this situation. For example, if a scroll backward needs to redisplay a row that has been since been replaced, QMF will reopen the cursor and again retrieve the data.

Q: *What changes, if any, should be made to the Dynamic Storage Area (DSA) in CICS when running QMF in a CICS/ESA (V3.x) environment?*

A: The storage requirements associated with running QMF in either a TSO or CICS environment will depend on a number of factors. The typical DATA and REPORT object sizes are determined by the amount of data requested in an SQL statement. In addition, space is required when QMF procedures invoke various MVS services. For the CICS/QMF environment, the Extended Dynamic Storage Area (EDSA) of CICS must normally be increased to approximately 40–50 megabytes, depending upon the number of concurrent users. For the TSO/QMF user, a virtual storage definition of at least 4 megabytes is usually recommended.

Q: *What is the QMF governor?*

A: The QMF governor is a resource monitoring and limiting facility which is provided as an integral component of the base product. Two IBM-provided governor programs are supplied with QMF, and the generic interfaces are documented and enabled to facilitate the implementation of user-written governor routines. A variety of exit points in the life of a QMF transaction can be accessed from a governor program, including start and end events associated with sessions, commands, database activity, think time, and so forth. A QMF resource control table establishes each individual resource group and its primary control parameters, while the profile of each user identifies the particular group associated with each QMF session.

Q: *A new user has a profile row which contains a blank in the RESOURCE_ GROUP column. Is this user exempt from QMF governor control?*

A: Assuming that the governor has been enabled, a user with blanks in the RESOURCE_GROUP column of his or her profile record will *not* be exempt from resource governing. The default governor group, as determined by the SYSTEM row in the Q.PROFILES table, will be applied to this user.

Q: *How would the administrator disable the QMF governor?*

A: The QMF governor is activated by storing a numeric value of '0' in the third column of the RESOURCE_GROUP table, when the second column (RESOURCE_OPTION) contains the character string of SCOPE. Changing the value to any other number, including NULL, will effectively disable the governor.

Q: *An interactive QMF/TSO session is started with an initial procedure which calls a local CLIST. After ending out of the CLIST, the user is placed right back into the initial CLIST prompt and cannot seem to break out of this sequence. What is happening?*

A: The establishment of a QMF session may include the invocation of an initial procedure via the DSQSRUN parameter. Care must be taken to ensure that the initial procedure does not terminate by returning the interactive session to the Home panel. When this occurs, the initial procedure will be rerun if the global variable called DSQEC_RERUN_IPROC is set to its default value of 1. A common error in the coding of initial procedures is to include END as the last QMF command. This will typically place the user session in the Home panel, from which the IPROC will automatically reexecute in what appears as an endless loop.

Q: *What does the character string _B accomplish when appended to a variable in a form panel?*

A: Many QMF form panels support the inclusion of standard form variables and global variables which enable the substitution of text string or numeric values in the customized form. QMF will normally strip trailing blanks from text data, and leading blanks will be removed from numeric values. The inclusion of the _B appendage will allow trailing and leading blanks to remain in variable substitutions, typically for alignment purposes within sections of a report.

Q: *What must appear in the first line of a QMF procedure with logic?*

A: Two types of procedures are supported in QMF V3.1: linear procedures and procedures with logic. Procedures with logic are, in effect, REXX language routines and, as such, must adhere to REXX coding rules. The first line of a REXX procedure must be a comment card with the ******REXX******* identifier included. This requirement applies as well to QMF procedures with logic.

Q: *Can QMF be accessed directly from within a 3GL program?*

A: The most common methods for accessing the QMF application include the TSO/CAF and the CICS attachment mechanisms to DB2. It is also possible to invoke QMF services through use of the SAA callable interface. This facility enables the SAA Common Programming Interface for Query, which allows application programs to perform QMF functions through direct calls to QMF. The callable interface does not require TSO or ISPF services, and it does not require an active QMF session to be established. A number of QMF-provided 3GL interface routines are available, depending on the application language being utilized. In general, the SAA callable interface is implemented through a standard language call which includes a variable-length parameter list.

Q: *What command could be used to start QMF from within a C-language program?*

A: An application program written in C can access QMF services through use of the SAA callable interface. The interface routine for the C language is DSQCICE for extended commands such as START and SET GLOBAL, and DSQCIC for standard QMF commands and SQL statements. In general, an application utilizing this facility must issue a START command to initialize the interface, and the EXIT command should be issued to properly terminate QMF access.

Q: *What is the STATE command?*

A: The QMF command interface provides another technique for accessing QMF services via an application process. There are several specialized commands associated with the use of the command interface. One of these, the STATE command, is used to refresh the values assigned to a number of variables which QMF maintains during execution. These variables are reflected in the QMF global variable pool, and can be retrieved by ISPF services.

Q: *Is it possible to run multiple releases of QMF within a single DB2 subsystem?*

A: The QMF product releases have grown in sophistication since the early V2.x days, and a number of compatibility issues must be considered before multiple versions of QMF can coexist in the same DB2. Nonetheless, it is possible to maintain multiple releases in the same DB2 system, provided certain precautions are taken. The migration from version 2 to version 3 of QMF introduced alterations to the QMF control tables and, as a result, certain default functions such as profile setup are not downward-compatible. EXPORT/IMPORT services involving FORM objects are typically not compatible across releases, although most of the other object types in QMF have not changed recently.

Q: *What program enables the QMF command interface?*

A: The application support facility known as the command interface is provided by a single QMF-provided program. This routine, DSQCCI, requires an active QMF session in an ISPF environment in order to function. In addition, the QMF command interface is usable in a CLIST or REXX environment only; the interface cannot be called from a 3GL program.

23

COBOL/COBOL II

Richard Miller

Introduction

COBOL is the most widely used application programming language in the world today, and its use is growing. A lot of this has to do with COBOL's power in handling the data processing needs of business. (The name COBOL stands for Common Business-Oriented Language.)

The questions in this chapter pertain to VS COBOL as well as VS COBOL II. However, before we get to the questions, some of the advantages of VS COBOL II will be discussed. VS COBOL II is the most current version of COBOL today, and has many advantages over VS COBOL. The advantages are as follows:

1. VS COBOL II makes the operation of computer programs more efficient.
   a. It allows code to be shared.
   b. It optimizes code.
   c. It allows faster sorting.
   d. It eases program debugging and maintenance:
      (1) Supports a debugging tool—COBTEST.
      (2) Program listings provide information in a user-oriented way.
      (3) Formatted dumps display status of programs and files in COBOL format including data names and content.
   e. VS COBOL II will run in the same environment as VS COBOL without impact on current operations.
   f. COBOL/CICS interaction is easier to work with because of defined interfaces.
2. VS COBOL II has a number of special features.
   a. A variety of programming features assist programmers. Among the more important of these features that can help programmers develop, test, and debug code are:

(1) Support for 31-bit addressing, which can make it easier for programmers to develop large applications.

(2) An improved interface to CICS, which can simplify the way programmers build COBOL to be used with CICS.

(3) *Nested copying*—VS COBOL II allows the nesting of COPY statements. Not only can independent blocks of code be copied into the main segment of a program during compilations, but the copied code can copy other code. This means that, in addition to PERFORM and CALL statements, COPY statements can be used to build a program in a structured way. Using nested COPY statements in this way avoids the execution overhead of CALL statement processing and allows programmers to maintain their segments of a program independently.

(4) *VSAM buffers*—VS COBOL II causes VSAM to put buffers above the 16-million-byte line.

(5) Programmers no longer have to define and manipulate a list of pointers if their COBOL programs need to access data in locate mode.

b. *Application efficiency*—VS COBOL II extends the program efficiency features that are available in VS COBOL. A programmer can request a VS COBOL II program be compiled to be reentrant. A reentrant program can be placed in a shared virtual area of storage, so that one copy of the program is used to satisfy all concurrent requests for the program.

c. *Debugging and maintenance*—VS COBOL II offers a debugging tool called COBTEST. It is a tool for examining, monitoring, and controlling VS COBOL II programs in a test environment. Programs can be debugged using a full-screen interactive mode, line interactive, or batch mode. Data may be altered, logic may be changed, and results can be viewed on-line. VS COBOL II also has an enlarged 6-byte VSAM return code which contains register 15 return code, condition code, and feedback field code.

Questions and Answers

The COBOL questions and answers that follow are intended to enhance a programmer's ability to answer questions relating to significant areas of programming in COBOL and to stimulate a more in-depth analysis of the areas involved in order to build on their existing programming techniques.

Q: *COBOL is an acronym. What does it stand for?*
A: Common Business-Oriented Language.

Q: *What are the structured development aids introduced in COBOL II?*
A: COBOL II offers the following options.
   EVALUATE: permits CASE construction.
   The in-line PERFORM: permits 'do' constructions.
   TEST BEFORE and TEST AFTER in the PERFORM statements: permit 'do while' and 'do until' constructions.

Q: *What feature in COBOL II is similar to feature(s) in other programming languages?*

A: The most obvious are the explicit scope terminators for most processing actions. An alphabetical list indicates the variety:

end-add	end-if	end-search
end-call	end-multiply	end-start
end-compute	end-perform	end-string
end-delete	end-read	end-subtract
end-divide	end-return	end-unstring
end-evaluate	end-rewrite	end-write

The scope terminator ',' (as well as the period '.') is still available.

Q: *What are the three categories of data defined in the DATA division?*

A: 1. The file section (FD) information
2. Working storage information
3. Linkage-section data definitions

Q: *When is using READ INTO not advisable?*

A: READ INTO performs two actions: the file is read into the buffer and the record is moved to working storage. The construct assumes that the LRECL of every record is the same. When used with variable-length records, the results may be "unexpected."

Q: *What are the techniques for achieving "top-down" programming?*

A: Top-down is an effort to avoid spaghetti code and is sometimes referred to as "go to less" programming. Processing is performed from the beginning to the end of paragraphs. Performs rather than "go tos" are used to move through code. The PERFORM . . . THRU structure should be used only when the THRU is to an EXIT paragraph.

Q: *What is the EVALUATE statement?*

A: EVALUATE is the alternative to the nested IF statements and is used to select from a list of processing actions. WHEN is used instead of IF to determine if the action is to be taken. Like the IF statement, the WHEN statement should be coded from the most likely to the least likely occurrence. Like the nested IF, once the condition is true, control passes from the evaluate statement to the next statement in the program.

Q: *What are two of the more common forms of the EVALUATE statement?*

A: The two most common forms of the EVALUATE statement are:
1. EVALUATE TRUE, which allows multiple variables to be checked for a true condition. The list of options being tested must be prioritized, as the EVALUATE statement selects only the first TRUE condition per statement.
2. EVALUATE VARIABLE-NAME checks multiple options for the TRUE condition of a variable.

Q: *What does the INITIALIZE statement do?*
A: The INITIALIZE statement initializes data areas to zeros and spaces.

Q: *How can you use INITIALIZE for specifying specific values?*
A: INITIALIZE GROUP-ITEM REPLACING ALPHANUMERIC DATA BY HIGH-VALUES. When the REPLACING option is used, only the specified type will be initialized.

Q: *What is reference modification?*
A: Reference modification is the name for substring manipulations. The ':' allows part of a data item to be used without defining the data item in the data division.

Q: *Give two examples of how you would use reference modification.*
A: 1. In a list of ZIP codes, the first three digits define a geographic area:
```
IF ZIP ( 1 : 3 ) = '100'
     AREA = MANHATTAN
END-IF
```
   2. MOVE 'MEXICO' TO STATE (5 : 6) could change NEW JERSEY to NEW MEXICO.

Q: *What is a nested program?*
A: A nested program is a program that allows the coding of multiple procedure division within a single program. It is like a CALL, but it is more efficient.

Q: *What is the difference between a directly contained and an indirectly contained program in a nested program?*
A: A directly contained program is in the next-lower nesting, while the indirectly contained program is more than one nesting below.

Q: *Can there be a problem using ROUNDED in a compute statement?*
A: Yes. The compute rounds *each* intermediate result in a compute statement and not just the final result.

Q: *Name some of the advantages of COBOL II.*
A: VS COBOL II makes the operation of computer programs more efficient:
   - It allows code to be shared.
   - It optimizes code.
   - It allows faster sorting.
   - It eases program bugging and maintenance:
     Supports a debugging tool: COBTEST.
     Program listings provide information in a user-oriented way.
   - Formatted dumps display status of programs and files in COBOL format, including data names and content.
   - VS COBOL/CICS interaction is easier to work with because of defined interfaces.

Q: *What are VS COBOL II special features?*

A: The support of 31-bit addressing permits programs to operate "above the line" and to use larger tables in larger programs. This added space allows VSAM buffers to be placed above the 16-meg line, therefore the buffers can be larger.

Q: *What options have been removed in COBOL II?*

A: COBOL II does not support ISAM and BDAM access methods and clauses which are specific to them. In addition, the following have been eliminated:

REPORT WRITER

EXAMINE

TRANSFORM

READY TRACE and RESET TRACE

REMARKS paragraph and NOTES statement

The ON statement (ON 1 PERFORM . . .)

Q: *What is a nested-copy statement?*

A: Independent blocks of code can be copied into the main sections of a program during compilation. COBOL II allows the copied code to copy other code.

Q: *What is an example of application efficiency provided by COBOL II?*

A: COBOL II will allow a program to be compiled as REENTRANT. A reentrant program can be placed in a shared virtual storage area, so that one copy of the program is used to satisfy all concurrent requests for the program.

Q: *What is COBTEST?*

A: COBTEST is a debugging tool for examining, monitoring, and controlling VS COBOL II programs in a test environment. Programs can be debugged using a full-screen interactive mode, as well as a line interactive or batch mode. DATA may be altered, logic may be changed, and results can be viewed on-line.

Q: *How has the return code for VSAM files been changed in COBOL II?*

A: The return code has been enlarged to 6 bytes and returns the VSAM return code when the FILE STATUS is not 00. The format of the expanded return code is:

REGISTER 15 Return Code	PIC 9(2) COMP.
FUNCTION CODE	PIC 9(1) COMP.
FEEDBACK CODE	PIC 9(3) COMP.

Q: *What type of documentation would you recommend for a COBOL program?*

A: Document code changes at the beginning of the program. The documentation should include chronological references following the date compiled statement and should include date in a fixed position and a brief description of the change in a fixed position.

Programming techniques such as the use of copybooks, meaningful variable name, use of 88 levels, and top-down code also provide informative documentation.

Q: *What is the file organization clause?*
A: The file organization clause identifies the logical structure of a file.

Q: *Can the logical structure of a file be changed once it has been created?*
A: No.

Q: *What is file organization indexed?*
A: The file organization indexed is where the position of each logical record within a file is determined by the indexes created with the file and embedded in a key in each record.

Q: *What is file organization sequential?*
A: The file organization sequential indicates that records are loaded into a file based on a record-to-record relationship of the data sequence. Sequential is the default file organization.

Q: *What is file organization relative?*
A: The position of each logical record in the file is determined by its relative record number.

Q: *What is the dynamic access mode?*
A: The dynamic access mode permits reading and writing file records by a specific read or write statement which can be sequential and/or random. The dynamic access mode assumes that a file is indexed.

Q: *What access modes are permitted with sequential organization?*
A: The sequential access mode only.

Q: *What access modes are permitted with indexed organization?*
A: All three access modes—sequential, random, and dynamic—are permitted. In dynamic access mode, the file can be accessed sequentially and/or randomly.

Q: *What access modes are permitted with relative organization?*
A: All three access modes—sequential, random, and dynamic—are permitted.

Q: *What is a START statement?*
A: The START statement is used with an indexed or relative organization file for positioning within the file for subsequent sequential record retrieval. The access key may be qualified to provide a record equal to the key, greater than the key, less than the key, greater than or equal to the key.

Q: *What is a subscript?*
A: A subscript is a positive integer that represents an *occurrence* within a table that has been redefined with an occurs clause. A subscript must be defined in working storage and can be manipulated like any numeric variable.

Q: *What is an index for tables?*

A: An index references data in a table, but does it differently than a subscript. The index is defined with the table and represents a displacement into the table.

Q: *What are the advantages of indexes?*

A: Indexes are more efficient when used with the SEARCH verb because the computer does not have to generate the displacement from the beginning of the table.

Q: *What are two SEARCH techniques?*

A: The sequential or serial search moves through a table one record at a time until a match has been made. For example, in a table of 10 numbers (1 to 10), to find the number 8 the search must check and eliminate numbers 1 to 7. The process is initiated by the verb SEARCH.

    The binary search is a dichotomizing search and must have a key that is in ascending or descending order. At each step of the search, half of the records in the table are eliminated. For example, in the SEARCH for the number 8, the first division would locate the number 5 and eliminate records 1 to 5. The second division would locate the number 8. The process is initiated by the verb SEARCH ALL.

Q: *What COBOL verbs can change table indexes?*

A: SET, SEARCH, and PERFORM can change the value of a table index.

Q: *Is a binary search efficient when compared to a sequential search?*

A: The binary search is more efficient because it finds the answer with fewer data checks. However, the process for each data check is less efficient because of the machine code generated. If the list/table of variables has fewer than 100 entries, a sequential search would be a better choice.

Q: *What is the most efficient method for locating data in a table?*

A: If you know the location of the data in the table, use it. For example, in a table of the names of months, use the numeric value of the month to locate the name. To convert 04/01/93 to April 01 1993, the 04 would be used as the subscript to locate the word April.

Q: *How could one subscript sequentially through a table of the 50 states, looking for NY?*

A: Given the subscript SUB-1 PIC 99, the following COBOL II code could be used:

```
PERFORM TABLE-LOOK-UP THRU TABLE-EXIT VARYING SUB1 FROM 1
    BY 1 UNTIL SUB-1 > 50 OR MATCH-FOUND.

CONTINUE-1. (CONTINUE WITH PROGRAM)

TABLE-LOOK-UP.

IF STATE (SUB-1) = 'NY'
```

```
            SET MATCH-FOUND TO TRUE
            MOVE TABLE-DATA (SUB-1) TO OUTPUT-DATA
    END-IF.

    TABLE-EXIT. EXIT.
```

Q: *Recode the foregoing table lookup using an in-line perform.*

```
PERFORM VARYING SUB-1 FROM 1 BY 1 UNTIL MATCH-FOUND OR SUB-1 > 50
        IF STATE (SUB-1) = 'NY'
            SET MATCH-FOUND TO TRUE
            MOVE TABLE-DATA (SUB-1) TO OUTPUT-DATA
        END-IF.
END-PERFORM.
```

Q: *Give the answer to the previous question using a binary search, given the 01 level table name as 01 TABLE-NAME, the occurs clause indexed by table-index, ascending key is table-item.*

```
SEARCH ALL TABLE-NAME
   AT END
      MOVE 'FILE-ITEM NOT FOUND' TO FILE-ITEM-DESC
   WHEN TABLE-ITEM (TABLE-INDEX) EQUALS FILE-ITEM
      MOVE TABLE-ITEM-A (TABLE-ITEM) TO FILE-ITEM-DESC
END-SEARCH.
```

Q: *Describe a paragraph-naming convention that would assist navigation through a COBOL program.*

A: Paragraph names should be descriptive of what is contained within the paragraph and preceded by a sequential number according to their position within the program. For example:

```
100-OPEN-FILES; 500-READ-MASTER etc.
```

Q: *What is one major advantage of COBOL II when operating in an MVS/XA environment?*

A: COBOL II can utilize 31-bit addressing and therefore operate "above the line" (above the 17-MB virtual memory restriction) in an MVS/XA environment—an advantage not available in VS COBOL.

Q: *What is the format of a COBOL internal sort using an input procedure and an output procedure?*

A:
```
    SELECT SORT-FILE
    SD  SORT-FILE
    SORT RECORD IS SORT-WORK-REC.

01  SORT-WORK-REC.
    05 SORT-DATA.
        07 DATA-PART-1    PIC X(10).
        07 FIRST-SORT-KEY PIC X(5).

        (continue with record description for fields
        necessary for sorting and fields to be sent
```

```
                                to the sort, the entire record need not be
                                sorted unless required by the program)


          PROCEDURE DIVISION.
              SORT SORT-FILE
                  ASCENDING KEY FIRST-SORT-KEY
              INPUT PROCEDURE SORT-INPUT-PROCEDURE-0200
              OUTPUT PROCEDURE SORT-OUTPUT-PROCEDURE-0500.

          SORT-INPUT-PROCEDURE-0200 SECTION.
              SORT-INPUT-READ-SELECT.

                     (use the input procedure to read the file to
                         be sorted, select all or portion of the data,
                         process the data in any way and move the data
                         to the sort-work-rec for subsequent release to
                         the sort.)

              RELEASE SORT-WORK-REC.

          SORT-OUTPUT-PROCEDURE-0500 SECTION.
              SORT-OUTPUT-PROCESSING.

                     (use the output procedure to return and process
                         the sorted records)

              RETURN SORT-FILE AT END ...
```

Q: *What are some advantages of a COBOL internal sort?*
A: ■ You can select only the records required by the program, reducing the sort resource requirements.

■ Records can be processed before and after the sort.

■ One or more sorts may be performed on the same data for different functions within the program.

■ The program will document the criteria for record selection and sort criteria.

■ Data from separate files can be combined.

Q: *Is the SORT utility a reasonable alternative to the internal sort?*
A: The sort utility would require an extra step in the JCL and would select, sort, and document criteria. It could not manipulate the data before the sort. The final decision depends on installation standards.

Q: *What is a bubble sort?*
A: A bubble sort is an efficient way of resequencing a small table that already resides in memory. The sorting algorithm that can be used is referred to as a bubble sort. The bubble sort compares the key of the first item in a table with

the keys of all other items in the table, each time moving the item with the lowest key to the first item's position. The process is continued, starting with the second item, comparing it to the third item, swapping pairs of items until the entire table is in order.

Q: *What is an in-line perform?*

A: COBOL II allows a performed procedure to be coded in-line. The perform statement is coded without a paragraph name, followed directly by the code to be performed. An END-PERFORM statement is required and coded at the end of an in-line perform.

```
PERFORM
      .
      .
END-PERFORM
```

Q: *What is the COBOL II statement WITH TEST AFTER?*

A: In a PERFORM, the UNTIL clause is examined before the PERFORM, not after. COBOL II allows the programmer to specify PERFORM WITH TEST AFTER, which will always execute a paragraph at least once.

Q: *How could 88 levels be used for validation of data for valid values and valid ranges?*

A: The 88 level is used to specify the valid values and/or ranges of values, and then the 88 data name is used in an if statement to test the data.

Q: *Give an example of how you would code an "88".*

A:
```
02  INPUT-LOCATION PICTURE 9(3).
    88 VALID-LOCATIONS VALUES ARE 100, 200 THRU
       299.
```

Q: *How could 88 levels be used to determine the next step in navigating through a program?*

A: The 88-level data name can be used to specify a condition in both if and evaluate statements.

```
IF VALID-LOCATIONS
    PERFORM PARA-A
END-IF

EVALUATE TRUE
   WHEN VALID-LOCATIONS
     PERFORM PARA-A
   WHEN OTHER
     PERFORM PARA-B
END-EVALUATE
```

Q: *What is a CALL statement in COBOL?*

A: A CALL is a statement that transfers control from one object program to another object program within the same run-unit.

Q: *What does the COBOL "CANCEL" statement do?*
A: The CANCEL statement ensures that the next time the referenced sub-program is called it will be entered in its original state.

Q: *What is the LINKAGE SECTION in COBOL?*
A: The LINKAGE SECTION of a called program defines the data that is available (from a calling program) to a called program.

Q: *Which program can reference the data items described in the LINKAGE SECTION?*
A: The data items in a LINKAGE SECTION may be referenced by the calling program as well as by the called program.

Q: *What is the USING phrase of the CALL statement?*
A: The USING phrase makes available data items from the calling to the called program.

Q: *When can the USING phrase be included in the CALL statement?*
A: The USING phrase can be included in the CALL statement only if there is a USING phrase in the Procedure Division header or the ENTER statement through which the called program is invoked.

Q: *Can the number of operands in the USING phrase in the called program be different than the number of operands in the USING statement of the calling program?*
A: The *number* of operands in the calling program USING phrase and the called program USING phrase must be identical.

Q: *How do the operands of the calling program USING phrase align with the operands of the called program USING phrase?*
A: The correspondence is by position—not by name.

Q: *Can a called program contain CALL statements?*
A: Yes. However, a called program may not CALL the calling program directly or indirectly.

Q: *What is a COPY statement?*
A: The COPY statement copies existing text from a copy library into a COBOL program. For example:

```
COPY text-name.
```

Q: *What is a copy library?*
A: A copy library is basically a COBOL source library containing members that can be copied into COBOL source programs.

Q: *What type of text can be copied using the COPY statement?*
A: The type of text that can be copied into a COBOL program includes all types of components of a COBOL program, including file definitions, working storage, and procedure division code.

Q: *What is the REPLACING option of a COPY statement?*

A: The REPLACING option of a COPY statement contains two operands and performs the COPY, replacing all occurrences of the first operand within the copied library member text by the second operand.

Q: *Can the text of a copy library member contain nested COPY statements?*

A: In COBOL II a copy library member may contain nested COPY statements. This is not the case in VS COBOL.

Q: *Can a copy member with nested COPY statements contain the REPLACING option?*

A: No, a nested COPY statement cannot contain the REPLACING option.

Q: *Can a COPY statement with the REPLACING option contain nested COPY statements?*

A: No, a COPY statement with the REPLACING option cannot contain nested COPY statements.

Q: *What are some advantages to using COPY statements?*

A: An installation can develop standard file descriptions and mandate their use for standardization and ease of testing and maintenance. Also, standard working storage descriptions, record descriptions, and procedure division code can be developed, enhancing development and maintenance efforts.

Q: *What is the BY CONTENT phrase in COBOL II?*

A: The BY CONTENT phrase permits constants to be passed to a called program using the CALL statement.

Q: *What is the BY CONTENT LENGTH phrase in COBOL II?*

A: The BY CONTENT LENGTH phrase permits the length of a data item to be passed to a called program using the CALL statement.

Q: *What is the PICTURE clause?*

A: The PICTURE clause defines an elementary item's basic characteristics and editing requirements.

Q: *What would be the result of moving 030193 to a PICTURE clause of PICTURE 99/99/99?*

A: The result would be 03/01/93—but only if the month, day, and year were moved separately.

Q: *How are numbers stored in the computer?*

A: Each digit is stored in a single byte; the first 4 bits contain the "zone." The last 4 bits contain the digit. For numbers, the zone indicates positive numbers (a C or an F) and negative numbers (D).

Q: *What is EBCDIC?*

A: EBCDIC is an acronym for Extended Binary Coded Decimal Interchange Code.

Q: *In EBCDIC, how would the number 1234 be stored?*

A: The number 1234 would be stored as: F1 F2 F3 F4.

Q: *What is packed decimal?*

A: It is a method of storing numbers in less space. The zone is eliminated from each of the digits except for the last digit, which contains the sign for the number. Packed decimals are always stored in an even number of bytes, and the last byte is always the sign. The number of bytes used is determined by adding 1 to the total bytes requested and dividing by 2. The answer is always an even number.

Q: *How would the number +1234 be stored if a PIC clause of PICTURE S9(4) COMP-3 were used?*

A: The answer will use 3 bytes (4 + 1 = 5 / 2 = 2.5 or 3), so a leading 0 will pad the answer: 01234F.

Q: *What are binary numbers?*

A: Binary numbers are strings of 0s and 1s which are stored in half word, full word, or double word, depending on the size of the number.

- Up to 4 digits are stored in 2 bytes or a half word.
- 5–9 digits are stored in 4 bytes or a word.
- 10–18 digits are stored in 8 bytes or a double word.

Q: *What is a common problem when doing a table lookup?*

A: The maximum occurrences of the table are exceeded as a result of exiting the perform based on testing the subscript for "equal to" the maximum number of occurrences rather than "greater than" the number of occurrences. By manipulating the subscript, the subscript can become greater than the maximum number of occurrences, permitting the perform to continue beyond the bounds of the table.

Q: *What will be the result of executing a VS COBOL II program when a subscript exceeds the table limits?*

A: The table data overwrites the program code and will continue to do so until there is an abend. The abend message will reference gibberish code rather than a subscript out of range.

Q: *What will be the result of executing a VS COBOL II program that was compiled with the SSRANGE option, when a subscript exceeds the table limits?*

A: The program will terminate.

Q: *What is a common problem associated with reading a data file in a test environment?*

A: A read is executed on a file that has not been opened by the program.

Q: *What problem could occur when a file is read with an incorrect file definition?*

A: A data exception could occur, causing the program to terminate.

Q: *In a production environment, what should be programmed when an abnormal condition is encountered and it is undesirable to continue processing?*

A: The program should go to a programmed abnormal exit and pass a condition code to the job control language via an installation standard abend procedure. The job control language should, in turn, test the condition code and force the job to terminate with an abnormal condition code.

24
SAS

Sheryl Hert Harawitz

Introduction

Statistical Analysis System (SAS) is a leased product of the SAS Institute of Cary, N.C. SAS is utilized on mainframes running under MVS, CMS, and VSE; minicomputers using VMS, AOS/VS, PRIMOS, and UNIX workstations; and personal computers using DOS, OS/2, and Windows. SAS can access a variety of file types, including VSAM (sequential and direct access), BDAM, ISAM, and partitioned data sets.

The latest SAS release has a new engine which uses MultiVendor Architecture (MVA). MVA is platform-independent in that a SAS program written for the personal computer will also work on a mainframe computer. Since SAS is platform-independent, it is an ideal tool for environments with a multitude of computer systems. The SAS programming language and procedures remain constant across systems.

SAS Products

The core product of SAS is BASE/SAS software. BASE/SAS enables you to access a variety of data sources, manipulate the data, write reports, build simple graphs, analyze data, and perform simple statistical analysis. Over the years SAS has not only expanded the range of hardware and operating systems on which it will run, but has also expanded the number of products. Bear in mind that SAS is a leased product and each of the following components is leased separately from BASE/SAS described here.

1. SAS/STAT software used to be included with the BASE/SAS, but with the new release it became a separate package. This component product offers

ANOVA (Analysis of Variance), regression analysis, categorical analysis, multivariate analysis, psychometric analysis, cluster analysis, and nonparametric analysis.

2. SAS/FSP is the software package used for full-screen data entry, letters, and spreadsheets.

3. SAS/AF software module is used for creating menus and screens.

4. SAS/GRAPH software is a complete graphics package, including mapping capabilities. It is compatible with a wide range of graphic interfaces and plotters.

5. SAS/ACCESS is the interface product for linking SAS to DB2, Oracle, Adabas, and other databases.

6. SAS/CPE is an interactive system used to monitor computer performance.

7. SAS/ETS software package is for economic and time-series analysis.

8. MXG is a related package which can be leased from Merill Consultants in Texas. With this package data can be extracted from MVS, VM, VSE, etc., operating systems. The software consists of data input and formats statements for these data types and the procedures necessary to convert these data types into SAS data sets.

Terminology

SUGI: SAS Users Group International. Every year SAS holds a conference in which SAS users are invited to submit papers on application development, computer performance, database management, econometric and operation research, graphics, and other topics.

Observation: Refers to a line of data or a record.

Variable: A field or data element.

SAS Log: SAS Log is where SAS puts information about the processing of the data step. Items typically included are the number of observations, error messages, warning messages, the name of the data sets accessed, and number of variables on the data sets.

SAS output file: This is where SAS puts the output from SAS procedures.

Options: Options sets the options such as page size, line size, block size, and some 100 other options.

SAS data sets: SAS data sets are created by Data Step and/or Procedures. These files differ from ordinary data sets in that they contain both the data and information about the data. They store the following information: the variable names (field or column names), data types (alpha or numeric), length, informat names, format names, and associated labels.

A SAS Job Interview

When a job calls for:

A beginner. Almost anyone who has written programs in COBOL or any other computer language and has the basic programming skills can program in SAS. It should be remembered that SAS programs are often written by noncomputer professionals.

An intermediate. The interviewer would expect you to be familiar with (1) formatting data and (2) some macro language.

An expert. You would be expected to be able to (1) use the macro language and (2) create an intricate production program system.

Some of the following sections will demonstrate how to write a small program. When asked to do this, keep the programs as simple as possible. Other questions in an interview may require you to find out what is wrong with the program. Still other questions will ask you to solve typical programming problems using basic logic skills.

The Structure of a SAS Dataset

SAS, because its roots are in the statistical world, uses the word *variable* as a synonym for *field*, and the term *observation* in place of *record*. Every sentence in SAS ends in a semicolon.

The following conventions are used: Keywords are *capitalized* and must be written as is. Variables (fields) are written in *lowercase*. Variables can be any 8-byte word which begins with an alpha.

A "Basic" SAS Program

```
//sas        EXEC PGM=SASAI
//SASLOG     DD DSN=                    SAS log information
//SASLIST    DD DSN=                    SAS output
//ddname1    DD DSN=file1.data,DISP=SHR  input data set
//ddname2    DD DSN=file2.data,DISP=OLD  output data set

  DATA anyname;
   INFILE ddname1;
   INPUT name1 name2 name3 number1 number2;
   IF name1 > name2;

   total1 =number1+number2;
   ...etc..;
    /*  comments ....... */
  PROC PRINT;
  PROC FREQ;
    TABLE name1;
```

A SAS program consists of two divisions: the DATA STEP and the PROC STEP. The data step begins with the word "DATA" while the proc starts with the word "PROC."

Components of a SAS Program

SAS programs begin with a DATA STEP. The data step begins with the word "DATA." The data step is where SAS is given instructions about the location of the data set and the description of the data elements. As SAS executes the data step, the data is evaluated and brought into SAS's working storage.

The data step contains the basic data retrieval, programming, and data manipulation language. It is the section of the program where you can create new variables and select specific records for processing (if statement, do loops, etc.). The end product of a SAS data step is the creation of a SAS data set for use in the SAS Proc or as an output file.

Keywords Used in a Data Step

DATA: The first word used in a SAS program. For example:

```
DATA anyname;
```

says start a data step and call the data set anyname. (Please note that SAS statements start with a key word and end with a semicolon.)

INFILE statement: Used for locating the external source of a data file. For example:

```
//file1   DD DSN=what.ever.it.is.called
DATA anyname; INFILE file1;
```

Here INFILE file1 says refer back to the line of JCL with the ddname file1. This is where the data is located.

INPUT statement: Tells SAS what the data elements are to be called and where in the data set they are located. The two most common input statements are column input and formatted input. An example of a column input statement is the following:

```
INPUT   dept $1-10
        salary 25-30;
```

This statement says the data in columns 1–10 is alphanumeric (the $ indicates alphanumeric data) and the data in bytes 25–30 is numeric. The first variable (field) will be called dept and the second variable will be called salary.

A formatted input statement is as follows:

```
INPUT   @1 dept $10.
        @25 salary 5.;
```

This statement says that the variable dept starts in byte 1 and continues for 10 bytes, while salary starts in byte 25 and continues for 5 bytes. (Please note that the period after 10 and 5 indicates to SAS that this is formatted data. A common error is to leave out the period.)

PUT: The opposite of an INPUT statement. It tells SAS how to write the variable. For example, the following statement:

```
PUT  @25 name $20.
     @89 dept $10.;
```

says to write the variable name at byte 25 as a character 20 bytes.

FILE: The opposite of an INFILE statement. The following statement tells SAS that the data should be put into an external data file with the ddname of new.

```
FILE new;
```

SET: Locates a SAS data set, that is, a data set that had been previously inputted into SAS and outputted as a SAS data set. When you use the SET statement, you do not have to supply an INPUT statement, since SAS stores format, labels, and attributes with the data set.

```
SET dept1;
```

LABEL: The keyword that associates a SAS variable with a longer name. Since SAS variables can be only 8 bytes, it is often necessary to associate a longer name with the variable for use in procedures such as Report.

```
LABEL dept='Department';
```

MERGE: Brings together multiple data sets by matching on a variable.

```
MERGE  file1 file2; BY name1;
```

where file1 and file2 are SAS data sets and name1 is the variable (field) that you want to match on.

FORMAT statements: Inform SAS about outputting the variable.

```
FORMAT date1  mmddyy8.;
FORMAT date2  yymmdd8.;
```

will result in the data looking like 08/08/92, while FORMAT yymmdd8. will result in the data looking like 92/08/08. SAS has an extensive list of formats. (Please note that formats end with a period.)

PROCs

The word "PROC" is used to invoke SAS procedure. A SAS Proc is basically a prewritten program that produces statistical analysis, creates reports, and/or outputs data sets. The following are some of the Procedures available in BASE/SAS:

PROC PRINT: Produces basic columnar reports. For example:

```
PROC PRINT; VAR date1 name;
```

will produce a report with two columns of data: date1 and name.

PROC FREQ: Produces cross-tabulation tables, mainly for categorical data.

```
PROC FREQ; TABLE dept*sex;
```

will produce a table such as the following:

```
              TABLE OF DEPARTMENT BY YEAR
    DEPT          SEX
                   | FEMALE  |   MALE  |     TOTAL

    SALES             200        100          300
    PERSONNEL         100        200          300
    TOTAL             300        300          600
```

PROC SORT: Sorts the data set.

```
    PROC SORT; BY name1;
```

will produce a data set sorted by name field.

PROC MEANS: Produces descriptive statistics such as mean, standard deviation, minimum and maximum values.

PROC PLOT: Produces simple plots. For example:

```
    PROC PLOT; PLOT total*shares;
```

PROC CALENDAR: Produces a calendar or a schedule. For example:

```
    PROC CALENDAR;  ID date1; VAR item1 item2;
```

PROC CHART: Produces bar charts, block graphs, and pie charts. (Bear in mind that this proc is different from SAS/GRAPH, which is another component with many more graphic capabilities.

```
    PROC CHART; VBAR sex;
```

(VBAR is a keyword indicating vertical bars.)

PROC COMPARE: Compares two data sets and lists the differences between them.

```
    PROC COMPARE DATE=file1 COMPARE=file2;
    VAR phone address;
    ID name;
```

This program will compare the two files (file1 and file2) by matching on the variable name, and will list the differences found on the variable's phone number and addresses.

PROC FORMS: Most commonly used for producing labels.

PROC SUMMARY: Produces summary statistics on numeric fields.

```
    PROC SUMMARY; CLASS dept; VAR salary; OUTPUT OUT=anyname
    MEAN=;
```

This program says create a data set called anyname and for each dept calculate the mean salary. To print this data set, use the following:

```
    PROC PRINT DATA=anyname;
```

Questions and Answers

Q: *Why would a staff person alter a SAS program from*

```
    DATA group1; INFILE file1; INPUT name $20. salary pd6.2;
```

to

```
DATA group1;
INFILE file1;
INPUT name $20. salary pd6.2;
```

A: Technically, the two programs are identical; therefore, the staff person changed the program for readability or personal preference.

Q: *Describe the data extracted with the following SAS statement:*

```
INPUT @1 test $10. @25 test2 PD6. @40 test3 MMDDYY6.;
```

A: Test would be an alphanumeric variable which was 10 bytes. Test2 would be a 6-byte packed decimal with no decimal places which started at byte 25. Test3 would be a date field (i.e., 010646) starting at byte 40.

Q: *Write an INPUT statement for a data set with department in bytes 35 through 45 and salary starting in byte 62, ending in byte 69, with two implied decimal places.*

A: INPUT dept $35–45 @62 salary 8.2;

Q: *Write a SAS INPUT statement for the following COBOL record:*

```
01  name-file-record.
    02  social-security-num      pic x(9).
    02  last-name                pic x(15).
    02  first-name               pic x(10).
    02  date-of-birth.
        03  month-of-birth       pic 9(2).
        03  day-of-birth         pic 9(2).
        03  year-of-birth        pic 9(2).
```

A: INPUT ssn $9. lname $15. fname $10. dob mmddyy6.;

Q: *Our company would like to put SAS programs into production. Is there a SAS equivalent to a COBOL copybook?*

A: Yes. By using SAS macro's language, you can store the INPUT statements in a library that can be called by multiple programs.

Q: *Write a SAS statement for a file which has five salaries, each 6 bytes wide.*

A: The statement INPUT (salary1-salary6) (6.); declares five variables: salary1, salary2, etc., each 6 bytes long.

Q: *Write a SAS statement for a data file that contains two different record types. The record type is located in byte 6 of the file. Record type 1 has the client's name in bytes 35–55 and Record type 2 has the client's name in bytes 20–40.*

A:
```
Input @6 type 1. @;
   IF type=1 THEN INPUT name $35-55;
   IF type=2 THEN INPUT name $20-40;
```

(Note the @ sign at the end of input statement holds the pointer for further processing with the next input.)

Q: *We want to reformat a file. Write a program which reads a data set with the variable name in bytes 24–34 and salary in byte 85–95 and writes the data to a file with name in byte 1–10 followed by salary.*

A:
```
//filein      DD  DSN=....
//fileout     DD  DSN=....

DATA rewrite;  INFILE filein;
               INPUT  salary 10-15 name $24-34;

               FILE fileout;
               PUT  name $1-10    salary 11-16;
```

Q: *How would you alter the foregoing program to include a calculated variable called salary2, which is calculated by multiplying salary by 1.10?*

A:
```
DATA rewrite;  INFILE filein;
               INPUT salary 10-15 name $24-34;
               salary2=salary*1.10;

               FILE fileout;
               PUT name $1-10  salary 11-16 @17 salary2 8.2;
```

(Note you can mix columnar and formatted data.)

Q: *The personnel department requested a report which lists the name of all employees and their social security numbers. After receiving the report, they requested that the social security number 123456789 be changed to 123-45-6789. How long would you expect it to take to recode the program?*

A: It should take about 5 minutes since the only line of code needed to be changed is the following:
```
FORMAT socnum SSN.;
```

Q: *An employee that you supervised gave you the following program. How would you rate his work?*
```
DATA test1; INPUT name 1-30 date_of_birth 31-35;
```

A: This employee has little experience with SAS programming. First, SAS variables can be only 8 bytes. The data step has no INFILE or SET statement; thus, no data.

Q: *How do you differentiate macro variables from regular SAS variables?*

A: Macro variables begin with the % sign.

Q: *What is the difference between the following two SAS statements?*
```
DATA dept1; INFILE file1; INPUT dept $1-4 name $20-40;
```
and
```
DATA dept1;
INFILE file1;
INPUT dept $1-4
      name $20-40;
```

A: There is no difference. The SAS programming language is not space-sensitive. Each statement begins with a keyword and ends with a semicolon.

Q: *What is wrong with the following statement?*
```
INPUT dept $1-10 filler $11-20 name $21-40 filler $41-60;
```

A: The variable name "FILLER" is used twice. Unlike COBOL, SAS does not use filler. If you do not need the data in a field, just skip over it, or else you have to use a unique name such as filler2.

Q: *What is wrong with the following statement?*
```
DATA dept1; SET dept; INPUT name $1-20;
```

A: There is no need for an INPUT statement when SET is used. SET indicates an existing SAS data set.

Q: *How would you print a list of department salaries with dollar signs, commas, and two decimal places?*

A: First format the data with the following statement:
```
Format salary DOLLAR12.2;
```
Then use PROC PRINT.

Q: *Write a program to calculate the age of our clients.*

A:
```
DATA age;
INPUT name  birth MMDDYY6.;
age=(DATE()-birth)/365.25;
```

Q: *Write a program that would process records 5000 through 6000.*

A:
```
INFILE dept5 OBS=1000 FIRSTOBS=5000;
```
This statement limits SAS to 1000 observations, with the first observation starting at record number 5000.

Q: *Write a program to merge two data sets.*

A:
```
MERGE file1 file2;
```

Q: *Write a program to match two data sets on id number and include only those records that were on the first data set.*

A:
```
MERGE file1 (IN=data1) file2 (IN=data2); BY id;
  IF data1;
```

Q: *Our company has two files. File 1 has the names of our departments and the manager's names. The second file has the salespersons' names, amount of their annual sales, and their department. Write a program to list the salesperson, his or her annual sales, and manager's name.*

A:
```
DATA file1; INFILE mgmt; INPUT dept $ manager $ ;
        LABEL manager='Manager's Name';
   DATA file2; INFILE sales; INPUT sales $ amount dept $;
        LABEL sales='Salesperson's Name'
              amount='Total Sales';
   PROC SORT DATA=file1; BY dept;
   PROC SORT DATA=file2; BY dept;
```

```
DATA file3; MERGE file2 file1; BY dept;
PROC PRINT LABEL; VAR sales amount manager ;
```

Q: *Write a second program that prints a summary of the number of sales-persons, and the total amount of sales per manager.*

A: Add the following to the preceding program:

```
PROC SUMMARY DATA=file3 NWAY; CLASS manager;
     VAR amount;
     OUTPUT OUT=summary1 SUM=;
PROC PRINT;
```

Q: *Change the preceding program to find the average amount of sales per manager.*

A: The only line of code that has to change is:

```
OUTPUT OUT=summary1 MEAN=;
```

Q: *What procedure could you use to calculate the standard deviation?*

A: The standard deviation can be calculated with PROC SUMMARY, PROC UNIVARIATE, PROC TABULATE, PROC CORR, and PROC MEANS.

Q: *Our company has been collecting data on the age of our customers and the amount of their purchases. We would like to know if there is a relationship between the customer's age and the amount of money spent per year. How would you proceed?*

A: First, check the accuracy of the data set by looking for outlying data elements. That is, find the youngest and oldest customers and see if these ages are correct. The following program would do that.

```
PROC FREQ; TABLE age amount;
```

Next, prepare a graphic and analytic presentation of the data by using PROC CORR and PROC PLOT.

```
PROC PLOT; age*purchases;
PROC CORR; VAR age purchases;
```

Q: *What procedure would you use to perform a T test?*

A: `PROC UNIVARIATE`

Q: *Our company would like to know the percent of males and females in each department. How would you go about answering this user inquiry?*

A: Obtain or create a file with the employees, their departments, and their gender. The following program would produce a table with each department, the percent of females and males in each department, the number of males and females in each department, and the overall count and percent of males and females.

```
PROC FREQ; TABLE dept * sex;
```

Q: *The personnel department would like to know the average salary for each job title. What procedure would you use to find the average salary for each job title?*

A: Proc summary is an efficient way to provide means for variables. A typical program would be the following:

```
PROC SUMMARY;
CLASS title;
VAR salary;
OUTPUT OUT=file1 MEAN=;
PROC PRINT;
```

Q: *Are there any other procedures which could be used to find the average salary for each job title?*

A: A combination of PROC SORT and PROC MEANS, as in the following program, will work.

```
PROC SORT; BY title;
PROC MEANS; BY title;
VAR salary;
```

Q: *Our company has a very large database, with over 1 million records. We would like to find out the distribution of our customers by zip code, but each time we try to run the program we run out of space. How would you handle this problem?*

A: One way to handle this is to take a random sample of the records by using the following:

```
If ranuni(0) LE .25;
```

would produce a sample with approximately 250,000 customers.

Q: *Our company placed addresses in a free-form field; that is, the street name can be anywhere in a 30-byte field. We need to locate the customers who live on Wilson Street. How would you go about solving this situation?*

A: First, define the 30-byte field, then use index feature to locate the words "Wilson" and "Street," as in the following program:

```
INPUT address $30.;
IF INDEX(address,'wilson') AND INDEX(address,'st');
```

Q: *The following program produced no output. Why?*

```
PROC SUMMARY; CLASS sex; VAR salary; OUTPUT OUT=test MEAN=;
```

A: Proc summary does not produce printed output, but outputs the data to a SAS data set that could be printed with Proc Print or used as input to another procedure or data step. To see the output of Proc Summary, it needs to be followed with a Proc Print.

Q: *How would you output the data to disk rather than paper?*

A: If using SAS5, then change the //FT12 ... line to indicate the location for the output data set. If using SAS6, then change the //SASLIST line to indicate an output data.

Q: *What procedure would you use to print a quick report?*

A: Proc Print will produce a reasonable report with the following statement:

```
PROC PRINT;
```

Q: *What is the difference between the following two statements?*

```
total=salary1+salary2+salary3;
total=sum(salary1,salary2,salary3);
```

A: The difference is the way SAS handles missing values. In the first statement, if any of the variables have a missing value, then the total will have a missing value. In the second, SAS will add the variables even if one of the variables is missing.

Q: *Our company has decided to install Version 6 of SAS. How would you go about converting programs from Version 5 to Version 6?*

A: You should analyze the programs and check to see if any program modification is necessary for the conversion. Most programs will run without modification under the new SAS.

Q: *What version of SAS have you worked with?*

A: Try the truth. Version 5 is the old version; the current version is 6.07. If you have used Version 5 you will have no problem with Version 6.

Q: *What is the major difference between Version 5 and Version 6 of SAS?*

A: The major difference between SAS 5 and SAS 6 is the storage of SAS data sets. With SAS 6, you can now compress the SAS data sets, thus saving disk space.

Q: *Our company is experiencing a shortage of DASD space. How would you address this problem among the SAS users?*

A: First, I would expect the SAS users to eliminate duplicate files, and then I would compress the data sets.

Q: *How would you alter the following program to use less work space?*

```
DATA dept1; SET dept;
PROC PRINT; WHERE age LE 18;
```

A: Put the select statement in the DATA step.

Q: *What is the difference between an informat and a format statement?*

A: An informat is used to read data into a SAS data set, while a format is used for printing and/or writing the data.

Q: *What kind of graphics can SAS produce?*

A: This is dependent upon which components of the SAS system your company has. BASE/SAS has very limited graphing capabilities. It can produce bar and block charts, time lines, and two variable plots. On the other hand, SAS/GRAPH can produce basic graphs, three-dimensional color charts, and maps.

Q: *What is the difference between a Data Step and a Proc Step?*

A: Basically SAS Proc Step operates on SAS Data Sets.

Q: *Where in a SAS program would you find the following statement?*

```
IF age GE 55;
```

A: This would be found in a Data Step. This statement says select only those records where age is greater than or equal to 55.

Q: *Where would you put the following statement in a SAS program?*

```
TITLE "This is the title of my report";
```

A: This statement can be placed anywhere in a SAS program.

Q: *Have you ever installed SAS?*

A: Yes or no, depending upon your experience. If you have never installed SAS on the mainframe, don't worry. SAS technical support will walk you through, if needed. Installing SAS on a personal computer is as simple as installing any other software.

Q: *What would you recommend as minimum requirement for SAS on the personal computer?*

A: As a minimum, you would recommend 4 megs and a math coprocessor.

Q: *How do you handle lease expiration?*

A: Each year you must use PROC SETINIT to inform the software that you have paid your yearly fee. After paying your bill, SAS will send you the information necessary to use the procedure Setinit.

Q: *What is wrong with the following SAS program?*

```
DATA department; INFILE mydata; INPUT dept $3. date MMDDYY6.;
```

A: SAS variables can be only 8 bytes long; department is 10 bytes.

Q: *What is the difference between the following two SAS statements?*

```
DATA dept; SET dept1;
DATA dept; INFILE dept1;
```

A: The first statement says that the data being brought in is already a SAS data set. The second statement requires an input statement because it is a regular data set.

Q: *We need to make labels from a SAS data set. How would you go about doing this?*

A: First you should find out the size of the labels in stock (on hand). The information needed is the size of the labels and the number of spaces between the labels.

Q: *SAS is using a lot of computer resources. What would you do to lessen the impact?*

A: First, you would ascertain which type of computer resource SAS was using a lot: CPU, I/O, or Disk Space. To save I/O, I would use SAS data sets. To save disk space, I would write out only those variables that I needed for the current analysis. To save CPU, I would put the select statements as early as possible in the program.

Q: *What problems have you experienced in working with SAS?*
A: One problem is that SAS uses a lot of computer resources.

Q: *What are some limitations of SAS?*
A: The three limitations of SAS are (1) Proc Print produces a very limited range of reports, (2) the SAS manual is not only unwieldy, but the index is incomplete, and (3) the variable names are limited to 8 bytes.

Q: *How did you overcome these limitations?*
A: To overcome the problem of customized reports, I would use the SAS programming language. As for the variable name, use SAS label statements to attach a more meaningful name to the variable.

Q: *How would you go about setting up a training class for our staff?*
A: First, determine if the class is for computer professionals who need to add SAS as another tool or for noncomputer professionals. Based upon that information, contact SAS for their training kit.

Q: *What would you do to decrease SAS consumption of CPU time?*
A: Assign as many variables as possible with one statement. Write conditional statements in order of their probability of occurrence.

Q: *What would you do to decrease SAS usage of disk space?*
A: An easy way to decrease disk space usage is to store numeric data as characters.

Q: *The output data set contained no observations. What could have caused this?*
A: Unless otherwise specified, all data sets are temporary and are deleted at the end of the SAS session. To create a permanent data set requires a two-level name (i.e., mydata,setone), where mydata tells the location of the data set, and setone is the member name.

Q: *What is wrong with this program?*

```
DATA mydata; INFILE dept; INPUT ssn $9. name $20.
PROC PRINT;
IF SUBSTR(name, 1,1)='A';
```

A: The "IF" statement belongs in the Data Step, not in the Proc.

Q: *What do the initials SAS mean?*
A: SAS stands for Statistical Analysis System, which is a product of SAS Institute of Cary, North Carolina.

Q: *Our company is trying to decide between SAS and SPSS. How would you compare the two products?*
A: Both products are similar in that both can handle basic statistical analysis. However, SAS is a business-oriented product capable of handling more data types and file structures, while SPSS is more research-oriented, with more sophisticated statistical analysis.

Q: *How would you correct this error?*

```
127    DATA STOCK1; SET STOCK;
NOTE: The data set WORK.STOCK has 40 observations and 10 variables.
128            set stock;
129            total=price*shares
130
131    DATA stock2; SET stock;
DATA stock1; SET stock;
----
ERROR: Syntax error detected.
NOTE: Expecting one of the following:( [ {
```

A: The error is in line 129. There is a semicolon missing after the word "shares."

Q: *What does the following NOTE message mean?*

```
139    DATA stock3; SET stock;
140            FORMAT bought DOLLAR8;
141            FORMAT shares COMMA4;
```

NOTE: Variable COMMA4 is uninitialized.

A: Variable COMMA4 is uninitialized, meaning that SAS is looking for a variable called COMMA4, but the program is calling for a format call COMMA4. (with a period at the end). The period is missing after the COMMA4.

Q: *Why does COMMA4 have a ".", while NAME is blank?*

OBS	YEAR92	TEMP	YEAR	COMMA4	NAME
1	227.63	−0.0067	1992	.	
2	195.74	−0.0046	1992	.	
3	140.73	0.0777	1992	.	
4	152.88	0.0033	1992	.	

A: "COMMA4" is numeric; thus, missing values are indicated by ".", while NAME is alphanumeric. Data and missing values are spaces.

Q: *What is meant by the following SAS NOTE?*

```
142            FORMAT name $25.;
```

NOTE: Variable NAME is uninitialized.

A: Variable NAME being uninitialized probably means that there is no such variable on the data set. This is probably due to a spelling error on the variable list.

Q: *What is the problem with the following program?*

```
132            total=shares*price;
133
134            IF total GE 5000
135
136    PROC PRINT;
PROC PRINT;
```

```
    - - - -
ERROR: Syntax error detected.
```

NOTE: Expecting one of the following:** <> >< MAX MIN.
A: The problem with the program is a missing semicolon on line 134. Without the semicolon, SAS continued reading.

Q: *Why was the error message in the preceding question different from the error message on p. 356, even though the error was the same in both questions?*
A: The error message in the preceding question is related to the IF statement, while the error message on p. 356 is related to an assignment statement. Neither error message indicates that it is a missing semicolon.

Q: *What is the difference between these two SAS sentences?*
```
PROC SORT; BY id;


PROC SORT;
BY id;
```
A: There is no difference between the two sentences. SAS language is not space-sensitive. Each sentence begins with a keyword and ends with a semicolon. The layout of the program has more to do with easy reading and personal preference.

Q: *What is the difference between the Data Step and the Proc Step?*
A: Basically, SAS operates by either creating SAS data sets or analyzing SAS data sets. Data sets are created in the data step and used by the procs.

Q: *Can SAS use COBOL copybooks as input?*
A: No, SAS has its own input statement language.

Q: *We have SAS on our personal computers, and your experience is with mainframe SAS. Is your experience transferrable?*
A: Yes, the SAS programming language and procedure are independent of the computer hardware and operating system. Thus, all experience on the mainframe will be transferable to the personal computer version of SAS.

Q: *When would you use SAS over COBOL?*
A: I would use SAS when the programs need to be written quickly and the user request matches one of SAS's built-in procedures.

Q: *When would you use COBOL over SAS?*
A: I would use COBOL when computer resources were at a premium.

Q: *How would you access COBOL com3?*
A: COBOL comm3 translates to a SAS PD$x.n$, where x indicates the number of bytes occupied and n indicates the number of decimal places.

Q: *What does the following SAS statement mean?*

```
INPUT @1 salary PD4.2;
```

A: This statement says the salary is a 4-byte packed decimal field with two implied decimal places.

Q: *What is the difference between these two statements?*

```
A.  name EQ 'gat';
B.  name =  'gat';
```

A: Line A is a logical statement indicating that name should equal "gat," while B is an assignment statement where the "gat" should be placed into the variable called name.

Q: *What does the following SAS "note" mean?*

Note: The data set WORK.STOCK has 40 observations and 10 variables.

A: This is a message found on the SAS log and indicates that the data set had 10 variables (fields) and there were 40 records in the data set.

Q: *What is the difference between a SAS "note" and a SAS "warning"?*

A: An SAS warning contains information about input statements that could seriously compromise the results of the data analysis. An SAS note contains information about the data sets.

How well can you read SAS output? The next series of questions is based upon the following output from a SAS program, where Stock is the number of purchase orders and Year is the year in which the purchase took place. (*Hint:* There is no need for a calculator to answer any of the following questions. Every answer in the table.)

```
TABLE OF COMPANY BY YEAR

STOCK                   YEAR
```

Frequency Percent Row Pct Col Pct	1991	1992	Total
APPLE	0 0.00 0.00 0.00	8 20.00 100.00 25.00	8 20.00
IBM	3 7.50 21.43 37.50	11 27.50 78.57 34.38	14 35.00
Vanguard	5 12.50 27.78 62.50	13 32.50 72.22 40.63	18 45.00
Total	8 20.00	32 80.00	40 100.00

Q: *What procedure created this output?*
A: This was created by Proc Freq; Table company * year;

Q: *How many orders were placed in 1992 for Vanguard?*
A: Thirteen.

Q: *Of the total number of orders, what percent went to Vanguard?*
A: 45 percent.

Q: *Of the total number of orders, what percent went to IBM in 1992?*
A: 27.5 percent.

Q: *Of the 1991 orders, what percent went to IBM?*
A: 37.5 percent.

Q: *Of the Vanguard orders, what percent took place in 1992?*
A: 72.22 percent.

The following questions are based upon hypothetical data set listed.

File 1 layout	From	To
Last name (alphanumeric	1	15
First name alphanumeric	16	25
Social security number	26	34
Sex (m or f)	35	35
Blank	36	36
Date of birth (mmddyy)	37	42
File 2 layout		
Social security number	1	9
Salary (2 decimal places)	10	17
Commission (no decimal)	18	25

Q: *Given the preceding file layout, write a SAS program to input these files:*

```
     DATA file1;
     INFILE ddname1;
     INPUT  lname $1-15    fname $16-26
            ssn   $26-34  sex    $35
            blank $35       @37  dob mmddyy6.;
```

A:
```
   DATA file2;
     INFILE ddname2;
     INPUT  ssn $1-9    @10 salary 8.2   @18  comm 8.;
```

Q: *Produce a list of all the personnel and a sum of the salary and commissions.*
A:
```
   PROC SORT DATA=file1; BY ssn;
   PROC SORT DATA=file1; BY ssn;
   DATA both; MERGE file1 file2; BY ssn;
   PROC PRINT; VAR lname fname ; Sum salary comm;
```

Q: *Write a report showing the relationship between age and salary.*
A: `PROC CORR; VAR age*salary;`

Q: *Write a SAS to produce a report giving the average salary for males and females.*
A: `PROC SORT; BY sex;`
   `PROC MEANS; BY sex; VAR salary;`

Q: *Write a program to list those persons who received no commissions.*
A: `PROC PRINT; WHERE comm LE 0; VAR lname fname;`

Q: *Write a program to create a calendar of our employees' birthdays.*
A: Add a statement in the Data Step to create a variable which contains the date of employee's birthday and a duration variable (which is needed for Proc Calendar) containing the constant 1 (the number of days the birthday will last).

```
long=1;
birth=COMPRESS(MONTH(dob) || DAY(dob) || '1993';
birth2= INPUT(birth,mmddyy8.)

PROC CALENDAR;
     START birth2 ; VAR name; DUR long;
```

Q: *What is the SAS Display Manager?*
A: That is the interactive component of SAS.

Q: *What kinds of information will you find on the output log?*
A: The output log contains the results of SAS procedures.

Q: *In which language is SAS written?*
A: SAS is written in C.

Q: *What denotes a SAS system variable?*
A: A system variable is denoted by two underscores. For example, _FREQ_, _NULL_, _N_ are variables created by SAS.

Q: *What is wrong with the following statement?*
   `If age EQ 45 OR 49 OR 52;`
A: The statement should read:
   `IF age EQ 45 OR age EQ 49 OR age EQ 52;`

Q: *How do you code for a variable-length file?*
A: First, create a variable for the counter. Then input the variables with a do loop using the counter to position the pointer.

Q: *What information is available with Proc Content?*
A: Proc Content provides a list of the variables in the data set, along with the length, type of variable, and any labels associated with them.

Q: *How do you define your own formats?*
A: Formats are defined with Proc Format. These can then be used in the data step or in the procedures.

Q: *How do you create a running total?*

A: Use Retain to prevent SAS from reinitializing a variable each time a new record is read into the data step. For example, the following will create a running total of sales:

```
RETAIN sales
sales=sales+sales
```

Q: *How do you create two data sets from one?*

A:
```
DATA good bad; SET total;
      IF status='good' THEN OUTPUT good;
      IF status='bad' THEN OUTPUT bad;
```

will create two data sets: one data set named good and one named bad.

Q: *What does First.byvariable Last.byvariable mean?*

A: After sorting a data set and using the by statement, SAS creates a variable last.xxx which marks the end of the group.

Q: *How would you write a statement to calculate the age of a person as of January 1, 1993?*

A: `Age=('01jan93'd -dob)/365.25;`

where dob is a variable with the person's date of birth.

Q: *Are these two statements always identical?*

```
      IF gender EQ 'f' ;
      IF gender EQ 'm' THEN DELETE;
```

A: The two statements produce different results if gender contains missing values.

Q: *A Proc Freq on salary produced reams of paper. Why?*

A: Proc Freq will produce a count for each different value of salary, even if the value varies by one cent.

Q: *What are some system options that can be set?*

A: Some options that are available for setting are CENTER/NOCENTER, OBS=xx (where xx is a number), DATE/NODATE, LINESIZE=xx, and PAGESIZE=xx.

References

1. *SAS User's Guide: Basics*, SAS Institute, Cary, N.C.

2. Monte Aronson and Alvera L. Aronson, *SAS System: A Programmer's Guide*, McGraw-Hill, Inc., New York, 1990.

25
Structured Methodologies

Marvin Rubenstein

Introduction

The structured methodologies emerged in the early 1970s. This "structured revolution" came about as a result of dissatisfaction with the then prevailing narrative style of prose documentation that was used to describe system requirements. This dramatic innovation evolved in the classical way, from structured programming to structured design, and then came to rest in structured analysis.

In order to rectify the many deficiencies of the traditional narrative way of preparing requirements documents, structured methods were developed. When manual methods and early text or word processors were employed to prepare requirements specifications, there wasn't a satisfactory way to check the documents for consistency, accuracy, and completeness. Consequently, documents produced by these methods were often riddled with errors that were not apparent until implementation time.

The volume of documentation produced for large systems was often so huge that it was referred to as the "Victorian novel" by Tom DeMarco, one of the early developers of structured analysis. When generated for large to very large systems, the sheer size of the requirements document made it difficult to produce, edit, and control its production. There were times when the documents literally required two, three, or more hand trucks to deliver to the client/user.

In lieu of the "sign-off" by clients/users that was supposed to connote understanding and agreement with the document contents, it was signed off merely to get rid of it, because it was virtually impossible to read and understand a figurative mountain of verbiage in any reasonable time. Consequently, the clients/users did not really know what was going to be delivered to them until the system was installed. Quite often, systems were delivered with incorrect requirements or, even worse, gross errors of omission.

One of the most salient characteristics of the traditional method was that it took such a long time to prepare. In terms of the total percent of time devoted to requirements analysis for large to very large systems, quite often it often took up to 50 percent of the total time to develop the entire system. As a result, systems analysis in attempts to shorten the development cycle was abbreviated to the point that incomplete and omitted specifications soon became the rule instead of the exception.

English is a difficult medium to handle with precision and ease. The description of complicated processes in English requires painstaking effort and volumes of prose. It is virtually impossible at this time to machine process English prose so that intent, connotation, and implication are understood. Because "a picture is worth a thousand words," when an agreed-upon diagram is used for descriptive purposes, reams of words and paper disappear. The system diagrams (structured techniques) can be thought of in the same light as being akin to international road signs. The signs have international acceptance, so that everyone, regardless of their language, can understand them, even if in a foreign country. For example, when driving your car down a mountain road you see a road sign that is composed of a red circle with a red slash mark from northeast to southwest with a line drawing of a car going downhill with skid marks behind it in the center of the circle, you immediately sense danger, and drive slower or in a lower gear. If you had to read text, in whatever language, for everything that the sign connoted, you might be dead before you finished reading it!

Main Features Comprising a
Generic Structured Methodology

Diagrams. James Martin has written, "When several people work on a system or program, the diagrams are an essential *communication* tool. A formal diagramming technique is needed to enable the developers to interchange ideas and to make their separate components fit together with precision." Communication is the very essence of what diagramming and the structured methods are all about. Just like international Morse code, diagramming standards used in the structured methods have gained international acceptance.

Depending on the particular structured method employed, the symbols used in their diagrams vary slightly from method to method. Most methods use only a handful of symbols for their particular diagrams. This makes the method easy to learn and easy to use.

Circles are used to denote a process in one methodology, while a rectangle with rounded corners is used in another. A rectangle is used to denote an external source or destination of data in one methodology, while squares are used in another.

Functional Decomposition.   Functional decomposition, also known as *step-wise refinement,* is the process whereby the "whole" is decomposed, or broken down into its component parts. Each of the parts is then considered to be the whole and, in turn, is decomposed. The process is repeated until an agreed-upon level of granularity, or detail, is reached.

The functional decomposition technique is what gives the structured methods their power in terms of system quality improvement. Compared to the traditional methods of/analysis and design which were, in effect, merely the recording of the client user requirements and the design concepts, the structured techniques made it possible to improve system quality by an order of magnitude.

Think about this concept for a few moments. The two-dimensional description of a proposed system is only a superficial, broad, brush-stroke view of the major system concepts. This is what we used to get with traditional methods. Now, for the first time, we began to get engineering-like precision!

Here are two *Random House Dictionary* definitions of analysis:

1. "the separating of any material or abstract entity into its constituent elements (opposed to synthesis)."

2. "this process as a method of studying the nature of something or of determining its essential features and their relations."

With structured methodologies, real in-detail analysis of the system and its system components had begun to take place at a level that was hardly practiced heretofore. It was as if we were peering through a microscope and, while moving the ocular horizontally and vertically, we were able to view the entire system terrain, noting the relationship of one part to the others. Then, if we chose to, we could even move into the third dimension of depth by utilizing the higher powers of magnification to view the very essence of any single system component. Now, if this view was insufficient for our needs, higher powers of magnification could be utilized to view the structure of the structure. In a sense, it was equivalent to observing a single cell that was part of a larger body of tissue and then being able to view the very nucleus of the cell itself.

We had finally begun to understand the nature of the system beast!

Various Methodologies and Their Operating Environment(s)

Some of the Different Types of Structured Methodologies Available

In the following discussion, pluses (+) will denote advantages and minuses (–) will denote disadvantages of the various methodologies.

De Marco Structured Analysis

+ Approximately four basic symbols are used to produce the diagrams. This makes this methodology easy to learn and easy to use.

+ It is the most widely used of the structured methodologies. This attribute guarantees that a large number of practitioners have been trained and are experienced in its use.

+ The system specification has changed from a largely incomprehensible document to a straightforward graphic model.

+ With the inclusion of event analysis in later versions of structured analysis, the power of this methodology increased enormously.

– Because of its deceptive appearance of simplicity and ease of use, its many practitioners often practice it at a superficial level.

– Its diagrams are often so simplistic that they fail to convey a wealth of knowledge. This means that they are often required to be accompanied by, in some cases, generous explanatory and interpretive text.

– Because of its simplistic nature (lack of recording mechanism), it often fails to capture the richness of detail required for very complex systems. (i.e., data modeling is absent).

– In its manual non-CASE mode, when used for larger systems, so much paper can be generated that corrections and additions to the documents are extremely time-consuming and difficult to make.

Gane and Sarson (Notation)

+ Contains a richness of detail suitably employed to analyze large projects.

+ More system subtleties can be documented without supporting text than in most other structured analysis methodologies.

+ It was one of the very early methodologies to be automated in a CASE-like tool, having proved its worth over time (Stradis/Draw from McAuto).

– Because it has greater detail than some of the other structured methodologies, it is a little more difficult to learn quickly and easily.

– The users of this methodology were in the minority. Consequently, few practitioners who knew it well were available.

– Until fairly recently, it was expensive to operate on a mainframe.

Jackson Design Methodology

+ This was one of the first methodologies to recognize the importance of data structure in order to derive the processing structure.

+ Precise representations of both input and output data can lead to precise program structures.

+ The system network diagram is similar to the data-flow diagram, while the program structure chart is similar to structure chart diagrams. For those who know and understand the traditional structured techniques, the Jackson diagrams can be learned quickly.

 −   It is usually used for program and file structures and is cumbersome to use at the system level.

 −   It is used mostly in Europe, and therefore experienced users in the United States are in short supply.

 −   It is not easy to learn to use quickly, but not so difficult as to be daunting. Those who understand structured design will find it familiar.

 −   It handles database systems as if they were the same as file systems.

Warnier-Orr (Alternation Structure)

 +   Warnier-Orr diagrams can represent hierarchical data structures or reports as well as program structures.

 +   With only four basic diagramming techniques, they are easy to learn and use.

 +   One of the major benefits of Warnier-Orr diagrams is the creation of good data-structure documentation.

 −   When used at a low level of detail, Warnier-Orr diagrams can become large and difficult to read.

 −   Warnier-Orr diagrams do not show conditional logic as well as other techniques.

 −   A major problem is that the Warnier-Orr diagrams are not database-oriented. They can represent only hierarchical data structures.

Yourdon Structured Design Methodology

 +   Because it is the most widely used structured design methodology, the availability of professionals that have learned and used it is large.

 +   It represents the system graphically in terms of its "top" modules/programs down to the lowest level of detail in terms of called and caller modules/programs. This technique makes the system's program component relationships clear.

 +   The methodology is utilized in most of the major CASE tools.

 −   There is no clear bridge from structured analysis to structured design. This shortcoming negates much of the rigor obtained in analysis.

 −   Those unfamiliar with the basic background constructs of structured design (i.e., coupling and cohesion) may find the learning curve formidable.

 −   There isn't an empirical method of determining the best overall design until execution time. Transform and transaction analysis are still art-form-like.

Entity Relationship Diagrams

 +   This is one of the most excellent techniques for describing datum, data, its relationship, interrelationships, attributes, and cardinalities. It is capable of creating data model from a very high enterprise level to a detailed business-area level.

 +   It requires and has strong end-user involvement.

 +   It is independent of technology (because technology will change).

- It uses classical data administration and modeling techniques.
- Its appearance is deceptively simple. It is easy to learn, but requires much practice to do well.
- It is an iterative process, and rethinking is required in many steps. Often, the pressure to get things done quickly mitigates against this approach.
- Beginners have a tendency to put too much clutter and detail into their diagrams.

Where and When These Methodologies Can/Should Be Used

De Marco Structured Analysis.   If you are attempting to do the requirements analysis phase of a project, and the project is relatively small or relatively simple, without too many data complexities, this structured analysis technique should be used. On the other hand, if the project is large to very large, and is still relatively noncomplex, a CASE tool that employs this technique should be used. Manual methods for these kinds of projects become untenable.

Gane and Sarson (Notation).   If the proposed system is of medium size, and more than just average in complexity, with not too many serious data considerations, this structured technique should be used. Because of its capability of documenting detail in more than just an ordinary way, it will prove to be a productivity and quality boon. But beware—for the large to very large project, a CASE software product that includes this structured analysis technique should be used.

Jackson Design Methodology.   When your project is more data- than process-oriented in nature this structured analysis technique is recommended. But it should be borne in mind that, where possible, a CASE software product should be used, except for the small or simple project.

Warnier-Orr (Alternation Structure).   When a serious consideration of data is a system development goal, this structured technique should be used. But be forewarned, if the project is large or very large, a CASE software tool should be used. If not, the profusion of manually produced documentation will soon become unmanageable.

Yourdon Structured Design Methodology.   When the system project is small to almost large, and the data and process are about equally significant, this is the analysis technique that should be used. The majority of system professionals have been trained in its use; it is simple to use and simple to understand. Productivity is quite high with this approach. The leading CASE tools utilize this methodology.

Entity Relationship Diagrams.   When you want to examine the data part of data processing, entity relationship diagrams are the way to go! If you want to understand how an enterprise's data defines the enterprise, and how each datum relates to all the others and to the organization as a whole, entity relationship diagrams are your strongest techniques. With the advent of information engineering and its primary relationship on data as the driving force in system development, we now have a method for looking at data with a microscope in that we can now delineate data objects with its attributes, their relationship to each other, and the cardinalities of the defined relationships. Most respectable upper CASE tools include entity relationship diagramming within their repertoire of diagramming techniques.

How the Components of Various Structured Methodologies Interact with Some of the Automated Tools That Are Available

De Marco Structured Analysis.   Most of the modern sophisticated CASE tools include some form of structured analysis, and the De Marco structured analysis method is by far the most widely used. Usually, the method is loosely joined via the CASE encyclopedia to some type of planning module that precedes it and the design module that follows it. For the most part, the planning module is given short shrift or totally ignored, because most CASE users dive right into the analysis phase wherein structured analysis is encountered. Another major interaction is with entity relationship diagrams that are often found in the analysis modules of sophisticated CASE tools. Usually, the interaction is in the form of matrices wherein the data on one axis is related to the processes found on the other axis.

Gane and Sarson (Notation).   The CASE tools that utilize the Gane and Sarson notation employ the same interactions of the less sophisticated structured analysis methods (i.e., De Marco).

Jackson Design Methodology.   The Jackson design methodology is widely used in Europe. There is a small number of adherents in this country. The methodology is heavily weighted in favor of data analysis as the means to achieving the processing structure and, consequently, has less interaction or components than other methodologies.

Warnier-Orr (Alternation Structure).   A small percentage of structured methodology users in this country employ the Warnier-Orr methodology. Similar in nature to the Jackson design methodology, it is highly data-centered and, consequently, has little interaction with any of the other components that might be found in CASE tools.

Yourdon Structured Design Methodology.   For the most part, the Yourdon structured design methodology that can be found in sophisticated CASE tools has minimal interaction with the structured methodologies found in the same tool. It has its greatest interactions with the code-generation modules that are found in such CASE tools. The main component of structured design is the Structure Chart, wherein the processing hierarchy is depicted (which caller module calls a subordinate module), the parameters are passed between modules, and the basic processing symbols are indicated (i.e., iteration and case). The automated structured design also produces action diagrams (a procedural description of the processes) and screen and report layouts. These are then passed to the code-generation module.

Entity Relationship Diagrams.   Within the past five years, Entity Relationship Diagrams have come into prominence. The acceptance and utilization of this methodology has been accelerated with the advent of information engineering as a system development methodology, and the increasing use of relational databases. There is hardly a major CASE product that does not include entity relationship diagramming as one of its components.

The entity relationship diagram is most useful in creating the logical database design, and interacts with the construction module in order to create the physical design. Entities (business objects), the interrelationships between the entities, the cardinalities of the relationships, and those attributes that are "keys" are indicated. "Normalization" then takes place and the next phase—construction—takes place.

The other interaction is with the processes that are derived via the structured analysis methodology. A comparison between the processes and data is indicated via matrices. The matrices show which process use what data, and which data is used by each process.

Terminology

The following are the major terms and "buzz" words and/or abbreviations that are used by the technically knowledgeable.

Associative entity: An entity that exists primarily to interrelate other entity types.

Attribute: A type of characteristic or property describable in terms of a value that entities of a given type possess.

Attribute value: The number, character string, or other element of information assigned to a given attribute of a given record instance at a given time.

Balancing: The correct correspondence in leveled data-flow diagrams between a process and its decomposition in a lower-level diagram, particularly with regard to its input and output data flows.

Black-box function: A reusable module developed during the construction and implementation phase.

Black hole: A process that receives input but does not produce output.

Business event: A significant occurrence, initiated by external agents or by the passage of time, which triggers a process that must be recognized and responded to.

BSD: Business System Design. The period in the systems life cycle in which a complete and detailed specification is produced of the application system needed to support a defined area within the enterprise.

Cardinality: The number of instances of one object type associated with an instance of another type.

Cohesion: The degree of dependence of one module on another; specifically, a measure of the chance that a defect in one module will appear as a defect in the other, or the chance that a change to one module will necessitate a change to the other.

Conceptual model: The overall logical structure of a database, which is independent of any software or data storage structure.

Coupling: A measure of the strength of functional association of processing activities (normally within a single module).

CRUD matrix: A tabular representation of the relationship between processes and entities with an indication as to whether the type of involvement is created, retrieved, updated, deleted, or a combination of these.

DFD: Data-Flow Diagram. A diagram of the data flows through a set of processes or procedures. It shows the external agents that are sources or destinations of data, the activities that transform the data, and the data stores or data collections where the data is held.

Data model: A logical map of data which represents the inherent properties of the data independently of software, hardware, or machine performance considerations. The model shows data items grouped into third-normal-form records, and shows the associations among those records.

Domain: The collection of data items (fields) of the same type, in a relation (flat file).

Information engineering: An interlocking set of formal techniques in which business models, data models, and process models are built up in a comprehensive knowledge base and are used to create and maintain information systems.

Methodology: A guideline specifying how to develop an application system. A methodology describes the managerial and technical procedures that facilitates development of an application system.

Object: A component of a logical database description that represents a real-world entity about which information is stored.

Technique: A set of interrelated procedures which together describe how a task in the methodology can be accomplished.

Questions and Answers

This section entails an introductory discussion (in a question-and-answer format) of the technical areas that are covered in an interview.

"Definition" Type Questions.   This is where the interviewer asks the applicant, "What is _____ or what does _____ mean (or do)?"

Q: *What is an afferent stream?*
A: A hierarchy of afferent modules on a structure chart or, on a data-flow diagram, a string of processes whose chief function is to collect or transport data from its physical source, or to refine input data from the form provided by its source to a form suitable for the major functions of the system.

Q: *What is a balanced system?*
A: A system that is neither physically input-driven nor physically output-driven; a system in which the top modules deal with logical rather than physical data.

Q: *What is the central transform?*
A: The portion(s) of a data-flow diagram or structure chart that remains when the afferent and efferent streams have been removed; the major data-transforming functions of a system.

Q: *What is a context diagram?*
A: The top level of a leveled set of data-flow diagrams.

Q: *What is an efferent stream?*
A: A hierarchy of efferent modules on a structure chart or, on a data-flow diagram, a string of processes whose chief function is to transport or dispatch data to its physical sink, or to format output data from the form produced by the major functions of the system to a form suitable for its sink.

Q: *What does elementary data mean?*
A: A data type that is not decomposed into other items of data.

Q: *What does fan-in mean?*
A: The number of immediate superordinates of a module.

Q: *What does fan-out mean?*
A: The number of immediate subordinates of a module.

Q: *What is a functional primitive?*
A: A process on a data-flow diagram that is not further decomposed on a lower level; a bottom-level bubble.

Q: *What does logical cohesion mean?*
A: A grouping of activities based on a real or imagined similarity of implementation (without regard to data flow, order, or time of execution).

Q: *What is a minispecification?*

A: A statement of the purpose and procedure that govern the transformation of input data flow(s) into output data flow(s) for a given functional primitive.

Q: *What is transaction analysis?*

A: A design strategy by which the structure of a system is derived from a study of the transactions that the system comprises.

Q: *What is transform analysis?*

A: A design strategy in which the structure of a system is derived from a study of the flow of data through a system and of the transformations to that data.

Q: *What does candidate key mean?*

A: A key that uniquely identifies normalized record instances of a given type.

Q: *What does normalization do?*

A: It simplifies more complex data structures according to E. F. Codd's rules, which are designed to produce simpler, more stable structures.

Q: *What is meant by plex structure?*

A: A typical "plex" structure is a relationship between records (or other groupings) in which a child record can have more than one parent record.

Q: *What does a prototype do?*

A: A prototype is a representation of the system which simulates the main user interfaces so that users can understand and critique the system.

Q: *What is relational algebra?*

A: A language providing a set of operators for manipulating relations. These include "project," "join," and "search" operators.

Q: *What is meant by schema?*

A: A map of the overall logical structure of a database. Contrast with data model. A schema consists of DDL (Data Description Language) entries and is a complete description of the area, set occurrences, record occurrences, and associated data items and data aggregates as they exist in the database (CODASYL).

Q: *What is a strategic information systems plan?*

A: A plan that sets out the overall objectives for information systems development over a three- to five-year period.

"Problem Solving" Type Questions.   With this type of question the interviewee describes a situation (either verbally or by means of an illustration) that has happened or something that has to be done—with the question being either "What would you do to solve the problem?" or "What would you do to achieve this objective?"

Q: *What would you do to achieve a system design via central transform analysis?*

A: Transform analysis is composed of the following five steps:

1. Drawing a DFD of a transaction type
2. Finding the central functions of the DFD
   - Strip of the afferent (input) and efferent (output) branches of the DFD
   - That/those process(es) (known as the central transform) that convert input to output
3. Converting the DFD into a rough-cut structure chart
4. Refining the structure chart by means of Structured Design criteria
5. Verifying that the final structure chart meets the requirements of the original DFD

Q: *What would you do to achieve partioning of the context diagram?*

A: Briefly, there are four steps in this procedure:

1. Identify the events to which the existing system responds.
2. For each event, identify the activities, data flows, and data stores that make up the system's entire immediate response to the event.
3. Depict the set of activity and memory fragments for each event on a separate data-flow diagram.
4. Draw (or create) an upper-level data-flow diagram on which each response to an event—each essential activity—is represented by a single process. If there are too many essential activities to put on one data-flow diagram, create even higher-level DFDs to group essential activities that respond to related events.

Q: *What would you do to make certain that* each one *of your data items is used by at least one process?*

A: Using CASE tools (or manually), build a matrix. On one axis the data are indicated, while on the other the processes are shown. Each data item, be they in rows or columns, should have at least one process (indicated by a check mark or asterisk) that uses it.

Q: *Your data-flow diagram requires that an output data flow of a process is received by two different successor processes at different points in time. What would you do to achieve this objective?*

   (Note that data-flow diagrams do not imply sequence! As drawn, the implication is that all of the processes are being executed simultaneously, as if many small computers were operating via a distributed network.)

A: The specific answer to this question is: When creating DFDs manually, split the data flow by means of bifurcation, which will allow you to indicate two destination points. When using a CASE tool, a junction is used. This is a point at which a data flow ends in a small darkened circle and then continues on to two different destination points.

Q: *Your data-flow diagram includes 44 different transaction types. What would they do to achieve a structured design?*

A: Via transaction analysis, which is the technique of identifying the transaction types of a system, use them as the units of design. After identifying the transactions, each one of them is designed separately by means of transform analysis. You can identify transaction types on the essential model of the system by studying the discrete event types that drive the system. If the essential model has been created through a technique such as event partitioning, then the transaction types of the systems will be clearly separated and clearly identified.

Q: *On your Entity Relationship Diagram (ERD), you have an entity type named "creature." You also have entities named "animal," "fish," and "bird." Each of these entities have different associations to other entity types. What would you do to indicate all these relationships on your ERD?*

A: You should divide these entity types into *entity subtypes* if they have associations to other entity types. If, on the other hand, we store essentially the same information about animals, fish, and birds, you should regard these three categories as merely attribute values of the entity type *creature*.

Q: *What is the objective of leaving the data flow that enters or leaves a file sometimes unnamed?*

A: The objective of leaving such a data flow unnamed is to indicate that not much information can be gleaned from a data flow—that the data flow has essentially the same name and contents as the data store (i.e., data store = customer file and data flow = customer record). The only time that annotating a reference to a file would tell you anything extra is when the data flow carries only part of a record from the file (i.e., data store = customer file and data flow = customer phone number).

Q: *Describe entity life-cycle analysis.*

A: Entity life-cycle analysis is analyzing each entity in terms of where and the conditions under which it is created: where/how the entity is updated; where/when it is shared; and when/where the entity is removed from the system.

Q: *What is the objective of performing entity life-cycle analysis when you have finished the ERD?*

A: It is a useful quality check to select about 10 of the most important entities and consider their life cycles. This may indicate missing attributes, relationships, entities, and both events and business functions that act on these entities.

Q: *How would you determine the measure of strength between one module and another in order to improve its coupling relationship?*

A: Coupling is a measure of the strength of interconnection between one module and another. "Tight" coupling occurs when many interconnections exist between modules. This makes it difficult to modify the module with a degree of certainty that ensures that nothing has been disturbed and that the module will execute correctly. With "loose" coupling, just a few or even one interconnection is present. Modifications are therefore simpler to achieve. Ascertaining the number of interconnections and reducing them, if possible, is the objective.

Q: *The objective of building entity-relationship diagrams and data models is to create a description of the semantics of data that reflects the actual enterprise and its informational requirements. The task of the data modeler is to capture reality and to communicate it accurately. Describe how you would use one of the techniques to accomplish this objective.*

A: Here is one suggested technique. Upon arriving at a first-draft ERD, the users should be involved in a structured *walk-through* with the data modeler. This will help assure the data modeler that the entities, relationships, and cardinalities are complete, accurate, and consistent.

The next step would be to "play relational database" by manually navigating through the relationships in an SQL-like fashion in order to determine that all the paths represented by the relationships are present and will satisfy the user's requirements.

Q: *Your ERD data is extremely complicated with many-to-many relationships. What would you do to simplify the data represented on the ERD?*

A: Employ the normalization technique.

1. *Unnormalized data.* (Records with repeating groups.) Decompose all nonflat data structures into two-dimensional records.

2. *First normal form.* (Records with no repeating groups.) For records whose keys have more than one data item, ensure that all other data items are dependent on the whole key. Split the records, if necessary, to achieve this.

3. *Second normal form.* (All nonkey data items fully functional dependent on the primary key.) Remove all transitive dependencies, splitting the record, if necessary, to achieve this.

4. *Third normal form.* (All nonkey data items fully functionally dependent on the primary key and independent of each other.) Remove all conditional dependencies, splitting the record, if necessary, to achieve this.

Q: *During analysis, the objective is to eliminate identical functions wherever possible. What would you do to achieve this objective?*

A: Eliminate identical functions wherever possible by overlapping, making them more generic, or recognizing that they were not identical in the first place. When this is not practical, one or more common functions may be created, each of which is a slave to (copy of) a master function. Only the master function may then be further described, while the functions can appear in different parts of the function hierarchy, as required.

Q: *A "black box" is a system (or, equivalently, a component) with known inputs, known outputs, and generally, a known transformation, but with unknown (or irrelevant) contents. The box is black—we cannot see inside of it. Explain why you would want to create black boxes.*

A: A true black box is a system which can be fully exploited without knowledge of what is inside of it. Given a specific input, it will always produce a specific output. To the average driver, an automobile is a virtual black box transforming fuel, directional, accelerative, and decelerative inputs into motion at the desired speed in the desired direction. This is fortunate, for if we needed to know the involved electromagnetic, mechanical, hydraulic, and other techniques employed in these systems in order to make use of them, we would be greatly inconvenienced, if not paralyzed. When we deal with nonblack boxes, and we desire to make even the smallest change, we must understand the innermost workings of the logic, which takes resources and time.

Q: *Your objective is to indicate all the net inputs and outputs of a system. How would you achieve this objective?*

A: Create a *context diagram!* This is a *top-level* diagram of a leveled DFD set— Data-Flow Diagram that portrays all the net inputs and outputs of a system, but shows no decomposition.

Q: *What would you do to achieve an improved degree of functional relatedness of processing elements within a single module?*

A: There are seven levels of cohesion from good to bad: functional, sequential, communicational, procedural, temporal, logical, and coincidental. An examination of the type of cohesion is required in order to determine its place on the scale of good to bad values. If it can be raised to a higher level of cohesion on the scale of values, its modifiability, understandability, and its overall effect on system maintainability will be improved.

Q: *You would like to create a module that is both subordinate and/or superordinate to itself. Can this be accomplished: yes or no? Explain how you would or would not accomplish this objective.*

A: Yes! This objective can be accomplished by creating a recursive module (a module that calls itself or calls one of its superordinates) that has this property.

Q: *Your objective is to create modules with a high degree of functional cohesion. Would you be able to achieve your objective if there is a function-interface inconsistency in a module that performs the function "get master record" and where one of the output parameters is an error code defined as "no record found"?*

A: Absolutely not! The error code is pertinent to the module's function.

Q: *You want to access specific named columns only. What would you do to achieve this objective?*

A: A "view" would be created so that a subset of the database is accessed as if it were a table. The view may be restricted to named columns, be restricted to specific rows, change column names, derive new columns, and give access to a combination of related tables and/or views.

Q: *Your objective is to create an entity relationship diagram via bottom-up analysis. Explain how your objective can be achieved.*

A: Bottom-up analysis is often perceived as looking at the *current* data in an organization and modeling it. This can be done by analysts from the data processing department and does not involve analysis of future data needs, which is more difficult to acquire. The approach to take is top-down planning, which is also known as "strategic" planning. Strategic planning is intended to identify the data resources which the enterprise needs to support its future evolution. It is top-down design that creates an entity relationship diagram which gives an overview of the data entities that the organization should work with, not bottom-up analysis.

Q: *Describe what you might do to achieve the desired objective of creating a nonredundant data model.*

A: There is one and only one nonredundant model of a given collection of data. This is called the *canonical model*—the simplest standard model. Canonical synthesis is the technique that takes any number of user views of data and combines them into a minimal set of canonical records with the requisite links between records. Done manually, the process is laborious and time-consuming, but done by computer, it is easy and accurate. The input to the process must correctly identify the associations among data items in each user's view.

References

1. Richard Barker, *CASE*Method-Entity Relationship Modelling*.

2. Tom De Marco, *Structured Analysis and System Specification*, Yourdon, Inc., New York, 1978.

3. Chris Gane, Trish Sarson, *Structured Systems Analysis: Tools and Techniques*, Prentice-Hall, Inc., Englewood Cliffs, N.J., 1979.

4. M. A. Jackson, *Principles of Program Design*, Academic Press, New York, 1975.

5. Robert Keller, *The Practice of Structured Analysis—Exploding Myths*, Yourdon Press, New York, 1983.

6. James Martin, *Recommended Diagramming Standards for Analysts & Programmers— A Basis for Automation*, Prentice-Hall, Inc., Englewood Cliffs, N.J., 1987.

7. James Martin, *Information Engineering—Planning & Analysis—Book II*, Prentice-Hall, Inc., Englewood Cliffs, N.J., 1990.

8. James Martin, Carma McClure, *Structured Techniques for Computing*, Prentice-Hall, Inc., Englewood Cliffs, N.J., 1985.

9. Stephen M. McMenamin, John F. Palmer, *Essential Systems Analysis*, Yourdon Press, New York, 1984.

10. Meilir Page-Jones, *The Practical Guide to Structured Systems Design*, Yourdon Press, Englewood Cliffs, N.J., 1988.

11. Glenford J. Myers, *Composite Structured Design*, Van Nostrand Reinhold, New York, 1978.

12. Michael Rothstein, Burt Rosner, Michael Senatore, and David Mulligan, *Structured Analysis and Design for the Case User*, McGraw-Hill, 1993.

13. Wayne P. Stevens, *Using Structured Design*, John Wiley & Sons, New York, 1981.

14. Paul T. Ward, Stephen J. Mellor, *Structured Development for Real-Time Systems*, Yourdon Press, Englewood Cliffs, N.J., 1986.

15. K. Wigander, A. Svensson, L. Schoug, A. Rydin, C. Dahlgren, *Structured Analysis and Design of Information Systems*, McGraw-Hill Book Company, New York, 1984.

16. Edward Yourdon, Larry L. Constantine, *Structured Design—Fundamentals of a Discipline of Computer Program and Systems Design*, Prentice-Hall, Inc., Englewood Cliffs, N.J., 1979.

17. Yourdon, Inc. (Subsidiary of DeVry), *Structured Analysis Workshop*, "Defining Requirements for Complex Systems," Yourdon, Inc., New York.

26

CASE Fundamentals

Burt Rosner

Introduction

One of the effects of the personnel computer explosion of the 1980s was the realization that theories and concepts developed regarding system development in the 1960s and 1970s could now be bundled into software packages. System development work that was considered to be laborious, if not impossible, to perform, let alone manage, started to look doable via the use of a PC. Many companies incorporated CASE tools into their work environments and, although a company may have chosen a specific CASE tool, a primary concern was knowing what skills were needed by their staff in order to use the CASE tools effectively.

CASE has taken its rightful place in the Systems Development Life Cycle (SDLC). CASE has matured, similar to the way code generators have matured, not as an end in themselves, but as part of a suite of tools needed to perform systems analysis and design as well as to act as an integrity check in the early phases of development. Studies have shown that it cost from 10 to 100 times more to "correct" design flaws during the last stages of development than if they were caught in the early stages. CASE is especially useful in identifying these types of design flaws long before they become apparent in the code and testing of the system. CASE has proven, when used appropriately, to be cost effective over the long term of a systems life.

This chapter's questions and answers are focused on helping a person discuss, during a job interview, the fundamental features, concepts, techniques, and procedures of CASE and what is needed to ensure their success during their introduction, installation, and operation.

Questions and Answers

Q: *What is and is not CASE?*

A: CASE (Computer-Aided Software Engineering) is a computerized tool used to perform *analysis* and *design,* preferably for new systems. A CASE tool is not a code generator. Although a CASE tool can have or be a bridge to a code generator.

Q: *To which areas will a CASE tool allow you to link your systems work?*

A: A CASE tool allows you to link:

- Business strategies
- User requirements
- System prototypes
- Data model diagrams
- Data flows
- System flows
- Construction
- Testing
- Quality assurance
- To other products

Q: *How can CASE tools help perform business strategy?*

A: CASE tools have features that allow efficient organization of economic, industrial, and business decision information (matrices). These matrices can be linked to systems and give users a concise view as to the impact of their decisions and the amount of involvement and resources required to meet stated objectives.

Q: *What prototyping features should be included in a CASE tool?*

A: Screen and report formatting features linked to data and processes should be part of a CASE tool. Theoretical load balancing and volume testing features can also be of use during prototyping sessions.

Q: *What data model methodologies are compatible with currently available CASE tools?*

A: Chen, Yourdon, Gane and Sarson, and Martin are some of the more popular.

Q: *What data modeling features should be included in a CASE tool?*

A: A CASE tool should have the ability to represent cardinality, entities, associative and characteristic entities, along with their attributes (elements). In addition, they should have the ability to perform normalization automatically, create physical records, and be able to link data to processes.

Q: *What process modeling features should be included in a CASE tool?*

A: A CASE tool should have the ability to represent processes, interfaces that are external to the system, data storage areas, and lines of flow.

Q: *How can the process modeling features of a CASE tool be used?*
A: Process modeling features are used to construct data-flow diagrams. In addition, state transition diagrams can also be used to represent the state of an entity and event objects. Process hierarchy diagrams are also used to represent the flow of processes.

Q: *What limitations (if any) should the user be aware of?*
A: Data-flow diagrams, for example, do not represent time constraints. Therefore, additional object representation in the way of control flows must be established, when required. State transition diagrams do not represent external inputs or outputs from the system, and hierarchy diagrams do not show sequence of events.

Q: *How are CASE tools classified?*
A: CASE tools are usually categorized as follows:

Front-end CASE tools	Focus the attention of systems personnel on developing user requirements and sequence of processes in a conceptual environment.
Back-end CASE tools	Focus the attention of the systems personnel on developing physical design of data and processes.
ICASE tools	Integrated CASE combines the front-end and back-end activities into one tool and is linked to a code generator.

Q: *What role does a methodology play when using a CASE tool?*
A: A methodology is the vehicle that guides all work the CASE tool must perform. If you do not have a methodology, it would be the same as driving a car without having a specific destination in mind.

Q: *What are the predominant methodologies used in developing systems?*
A: Structured Analysis and Design and Information Engineering.

Q: *What would you consider the most important aspect of a CASE tool?*
A: Its automation and customization. Besides storing analysis and design information, a CASE tool must be able to be modified (or adjusted) to reflect the unique methodology employed by the firm's system area. In addition, a CASE tool must be able to allow the user to change relationships of the objects within the tool.

Q: *What does it take to introduce a CASE tool into the development environment?*
A: A firm would need in place a realistic methodology that is being correctly used and a "complete" training program. The training program would be used to reinforce the methodology and should include the following subject areas:
- PC familiarization
- Business analysis

- Data modeling concepts
- Design concepts
- Mainframe environment
- Project management techniques

Q: *What is meta data?*

A: Meta data is information about data. For example, a customer has an address. You don't know the exact customer or address, but you do know that if you have a customer, you will also need to have an address.

Q: *How is a meta data model used?*

A: A meta data model is used to show the relationship of data to other data. For example, a road map would be considered a meta data model of the road system within a specific geographical location.

Q: *What is the predominant feature of a CASE tool?*

A: Its repository. Navigating through the CASE tool's repository and identifying the many different ways information can be viewed will give you an idea of what the tool can, or cannot, do.

Q: *What type of technology is required to make CASE effective in your area?*

A: A CASE tool is not technology-reliant. It is more important to know what information is related and whether that information is needed to support the systems methodology. A simple drawing software package and a word processor could be used if relationships to other systems are not required.

Q: *What type of hardware/software would a company need to support CASE activities?*

A: A generic environment for using CASE would include:

1. *A Local Area Network (LAN).* The LAN would be used to centralize the CASE repository and allow communications between work groups. Depending on the CASE tool, a mainframe link may also be necessary.
2. *PCs.* Also known as *workstations,* their exact power would depend on the type of software (CASE tool) being used and how much information each workstation is expected to hold.
3. *Security software.* This would restrict the access of personnel to sensitive information and code.
4. *On-line help.* Most software packages have their own help files, but you will also need to have an on-line methodology and standards help facility available.

Q: *What types of organizations will you need to support a CASE tool?*

A: 1. A methodology and standards group to centralize and procedures and perform consulting activities
2. A technical support group to assist developers—basically an in-house hot line for the CASE tool, LAN, Mainframe, and peripherals, (e.g., Printers)
3. A data resource management group to assist in developing data models and maintain the repository

Q: *How would you measure the success of a CASE tool?*

A: Measurement guidelines for developing systems will need to be created "on-site." Each company needs to create their own measurements based on the "new" way systems will be developed versus the "old" way. This would require the documentation of time, resources used, and complexity of systems being developed.

Q: *If you were to establish a CASE base development environment, what would you do first, second . . . ?*

A: 1. First, obtain strong executive management support. Not simply a "yes go ahead and do it" support, but a well-documented intent of what is expected and what upper management will do to support the effort.

   2. Second, study the existing systems environment, focusing on how actual work is being performed. By listening to the people and including their concerns, you should be able to get their buy-in and reduce the "culture shock" of introducing a CASE tool.

   3. Third, develop a training package. The training would include learning the concepts behind CASE and the use of the CASE tool purchased.

   4. Fourth, create support groups to act as in-house hot-line technical and methodology consultants.

   5. Fifth, select project(s) that will use the selected CASE tool.

   6. Sixth, monitor the projects closely to adjust training and methodology practices and standards.

   7. Seventh, continue to deploy CASE tools to additional project development efforts.

Q: *What is a repository?*

A: A repository is a facility provided for storing and linking objects—objects being business units, processes, and data items along with their attributes.

Q: *What is a data dictionary?*

A: A data dictionary is a facility provided for storing and linking data items and their descriptions, along with other field-related information.

Q: *What is a database?*

A: A database is a grouping of fields and their values.

Q: *What is the difference between logical and physical analysis/design?*

A: Logical analysis/design focuses on *what* a system is expected to perform. Physical analysis/design focuses on *how* a system will do it.

Q: *What techniques should be introduced when deploying CASE tools?*

A: Data-modeling techniques, structured analysis techniques, information engineering techniques, human factors engineering, and logical concepts.

Q: *What basic skills does a person using a CASE tool need?*

A: Written, oral expression, and analytical skills.

Q: *How many years of experience do you feel a person needs to be proficient with a CASE tool?*

A: An average person, with the aptitude and interest, should require between six months and a year of working with (or having access to) a senior person in order to be proficient with a CASE tool.

Q: *What is Integrated Computer-Aided Software Engineering (ICASE)?*

A: ICASE is the combination of a front-end CASE tool linked to a code generator, prototyping tool, and a project management tool.

Q: *What is CUA?*

A: CUA is a set of standards for formatting terminal-screen (panel) outputs. CUA standards cover the placement of specific types of data characteristics on terminal and workstation screens to increase consistency and intuitiveness. The title on the screen, for example, will always be in the center on the top line using both upper- and lowercase letters; function keys will be displayed on the last line of the screen, etc.

Q: *What basic types of information must be captured in a CASE tool?*

A: Entity relationships, logical process flows, and linkages between entities and processes.

Q: *What skill(s) would you look for in a person who works with CASE tools?*

A: Analytical ability. The person should be able to express and document an abstract idea and communicate it to others.

Q: *Will a CASE tool reduce the time it takes to develop a system?*

A: Usually, no. CASE will allow you to focus your attention on the analysis and design of a system, thus reducing the time to construct and implement it.

Q: *Does CASE actually increase the quality of the system developed?*

A: People are responsible for quality. CASE is a tool that will *aid* a person in achieving that goal. Another way of asking the question would be: Do expensive carpenter tools increase the quality of a cabinet?

Q: *How would you select a CASE tool?*

A: By what is needed to perform the work required in conjunction with the methodology that is (or will be) used along with the CASE tool.

Q: *Can you develop a system without the use of a CASE tool?*

A: Yes, but you run the risk of not having enough time to perform the analysis required for the long-term impact of the system. You also don't have the advantages of the automated features provided by CASE. In addition, you may run the risk of inconsistencies developed during analysis coming to light during coding and testing (rather than during analysis)—thus increasing development costs.

Q: *Do you think that CASE has a future or is it just a passing phase?*

A: CASE is an integral part of systems development. The concepts of performing the work using CASE allows the automation of many previously performed manual procedures.

Q: *What is the difference between structured analysis and information engineering?*

A: Structured analysis follows a linear approach of developing a system and is usually used to develop a single-purpose system. Information engineering follows a top-down approach of developing a corporatewide data processing environment. This is used to integrate business objectives to individual business unit requirements.

Q: *Of the following eight phases of a Systems Development Life Cycle (SDLC)—proposal, requirements, definition, analysis, design, construction, test, and implementation—which phases are aided by purchasing a CASE tool?*

A: Definition, analysis, and design are the phases of an SDLC which are aided by CASE.

Q: *What is the advantage of purchasing a graphics-based CASE tool rather than a character-based CASE tool?*

A: Graphics-based CASE tools are not restricted by the number of ASCII characters available or screen size.

Q: *What are some additional advantages of CASE?*

A: CASE makes structured techniques practical, enforces the methodology, allows the capture and link of required information electronically, moves prototyping closer to the analysis phase of development, and enables the possibility of reusing existing processes.

Q: *Name some additional capabilities and potential capabilities of CASE tools?*

A: Common interfaces to users; data transfer between CASE tools; and system development phase integration, centralization, sharing, and security of project data.

Q: *Name one type of prototyping that CASE tools provide the developer?*

A: On-line user interaction.

Q: *What is the main advantage of performing on-line prototyping with a CASE tool?*

A: Screens and reports can be developed for users based on direct (real-time) input from the users. Output formats can be captured and linked to processes that will support their creation.

Q: *What is the main advantage of performing batch prototyping with a CASE tool?*

A: Processes can be drawn, documented, and designed for maximum efficiency, preparing them for the construction phase of development.

Q: *What are some of the types of diagrams, within a CASE tool, that can be used to define real-time systems?*

A: Control flow diagrams, state transition diagrams, transformation graphs, and state event matrices.

Q: *What type of information does a hierarchical diagram represent?*
A: A hierarchical diagram shows the relationship between program modules and data.

Q: *What is the difference between a hierarchical diagram and a structure chart?*
A: None; they are two names for the same thing.

Q: *What do action diagrams consist of?*
A: Pseudo or structured English text that represents the detail logic of a program without using a specific programming language.

Q: *What type of information does a data-flow diagram represent?*
A: A data-flow diagram shows the logical (conceptual) relationship between processes, data, external entities, and data storage areas.

Q: *Of the following—DeMarco, Gane-Sarson, Yuordon, Jackson, Orr, and Martin—who is most closely associated with Information Engineering?*
A: James Martin.

Q: *What is the most significant impact of introducing CASE into the work area?*
A: The most significant impact of CASE is the shift of focus when developing systems: from the construction phase to the analysis and design phases of the SDLC.

27

Artificial Intelligence/ Expert Systems

Joseph S. Rubenfeld and Jeffrey O. Milman

Introduction

Artificial Intelligence (AI) is a branch of computer science devoted to making machines exhibit intelligent behavior (as opposed to dumb machines). Conventional computer programs typically make use primarily of only the computational and storage and retrieval facilities of a computer. Business applications such as accounting and word processing accept data, massage it, store it, and report on it. AI systems, however, are primarily directed to make use of the logical facilities of a computer, permitting the computer to "make decisions." AI systems basically simulate various aspects of intelligence on a computer. They involve advanced programming, often dealing with extremely difficult programming problems and with levels of complexity which far exceed the limits for conventional systems.

Artificial intelligence systems include:

- *Natural language recognition*—Conversing via English sentences
- *Speech recognition*—Recognizing spoken words
- *Machine vision*—Recognizing scenes through a TV camera
- *Machine learning*—Getting smarter automatically through experience
- *Robotics*—Moving through space and manipulating objects
- *Expert systems*—Making decisions by applying rules

While all of the these subfields have now produced commercially valuable results in real-world applications, this chapter will concentrate on the subfield known as "expert systems"—i.e., those systems that have "knowledge" of some domain and can make decisions within that domain in the following capacities:

- *Expert clone.*   Makes decisions or gives advice in place of a human expert.
- *Expert assistant.*   Helps the expert make decisions.
- *Autonomous.*   System acts on its own in response to one or more streams of inputs, often from sensors and often in real time.
- *Self-learning.*   The system modifies its own behavior based on its experience.

There are several dozen commercial expert system development environments on the market.

The Interview

The technical areas covered in interviews include a familiarity with the concepts of expert systems development, heuristic programming, and knowledge engineering. Interviewers usually are looking to see if you are articulate, accurate, and exhibit creativity, problem-solving ability, flexibility, good listening skills, advanced programming skills, tact, and (often) a sense of humor.

Questions and Answers

Q: *What is the difference between expert systems and knowledge-based systems?*
A: Although often used interchangeably, knowledge-based are a broad class of systems that includes expert systems.

Q: *Name some of the functions served by expert systems.*
A: Expert systems serve the following intellectual functions:
- Input (information collection, monitoring, selection)
- Analysis (interpreting information and diagnosis)
- Creation (design, synthesis, planning, scheduling)
- Implementation (dispatching, process control)
- Evaluation (testing, measuring)

Q: *In what important applications are expert systems having a major impact?*
A: Expert systems are having a major impact in the following applications areas:
1. Allocating gates at airports to incoming planes under quickly varying conditions of weather and connecting traffic delays
2. Scheduling personnel in hospitals among shifts, patient loads, and specialties—taking into account nursing preferences, training, unexpected absences, and overtime budgeting constraints

3. Managing revenue yield in airlines and hotels
4. Managing information overload in situations such as those occurring in power stations
5. Prescreening large amounts of incoming data, making decisions where applicable, and recommending suggested remedial action(s)

Q: *In what other areas/applications are expert systems expected to have a large impact in the near future?*
A: Expert systems are expected to have the largest impact in the near future in the following applications areas:

1. Real-time plant operation and control, particularly in the chemical and oil industry.
2. On-board and portable maintenance and repair expert systems to be shipped with every major machine or equipment such as newspaper printing presses, numerical milling machines, and large commercial copying machines.
3. Parsing electronic messages for priority, emergency announcements and distribution. The Coast Guard already utilizes such a system to analyze emergency radio calls from vessels in trouble.

Q: *Almost all specialized languages for building expert systems which were developed in the United States are of a type known as the "MYCIN paradigm." What does this mean?*
A: Developed at Stanford University in the early 1970s, the MYCIN system became an expert at diagnosing certain blood diseases. The key concepts of the MYCIN paradigm include the opportunistic application of production rules to a set of facts in a work space.

Q: *Why are expert system development environments called* shells?
A: Because when the domain-specific knowledge is removed, what remains is an "empty shell."

Q: *What is the difference between an expert system shell and a UNIX shell?*
A: An expert system shell is a full-development environment for building expert systems. It contains an inference engine, debugging facilities, a user interface, and other facilities. It is a very high level language for representing knowledge and decision-making processes. UNIX shell programs are akin to what other operating systems call *batch files* or JCL.

Q: *When are goal-driven expert systems most appropriate?*
A: Goal-driven expert systems are most appropriate when the expert system must be able to justify its decisions (such as in a medical advisory system) when the number of outcomes is relatively limited and when large numbers of outcomes require the expert system to search each goal in the knowledge base.

Q: *When are data-driven expert systems most appropriate?*

A: Data-driven expert systems are most appropriate when it is not necessary to compare a number of competing solutions, and problems permit large numbers of potential outcomes.

Q: *When is a mixture of goal-driven and data-driven techniques most appropriate in an expert system?*

A: A mixture of goal-driven and data-driven techniques is most appropriate for complex problems such as speech recognition. The goal-directed segment hypothesizes whether certain syllables are represented within the isolated phonemes. The outcomes have been limited sufficiently by the data-driven segment for the goal-directed segment to effectively search the outcome space for correctness.

Q: *How many experts should a knowledge engineer interview to build an expert system?*

A: Some feel that only a single expert should be used because of the extra time and difficulty involved in reconciling differences of opinion that are bound to arise when multiple experts are consulted. Others feel that fresh approaches and broader coverage of the subject area outweigh the added difficulties.

Q: *What part does knowledge acquisition play in expert systems development?*

A: Knowledge acquisition is considered the bottleneck of expert systems development. It is the most time-consuming, the most critical, and the most error-prone of all the development steps.

Q: *What are some of the most important techniques of knowledge acquisition for building the knowledge base of an expert system?*

A: One technique is to ask copious questions about specific situations rather than general questions. A second technique is to use situation comparison. A third technique is to set up a "straw man" and have the expert "shoot him down" (i.e., the knowledge engineer proposes a solution to a problem and the expert explains why the solution is deficient).

Q: *What is the importance of designing rules that are opportunistic?*

A: One of the key concepts of rule-based programming is that of allowing rules to interact opportunistically (i.e., each rule is a stand-alone unit of information which "watches" for an opportunity to express itself as changes are made to the list of facts and objects in the work space).

Q: *What is the main advantage/benefit of expert systems technology?*

A: The main advantage/benefit of expert systems technology for companies is that expert systems, once developed, capture the expertise and provide advice indefinitely.

Q: *What are the disadvantages of expert systems?*

A: The main disadvantage of expert systems is that they tend to be expensive to develop. In addition, they require frequent maintenance to keep their expertise current.

Q: *When are expert systems absolutely not advised?*

A: Expert systems are absolutely not advised when knowledge about the problem is readily available in algorithmic form and conventional techniques are proven to satisfactorily and efficiently solve the problem.

Q: *Name an important beneficial outcome of induction expert systems.*

A: One of the most important beneficial outcomes of induction expert systems is the distillation of effective rules to the lowest possible number in a given situation. The ID3 algorithm has been demonstrated in real-world applications to reduce the number of commonly recommended tests. For example, in the diagnosis of heart attack, thyroid disease, soybean disease, and electronic bench testing, a number of tests were eliminated by ID3 *with better predictive results.* In many real-world applications, the number of diagnostic tests grows through caution (e.g., doctors order every possible blood test to prevent a lawsuit) and technology (use a new test if it is available). The new test results overlap with the old and, in many cases, simply add confusion rather than enlightenment. More tests may introduce more conflicting outcomes.

Inductive expert systems, which use information theory to prune decision trees by rejecting redundant information values, seek the smallest number of rules to accurately classify each recorded outcome. Induction systems are good for quick and dirty prototypes.

Q: *Describe some impressive successes of induction expert systems.*

A: Induction expert systems have uncovered new minimal chess end-game solutions undiscovered by grand masters throughout history. Westinghouse saved several million dollars by using an induction expert system to determine the correct settings among 30 parameters in six processes necessary to produce uranium dioxide fuel pellets from uranium hexafloride gas. These parameters included temperatures, pressures, and flow rates. Years of experience had still not taught the process engineers how to maintain consistently high yield. There were simply too many variables to control, and the hazards of nuclear fuel prevented careful, painstaking, parameter-by-parameter experimentation to determine exactly which ones mattered most. The induction expert system isolated the exact number of parameters and their settings, which affected the yield and discarded the rest, resulting in an immediate improvement of yield, consistency, and control confidence.

Q: *List several advantages of induction technology for expert systems.*

A: The following are advantages of induction technology for expert systems.

- Discovers rules from examples
- Avoids knowledge-acquisition problems
- Can produce new knowledge
- Can uncover critical decision factors
- Can eliminate unnecessary decision factors

Q: *List several disadvantages of induction technology for expert systems.*

A: The following are possible disadvantages of induction technology for expert systems.

- Difficult to choose factors to consider
- Difficult to understand complex rules
- Can find spurious relations
- Difficult to get complete historical decision data
- Requires both positive examples and negative examples

Q: *Describe the concept of database mining.*

A: Database mining refers to the use of AI techniques to examine the contents of a large database or several databases in order to discover significant patterns or relationships among the data. An expert system can constantly monitor a database and reveal valuable information contained within it that would escape notice by human information workers due to the overwhelming volume. The expert system can either make real-time decisions, such as buy and sell decisions in a trading system monitoring price fluctuations, or report its findings for human evaluation.

Q: *Why is the separation of knowledge from the general reasoning or inference mechanism in an expert system so powerful?*

A: The separation of knowledge from the general reasoning or inference mechanism in an expert system is very powerful because, with the addition of often just a few rules into the knowledge base, a running, if incomplete, system is available at a very early stage of development. Nothing earns an expert system developer more attention and support for a project than a demonstrable system to touch, feel, and improve.

Q: *What is the difference between forward chaining and backward chaining?*

A: Forward chaining is an inference technique which fires rules whose conditions are satisfied by executing the action part of the rule. The process moves forward from a set of facts to any conclusions that can be drawn. Backward chaining starts from a goal that is to be established. It fires rules "backward" by finding which rules when fired would establish the current goal or subgoal. It then adds the conditional part of those rules to the list of subgoals to be established. The process moves backward from a goal hypothesis to find if all the facts necessary to support the goal hypothesis are known.

Q: *When would you use forward chaining and when would you use backward chaining in an expert system?*

A: Forward chaining is used when any of a large number of conclusions can be reached. The facts are examined to see where they will lead with no particular direction favored over others. Backward chaining is used when only one or a few conclusions are expected. Backward chaining is goal-directed and therefore far more efficient than forward chaining in these types of searches. Backward chaining, because it is goal-directed, often leads to a more intelligent and natural set of inquiries when conducting a dialogue with a user.

Q: *What do rule-based expert systems lack that domain experts do not?*
A: Rule-based expert systems lack:

1. The ability to look at a problem from different perspectives
2. The ability to reason on several levels simultaneously
3. The ability to break their own rules when necessary
4. The ability to understand the reasoning behind the rules
5. Common sense

Q: *What are heuristics? How are they used in expert systems? Distinguish* heuristic *from* algorithm.
A: Heuristics are tricks of the trade or rules of thumb that make problem solving faster, although sometimes at the expense of guaranteeing the most efficient solution. In expert systems, heuristics can obviate the need for exhaustive searches by eliminating certain search paths based on various information. An algorithm is a list of steps for solving a problem. An algorithmic solution is usually guaranteed to find a solution, although not necessarily in a reasonable amount of time.

Q: *Give an example of the use of heuristics.*
A: Estimating (as in solving a problem in division or square roots) is a good example of the everyday use of heuristics. Sampling in surveys is a heuristic to determine public opinion about some issue.

Q: *Two languages widely used in artificial intelligence and occasionally in expert systems are LISP and PROLOG. Describe LISP briefly.*
A: LISP is a list-processing language that is interpretive. It contains many functions for acting upon lists, such as choosing the first, last, or *n*th element of a list or executing a given function for each element of a list. The format of a program itself is a list. Hence, a LISP program can modify itself easily. From a simple beginning, LISP has grown to contain a rich library of functions that enable LISP programmers to quickly prototype an idea and later modify it as it becomes clarified.

Q: *Describe PROLOG briefly.*
A: PROLOG is actually an extension of LISP. PROLOG is designed for logic programming, that is, the proving or establishing of statements. PROLOG gained more popularity in Europe and Asia than in the United States.

Q: *The LOGO language is a descendant of LISP. What is its specialty?*
A: LOGO is a simplified version of LISP specifically designed for teaching programming concepts, especially to young children. LOGO contains "turtle graphics" for doing elementary graphics programming in terms that young children have been able to master.

Q: *When is logic weak for expert system solutions?*

A: Logic is weak in some expert system solutions because pure logic does not enable an expert system to distinguish between fast and slow solutions or a concept that says that a test is effective but only if it is performed less than three times. Logic depends on using knowledge in rigorous, provably correct ways, arguing from progressive axioms that are immutable. If someone says that all mammals bear live young, how do you classify a duck-billed platypus or a dead horse? Conventional monotonic logic has distinct limits in expert system development.

Q: *What are the special difficulties of testing an expert system, above and beyond those of testing a conventional system?*

A: Expert systems are complex programs designed to respond intelligently to a large set of combinations of input values. It is impossible to exhaustively test all combinations of potential inputs to the system. In addition, if the system is interactive, it may be required to ask questions of the user in an order which seems reasonable. If the system is required to explain its advice, this must also make sense to the user. It may not be possible to know if the system is giving the best advice in certain situations. In conventional systems, the inputs and the associated processing of those inputs can be precisely described. If the system is a compiler, the input language is described by a set of rules which prescribe valid syntax. If the system is a business system, the organization has procedures and policies which must be followed by the system.

In expert systems, a certain amount of judgment is expected on the part of the system. The system must be able to weigh numerous factors which interact in subtle ways. Gaps in the system's rules can be fatal to the system's ability to be reliably trusted with important decisions.

Q: *What are some techniques used to test expert systems?*

A: There are no special techniques used to test expert systems. However, there is additional emphasis placed on certain aspects of testing expert systems than in conventional systems. Expert systems are built as a series of prototypes which are refined and tuned over a period of time. The knowledge engineer takes care to assemble a set of test cases which cover the most likely, the most critical, and various types of unusual situations that the expert system might encounter. The knowledge engineer attempts to ensure that each rule in the knowledge base is exercised at least once during the controlled testing process. After the knowledge engineer and the expert are satisfied that the system contains all the knowledge that it will need, the system is run in parallel production mode for a much longer period of time than is required for conventional systems. One major insurance company ran its new underwriting expert system in parallel production for an entire year before relying on any of its decisions. This caution persisted even though not a single insurance application was erroneously approved by the system during the test year.

As a system's knowledge base is updated even after a system is placed in production, its output must be frequently audited. The addition of even a single new rule may bring down an entire system. This "brittleness" requires extensive regression testing.

Q: *What are the major capabilities of expert systems technology?*

A: Expert systems can make decisions or advise in situations where a solution involves recalling a previous situation or classifying a situation into one of a fixed and known set of solutions. If the expertise needed to solve a type of problem is not known, it is possible that machine learning techniques may find a solution by generalizing past knowledge.

Q: *What are the limitations of expert systems technology?*

A: Expert systems are of little help in situations that require common sense or creativity. If the problems presented to the system are unique or highly variable, the system is unlikely to be effective. Also, machine learning techniques are relatively weak and cannot be trusted with important decisions. Expert systems with many rules can be quite slow and great resource hogs.

Q: *What is the Four by Four Expert System Methodology and why is it so effective in practice?*

A: The Four by Four Expert System Methodology was developed by a company called ServiceWare, Inc. to manage expert system projects. As the name implies, it divides the expert system building process into four distinct stages: planning, building, testing, and fielding. Within each stage are four distinct tasks:

Planning

1. Assess viability—Payoff high? Experts available?
2. Define requirements, purpose, function, end result.
3. Create systems specifications—Functional design.
4. Create project plan—Time, cost, personnel.

Building

1. Capture knowledge.
2. Enter knowledge.
3. Demonstrate.
4. Preverify—Knowledge engineers review their work.

Testing

1. Verify—Knowledge engineer and expert review work together step by step.
2. Validate against real-world samples.
3. Review language usage—Edit messages for understanding and impact to user.
4. Pilot test.

Fielding
1. Integrate system.
2. Deploy.
3. Support—Gather feedback from users.
4. Evaluate and extend.

This process is extremely powerful because it prevents the expert system builder from overlooking important steps that have proven to be vital to successful implementation under real-world conditions. The dramatic and rapid success of toy expert system demonstrations (rapid prototyping) often seduced expert system builders into shortcutting the development process. The scaling up of these demonstration systems into productive applications often failed because many of the time-tested procedures used for successful conventional system development and implementation were ignored.

Q: *When would you use inference in building an expert system?*
A: Inference can be used to build an expert system when the rules for making decisions are well known or can be expressed by a human expert (albeit with help from a skilled knowledge engineer).

Q: *When would you use induction in building an expert system?*
A: Induction can be used to build an expert system when decisions and the data on which the decisions were based are available in machine-readable form. Induction can be used to induce rules from the data. The rules can then be reviewed by experts to assure that they are relevant.

Q: *When would you use neural-net learning in building an expert system?*
A: Neural-net learning is similar to inductive learning in that the system learns from examples. Both positive examples and negative examples are necessary to enable the machine to learn by both generalization and discrimination. Neural-net learning is especially valuable for recognizing patterns. However, the patterns learned cannot be inspected to determine their logical consistency. The user has to "trust" the patterns if he or she wants to use neural nets in real-world situations. Also, neural-net learning is far more adaptive to noisy data than inductive learning.

Q: *When would you use case-based reasoning in building an expert system?*
A: Case-based reasoning (CBR) maintains a database of previous examples of decisions (called *cases*). As new cases are presented to the system, it attempts to match them to previous cases. This paradigm is especially useful in help desk and diagnostic systems where cases tend to be repetitive over time. CBR has been implemented in packages that make it very easy to use by end users without programming.

Q: *When would you use fuzzy logic in building an expert system?*
A: Fuzzy logic is used when experts deal with imprecise, relative terms. This allows them to express themselves in a natural way. For example, big and

small, hot and cold, new and old, simple and complex are all fuzzy terms. Although the expert need not define these terms initially, ultimately a function must be defined that allows the computer to make a clear classification. Fuzzy logic provides interpretations for logical connections ("and," "or," "not," etc.) and common modifiers ("very," "slightly," etc.) so that a system may evaluate natural expressions such as "It's not very hot or somewhat hardened."

Q: *Why is knowledge engineering so difficult?*

A: Knowledge engineering is difficult for several reasons:

- Experts typically have forgotten the explicit rules that they use to make decisions. The answer just comes to them intuitively.

- Experts have knowledge organized in a way that allows them to apply the knowledge, but not necessarily teach it.

- Experts have a lot of knowledge that can take a very long time to make explicit in the form of simple rules.

- General rules frequently have many exceptions.

- Often, the expert is the one person that the company cannot do without while the expert system is being developed, so that commandeering sufficient time with the expert is difficult.

Q: *SmallTalk is a language that came out of AI research and is gaining popularity in the commercial marketplace. Briefly describe SmallTalk.*

A: SmallTalk was developed in the early 1970s by the Xerox PARC Learning Research Group. SmallTalk is an interpretive, object-oriented language. It contains a rich set of predefined classes, subclasses, and metaclasses for handling many types of processing, including a graphical, interactive programming environment and list-processing facilities.

Q: *As a knowledge engineer (KE) you have been assigned to an expert who has no time and little patience for you. What can you do?*

A: When a knowledge engineer (KE) encounters an expert who has no time and little patience, the KE can save the expert time by reading background literature, procedure manuals, handbooks, etc., and talking with others prior to beginning knowledge-engineering sessions with the expert. It may be possible to observe the expert and even videotape the expert interacting with people presenting the expert with problems. The expert might be more willing to review the tapes later and explain the decisions. This is far less taxing and less frustrating for the expert than explaining his or her art.

Q: *As a KE you have been assigned to a group of experts who cannot agree on the rules. What can you do?*

A: When a KE encounters a group of experts who cannot agree on the rules, this is usually a sign that the real expert is not included in the group. Alternatively, this may indicate that real expertise is unavailable. It may be possible to validate some of the rules against historical records. It may be possible to go to higher authorities, either within the organization or to professional consultants who are recognized and accepted authorities.

Q: *As a KE you have been assigned to an expert who fears that the expert system you are building will put him or her out of a job. What can you do?*

A: When a KE encounters an expert who fears that the expert system will put him or her out of a job, the KE should explain the advantages of being the expert system domain expert. For example, one major insurance company built an expert system that allowed them to reassign (i.e., let go) half of their underwriters. Of course, they kept all the underwriters who had participated in the expert system development project because they were needed to maintain the expert system. Expertise is rarely static, and lending one's expertise to a system is more often a key to job security than not.

Q: *As a KE, the expert you are interviewing is convinced that he or she can "smell" a problem that a computer could never detect because it cannot be expressed in words. What can you do?*

A: When a KE interviews an expert who is convinced that he or she can "smell" a problem that a computer could never detect because it cannot be expressed in words, this is usually an indication that the expert cannot articulate the rules because they are too subtle. In such a case, the KE must draw on his or her interviewing skills—especially listening skills—to carefully analyze by detailed questioning these situations and identify the subtle cues that the expert is using. Occasionally, the "smell" test is a case of superstitious behavior on the part of the expert in which the rules were broken to satisfy a personal bias and the expert remembered one or a few successes while forgetting or not being aware of nonsuccesses. This requires a great deal of tact and discretion on the part of the KE.

Q: *You are developing an expert system using a shell that employs the RETE algorithm. Your system produces the correct answers but takes an inordinate amount of time. What can you do?*

A: An expert system using a shell that employs the RETE algorithm should observe the following guidelines for efficiency considerations:

- Put the most restrictive pattern elements at the head of the rules. This eliminates unwanted facts early in the process.
- Put expensive pattern tests at the end of the rules. For example, testing a multiple-valued slot in an object can be very expensive in time. Placing these tests last requires them to be performed less often.
- Write patterns which are very restrictive.
- Use wildcard patterns judiciously.
- Allow rules to share patterns when possible by placing them at the head of their respective rules and in the same order.
- Avoid rule patterns in which the same set of facts will activate a rule in multiple, unnecessary ways.

Q: *The RETE algorithm uses a pattern net and a join net. What is the difference?*

A: The RETE algorithm uses a pattern net and a join net. The pattern net sorts facts from the work space into the patterns that they instantiate. The join net then combines instantiated patterns to build rule activations. The set of activated rules comprises an agenda of eligible rules from which a single rule is chosen to fire. This algorithm, developed by C. L. Forgy and employed widely in rule-based inference engines, allows relational operations on facts to be performed incrementally. A fact or object in the work space must pass a series of specific tests to arrive at a terminal node which represents the instantiation of a pattern. The join net gathers collections of facts which produce partial matches of rule patterns until a complete match is produced, at which time the corresponding rule is activated.

Q: *What goes into the left-hand side of a rule?*

A: The left-hand side (LHS) of a production rule specifies the condition to which the rule responds. This is somewhat analogous to the domain of a mathematical function.

Q: *What types of things go into the right-hand side of a rule?*

A: The right-hand side of a production rule specifies the actions for the system to take when the left-hand side conditions are satisfied. These actions should modify the set of facts in the work space to make other rules eligible to fire. The actions may assert new facts, modify existing facts or objects, or retract previously asserted facts. The actions may also cause input or output activity such as printing or displaying decisions. In addition, the actions may invoke other systems which may control various devices.

Q: *Object-oriented programming relies heavily on inheritance. What is inheritance?*

A: Inheritance is a characteristic of hierarchy. When classes are arranged in a hierarchical fashion, attributes of lower classes tend to have the same attributes as classes above them in the hierarchy. For this reason, we say that the lower-level classes inherit values from higher-level classes. For example, if the class of insects called SPIDERS has an attribute, "8 legs," then for each subclass (a particular type of spider) the number of legs need not be repeated unless it is different from eight. This not only saves storage, but makes adding new types easier and updating information that changes much faster.

Q: *What is multiple inheritance?*

A: Multiple inheritance comes into play when two or more hierarchies share an object. In a strict hierarchy, each object can have only one parent. When objects are allowed to belong to two distinct hierarchies, they can inherit attributes from both sets of higher-level classes. For example, goldfish belong to the class of all fishes and inherit its attributes, such as fins and scales. But goldfish also belong the class of pets and inherit its attributes, such as owner and address.

Q: *Why is multiple inheritance important in building expert systems?*

A: Not all object-oriented systems support multiple inheritance. Multiple inheritance is important because it is a concept that frequently occurs naturally. Whatever makes the modeling process more natural and eliminates unnecessary redundancy is generally very valuable in dealing with the complex world. Multiple inheritance also presents potential problems in that conflicting values of the same attribute may be inherited from two different parent classes. There is no standard way of handling this situation.

Q: *Why can't I write an expert system in COBOL?*

A: In the functional sense of being able to make decisions, an expert system can be written in COBOL or in BASIC or in any conventional programming language. However, for all but the simplest systems, far too much effort will be required to code and debug the system, and the system will be virtually unmaintainable in a conventional language. Furthermore, expert system shells offer inferencing, object-oriented processing, explanation facilities, special debugging facilities, and a graphical user interface (GUI).

Q: *Why is rapid prototyping considered AI, since we also use it in conventional systems development?*

A: Although rapid prototyping is used these days in conventional systems development, its origins were in AI. In expert systems development, prototyping—as opposed to full system specification, including analysis and design—is an absolute necessity because the logic is extremely complex, the knowledge is difficult to extract, and the validation process is very long.

Q: *What is the difference between a database and a knowledge base?*

A: A database contains information describing various aspects or attributes of the objects in the database. For example, in a personnel database you will find descriptions of relevant aspects of the employees in the database. These include attributes such as name and address, job title, skills, benefits, and other pieces of information that would allow you to categorize and report on the personnel. A knowledge base contains information on how to interpret the information in a database, usually for the purpose of making decisions. For example, a knowledge base for personnel applications might contain rules for determining eligibility for various benefit plans, for determining compliance with government requirements, and for adherence to company policies and collective bargaining agreements. As you type data into a personnel database, for example, a supervisory expert system might tell you that the new employee's salary is insufficient for the grade assigned under the current union contract.

Q: *What does modeling have to do with expert systems?*

A: An expert system is essentially a model of how an expert solves a problem or makes a decision. For example, in diagnosing an equipment failure, an expert system would refer to a model included in its knowledge base that includes a number of cause-and-effect relations. The diagnosis would work backward, just as an expert would do to match reported malfunction symptoms to known effects to identify one or more possible causes. These possible causes would then be tested to determine the actual malfunctioning components.

Q: *What is the connection between CASE (Computer-Assisted Software Engineering) and AI?*

A: CASE (Computer-Assisted Software Engineering) technology is a category of software designed to help in the development of computer applications. The CASE field is divided into what are called "upper CASE" for systems analysis and design and "lower CASE" for code generation. Some of CASE technology is simply the application of graphics and database technology to the programming field. But the vision behind the CASE field and the direction toward which it is moving stems from the subfield of AI known as *automatic program generation,* or AP. Much research has gone into AP, resulting in several interesting experimental systems (PSI, CHI, SAFE, the Programmer's Apprentice, PECOS, DEDALUS, Protosystem I, NLPQ, LIBRA). However, much work remains before commercially valuable AP systems put programmers out of work forever.

Some of the firms specializing in expert systems technology have begun to call their products CASE tools because expert system shells are very high level languages which facilitate rapid system development. Since the primary goal of CASE is to reduce the time and effort necessary to develop systems, it is not unfair to include expert systems tools in that category.

Q: *What is the connection between Entity Relationship diagrams and AI?*

A: Entity Relationship diagrams are a form of data modeling used in performing systems analysis and creating functional specifications for a system. The concept of Entity Relationship diagrams comes from early AI research in an area known as *semantic nets.* Semantic nets were an attempt to enable computers to understand natural language (such as English) by associating various conceptual terms (entities) with other terms via links (relationships) in a network.

Q: *Give examples of appropriate uses of forward chaining and backward chaining.*

A: Forward chaining is best used when any one of many conclusions can be drawn from a given set of facts. For example, in a classification problem, such as classifying organic chemical compounds, a given case might lead to any of thousands of distinct answers. Backward chaining is most appropriate where only a small set of answers is possible and the reasoning process itself (not simply the answer) is important. One example is in diagnosing a medical problem which has been narrowed down to a small set of possibilities. The decision-making process requires various tests to be performed on the patient. Each test has a cost, a time consideration, and other factors associated with it. Only the necessary tests should be performed and the order in which they are performed is also significant. Backward chaining can weigh these factors as it reasons toward a conclusion (goal).

Q: *What is metaknowledge and how is it related to expert systems technology?*

A: Metaknowledge means knowledge about knowledge. An expert system shell includes metaknowledge in the sense that it deals with how knowledge about a particular domain is represented and how reasoning is performed to solve problems. Expert systems with extensive metaknowledge allow them to adapt gracefully and effectively to new situations just beyond the edge of their predefined rules, but so far not achieved.

Q: *What is the connection between expert systems and CAI/CBT (Computer-Aided Instruction and Computer-Based Training)?*

A: Computer-Aided Instruction (CAI) and Computer-Based Training (CBT) are two areas of computer science that have long been closely associated with AI. Since artificial intelligence is the intersection between computer science and cognitive science, AI practitioners have done much research into applying AI concepts to the problem of educating students. The decision-making processes to which expert systems technology is applied in CAI are (1) whether the student has mastered a topic or needs remedial help and (2) what misconceptions or erroneous rules the student has learned which cause the mistakes the student makes on tests. The concepts of knowledge representation take on new meaning in this domain, because it becomes critical for the computer to "understand" the student's representation of the knowledge. In theory, the same production rules which an expert system uses to make decisions could be used to teach novices the knowledge contained in the rules. In practice, this has been difficult to achieve.

Q: *Describe the concept of work space in expert systems.*

A: The concept of work space in expert systems is has its origins in LISP. During the reasoning process, the expert system stores its preliminary conclusions and intermediate results in the work space. These are usually facts which have been derived from the initial set of facts by the inference rules that make up the knowledge base of the system.

Q: *A knowledge base contains declarative knowledge and procedural knowledge. What is the difference?*

A: Declarative knowledge consists of facts and static relationships. Procedural knowledge consists of rules and methods. Methods are procedures attached to objects in object-oriented programming. For example, declarative knowledge might include information that a particular person, say John, is right-handed and that a human body typically has two hands, one left hand and one right hand. Procedural knowledge might contain rules for determining if a person is left-handed or right-handed.

Q: *Rule-based systems are said to be data-driven. What does that mean?*

A: The flow of control in a rule-based system is not dependent on the order of the rules or control structures in the rules as in conventional programming.

The flow is entirely dependent on the data which is presented to the rules. The inference engine fires rules which are relevant to whatever data is input to the system.

Q: *What is the concept of an agenda in expert systems?*

A: A production rule usually contains multiple conditions. Each time a condition is matched to a fact in the work space, that condition is said to be instantiated. When all of the conditions of a rule are instantiated, the rule becomes activated. Activations are placed on an agenda. The agenda, therefore, is a list of activations of rules which are currently competing for an opportunity to fire. Each inference engine has its own techniques for choosing the next rule to actually fire from the agenda.

Q: *Two types of inheritance relations among objects are "is-a" and "instance-of." What is the difference?*

A: An "is-a" relationship between two classes (sometimes called *schemas*) links one general concept (or class of objects) to another. For example, the class Dog would be related to the class Mammal via an is-a relationship. The "instance-of" relationship specifies that an object is a member of a class for inheritance. For example, the object Fido would be defined as an instance-of the class Dog.

Q: *The concept of wildcards makes the use of production rules a powerful knowledge-representation tool. Describe this concept.*

A: A wildcard is a part of a pattern in the conditional section of a production rule that will match any element. Some wildcard symbols match a single element. Others match any number of elements. For example, if the question mark (?) is a wildcard symbol, then this pattern in a rule:

```
(T H ? S E)
```

will match all of these facts in the work space:

```
(T H E S E)
(T H O S E)
(T H X S E).
```

Q: *Explain the concept of binding of variables in expert systems.*

A: In rule-based programming, a variable can be used to communicate information between the conditional part of a rule and its action part. The item or items that matched the variable (for the particular instantiation for which the rule is being fired—and therefore for which the action part of the rule is being executed) becomes the value of the variable. Since this is only a temporary value, the value is said to be "bound" to the variable as opposed to being "assigned" as in conventional programming.

Q: *How is truth maintenance supported by logical dependency in rule-based programming?*

A: Some expert system shells allow the assertion of facts to be logically dependent upon other facts. Truth maintenance allows the knowledge engineer to code rules which assert a fact or a whole series of facts which are only hypotheses. If it later turns out that the original hypothesis was wrong, retracting the original fact automatically retracts all other facts which are logically dependent on it.

Q: *Give an example of logical dependency.*

A: As an example of logical dependency, consider a darkroom which contains a light switch and an open sheet of photographic paper unexposed to light. When the switch is turned on, the room becomes light and the paper becomes exposed and ruined. When the switch is turned off, the room becomes dark again but the paper remains ruined. The darkness of the room is logically dependent on the state of the light switch. The paper, once exposed, is not dependent on the light switch.

Q: *Describe the concept of message passing. Why is it better than procedure calling?*

A: The concept of message passing is key to object-oriented programming. In object-oriented programming, objects are activated by passing them a message to perform a given operation. The procedure that the object uses to respond to the message is called a *method*. Although similar to calling a procedure in conventional or procedural programming, message passing has the advantages that the same message may be passed to several different objects, each of which reacts in its own unique way and, since objects are linked hierarchically, an object may pass a message up the hierarchy for handling. For example, an object may send a message to add a quantity to the value of a particular object. Since each object type that can support an add operation will have its own method, the sender of the message need not be concerned about whether the quantity is an integer number, a floating-point number, an imaginary number, a complex number, or even an entire matrix.

Q: *What is the difference between knowledge processing and data processing?*

A: Knowledge processing is an evolutionary advancement in the way people and computers interact to solve problems and conduct business. Knowledge processing technology extends data processing by increasing the diversity of information that can be represented within computers, by increasing the complexity of the relationships which can be managed by the system, by expanding the range of analysis techniques that computers can apply to information, and by making it easier for computers to interact with users.

Q: *What are some guidelines for choosing an initial expert systems project for an organization?*

A: For a first demonstration of expert systems technology, the problem should be:

- Likely to succeed
- Important to the organization
- Solvable by the technology
- Difficult or infeasible to solve with conventional methods

Q: *The following decision tree represents an initial position (as in a game of chess, for example) and two ply of moves and responses. Assign arbitrary values to the leaf nodes and show how the minimax algorithm would use them to compute a score for the initial and intermediate positions.*

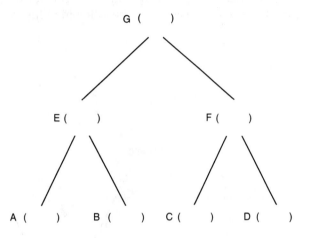

A: If the decision tree represents an initial position and two ply of moves and responses, and the values in the leaf nodes (the bottom row) represent a static evaluation of my replies to my opponent's moves from the current position (the top row), then the minimax algorithm would compute a score for the initial and intermediate positions as follows:

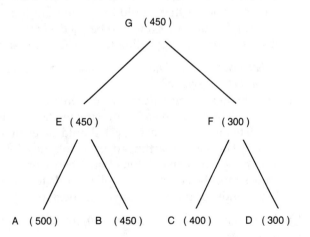

If I choose move E, my opponent will minimize my next choice by choosing move B which has a value of 450. Therefore, the value for move E is only 450. Similarly, if I choose move F, my opponent will choose move D, minimizing my replies so move F receives a value of 300. I will maximize my score by choosing move E over move F, so this position, G, is worth 450 for me.

Q: *In the same decision tree, assign arbitrary values to the leaf nodes that illustrate the alpha-beta heuristic and show how this reduces the number of nodes that must be searched to compute a score for the initial position.*

A: In the same decision tree, the following illustrates the alpha-beta heuristic.

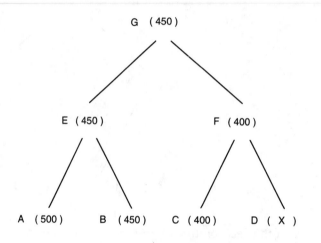

The value of position E is computed by the minimax algorithm, as previously, by minimizing between 500 and 450 to get 450. When computing a value for node F, we see that node C has a value of 400, which is less than the 450 of node E. Therefore, there is no need to compute a value for node D (or any other nodes that would be to the right of node D) because if the value were higher than 400, it would be rejected by F and if it were lower than 400, it would not be as appealing to node G as the 450 it can get by moving to E.

Q: *What search technique can be used to maximize the effectiveness of the alpha-beta heuristic?*

A: The alpha-beta heuristic can save more than 50 percent of the time needed to evaluate a move tree. To maximize the effectiveness of the alpha-beta heuristic, moves on each level should be evaluated in the order of best to worst. This can be arranged by combining breadth-first with depth-first searching. The name "alpha-beta" heuristic comes from the fact that two values must be compared. Alpha stands for the maximum at one level and beta stands for the minimum at the next level.

Q: *Name the three main concepts employed by genetic algorithms for machine learning.*

A: The three main concepts employed by genetic algorithms for machine learning are: mating, random mutation, and survival of the fittest.

28
BACHMAN

Walter N. Eachus

Introduction

With the advent of CASE tools in the 1980s, many market niches developed that are covered by CASE tools. There are the full development cycle repository-based CASE tools such as Pacbase* and IEF.[†] There are CASE tools that have a strong set of database migration and data modeling tools, of which BACHMAN has established itself as a strong leader.

Bachman started out as a reengineering tool to migrate from IDMS to relational data structures (DB2). The tool has grown to meet the demand of the data and process modeling components with a link through the designer tool to CSP and code generation into CICS/DB2 using COBOL. Today the BACHMAN[‡]/Analyst tool can run on a 386 or higher processor, 12 megs of RAM, and at least 30 megs of free space on the hard drive for the swapper.dat file to expand.

The BACHMAN toolset provides:

- Data modeling at an enterprise level
- Data modeling at the project level
- Shared work manager
- Process modeling (DFD, FDD)
- Logic model (PSD)
- DBA toolkit—DDL generation

* Pacbase is a product of CGI Systems, Inc., Pearl River, N.Y.

[†] IEF is a product of Texas Instruments.

[‡] BACHMAN toolset is a product of Bachman Information Systems, Inc.

DATA Modeling at an Enterprise Level.   The data modeling at an enterprise level is a top-to-bottom approach. This approach is usually taken when a complete validation process is desired in order to handle the relationships of the organization.

DATA Modeling at the Project Level.   The data modeling at the project level is a bottom-to-top approach. This approach is usually used when there are current systems that exist that must be converted and there are individual projects that will support the validation of each area of the model. The merging process of the model into an enterprise model is done as projects are completed. Both of the preceding approaches need the strengths of a strong data modeling tool which is the Bachman/Data Analyst.

Shared Work Manager.   The Shared Work Manager tool allows data modeling information to be shared between analysts on a project team and then reassembled into the enterprise data model. The items that are shareable are:

- Data models
- Entity methods
- External procedures
- Attribute derivations

Process Modeling.   The Process Modeling tool includes the Data Flow Diagrams (DFD) and Functional Decomposition Diagrams (FDD). The DFDs are broken down at a transaction level and then decomposed through the FDD tool for routine definition.

Logic Modeling.   The Logic Modeling tool (PSD—Process Specification Diagram) expresses in detail the input parameters, process logic, and the outputs of the logic. The output is then passed to the Designer tool, and ESF (External Structure Format) is then generated to be passed into IBM's CSP generator.

DBA Toolkit—DDL Generation.   This is the data model after the project is migrated to the DBA tool and forward engineered into DB2. There are DDL files that are generated to be input into the DCLGEN. After the forward engineering is complete, then the process of reverse engineering back into the analyst tool is done so that the physical data mappings will be saved in the enterprise data model.

Terminology

Entity: A term used to denote a person, place, or thing (noun) that is of fundamental interest to the business.

Entity type hierarchy: Term used to denote various types of entities which exist in a one-to-one relationship with the supertype and will inherit the key of the supertype (e.g., car: Chevrolet, Chrysler, Ford).

Business subject area: Used to group logically related entities for a related business function.

Relational diagram: Depicts the objects in the logical design that would exist in any relational model but which are not implementation-specific and do not contain tablespaces and indexes.

Physical diagram: Depicts the objects with implementation-specific objects, which would include tablespaces and indexes on specific storage devices (volumes) and access structures.

Data flow diagram: Represents the external agents, information flows, and stores of the data as it moves through a business function.

Functional decomposition diagram: Shows the process breakdown of a data-flow diagram which has to have been previously built.

External agent: A person (s) or another data processing system that is not within the current scope of the system being analyzed.

Forward engineering functions: Translate the logical data model into a physical model. Instead of entities there will be tables; attributes will be columns and keys will become primary indexes.

Attribute derivation: The formula for the calculation of an attribute, such as "interest is rate times price."

Attribute: A piece of information used by the business in either documents, screens, or reports.

Free attribute: A piece of information of the business which is not connected to an entity. As the analysis phase continues, these attributes will be used by entities.

Export utility functions: The method of placing in a .VAR file the data model which can later be imported and saved.

Entity relationship diagram: Represents the entities and the way they relate to one another (one-to-one, one-to-many, many-to-one, many-to-many).

Profile: The way in which user, data model, process model, and merge criteria will be used to perform various functions in the tool. It is the user profile that controls the placement of the data models and name of the reporting database.

Questions and Answers

The technical interview is a back-and-forth discussion of data modeling and the ways that the Bachman toolset solves the problems related to data. The interviewer is looking not only for correct answers, but correct discussions involving the pros and cons of the approaches to data modeling. The questions will relate directly to the product and also to of the way the tool can be used with different data modeling concepts. This means that the questions will be answered within a Bachman context.

Q: *What is enterprise modeling?*
A: The concept of enterprise modeling may be diagrammed as follows*:

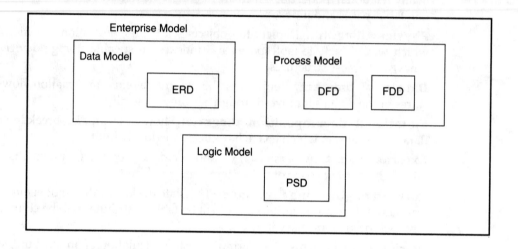

and involves the interaction of these three models on an organizational (corporatewide) basis.

Q: *What is data modeling?*
A: It is the logical representation of the information as it is used within the business. It is composed of entities, partnership sets, and attributes. The data model can interface with none, one, or more processes.

Q: *What is logic modeling?*
A: It is the processing representation of functions within the business that operate against the data model. The logic model is composed of data flow diagrams, process specification diagrams, and functional decomposition diagrams. This is the basis for transaction analysis to be given to the DBA group for physical modeling.

Q: *What is physical modeling?*
A: It is the process of taking the logical representation of data and the transaction analysis to analyze the performance of the transactions. The DBA will allocate disk volumes, indexes, and other performance enhancements needed on the basis of the analysis.

---

* BACHMAN/*Analyst Getting Started,* Bachman Information Systems, Inc., 1992, pp. 1–4.

Q: *What is Shared Work Manager?*

A: The ability to share the enterprise modeling information and its components through a controlled environment of check in and check out with analysts on a project team. The function also allows the reporting on these changes before the actual process is executed.

Q: *What is a check in?*

A: Checking in has two main levels of functionality at the base model and the subset model levels. At the base model level, it is the method where subsets and users get associated to the base model. At the subset model level, it is the method where analysts, after modification, place the subset back into the base model.

Q: *What is a reassembly?*

A: Through a series of reports after the check in has been completed, the subset is reassembled (merged) into the base. This function is similar to the merge function except in two major areas:

- Specification of the order of merging.
- Only net changes from the data model are merged.

Q: *What is a process working store?*

A: Within PSD it is thought of as a holding area for entity, attribute, and relationship occurrences that the process uses during the execution of the process. This object is a temporary object lasting only as long as the process.

Q: *What is the importance of exporting?*

A: The function of exporting a model is used to save a model to import later. The file is a straight ASCII file with a .VAR extension. It is done so that reports can be written against this file by the clients. Exporting is also a good backup facility.

Q: *What is the setup for reports?*

A: The function of setting up for reports is done so that the *filename*.AN file is exported into a file and then written to Query Manager by a REXX program in an off-line fashion so that other processing can take place on another model.

Q: *What function does Query Manager play in the BACHMAN/Analyst?*

A: The reporting function in Bachman is heavily dependent on the Query Manager database. This is the repository for all the reports produced by the Bachman product.

Q: *What things should you look at before merging enterprise models?*

A: There are three major areas of concern with merging:

- Entities
- Attributes
- Partnership sets

Entities, attributes, and partnership sets that exist in both models must be spelled identically so that the information can be merged correctly.

Q: *What is the function of the BACHMAN.IXF file?*

A: This file contains all the meta-model information for the Bachman tool that will be placed in the Query Manager database (e.g., tables, queries, procedures, and forms).

Q: *How do you open the data model form?*

A: Open a file with the mouse and choose a model. The model that will appear on the screen will be the enterprise model. Choose the diagram menu selection and click on ERD. This will bring up the ERD model. Then find background around the model and double-click. The data model form will appear.

Q: *What is a keyword?*

A: This is a name given to a group of objects to logically link them together for display purposes. Typically, keywords are used in conjunction with filters to display a portion of an enterprise model.

Q: *What is the quickest method for putting keywords in the data model for entities?*

A: First, lasso the logical entities together with the left button of the mouse and then select the Task menu from the bar. Click on the Transform task and select Attach a Keyword. The form will come up to select a current keyword or key in another keyword; then select OK.

Q: *What is the relationship between the printer definition in Query Manager and printing the E/R diagram?*

A: The BACHMAN/Analyst tool uses the printer definition that has been set up in OS/2 and that has been connected and active in the printer control of OS/2.

Q: *What is the function(s) of the Properties menu item?*

A: The most important functions of the properties menu on the ERD: allowing manual placement of entities in the model, turning off the palette for greater work space, and turning off the partnership set names so that only entities are seen along with the relationships.

Q: *How does Page Bound work?*

A: In the function of printing a diagram, the art of sizing a diagram to print is important. In order to size, the diagram must be bound to the grid layout.

Q: *What function does cataloging a database perform?*

A: In Shared Work Manager, cataloging a database is done so that the information for the database can be identified with the workstation and that the connection process can be done.

Q: *What function does connecting to a database perform?*

A: With the OS/2 Shared Work Manager server running minimized in the OS/2 desktop, connecting to the database allows the check-in and check-out functions of Shared Work Manager to work.

Q: *What is enterprise model merging?*

A: To merge an enterprise model means to take all aspects of the model and merge them into another model. This would include data model, process model, and any logic that has been written (e.g., PSD).

Q: *What part does the merge profile play in the merge process?*

A: The merge profile has every object within the BACHMAN/Data Analyst tool defaulted to whether the source or target should be used as the default for priority. Say you merged model A into model B, and A has DOMAIN CHARACTER-5 as an integer, and the B model has DOMAIN CHARACTER-5 as alphanumeric—if target was specified, model B's description of DOMAIN CHARACTER-5 would remain.

Q: *What is the function of the user profile?*

A: For a given signon, it will set the defaults for where the models are stored, which default merge profile to use, or in which database the setup for reports should place the model.

Q: *What is the reason for the signon box to BACHMAN/Data Analyst?*

A: Before 4.10, the signon box was used only to tag each object with which signon made the changes to an object. With 4.10, the aspect of security was added for shared work in signing in and out models.

Q: *What is the main purpose of the F6 key?*

A: The F6's main function is to act as a list key within an object. For instance, if you want to see the list of possible dimensions within the model, click on the Dimension box and hit F6, and all the possible dimensions will be listed. A selection can be done by clicking on the Dimension and clicking on OK.

Q: *What is Model Manager?*

A: The Model Manager is a tool within the Bachman/Utilities toolbox and is used to create, catalog, and connect to databases. Once connected to a database, the functions of deletion of files, modifying user information for the database, or running reports on subsets for Shared Work Manager can be executed.

Q: *What is the ANALYST.SQL file?*

A: After the installation of the Bachman product, one of the first steps to do is to create the Bachman database within Query Manager in order to be able to set up for reports. This creation of the Bachman database reads the ANALYST.SQL file in order to build the tables within Query Manager.

Q: *What is an information store?*

A: This is the place where entities and attributes from the data model are stored until they are defined in the model. This is an interim storage area.

Q: *What is a grid?*

A: The grid originates as defaults with your printer as defined to OS/2 at the time of installation (i.e., if an HP IV were installed with OS/2, then Bachman would use that printer as the defaults for the grids). The grids are the pages for the layout of the diagram.

Q: *How do you set Landscape and Portrait grids?*

A: The grids are set up in the file pull-down menu under Printer Options. Click on Printer Options and then click on Change Printer. When the Change Printer screen displays, click on SETUP and change the default to Portrait or Landscape.

Q: *What is importing a model?*

A: After an export function has been completed on a model, the import function can be performed, which will get rid of extraneous pointers within a model and reduce the size of the model.

Q: *What two types of files does an export create?*

A: The two files created by an export are (1) *filename*.VAR file and (2) the DBIMP.LOG file, both of which are ASCII files.

Q: *What is an entity method?*

A: The application of rules to an entity, which would include rules for insertion, retrieval, updating, and erasing them. The method is associated with one entity, and will reside in the data model for reuse purposes so that they can also be used by process models.

Q: *What is an external procedure?*

A: The view of this procedure is broader than the entity method in two ways: (1) its view is the entire data model and (2) it may reference one or more entities or no entities at all (e.g., calculation routines).

Q: *What are views?*

A: The purpose of views is to allow display of a portion of related entities and attributes by a keyword using a filter. The tool will try to keep the entities in their positions in the diagram.

Q: *What is the Revert function?*

A: The ability to go back to a previous version of the model is a function called *revert*. This menu pull-down allows a previous version to be retrieved in between the Save function.

Q: *What is a subset?*

A: This is a data model, process model, and/or Business Subject Area (BSA) which has been copied from the enterprise model at a point in time and placed into another model for the purpose of modification by analysts to meet project requirements. This subset is created through the use of the Shared Work Manager toolset.

Q: *What is a check out?*
A: The function of checking out a subset for modification. This checking out function will log the entry into the subset that has been taken out for modification.

Q: *What is the function of release?*
A: After a subset has been checked out and modified, the analyst may decide that the changes should not be copied back into the base model (i.e., checked in). The method to revert back to the previous check out subset is to release the subset in Shared Work Manager. This will update the Shared Work Manager database file and the check-out process can begin again.

Q: *How is the function of saving accomplished?*
A: In order to use this function, data changes have to have been made to the model. This will cause the menu pull-down to darken the SAVE function. When the model is saved, several things happen:
  1. Updates are written to the *filename*.AN file.
  2. A new index file (*filename*.AN) is created.
  3. The original index file is saved as *filename*.OAN.
  4. The undo list will be cleared. (This will gray the Undo selection on the menu pull-down.)

Q: *What does the function Save As accomplish?*
A: This function does not need changes made to the model to operate. When the SAVE AS function is performed it will do several things:
  1. Reduces the size of the model by doing deletions
  2. Saves the file by creation of a new model file and a new index file
  3. Clears the undo list
  4. Makes the new model the active model for modification

Q: *What is a* filename.*AN file, and how can you display it?*
A: This is a data model file which is displayed when you click on the following:
  1. the file pull-down menu item
  2. OPEN
  3. Analyst Model
  At this point, the list of *filename*.AN will be displayed.

Q: *What is* filename.*IAN file?*
A: This is the current index file which contains pointers into the data model. Since, during the SAVE function, objects are not physically deleted, this file contains the pointers to the active objects in the model.

Q: *What is a* filename.*OAN file?*

A: This is the previous active index file which was created during a SAVE function as a backup. It gives the ability to back up to the previous version of the data model.

Q: *What is a* filename.*AN1 file?*

A: This is a previous *filename.*AN file after the SAVE AS function has been performed. So, even after a SAVE AS, a return to the previous model is allowed by renaming the AN1 file and the OAN to the original *filename.*AN and *filename.*IAN files.

Q: *What function does the utility BACHCOPY do?*

A: The ability to copy models for the purposes of backup and distribution is done through the utility BACHCOPY, which automatically copies the *filename.*AN and *filename.*IAN files. This utility is executed from an OS/2 window or full screen using the format BACHCOPY *filename* at the command prompt.

Q: *What function does the utility BACHIX do?*

A: In case you forget to copy the *filename.*IAN file, if you use the regular OS/2 copy command, the BACHIX facility allows you to rebuild the *filename.*IAN file from the *filename.*AN file. The format is BACHIX *filename.*

Q: *What does the symbol ABC on the data model palette mean?*

A: On a data model, the ability to key in text into the model without any association to an object is performed by the ABC palette selection.

Q: *Which function key invokes the Find command?*

A: Some models, after many modifications and additions, become large models—especially at the corporate model level. In order to find entities or other objects, the Find command is very helpful. On the data model (ERD), press the F7 function key for a list of objects to find, and click on APPLY.

Q: *What are some reasons for using the Find command?*

A: On large models it is common to use the Find command to center an entity that must be modified. This Find will also put the entity in select status (i.e., highlighted for selection) and will put the entity in the select list. The Find command can also be used to delete keywords that are no longer needed by using the open form and center options and then backspacing over the name of the keyword.

Q: *What function does the F4 key perform?*

A: The F4 key performs the SAVE function.

Q: *What does the function SELECT PAGES do?*

A: The ability to select pages for printing is done by clicking on the SELECT PAGES feature after choosing PRINT DIAGRAM from the menu pulldown.

Q: *What do ALL and NONE on the SELECT PAGES screen do?*

A: Choose ALL to print the pages in the diagram and to manually click on each page that is *not* to be printed. This option is fine if most of the diagrams are to be printed. The NONE option is used if most of the pages are *not* printed. This option will deselect all pages for printing, and printing is activated for each page that is clicked on.

Q: *What are some ways to enlarge the data model diagram?*

A: There are three ways to enlarge the diagram:

1. On the palette or diagram pull-down menu, choose the zoom option.
2. Use the Page Up and Page Down keys, which will enlarge or shrink the diagram, respectively.
3. Using the right button on the mouse, drag the area in a box that is to be enlarged.

Q: *How do you add a process model (to a data model)?*

A: The function of adding a process model to a data model is to double-click on Enterprise Model, press PF8, and select Process Model or press the down arrow and go to the Process Model box. Enter in a process model name and select the ADD button: the model will be added to the enterprise model.

Q: *What is a node?*

A: A node is a display button which can get you to a list of functions. There are CRUD (i.e., create, retrieve, update, and delete) functions conditional statements (e.g., IF, CASE), iterations, screen options for sending or receiving information to an external agent, and miscellaneous functions (e.g., DO, STRUCTURE). These functions can be selected and used in the building of a PSD statement.

Q: *What does a retrieve statement in PSD do?*

A: The statement is used to retrieve information from the logical data model, which is entity information (e.g., entity occurrences, attributes, or partnership set information flows) or related information (e.g., attributes from related entities) from other entities. The output is the process working store which is overwritten with the new retrieve.

Q: *What function do input parameters perform?*

A: The input parameters are placed on external procedures or entity methods which are a process-working-store (PWS) attribute, partnership set, or entity which is input into this method or procedure.

Q: *Within a form, what function does the F8 key perform?*

A: The key is used to find an area in a form quickly. Press the F8 key and a list will appear with the names within the form. Then select the place in the form and the cursor will follow (e.g., within the entity form, press F8, then "A," and press Enter—this will position the cursor at attributes for an entity).

Q: *When forward engineering, what do the entity and attribute names become in the relational and physical diagrams?*

A: The entity name (e.g., not synonym names) become the table names that are used within the RD (Relation Diagram) and PD (Physical Diagram). The attribute names become the column names in the RD and PD. These will be used to generate the DDL which will be input into the DCLGEN.

Q: *What is NSSL?*

A: This stands for Naming Standards Specification Language, which is the method of intercepting logical model naming standards and replacing them with DB2 naming standards (e.g., entity CUSTOMER could be table CUST in DB2).

Q: *What purpose does NSSL perform in forward engineering?*

A: The naming standards for physical design can be enforced through the NSSL module as it intercepts the logical data model naming convention through forward engineering. This will guarantee, if applied uniformly through the modeling process, the exact naming at the object level (e.g., entity, attribute).

Q: *In the text form, is the NSSL statement usable by forward engineering?*

A: The ASCII source file that is created using OS/2 edit or another editing tool *cannot* be used, since the forward engineering program requires a binary compiled file to load in memory at run time.

Q: *What is a partnership set?*

A: This is an expression from each side of a relationship explaining how the entities relate to each other. This will define the business rule for that relationship and determine the cardinality and optionality of the entities (e.g., partnership set between customer and address could define that a customer must have at least one address and an address must have one customer).

Q: *What does an optional (o) partnership set mean?*

A: The open circle (o) indicates that a minimum number of occurrences will be set to 0 because there may not be any occurrences for the relationship.

Q: *What does a mandatory partnership set mean?*

A: The filled circle indicates that a minimum number of occurrences will be set to 1 because there must be at least one occurrence associated with the relationship.

Q: *What is an associative entity?*

A: This is an entity that resolves a many-to-many relationship in the physical diagram. This is represented in the logical data model as a double headed arrow (i.e., <————>) which must be resolved physically through an entity with keys from both entities.

Q: *What does the symbol ————> mean?*
A: This is the standard one-to-many relationship (1:M) which will mean that, for example, for each occurrence for entity A, there will be many entity Bs. Also, for each occurrence of B, there will be only one entity A associated with it.

Q: *What does the symbol ———— mean?*
A: This is the standard one-to-one relationship (1:1) where, for each occurrence of entity A, there will be only one occurrence of entity B. Also, for each occurrence of entity B, there will be only one occurrence of entity A.

Q: *What is a NULL map?*
A: A NULL map would be used so that an object (i.e., entity) is not forward-engineered and, therefore, no mapping is maintained between the logical and physical designs.

Q: *What is the default for Referential integrity for Bachman?*
A: The foreign key relationships are defaulted to a Delete Rule of Restrict. This can be modified to CASCADE, and the Bachman tool will retain the selection for that foreign key.

Q: *What is the primary key?*
A: The key is a unique identification of an entity which can be composed of one or more attributes or partnership sets.

Q: *What is a candidate key?*
A: A set of attributes that can access an entity but is not the primary key is called a candidate key.

Q: *What part does inheritance play in an Entity Type Hierarchy (ETH)?*
A: There are assumptions made when supertype and subtype relationships are built into an Entity Type Hierarchy (ETH).
   - All entities exist in a one-to-one relationship.
   - Each subtype is a type of the supertype (e.g., Customer would be the supertype and Retail/Wholesale would be the subtype entities).

Q: *Can primary keys allow null values?*
A: No. DB2 requires that all key attributes have values even though they maybe default values. If an attribute has the Null Allowed box checked in the attribute form, and the attribute is selected to be part of a key, Bachman will automatically change the attribute to Null Not Allowed.

Q: *What is process modeling?*
A: This is a high-level conceptual design for the business functions which access the data model. A process model cannot exist without the data model because the DFD accesses a data model which contains the constructs of the business.

Q: *What is a process triggering event?*

A: It is a controlling primitive process (i.e., lowest-level process) that will begin executing the logic specified.

Q: *What are the types of process triggering events?*

A: The four type of events are:

1. Clock/calendar event

2. Information flow event

3. Person event

4. Storage event

Q: *What is a clock/calendar event?*

A: Indicates the process will execute at a specific time on a weekly, monthly, daily, or yearly basis (e.g., end-of-day routines which initialize start-of-day attributes).

Q: *What is an information flow event?*

A: In the DFD, the information flow can trigger a process which originated with an external agent or another process. This is indicated on the information flow with a diamond-shaped icon on the arrow end.

Q: *What is a person event?*

A: This is a on-request process that runs at the request of a person.

Q: *What is a storage event?*

A: The primitive process executes whenever an attribute condition triggers the event (e.g., when the trade of stock sends the stock inventory to a short position, a buy for that stock is automatically generated).

Q: *What is a Placekeeper?*

A: This is a Shared Work Manager object only. It keeps track of all updates to the subset model when deletion and renaming of objects occur. It is used to safeguard the reassembly process against damaging.

Q: *What is the Expunge function?*

A: This process physically removes the placekeepers from the base model only. This function cannot run against the subset since this would allow possible model integrity problems to occur in the model.

About the Editor

Michael Rothstein is an independent consultant with more than 30 years' experience in computers and information technology. His clients include Shearson Lehman, Metropolitan Life Insurance Company, Empire Blue Cross/Blue Shield, Paine Webber, Citibank, and others. He is the coauthor of *Structured Analysis and Design for the CASE User* (McGraw-Hill, 1993) and two other professional books. Mr. Rothstein received his M.B.A. from City University, has lectured at New York University's Management Institute, and previously worked as a systems engineer for IBM.